PUBLIC MANAGEMENT AND SUSTAINABLE DEVELOPMENT IN NIGERIA

To

Mr Jones David Dibie and Mrs Sarah Eloh Dibie

I dedicate this volume to my beloved parents and trusted advisors who dedicated all their resources to make me whom I am today. They struggled to provide different things for their children, especially the much needed encouragement and support that galvanized my ambition for intellectual excellence.

Public Management and Sustainable Development in Nigeria

Military–Bureaucracy Relationship

ROBERT DIBIE

ASHGATE

Published by
Ashgate Publishing Limited
Gower House
Croft Road
Aldershot
Hampshire GU11 3HR
England

Ashgate Publishing Company
Suite 420
101 Cherry Street
Burlington, VT 05401-4405
USA

Ashgate website: http://www.ashgate.com

British Library Cataloguing in Publication Data
Dibie, Robert
Public management and sustainable development in Nigeria : military–bureaucracy relationship
1. Sustainable development - Nigeria 2. Nigeria - Politics and government - 1960- 3. Nigeria - Economic policy
4. Nigeria - Economic conditions - 1960-
I. Title
338.9'669

Library of Congress Control Number: 2001097974

ISBN 0 7546 1877 3

Printed and bound by Athenaeum Press, Ltd., Gateshead, Tyne & Wear.

Contents

PART III: ENHANCING PUBLIC MANAGEMENT CAPACITIES

PART IV: HOW TO ACHIEVE SUSTAINABLE DEVELOPMENT

List of Figures

List of Tables

Preface

This book examines public management and the trend of sustainable development in Nigeria from 1966 to 1999. The text analyzes the trend of change that occurred in Nigeria during the several military regimes and the short democratic government. It argues that Nigeria needs to change in both its public administration and military institutions in order to attain sustainable development. In the past four decades Nigeria has experienced negative transformation in its political leaders, public management, economic development, industrial organizations and quality performance. The major question is not public or private management style, rather it is, how does Nigeria get the public and private sectors to most effectively meet social needs? This is referred to as sustainable development in this book.

This book addresses why public administrators in Nigeria are happy with the status quo. It uses several case studies to present an argument that Nigeria must come to terms with its lack of capable public administrators to organize production, and manage industrial operations in an effective and efficient manner. One of the major factors, which have made Nigeria to experience the above negative transformation, is the social and economic environment that public administrators operate in. The public administration environment in Nigeria has taken various structural and cultural forms. As a result extended family, corruption, ethnic tie has affected the impartiality of public managers and private invested interests in competition for state patronage. These factors become very crucial in a nation such as Nigeria where the state has been the main agent of development. Thus, the text contends that the effective performance of public administration in the sustainable development process will require a high level of creative assessment and innovation on the part of political leaders. Further senior public managers that envisage not simply the improvement of administrative performance but a restructuring of existing government institutions, behavior, social and cultural change must be willing to show good examples. Therefore, the task of training competent public administrators and genuine industrial technologists in Nigeria is not only imperative, it is urgent. Greater emphasis must be placed on the development of public managers through formal education and industrial training.

Nigeria is blessed with abundant natural and mineral resources but these resources have not been used to provide sustainable development for the people of the nation. Why is it so? The answer according to this text is lack of competent public managers and grid. The inability of the Nigerian government to manage its resources remains the single most important problem that must be addressed by the new democratic administration of the nation.

Failure, success or transformation in the sustainable development process of a nation often depends on assessment of what it takes to protect, reform, manipulate, or do away with prevailing institutions and regimes. There is also an emerging consensus on the need for change in the role of the state. The World Bank and IMF have increasingly demanded that the Nigerian government should relieve itself of a number of functions. This need arises from the incapacity of the government to achieve its objective of enhancing economic and sustainable development. The civil service and government agencies that are instruments and apparatus for the attainment of these objectives are simply not equal to the task. This limitation in the public sector performance calls for immediate action on the part of the government in: (1) restructuring government involvement; (2) accountability and transparency; (3) training of competent public managers; and (4) changing some of the social and cultural values in the nation.

This book expands the empirical and theoretical analyses of development policy and its implementation that have traditionally relied on motives of "rationality" (costs/benefits) to explain bureaucratic behavior. It examines and juxtaposes the military-dominated policy making apparatus with the traditional bureaucracy, which has the responsibility for the execution of public policy. It also attempts to make some contribution to Nigerian and comparative literature in the field of industrial development policy.

This book also examines the type of public policy that emanated from the transformation role of the Government of Nigeria between 1966 and 1999. These policies range from deregulation to structural adjustment (including privatization). The text also evaluates a number of policies that the Nigerian government has implemented for the purpose of restructuring the public service. However, public administrators in the nation seem to embrace the status quo rather than taking advantage of these change instruments. This book analyzes the implication of this profound transformation and the unique characteristics of the civil services as an instrument of national development.

This book is unique and distinguishes itself by studying the political system model in a unitary and developing nation where actors operate in a highly centralized manner. It helps identify the differences between, and reveals the difficulties in applying the political system model to Nigeria rather than to the United States. The main question addressed is: What is the relationship between the Nigerian military junta and the country's bureaucracy in the development processes and how has this relationship been shaped by the colonial legacy? The major argument developed in this book is that Nigeria needs to build an institutional capacity for sustainable development on the basis of democratic values.

The book is based on field surveys in Lagos and Abuja, Nigeria. These survey involved interviews of selected federal ministers, senior bureaucrats and managing directors of major research and development corporations. Analyses of financial data of federal ministries, agencies, and the Central Bank of Nigeria are also utilized to relate the ministries and agency responses to the goals of the policy. The findings of the book suggest that bureaucratic support has been central to the minimal success of the Structural Adjustment/Make-or-Buy Policy even in so centralized a political administrative system as prevails in Nigeria.

The book was written for both practitioners and students of developing administration, public policy, and economic development. It is appropriate for use in a variety of undergraduate and graduate university courses. Although the mode of analysis introduced in the book applies to Nigeria's problems, it could be applicable to a wide variety of developing countries' political economy issues. It is my hope that all those engaged in analyzing development problems, particularly those wrestling with the challenging task of developing and maintaining successful political and economic development in Africa, will find this book informative and helpful.

Robert Dibie

Acknowledgements

I wish to acknowledge the many talented and hard-working individuals whose efforts have made this book possible. First, I thank my colleagues Professors Mohapatra, Samory Rashid (Indiana State University) and Dr. Sharron Herron (California State University, Fresno) who provided valuable suggestions and comments after reading various drafts of this book.

Second, I wish to thank Dr. Helenan Robin and Dr. Larry Ziring who helped me in clarifying my thinking and transfer my ideas into a presentable book.

Third, I gratefully acknowledge many of my graduate students in the Master of Public Administration program at both Indiana State University Terre Haute and California State University Fresno whose insight and curiosity energized the long process of research and writing. I am also indebted to the editorial staff of Ashgate publishers for their dedication and support in completing this book.

Field studies are only possible with the cooperation of others. I wish to express my appreciation to the officials of the national, state, and local governments of Nigeria for making the survey and data collection possible.

Finally, I wish to acknowledge the enormous sacrifices and contribution of my wife and best friend Josephine Dibie. Her keen eyes and good sense made the book more coherent and accessible to wide readership.

Robert Dibie

List of Abbreviations

ABU	Ahmadu Bello University
AD	Alliance for Democracy
AFRC	Armed Forces Ruling Council
AG	Action Group
APP	All People's Party
ASCON	Administrative Staff College of Nigeria
ASUU	Academic Staff Union of Universities
CBN	Central Bank of Nigeria
EMR	Energy Mines and Research
FGN	Federal Government of Nigeria
FEPA	Federal Environmental Protection Agency
FOS	Federal Office of Statistics
GDP	Gross Domestic Product
GNP	Gross National Product
IMF	International Monetary Fund
JPB	Joint Planning Board
MAN	Manufacturers Association of Nigeria
MIGA	Multilateral Investment Guarantee Agency
MPRI	Military Professional Resource Initiative
MOST	Ministry of Science and Technology
MTI	Ministry of Trade and Industry
NAFDAC	National Agency for Food and Drug Administration and Control
NEPA	National Electricity Power Authority
NCNC	National Council of Nigeria and the Cameroon
NCO	Non Commission Officer
NECON	National Electoral Commission of Nigeria
NIPOST	Nigerian Post Office
NITEL	Nigerian Telecomunication
NMB	National Manpower Board
NMC	Nigerian Mining Corporation

NNDP	Nigerian National Democratic Party
NNPC	Nigerian National Petroleum Corporation
NPC	Northern People's Congress
NPN	National Party of Nigeria
NRMRDC	Nigerian Raw Materials Research and Development Council
NRC	National Republican Party
NSITF	National Social Insurance Trust Fund
OAU	Organization of African Unity
OPEC	Organization of Petroleum Exporting Nations
PDP	People's Democratic Party
PRC	Provisional Ruling Council
R&D	Research and Development
RWAFF	Royal West African Frontier Force
SAL	Structural Adjustment Loan
SAP	Structural Adjustment Policy
SDP	Social Democratic Party
SMC	Supreme Military Council
UPN	Unity Party of Nigeria
WAFF	West African Frontier Force

Part I

History and Problems

1 Premise of a Dynamic Nation

Introduction

In the mid-1980s, Nigeria, a developing nation in Africa, with just over two decades of experience with independence, faced a severe economic and debt crisis. This problem was due to an oil glut on the world market and declining oil revenue. Petroleum had been the major source of revenue for this fledgling nation since its independence. Under pressure from and using the suggestions of the World Bank and the International Monetary Fund (IMF), the military government adopted a series of structural adjustment programs. These programs included the devaluation of its currency, the reduction of its government size, the encouragement of export of agricultural and other non-oil products, and the privatization of some of its government enterprises. Among these policies was one directed specifically toward the development of indigenous technology in the private sector with contracts and financial resources provided by the various ministries of the national government? It is this policy that the military government called the Structural Adjustment/Make-or-Buy policy.

In recent time, Nigeria has earned a reputation for graft, blatant corruption, and outright looting of public resources. The recent survey of the Transparency International rank it as the second most corrupt nation (after Russia) on earth. This unfortunate reputation of Nigeria is support by a World Bank member-organ, the Multilateral Investment Guarantee Agency (MIGA). According to this survey, private saving held by Nigerians outside Africa amounted to US $15 billion or 1.458 trillion Naire (Nigerian currency). The interesting issue here is that this amount of money was taken out of Nigeria between 1966 and 1996 under the cover of development policies that was never implemented.

This book examines public policy and economic development in Nigeria from 1966 when the military took control of the national government till 1999 when they handed over power to an elected civilian regime. In the past four decades political leaders and social scientists alike in most sub-Saharan nations want to know which patterns of politics are resistant to change and which are easily transformed. Most public policy analysts also want to know precisely what forces have the most impact on established norms and institutions.

The major rationale of this book is to examine the question of public management challenges that faced Nigeria between 1966 and 1996. It is the hope of the author that awareness of these public management challenges will help the new civilian government of Nigeria to address issues that they will confront in the twenty-first century.

The focus of this book is the roles played by the military juntas and higher federal public administrators, and how they interacted and reacted to the crisis represented by Nigeria's underdevelopment between 1966 and 1996. The major rationale is to evaluate the relationship between the military and the bureaucracy in public policy formulation and the subsequent interpretation and implementation of policy in Nigeria.

This book also addresses the question: What is the nature and scale of change that Nigeria will have to undergo in order to achieve development goals? How Nigeria does in the twenty-first century is a function of how it defines its future. For Nigeria, a major challenge is how it could effectively and efficiently manage its vast wealth. Nigeria is not poor because it is poor. The nation is poor because it cannot manage its development process. Barriers to effectively facilitating diversity in the public service in Nigeria include (1) public administrators who are unable to tolerate and channel the ambiguity, complexity, and confusion that arise over multiple meanings and miscommunication among members. (2) Ministries and government agencies costs that escalate because more time and efforts were not spent to obtain synergy through increase training and creating policies and procedures to integrate people. (3) Decrease morale, because of the presence of public administrators who are unable to channel diverse energies into focused action.

The shortage of managerial knowledge, skills and talents are pervasive, and the cogs in the wheel of Nigeria's development quest. The book argues that the task of developing managerial manpower in Nigeria is not only imperative, it is urgent. Until Nigeria evolves its endogenous managerial talents, economic development and structural change will continue to be elusive, and the process more agonizing and traumatizing.

No policy is created in a vacuum. To adequately examine the relationship between the military that decreed the policy and the bureaucracy that responded to it, depending upon the ministry, with support or resistance, it is important to provide a history of Nigeria and of the important actors involved in the policy formulation and implementation processes. Public management trend in Nigeria is the subject of this study. With the use of a political system decision-making model, the making and the implementation of this public policy in Nigeria will be examined.

The Geography and Demographic Setting

Nigeria was a British territory from 1861 until October 1, 1960, when it achieved independence as a sovereign nation. The Federal Republic of Nigeria was proclaimed in 1963. Nigeria is located on the Gulf of Guinea in West Africa. Its area of 356,669 square miles is entirely within the tropical zone between latitudes 4 and 14 degrees North and latitudes 2 and 14 degrees East. Nigeria is big, diverse, and is oil rich. It is as large as California, Arizona, and New Mexico combined. Appendix A shows a map of Nigeria. The River Niger, which is about 730 miles long (inside Nigeria) and from which the country derives its name, is the third longest river in Africa. The River Niger and its main tributary, the River Benue, divide the country into three major geographical sections: west, east and north. Nigeria is a tropical country. The climatic conditions along the coastal areas in the south are more stable than in the rest of the country. There are two main seasons in the year, the dry season and the wet season. In the southern half of the country, the rainy season lasts for about six months – from May to October – while the northern half of the country has a shorter rainy season. The dry season, which is of longer duration in the north, brings with it the dry, northeasterly cold wind – the harmattan. For the whole country, the hottest months of the year are March and April, while the wettest months are May, June, and October.

Nigeria is the most populous and potentially one of the richest countries of blacks Africa. The country has one of the world's most ethnically diverse societies, with over 250 identifiable ethnic groups. There are three very large ethno-linguistic groups – the Hausa-Fulani in the north, the Yoruba in the west, and the Igbo in the east. The Hausa-Fulani, Yoruba, Igbo, Kanuri, Tiv, Edo, Isoko, Nupe, Ibibio, and Ijaw groups together account for almost 80 percent of the population. The overwhelming majority of the northern population is Muslim, and Muslims are widely thought to compose more than 50 percent of the total population. Christianity is strong in the south, accounting for perhaps 35 percent of the country's total population, while the balance of the population remains animist. Latest estimates put the population at about 115 million people (Ihonvbere 1994; Walden Report 1995).

Most Nigerians are to be found in the rural areas. Some 70 percent live in the rural countryside, and about the same proportion of the labor force is engaged in agriculture and agriculture-related activities. There are, however, a number of very large cities, such as Lagos (estimated at 4 million in 1990), Ibadan (4.7 million), and Kano (2.6 million), besides a number of other secondary cities that now serve as state capitals in most of the thirty-six states. The national capital was recently moved from Lagos, on the coast, to Abuja, a more central, hinterland location, owing to considerations of space, centrality, and strategy, among others.

Political History

The post-independence history of the country has not been peaceful. The politics of Nigeria have been dominated by ethnic and regional antagonisms, with serious ramifications at all levels, from the civil war of the late 1960s to the politicization of normally technical activities. Upon independence, Nigeria had a federal constitution, with three semiautonomous regions – northern, western, and eastern, dominated respectively by the Hausa, the Yoruba, and the Igbo. The three regions and the federation as a whole had a parliamentary political system. This civilian government was deposed in a military coup in January 1966. Violence and ethnic tension between the Hausa and Igbos led to the Biafra secession and civil war (1967 to 1970). In October 1979 the military stepped down and ushered in a new civilian government, the Second Republic, with Alhaji Shehu Shagari as the president. The Second Republic operated under a new constitution that included a presidential system of government. New elections were held in August-September 1983, and a political elite, which had been accused of widespread corruption, won major offices. The 1983 elections met with numerous accusations of vote rigging and violence. This weakened the legitimacy of the government. The cited corruption of the political elite, combined with the severe slump in the economy set the climate for another military coup.

On the last day of 1983, a bloodless military coup, led by a group of senior military officers, overthrew Alhaji Shagari on the grounds that his administration was inept and corrupt. Public unrest, diminished oil income, and a declining economy showed this corruption. As chairman of the new Supreme Military Council, Major-General Muhammadu Buhari, suspended portions of the constitution, banned political parties, and launched a campaign against corruption and the lack of discipline. Plagued by worsening economic conditions and resistance to political repression, Buhari was in turn ousted in mid-1985 by General Babangida, who became the head of the governing military junta. In 1987, the Babangida regime set in motion a five-year schedule that was directed toward another civilian government. The agenda called for constitutional revision, terminating the ban on political parties (only two parties were sanctioned), elections to unicameral state legislatures in 1990, and federal presidential and legislative elections in 1992. The elections were held; but on June 12, 1993, General Babangida announced that the presidential election results, which were not yet published, had been annulled. This move was condemned at home and abroad. Social Democratic Party candidate Chief Moshood Abiola who, according to unofficial results, had easily defeated Alhaji Bashir Tofa of the National Republican Convention declared himself president-elect, but to no effect. The annulment precipitated serious political unrest, and the civil disobedience brought the Nigerian economy to a halt for weeks. On August 26, 1993, following the abortive presidential elections, General Babangida stepped down as president and handed power to an Interim National Government, a nonelected administration whose members were handpicked by him. Chief Ernest Shonekan was named as its head. The term of office of the new administration was set to end by March 31, 1994, during which time it would organize fresh presidential elections. Five years later, General Babangida who is now retired said that he was forced to cancel the presidential elections under "unimaginable pressure" from some military generals (including Abacha) and elites (including Shehu Shagari) of northern origin who could not stand a southern becoming the president of Nigeria (Babangida 1998; Umar 1998).

On November 17, 1993, the defense minister, General Sanni Abacha, ousted Chief Shonekan in a bloodless coup. The next day Abacha banned all political activity, scrapped the two political parties, dissolved parliament, and dismissed the thirty States Governors. He signed a decree on November 21, 1993, establishing a Provisional Ruling Council, and he ordered the restoration of the 1979 Constitution.

General Abacha, like his predecessor Babangida, instituted his own elaborate Transition to a Civil Rule Program on January 1994, the jewel of whose crown was paraded as a Constitutional Conference. Elections to that conference were boycotted nationwide, and Abacha in any case, nominated a third of its members. He pledged that the Constitutional Conference would deliberate with full authority, and that its decisions would not be tampered with. No sooner did the worthy legislators pass a resolution calling on Abacha to hand over power by January 1996, however, than he sent them packing. When the members of the Constitutional Conference reconvened, the retraction was predictable – Abacha's recommended exit date was expunged from the final conference report, with appropriate sentiments of self-abasement for their misguided dare.

During General Abacha's regime, the entire populace has been decreed out of the right of habeas corpus (due process of law). The judiciary has been ousted from the role of adjudication on any issue that involves the military, its regime, and its agents. In 1995, Abacha granted pardon to his fellow tribes man Umaru Diko, a former minister in the Shagari administration who was one of those accused on having looted Nigeria's treasury to the tune of some $5 billion and who had fled to Britain after the Buhari and Idiagbon coup of December 1983. It will be recalled that an attempt by agents of the Buhari regime to kidnap Dikko and bring him back to Nigeria to face charges of embezzlement was foiled by British security agents in 1984. Since 1994 Abacha has jailed, executed, or exiled legitimate political, cultural, and labor figures cited by other Nigerians as possible opposition leaders. His regime's human rights record has been dismal.

Abacha ruled by force and no credible alternative leadership has coalesced. Nigeria's economy continues to remain energy starved and is decaying toward the pre-independent level. In October 1995 Abacha announced a three-year program for transition to civilian rule, whereby a new president was to be inaugurated on October 1, 1998, following elections at local, state, and national level. He legalized five political parties in 1996, thus opening the way for a multiparty system in the nation. The new constitutional provision stipulated the division of the nation into a number of regions and the rotation of principal executives (president and vice president) as well as legislative offices between these regions for a period of thirty years. The constitution also established a National Judicial Council and a Constitutional Court. General Abacha also created a number of committees as part of the transitional programs including the National Electoral Commission of Nigeria, which divided the nation into seven regions. Tension rose in April 1998 when Abacha's aids engineered his nomination as the sole candidate for the presidency of a civilian government scheduled to take power from his military regime in October 1998. This move quashed Nigeria's hope for a peaceful political competition. On April 25, 1998, Nigerians underscored the unpopularity of General Sani Abacha by boycotting an election crafted to help him prolong his tenure as the president of the nation.

On June 8, 1998, Abacha died having arranged for himself to be the sole presidential candidate of five different political parties, which his junta had handpicked earlier. Another general of northern origin, General Abdusalam Abubakar became the new head of state on June 8, 1998. On July 20, 1998, Abubakar void all the elections that was held during Abacha's tenure, and announced yet another transition programs that would end on May 29, 1999. He also releases majority of those who were sent to prison without trial by Abacha. Nigeria continues to face the dilemma of establishing a legitimate government.

General Abdusalam Abubakar's administration conducted series of elections from December 1998 to February 1999, that culminated in the inauguration of General Olusegun Obasanjo as elected president in May 1999. The death of Moshood Abiola in jail, just after few weeks of Sani Abacha's sudden death almost spoiled General Abubakar's transition program.

These two sudden deaths however, set the stage for the Abubakar's transition program, as a measure to defuse tension in the nation. General Abdusalam Abubakar's government introduced a transition program, which encouraged political associations to form political parties. Nine of these associations met the requirements to receive interim registration as political parties and thereby became eligible to contest the local government elections on December 5, 1998. Those that received at least 5 percent of the votes in 24 of the nation's 36 states were given full registration and allowed to compete for offices at the state and federal levels. Only three parties met this criterion: the People are Democratic Party (PDP), the Alliance for Democracy (AD), and the All People's Party (APP). The excellent performance of PDP in the State-level elections of January 9, 1999, made the AD and the APP to form an electoral alliance for the presidential elections, nominating Chief Olu Falae of the AD as their presidential candidate. The PDP, after a hard-fought nomination struggle, nominated Obasanjo, who clearly had the backing of important retired military leaders from Hausa-Falani North. Obasanjo defeated Dr. Alex Ekwueme, a former vice president widely seen as the leader of the Igbo people of the Southeast. Two Yoruba leaders from Southwest then competed for the presidency on February 27, 1999. This unusual situation in ethnically charged Nigerian politics was brought about in part because of a widespread feeling that a power shift was necessary. This is because Northerners had ruled the nation for the vast majority of its independence, and because the freely elected Abiola had been Yoruba, political elites informally agreed that a Southerner, probably a Yoruba, should be the next president. Obasanjo, with a significant international standing as an elder statesman as well as with the open support of former military leaders, won the election easily, though amid widespread accusations of fraud and a court challenge from his opponent. International election monitors saw the process as flawed but not irredeemably so, and major international actors quickly recognized Obasanjo's victory.

The Nigerian military has been engaged in a program of transition to democratic rule since 1985. Since the 1980s the nation's military rulers have developed transition politics into a strategy of transition without end, a ruse to prevent democratization. The strategy, however, changed when General Abdulsalam Abubakar assumed power in June 1998. He systematically took measures to defuse tension that Abacha left behind after his death. Of the many political associations that sprouted and sought registration as political parties under Abubakar's transition plan, only three were eventually registered based on their performance in the local government election of December 1998: The People's Democratic party (PDP), the All people's Party (APP), and the Alliance for Democracy (AD).

General Obasanjo was a relatively late entrant into the PDP, and the party performed woefully in his home state, not even winning at his own polling station. In addition, the mainstream pan-Yoruba organization rebuffed the general, solidly supporting Falae (the presidential candidate for APP and AD alliance) instead. Why, then did the PDP nominate Obasanjo, and how can his victory in the party nomination and the presidential poll is explained? Three explanations stand out.

First, the single most important factor in Obasanjo's triumph was the support of his fellow retired generals, including Babangida and Danjuma. Obasanjo's retired military general friends and supporter were the source of the donation that he gave to the party and were well represented at the occasion at which 400 million naira was raised for his campaign. The general's camp was also alleged to have funded the candidacy of Chief Jim Nwobodo, an Igbo, in order to discomfit Dr. Alex Ekwueme and divide his support base among the Igbos. All candidates used money to win delegates votes. Therefore, it was not hard to imagine that the candidates with the most resources enjoyed an advantage.

Second, unlike its rival, the PDP remained united after the party nominated Obasanjo. The defeated Ekwueme not only remained a loyal party member but also was active in Obasnajo's campaign. He chaired the general's fund-raising dinner and was always in Obasanjo's entourage during his campaign in the East.

Third, the feared Igbo protest vote did not materialized. The call by the Ohaneze for Igbos to vote APP was largely ignored. General Obasanjo, for instance, won 76 percent of the votes in Ekwueme's home state of Anambra. Igbo political leaders in the PDP may have felt reluctant to risk their investment in the PDP for an uncertain welcome in the AD/APP alliance.

General Olusegun Obasanjo emerge victorious even though he was rebuffed and resisted by Afenifere, the mainstream umbrella organization of his Yoruba ethnic group. Indeed, the four states – Lagos, Ondo, Osun, and Oyo – in which he failed to score the mandatory 25 percent, are his entire home zone. The solidarity and support Obasanjo received from Nigeria's military elites in reserve facilitated his victory. His election signals the emergence of the military in retirements as the most potent political force in Nigeria, based on its massive fortunes accumulated, and social networks established, during its long stay in power. There can be no doubt that this retired military generals have their own agenda and will seek to wield influence in the new administration of President Obasanjo which started May 29, 1999.

President Obasanjo's administration has not been very smooth. Two years after his election, his government has not been able to deliver its promise to the people of Nigeria. Electricity and water supply is still a major problem in Nigeria. Every forth night the people of Nigeria still struggle to get petrol to operate their automobile. Sometimes it takes almost a day to queue up in gas stations in order to buy fuel. One wonders why the four refineries in the nation would break down at the same time. A sudden increase in the price of gasoline in 2000 almost paralyzed Obasanjo's government. Further, his education goals and promise to the people of Nigeria is something yet to be accomplished. Universities in the nation has been shot down for up to six months at time. In 2001, a newly appointed minister for education Professor Aborisade repudiated the agreement mutually entered between his predecessor Professor Adeniran and the Academic Staff Union of Universities (ASUU). While Professor Aborisade declared that the federal government of Nigeria cannot afford to spend 150 naira to up grade universities and other tertiary institutions in the nation, the National Assembly passed a bill which proposed 250 billion naria purchase of five jets. The five planes were for some members of the Executive and Legislative branch of government. This shows that while the government can afford to spend 250 billion naira to purchase planes for five government officials, it could not spend half of that money for over a million Nigerian children in universities. Obasanjo's administration continues to loose public sympathy in Nigeria. The legislative branch of government has not been without legitimacy problems. Two Senate presidents (Enwerem and Okadigbo) and one speaker of the National House of Representative have been fired from office due to corruption and forgery. The first speaker of the new House of Representative was impeached because he was exposed as a high-flying officer who forged certificates and lied under oath to get elected into the National Assembly. Former Senate President, Evans Enwerem was impeached on accounts of forgery and financial impropriety. Chuba Okadigbo was impeached following allegation of large-scale corruption. Elements of corruption that prevailed during the military administration are still available in the civilian administration. The rate of armed robbery has increased in the nation and the life of citizens and properties are no longer secured in most pasts of the nation.

President Obasanjo has been credited for keeping the Nigeria military in check since 1999. Few weeks after he was sworn in as president he retired several senior military officers. Himself and his defense minister retired general Danjuma has been able to restructure the military leadership and structure around the nation. In fullfilment of his electoral promises to fight corruption and restore human dignity, President Obasanjo retired military and police officers who has at a point or the other held political positions in previous regimes. President Obasanjo, who is also the commander-in-chief of the armed forces, retired general Malu the army chief of staff for taking a position contrary to that of the government that he served. General Malu also was punished for criticizing his commander-in-chief in a national new broadcast for allowing American military officers to interfere in Nigeria's defense matters. President Obasanjo had requested the American military assistance to re-professionalize the Nigerian army. Obasanjo action was regarded as strictly an act to educate the military that the president and commander-in-chief under a civilian administration have the power to appoint and remove any officer of the Nigerian armed forces.

The new democratic civilian administration of Nigeria has no doubt experienced some ugly events. Some of the events were sparked by the crisis of confidence that broke out between the Executive and Legislative branches of the government. The constant fuse between the President and the National Assembly over issues of supremacy at times seem to threaten the well being of the nation's new democracy. Similar political problems have been reported at the state level. In some states the Speaker of the State Assembly were impeached and State governors continue to be at loggerheads with the legislative branch of their government.

Public Management

The history of Nigeria shows how the nation's civil service has been subjected to three major influences – the British colonial administration, the Nigerian military, and three elected civilian administrations. The starting point of indigenous public administration in Nigeria is the "indirect rule" by which officers of the British colonial administration ruled through intermediaries of Nigerian tribal leaders. While there was no doubt during the colonial period of Nigeria's history about the ultimate authority of the colonial officers, what "indirect rule" meant was that traditional structures were left intact and tribal leaders played administrative roles in the colonial government at the local level. Indirect rule was styled as a colonial regime division of labor. On the one hand, the colonial rulers were supposed to attend to foreign affairs, the development of national institutions – such as the legislative councils and civil service – and the management of the macro-economy. On the other hand, it fell to the emirs, obas, and chiefs (where these existed) to carry out judicial and policing tasks, raise local revenues, administer the social units under domain, and in general carry on the development process determined by the higher authorities. In this way, the traditional society was supposed to advance gradually and effortlessly toward modernization, development, and ultimately independence and self-rule. The pattern of "Anglo-African" administration and partnership varied in different parts of the country. The pattern in the northern parts of the country was regarded as a fairly successful model, whereas varying degrees of difficulty were experienced in the southern parts. When the decolonialization process set in after World War II, the colonial administration officers agreed on the transplantation of the British-style parliamentary government commonly referred to as the Westminster model (Adamolekun and Ayeni 1990).

At independence in 1960, it was accepted that the government and administration of Nigeria would follow the Westminster-Whitehall arrangement in Britain. For various reasons, the experiment collapsed in January 1966, and a military government that remained in power (with four different heads of state) until September 1979 succeeded it. With these four heads of state and three recent military governments, the country has passed through seven different military regimes since independence.

Nigeria has a three-tiered government structure consisting of federal, state, and local levels. The major institutions in the Nigerian political system are the executive, the judiciary, and the legislative branches of government. These three institutions also exist at the federal state and local government levels of government. There were thirty-six states and 589 local governments in 1996. The number of local governments was increased to 776 in January of 1997, excluding the mayoralty of Abuja, which has four mayoral districts. The federal system has been restructured periodically since 1966, when the military took power from civilian politicians. The uneven structure of four regions was reorganized first into twelve states (1967), nineteen states (1976), twenty-one states (1989), thirty states (1991) and then into the current thirty-six states in 1996.

The Nigerian national government has the same organizational structure as those of the 36 states of the federation. As mentioned earlier the government has executive, legislative and judicial institutions. The President of Nigeria is both the head of state and head of government. At the state level, the governor is the chief executive. The head of the local government is the local government chairperson. A major variation between the military regime and the civilian administration is that during the military administration state executive council combined the legislative functions with the cabinet functions of policy formulation and implementation. However, during the civilian administration that started in 1999, the head of the state executive institution is an elected governor. Under the new civilian administration the state legislative and executive institutions are separate. The 1999 constitution also gives both the national and states legislators the power to impeach the head of the executive branch. This provision was not available during the military regime. As a matter of fact, during the military regime, the head of the national government had the power of appointing the 36 states military administrators (now governors).

The size of the National civil service has grown from about 30,000 in 1960 to about 200,000 in 1999 (Otobo, 1999). The Nigerian civil bureaucracy has played a prominent role both during periods of military rule and periods of civilian rule, in part because of the frequency of regime oscillations (Heady 1991). Nigeria is an example of a nation characterized by greater stability and continuity in its public administration than in its politics. At both the federal and state levels, the central feature of governmental administration is the ministry, an administrative organization whose structure and functioning have remained largely unchanged since ministries were first constituted in the 1950s. The number of ministries has changed over the years, but the hierarchical organization of the ministry and the divisions of the work within the ministry have broadly remained unchanged. The structure of the presidential executive of the Second Republic differed in some important respects from what had existed under the parliamentary government during the First Republic, and the structure of the military executive has added certain characteristics that were unknown under the various civilian governments.

During the parliamentary government, the Prime Minister, as head of the federal government, was responsible for the coordination of government work. The secretary to the government was the Prime Minister's key collaborator in carrying out this function. In addition to his role as the head of the government secretariat, the secretary to the government also served as the head of the federal civil service whose members staffed the individual ministries. At both the federal and regional levels, the coordination of government activities proved difficult. The president and Prime Minister competed for dominance. Cabinet ministers, legislators, and civil servants retained autonomous powers. Higher bureaucrats such as the permanent secretaries, deputy permanent secretaries, and assistant secretaries provided whatever coordination did emerge from this pluralist network. Ministers then headed the ministries.

This structural arrangement was replicated at the regional/state level, and the coordinating role of the premiers (title of regional heads of government) was the same as those at the federal level.

The major change introduced under the presidential form of government was the heightened emphasis placed on the executive office of the president. The president was intended to serve as the center of power of the federal government in a manner that was different from the coordinating role of the Prime Minister in the parliamentary form. A vice president and a number of special advisers assisted the president. A secretary headed the executive office of the president to the federal government who coordinated the work of government. The head of the federal civil service provided leadership for the career civil servants that staffed the individual ministries (Ademolekun and Ayeni 1990). At the state level, there was an executive office of the governor headed by a secretary to the government, as well as a deputy governor and a number of special advisers to assist the governor.

In 1988 General Babangida reformed the Nigerian civil service structure. He abolished the post of permanent secretary because it had become too political, and he designated the minister/commissioner as the chief executive and accounting officer of the ministry. A senior civil service position called Director-General was created to assist the minister in each ministry. The reform also prescribed that a Director-General should leave office with the administration that appoints him (Phillips 1990). One major implication of the 1988 reform of the Nigerian civil service is the enhanced professionalism. The former administrative class was abolished, and all civil servants now belong to a professional class. The previous Administrative Officers and General Executive Officers now specialize in one of the newly established professional divisions. These divisions include personnel management, finance, supply, planning, research, information/data management, operations, and so on. In fact, the title Administrative Officer no longer exists and has been replaced by professional titles such as Personnel Officer, Economist, Supplies Officer, and Planning Officer (Phillips 1990). The staff structure in the civil service has been broken down into three professional categories: namely, Assistant, Officer, and Director. The Assistant is a sub-professional; he is not required to have a university degree or other professional qualifications. The Officer, however, is a full professional and is required to have a university degree or equivalent professional qualifications. The Director is also a full professional who has been given general management functions as the head of a branch, a division, or a ministry.

The professional officer requires regular periods of in-service training and retraining. Therefore, staff training is an obligatory and periodic exercise in the Nigerian civil service, and as such it appears to have enhanced administrative reform. President Obasanjo changed the position of Director-General to Permanent Secretary in 1999, few months after he was sworn as the new President of Nigeria.

Nigerian civil bureaucrats have played a major role in public policy making, supported both by pre-independence tradition and post-independence practice. Peter Koehn asserts that higher civil servants have been central, and often dominant, participants in the policy-making process throughout Nigeria's history (Koehn 1984). In a political setting with frequent shifts back and forth from transient military to weak civilian governments, civil administrators have found an optimal environment to participate in policy making and to profit personally and collectively from their policy implementation opportunities.

Structural Adjustment Policy

Nigeria introduced a Structural Adjustment/Make-or-Buy Policy in July 1986. This policy represented the culmination of a series of efforts by the federal government of Nigeria to encourage the development of an indigenous technological capability in the country. The Structural Adjustment Policy marked a watershed in Nigeria's economic history. It represented the beginning of the adoption of conscious policies aimed at drastically changing the structure of the nation's economy that since the mid-1970s, has been suffering from the "Dutch" or more recently the "Nigerian, disease." This disease refers to the damage done to the economy as a result of reliance upon one sector. The modern economy of Nigeria, heavily dependent on oil earnings, is overlaid on a traditional agricultural and trading economy. The colonial regime from 1900 to 1960 introduced cash crops, developed harbors, railroads, and roads, and sought to develop a market for consumer goods. At independence in 1960 agriculture accounted for well over half of GDP and was the main source of export earnings and public revenue, with the agricultural marketing boards playing a major role, a role that has now been taken over by the Nigerian National Petroleum Corporation (NNPC).

The overwhelming importance of oil in recent years is evident from the fact that this one commodity accounts for about three-quarters of federal government revenue and well over 90 percent of export earnings

(Central Bank Report 1991). During the 1970s, the world oil price rose, Nigerian oil exports grew rapidly, and Nigeria had a balance of trade surplus almost every year. Although most of the exploration and production was undertaken by foreign oil companies, Nigeria kept a majority share holding in the oil industry through the nationally owned Nigerian National Petroleum Corporation (NNPC), and thus was able to restrict the proportion of the profits that left the country. The economy grew by about 8 percent annually, more than twice the rate of growth in the United States during the same time period. As a member of the Organization of Petroleum Exporting Countries (OPEC), Nigeria was one of the countries that engineered the oil price rises of the 1970s that resulted in huge new profits. Nigeria today is the fourth largest petroleum producer in OPEC and is the second largest exporter of oil to the United States, after Saudi Arabia.

As a result of the price rises, annual Nigerian oil income grew from $400 million in 1965 to $9 billion in 1970 and to $26 billion in 1980 (Central Bank Report 1991). With money flowing into its coffers, the government launched the biggest development plan ever considered by an African country. The plan called for spending $100 billion to transform Nigeria from a traditional to a modern society in five years. The minimum wage was doubled and all civil servants were given a 60 percent pay raise. More than 50,000 Nigerians were sent to the United States and Europe to learn new skills, and plans were announced for seven new universities, three new airports, thirteen new television stations, and a new federal capital at Abuja. The United States, the former Soviet Union, and Western Europe showed new interest in closer ties with Nigeria, which was now seen as a major regional economic power.

The collapse of OPEC unity, however, led to a collapse in the price of oil. This collapse in oil prices caused Nigerian oil revenues to drop from $26 billion a year to $10 billion a year between 1980 and 1983, just as its foreign debt was coming due. Nigeria's oil share of Gross Domestic Product (GDP) fell from 25 percent in 1980 to 14 percent in 1988. Moreover, Agriculture was still the principal activity of the majority of Nigerians but it only accounted for 30 percent of the nation's GDP (at factor cost) in 1988. By 1992 Nigeria's foreign debt stood at $34 billion, and servicing the debt was costing $5.5 billion annually, the latter accounted for nearly one-third of Nigeria's export earnings (McCormick 1995).

Through this "Nigerian disease" phenomenon, the petroleum sector of the economy had become more profitable than the agricultural export sector. This difference in intersectional profitability move resources from the agricultural export sector into the petroleum and service sectors and therefore led to the decline of agricultural production and export. Technological development was ignored. Instead the government concentrated on the provision of physical and economic infrastructure refinements. Some of these economic infrastructures (i.e., stadiums, airports, seaports, army barracks, etc.) were later found to be nonviable, and others were beyond the capacity of government agencies to execute. Instead of making the economy more self-reliant, the policies pursued during the 1970s made the economy vulnerable to further external shocks. Price distortions created by a highly overvalued currency and inappropriate institutional arrangements led to inadequate pricing of agricultural and other local products. The policy incentives and control measures only encouraged the setting up of manufacturing ventures based on wholesale imported inputs. The public sector involvement in economic activities became pervasive such that it accounted for half of the GDP and two thirds of Nigeria's modern sector employment (Central Bank Report 1991).

By the mid-1980s, the economy was in shambles. The public services were so poorly maintained that water and electricity supplies broke down on a daily basis. Nigeria's roads and railroads were in a poor state of repair. Although education had been one of the priorities of the government, Nigeria's educational system was foundering for lack of funds, and some schools in some states had to be closed for months. There were few teachers and classrooms, and the provision of education was uneven: for example, southerners had better facilities and more graduates than the northerners, and the universities were turning out too few scientists and professionals. According to the Central Bank Report (1991), 38 percent of Nigerian men and 60 percent of women were illiterate, hindering Nigeria's hopes of building a modern, successful society. Health care was also inadequate. Nigeria had one doctor and four nurses for every 100,000 people. Infant mortality was twelve times the rate in the United States (McCormick 1995). Only one in five rural people had access to safe drinking water. While these figures are not unusual by sub-Saharan African standards, they show how far Nigeria had yet to go to meet the basic needs of its people.

In order to prevent a collapse of the economy, the government initially introduced various demand management measures, for example, abandoning major capital projects (but those at Abuja, the new federal capital city, were allowed to continue). When it became clear that the economic situation would not improve, General Babangida's administration attempted to negotiate a $2.5 billion loan from the IMF. The IMF listed a number of conditions that Nigeria would have to meet to get the loan. Although many of these conditions made good sense, the idea that they were conditions to be levied on the nation led to their being opposed in the Nigerian press. The vehemence of opposition led the government to abandon the loan talks with IMF. However, the military government introduced several IMF-style austerity measures that called for a large reduction in petroleum subsidies, the reordering of the national economy into a market system, and the devaluation of the currency. The economic policy also called for a reduction of government size, privatization, the encouragement of agricultural export and handicrafts and investment in the manufacturing of local products.

The structural adjustments introduced in Nigeria were typical of the types of adjustments being recommended to and adopted by developing countries throughout the world at the time. The adjustments represented a change in strategy on the part of international assistance organizations, led by the World Bank. In the early 1980s these organizations shifted their priorities from programs to increase the income, productivity and living standards of the poor to programs for macroeconomics restructuring. Structural adjustment policies were aimed at helping developing countries cope with their severe debt problems by stimulating rapid economic growth. The policies sought to overcome problems associated with severe international recession and inflation, declining demand for exports, rising prices for imports, and decreases in international financial assistance. The shift in concern among international organizations from the alleviation of poverty to promoting macroeconomics growth also refocused their perspective on development. For example, the World Bank (1983) moved from the equity concerns that it had been pursuing for a decade to reforming monetary, fiscal, exchange rate, trade, and wage policies. World Bank structural adjustment loans (SALs) provided funding to support a comprehensive program of economic reform agreed to by a government and the Bank. The IMF and World Bank defined the solution to the debt-servicing problem as drastic economic reforms that would accelerate the growth of GDP. The reforms would promote open trade, export production, deregulation of industry, reduction of public expenditure and the public wage bill, and expansion of private-sector output. Many of the IMF's austerity programs and the World Bank's SALs were aimed at drastically cutting back the role of government in the economy. But in the rush to reduce the size of government in developing countries, the IMF and World Bank overlooked the critical role that governments had played in Western economic growth and in the success of the East Asian economies.

The Structural Adjustment Policy (SAP) including the make-or-buy provisions, was adopted in July 1986 by the Nigerian government in response to its debt crisis and the declining state of the domestic economy. The policy has two interrelated aspects. The first aspect aims at stabilizing the economy by ensuring external balance and fiscal viability. The second focuses on the restructuring of Nigeria's technological and production patterns. The policy was also designed to redress the fiscal imbalances and structural distortions in the economy with the view to propelling Nigeria toward self-sustainable growth. The general implementation format of the SAP is based on neoliberal strategies, which emphasize deregulation, devaluation, denationalization, trade liberalization, and technological development. Although many of the reforms prescribed by structural adjustment policies were needed to create an economic environment conducive to development, it remains to be seen how effective they will be in transforming planned economies into market economics and in improving the incomes and living conditions of the poor in Nigeria. Difficult economic issues loom on Nigeria's horizon. The oil revenues have been depleted without a legacy of long-term economic development, and the short-term prospects of the SAP are for serious domestic deprivations. These divisive issues will continue to be argued in the context of which region should dominate the others and in terms of the question of regime legitimacy.

Purpose of the Book

This book examines the Federal Structural Adjustment/Make-or-Buy Research and Development Policy. It uses a hybrid version of a political system decision-making model to analyze the formulation and implementation of the policy. The purpose of this approach is to evaluate the relationship between the military and the bureaucracy in public policy formulation and the subsequent interpretation and implementation of policy in Nigeria. More particularly, the study will attempt to account for variations in the degree of support for the Structural Adjustment/Make-or-Buy Policy, by four major research-and-development (R & D) ministries in the federal government (i.e., Agriculture, Communications, Defense and Energy, Mines and Resources).

The primary focus of this book is on the roles played by the military junta and higher federal public administrators and on how they have interacted with each other and have reacted to the crises represented by Nigeria's underdeveloped technology. The study has several important components (a) an historical examination of Nigerian political development and its British colonial legacy; (b) the origin and development of the Nigerian military; (c) the structure and development of the Nigerian bureaucracy. (d) The political economy of Nigeria and the situation that led the military regime to formulate the structural adjustment program in 1986. (e) The objectives of the Structural Adjustment/Make-or-Buy Policy; (f) the actions and reactions of the federal ministries in implementing the policy; (g) the connection between the Structural Adjustment/Make-or-Buy Policy and Nigeria's quest for appropriate technology.

The centerpiece of this research is the formulation of the policy in 1986 by the Armed Forces Ruling Council (AFRC) and the role of the federal bureaucrats in implementing it. The Structural Adjustment/Make-or-Buy Policy was enacted with the intention that it would resolve the crisis of technological underdevelopment, and perhaps the wider problem, namely, the privatization of R & D. The policy faced enormous problems from its inception. The public was not immediately supportive because in the prior three decades externally directed policies had intensified poverty for the vast majority of Africans (Mayer et al. 1996; Olukoshi 1992). Foreign-directed programs had also brought wealth and privilege to the few.

The implementation of a policy is faulty and questionable if it does not have a solid base of domestic support. Most important, some of the federal ministries appeared to oppose the policy. The reasons that certain ministries supported and others opposed the policy will be investigated. Also important to this study is the role-played by international institutions and their influence on the outcome of the Structural Adjustment/Make-or-Buy Policy.

Deliberate efforts to bring about changes in public policies and in the structure and function of public institutions are normal and ongoing processes of government. In this study, I intend to use a framework that helps us to understand the emergence, implementation, and sustainability of reform initiatives. In particular, I focus on the role played by military and bureaucratic elites in shaping and making policy decisions, how they consider available options, and how they manage the political and bureaucratic questions of implementation. By analyzing the military/bureaucracy role in the change process, I attempt to show how the Nigerian government functions and how it determines the range of its policy choices.

Organization of the Book

This book centers on the relationship between Nigeria's military and bureaucracy and on the role of the military and bureaucratic personnel in policy formulation and implementation, their need for cooperation as well as the potential for conflict between military junta and bureaucrats. The book has several important components: (a) an historical examination of Nigerian political development and its British colonial legacy. (b) The origin and development of the Nigerian Military; (c) the structure and development of the Nigerian Bureaucracy; (d) the political economy of Nigeria and the situation that led the military to formulate the structural adjustment and other polices between 1966 and 1999; (e) the objectives and implication of the various policies formulated by the military; (f) the actions and reaction of the federal ministries in implementing the development policies; (g) the connection between the development policies and the Nigerian quest for appropriate technology. The book is organized thematically into three parts, each of, which tackles major components of public management challenges that Nigeria must address in the twenty-first century in order to improve the welfare of its citizens.

Part I comprises Chapters 1-4. This part provides not only the history of Nigeria, but also more importantly the framework for understanding the nature, scope, and magnitude of the military and public management problems in Nigeria. The chapters in this part identify and explain certain generic and specific ethnic and public management issues that are unique to Nigeria. Chapter 3 concerns the historical development of the Nigerian bureaucracy, the various post-independence reforms of the civil service, and the role of the bureaucracy in policy formulation and implementation during a military regime. Chapter 4 describes the origin of the Nigerian military and examines the factors that galvanized the military to intervene in post-independence politics. This part also undertakes critical analysis of the military and the bureaucracy as well as the dilemma that they face.

Part II contains Chapters 5-8. This part of the book deals with public administration institutions that make public policy and implement them in the Nigeria political arena. This section examines the operations of the national bureaucracy as well as operations at the local government levels. The analysis of this session also reveals the military and the bureaucracy relations in Nigeria, as well as the dilemma that they face. Chapter 6-8 used case study to highlight the dilemma in both the military and bureaucracy in Nigeria. These dilemmas range from bad public management, ethnic conflict, inadequate information network, to poor market-based economy. Ethnic conflict and lack of managerial skills has seized the center stage in modern public management operations. On the one hand, public bureaucrats and military officers needs reliable accounting information in order to make timely and rational decisions. On the other hand, Nigeria will be better off by acquiring information and managerial skills needed in these institutions to improve on its poor market-based development strategies.

Part III consists of Chapters 9-11. The part examines the route that Nigeria could take in order to enhance its public management capacities. This underscores the need to reexamine the management development programs in vogue in the nation. Chapter 9 and 10 contends that any strategy aimed at enhancing public management capabilities in Nigeria must be rooted in the idea of maximum self-reliance and relative self-sufficiency. Chapter 11 uses a case study to examine the relationship between the military and the bureaucracy in the formulation and implementation of the Structural Adjustment/Make-or-Buy Policy with the aid of the political system decision making model.

Part VI consists of Chapters 12-15. This part is mainly concern with providing possible recommendations on what Nigeria can do in the twenty-first century in order to attain sustainable development. Chapter 12 addresses the way women have been treated in the nation. It contends that one of the possible ways of improving manpower in Nigeria is for the government to empower or recognize women as equal to men. Protection of women's right and equal opportunity would give Nigerian women the access to various professional positions that they have been denied in the past.

Chapter 13 addresses the vexing dilemma of corruption in Nigeria. It contends that Nigeria need to search for increased productivity and alternative strategies to improve public accountability. It stresses that the search is for Nigeria to seek strategies and techniques for re-orientating the behavior of individual administrators and military officer as public servants, managers, and decision-makers. As public servants, the need is sometimes expressed for administrators to maintain standards of leadership, integrity and democracy in their relations with clients.

Finally, Chapter 14 reviews the book in its entirety. The chapter describes what Nigeria can do to achieve broad-based sustainable development, democracy and a bright twenty-first century. Particular attention is given to the relationship between decision-makers (the military) and the subsequent interpretation and behavior of the implementers of the policy (the bureaucrats). The chapter argues that the environment that Nigeria's public administrators and military operate shapes their attitude. In order for Nigeria to attain sustainable development in the twenty-first century it's citizens, public administrators, and the military must be re-trained to accept the fact that self-interests need not take second place to rights, justice, fairness and national interests.

References

Adamolekun, O. (1999). Public Administration in Africa (ed.). Boulder, Colorado: Westview.

Adamolekun, O. and Victor Ayeni. (1990). "Nigeria." In Public Administration in the Third World edited by V. Subramanian. London: Longman.

Central Bank of Nigeria. (1991). Annual Report and Statement of Account. Abuja, Nigeria: CBN Press.

Heady, F. (1991). Public Administration: A Comparative Perspective. New York: Marcel Dekker.

Ihonvbere, J. (1994). Nigeria: The Politics of Adjustment and Democracy. New Brunswick: Transaction.

Koehn, P. (1984). "The Evolution of Public Bureaucracy in Nigeria." In Administrative System Abroad edited by P. Tummala. Boulder, Colorado: Westview.

Mayer, L., J. Burner, and S. Ogden. (1996). Comparative Politics: Nations and Theories in Changing World. Upper Saddle River, New Jersey: Prentice-Hall.

McCormick, J. (1995). Comparative Politics in Transition. New York: Wadsworth Publishing Company.

Olukoshi, A. (1992). The Politics of Structural Adjustment in Nigeria. London: James Carrey Press.

Otobo, E. (1999). "Nigeria" Public Administration in Africa (ed.). Boulder, Colorado: Westview.

Phillips, A. (1990). The 1988 Nigeran Civil Service Reforms and Their Post-1992 Prospects. Ibadan, Nigeria: NISER Publication.

World Bank. (1992). World Development Report. New York: Oxford University Press.

2 Managing Nigeria's Ethnic Legacy

Introduction

Nigeria was until October 1960 a British colony, and from the colonial experience, it inherited a number of British institutions and values. The political tensions, which Nigeria has experienced since independence, are rooted in part in the regional structure of administration imposed by the British. The territory of present-day Nigeria was defined, not on the basis of shared historic, economic or social experiences, but by the arbitrary amalgamation of a number of disparate ethno-cultural units which happened to occupy contiguous land areas then under British colonial administration. Nigeria's independence exaggerated and intensified ethnic and tribal rivalries, and a savage civil war threatened its republican status between 1967 and 1970.

Nigeria has several ethnic groups and a diverse and rich cultural heritage. The different ethnic groups differ in physical features, reasoning capacities, talents, strength, musical aptitude, and so on. All these inequalities are a product of colonial legacy, social learning and cultural inheritance though, the significance of each of these factors is not always clear. Perhaps more important, however, the ethnic groups are also unequal in their access to social rewards; that is, various forms of wealth, power, economic development, and prestige. These differences, all primarily of social origin, are of greatest consequence in accounting for the crisis among these various ethnic groups that constitute members of one nation-state.

In Nigeria no problem has more fiercely challenged political order and state cohesion than ethnic and religious conflict. Non Hausa and Fulani indigenes have often been attacked in Kaduna and Kano. Between 1999 and 2001 such religious attacks has led to the death over 1000 southerners in the north. In February 28, 2000, reprisal attacks were carried out on Hausa communities at the Igbo cities of Owerri and Aba on Sharia issues. In June of 2001, the former head of State of Nigeria retired major general Muhammadu Buhari was alleged to have called on Islam to vote for only Moslem candidates in future elections in Nigeria. It is ironic to note that Buhari who had a bad record of human right violation and the unbridled pursuit of ethnic agenda during his administration in the late 1980s would now turn around to use religion to his advantage. As head of state Buhari could not prove himself as a true Moslem believer. He could not avowed his commitment to Islam nor overcome his ethnic prejudice for total support of Moslem-Moslem ticket when Abiola-Kingibe ran for the presidency in 1993. When Buhari was appointed by General Abacha to head the Petroleum Trust Fund his tenure was frittered with allegation of mismanagement, nepotism, and waste. Buhari and his cohort feels the oil money that comes from a predominantly Christian South should be used to Islamize Nigeria, while denying the producers (indigenes from the oil producing areas) any chance of having a say in how the resources are allocated (Samuel 2001). There are so many Northern Moslems like Buhari who believe they are born to rule Nigeria. These group of Northern Moslem has often instigated street urchins known as "Almajiris and Yaandabas" to attack Southerners and non-Moslem in Northern Nigeria Cities. Idowu Samuel (2001) pointed out that several retired generals have been behind the plot to use Sharia religious issue to cause confudion and thereby bring the new democracy in Nigeria to an abrupt ending.

The recent debate on dual citizenship and the relevance of ethnicity to democratic politics has focused on which institutions are appropriate to govern a multi-ethnic nation-state (Ndegwa 1997; Lemarchand 1995; Esman 1994; Diamond and Plattner 1994). The intrusion of the military (1966 in Nigeria) into civil politics is the ultimate factor in the wake of ethnic conflict and political violence in these countries. It would therefore appear that the incident was indeed one that was not only inevitable but also desirable. In the 1990s, it has become quite clear that such move by the military was not a blessing in disguise. For as was the case with ethnic conflict and political violence in the past, military incursion into politics could be said to be related to the status quo of inter-ethnic rivalry and chauvinism, intra-class struggle for power, the oppression of minorities, as well as the institutional decay of the armed forces.

Conflict is an important aspect of ethnicity. This is inevitable under conditions of inter-ethnic competition for inequality is accepted as natural, and wealth is esteemed. The fear of inequality generates divisive and destructive socioeconomic competition, which has anti-social effects. Conflict makes it possible for the "in-group" to accept the expression of hostility toward the "out-group". For instance the Biafra secession (civil war) of Nigeria 1966-1970 by the Igbos was a result of hostility towards them by the Hausa-Fulani groups.

In political terms, coming to grips with the Nigerian systems is complicated by the lack of settled and predictable political patterns. Independent Nigeria has had two civilian governments (one based on the Westminster model, one on the American presidential model), five successful and several attempted military coups, a costly civil war, and ethnic and religious strife that has taken thousands of lives. The various ethnic groups in Nigeria have suffered both economic and political marginalization.

The purpose of this chapter is to demonstrate how British colonial policy influenced Nigeria's post independence political life. Three aspects of this legacy and their consequences are noteworthy. The first provides an understanding of how "tribalism" was introduced in Nigeria, and the way it relates to the economic and social structure of the nation. The second is what we will refer to as pre-independence politics. It will trace the stages of British entry into the area now known as Nigeria. It will also show how the integration of several ethnic groups by the colonial regime in tandem with the emergent nationalist elites created an early tendency towards tribal rivalry in the political system. Third, the post-independence federalism section shows how development needs permitted wide discretion for public intervention. This also led the nation to formulate policies geared towards stimulating demands for public amenities, protection, subsidy and patronage. The consequences of these policies further led to the struggle for opportunities and wealth among the different ethnic groups.

Diversity and Cross-cultural Dynamics

Judging from news accounts of violence and general hostilities in multiethnic societies, it would seem that ethnic relations are as a rule conflictual. Indeed, almost all theorists have viewed conflict as a fundamental, if not permanent, feature of relations between ethnic groups. Conflict theory and ethnic competition constitutes radical approaches to social and political problems (Gurr 1993; Esman 1994). They put the call for change high on the public agenda, and suggest that custom, practice, and tradition, instead of being useful to an orderly society, may create its problems. They start with the assumption that individual needs and potential should be fulfilled. Any situation that interferes with the desired fulfillment is therefore seen as a social problem, which should be examined. According to Peter Ekeh (1974), Richard Sklar (1993), (Martin Marger (1997) Milton Esman (1994) and Saxton and Kaufman (1971), the emphasis in conflict theory is upon restructuring society so that it can better fulfill the needs of its members, rather than upon adapting the individual or groups to the existing order.

The literature on ethnic identity and solidarity defines these terms in two perspectives: (1) narrow perspective and: (2) broader perspective. The narrower perspective denotes a community that claims common origin, often including common descent or kinship; that posses distinctive and valued cultural markers in the form of customs, dress, and especially language; that traces a common history and expects to share a common destiny. Persons born into such a community generally share a collective identity and constitute a distinct people (Harowitz 1985; Nyangoro 1994; Esman 1994; Halisi 1997).

The broader characterization of ethnicity incorporates other ascriptive solidarity groups such as race, religion, and nationality. In this study, the broader definition is used, and it includes a collective identity and solidarity based on inherited culture, racial differences, belief systems or sentiments of common nationality. In Canada for example, the main cleavage is defined as cultural-linguistic – Anglophone versus Francophone – though in the twentieth century it contained an important religious element, Catholic versus Protestant. Today, the claims of Canada's aboriginal people introduce racial as well as cultural differences. In Malaysia, the differences between Malays and Chinese include racial and religious as well as cultural dimensions. In Northern Ireland, the dispute between Catholic and Protestants do not in fact concern theological issues but the relative power, status, and resources available to each community (van den Berghe 1975; Crawford 1976; Horowitz 1985; Richard 1987; Malcolm 1989; Esman 1994). Although the parties in Southern Africa have been defined by race, the majority Black society encompasses highly mobilized peoples differentiated by distinctive cultures and institutions. The ultimate consideration in this study is ethnic pluralism, that is two or more ascriptive solidarity groups, "us and them" coexisting under a single political national government.

Liberal theory on ethnicity regards the individual as the main unit of social value and predicts that progress will inevitably break down artificial barriers based on parochial, ascriptive allegiances. In the emergent society, free of ascriptive or communal constraints, people would participate and compete as self-determining individuals valued and rewarded according to their individual contributions and performance (Esman 1994; Crawford 1976; Parson 1975; Glazer and Moynihan 1975; Deutsch 1953). No preferences, no discrimination a level playing field for every individual. Ethnicity would survive only as nostalgic vestiges of an earlier and less enlightened stage of historical development.

The influential modernization variant of classical liberalism argues that voluntary associations based on occupational and other "rational" interests would supplant status groups based on particularistic and parochial solidarities. In the wake of economic development and nation building ascriptive loyalties would lose their social function and gradually wither away (Esman 1994; Parsons 1975; Glazer and Moynihan 1975).

Ethnicity as politics is meaningful only in a relational framework. As a collective identity ethnicity is shaped not only by self-definition but also by constraints imposed by outsiders. Thus the internal "we" must be distinguished from the external "they." Where no relevant others exist, the need for solidarity disappear and society fragments on the basis of internal differences (Ndegwa 1997; Esman 1994; Rothchild 1981; Crawford 1976). The need for ethnic solidarity arises only when strange, threatening, competitive outsiders must be confronted. Only then is distinction between "us" and "them" arising. Consequently, this would lead to the need for internal solidarity and discipline. Thus, ethnicity is shaped by environment, by the threats and the opportunities it affords.

Different levels of ethnic inequality can be combined with the processes of assimilation and pluralism to shape a topology of multi-ethnic societies. Milton Yinger (1981) defines assimilation as a process of boundary reduction that can occur when members of two or more societies or smaller cultural groups meet. Robert Park (1920), Donald Horowitz (1990) and Milton Esman (1994) in their theory of assimilation explain that groups first come into contact through migration and subsequently, engage in competition, often characterized by conflict. Out of such competition eventually emerges some form of accommodation among the groups, leading finally to assimilation. Like Robert Park (1920), Milton Gordon (1964) and Milton Esman (1994) explains assimilation as a series of stages, or steps through which various groups pass. But rather than following a straight line leading from contact to eventual absorption, groups may remain indefinitely at one or another of these stages. Out of the seven stages that Gordon (1964) outlined, cultural assimilation and civic assimilation are the most complete. The first two, cultural and structural assimilation are, however, the most important. Cultural assimilation or acculturation according to Martin Marger (1997), Ekeh Peters (1974) and Donald Horowitz (1985; 1990) denotes the adoption by a minority ethnic group of the dominant group's cultural patterns, language, political beliefs and so on. But acculturation, though a prerequisite, does not assure movement to the next phase. Gordon explains that groups become very much like the dominant group in behavior and values but still remain structurally segregated. Structural assimilation, the second stage, is seen essentially as what we can refer to as primary or informal structural assimilation. This stage is the most critical because it is the key to all subsequent stages. Gordon asserts that once structural assimilation has occurred, either simultaneously with or subsequent to acculturation, all of the other types of assimilation will naturally follow.

Pluralism according to Glickman (1995), Ottaway (1994), Martin Marger (1997) and Peter Ekeh (1974) is a set of social processes and conditions that encourage group diversity and the maintenance of group boundaries. Pluralism must be understood as a variable for groups and societies. Ethnic pluralism never entails an absolute separation of groups. Ethnic groups in this chapter refer to a distinguishable group within a lager society. In a pluralistic society we assume that there will always be some common political or economic system that binds various ethnic groups together.

There are two forms of ethnic pluralism in modern multiethnic societies. The first group is referred to as equalitarian pluralism. In this pluralism, groups maintain cultural and structural autonomy but remain relatively equal in political and economic powers. The separation of groups under this pluralism is voluntary. The second pluralism is called inequalitarian pluralism. Under this pluralism, groups maintain structural segregation and perhaps cultural distinctness as well as unequal political and economic powers. Group separation in inequalitarian pluralism is involuntary. Inequalitarian pluralism is the chief feature of the Nigerian society or any other society that has experienced colonialism. In the Nigerian cases, one group exerts maximum political and economic powers, which enables it to shape the nature of the military, as well as inter-ethnic relations in such a way as to sustain its interests.

In the societies of nations such as Belgium, Canada, Malaysia and Switzerland structural and cultural differences among ethnic groups are protected by the state and institutional provisions are made to encourage an ethnically proportionate distribution of societal rewards. This type of pluralism is referred to as corporate pluralism. In corporate pluralistic system, the government formally recognizes ethnic units, and political and economic powers are allocated on the basis of an ethnic formula. Such systems are sometimes referred to as consociational federalism (Rothchild 1964; Bates 1974; Lijphart 1977; van Berghe 1981; Horowitz 1990). In corporate pluralistic societies, the groups are relatively balanced in political and economic power, and no single one is able to exert its will on all vital society issues. Moreover, group segregation is mainly voluntary. As Hunt and Walker (1974), Peter Ekeh (1974), Horowitz (1990), Richard Sklar (1993) and Milton Esman (1994) describe it, group relationships are so ordered that the extremes of inequality found in segregation are avoided and each group feels that it is gaining some benefit from association in the common society.

Conflicts therefore rests on four premises: (1) that contention and disputation can be a useful way of forcing problems to the attention of those in position to solve them; (2) that change and disequilibrium are not to be shunned or avoided; (3) that the causes of social and political problems often reside within social and political institutions; and (4) that changes in institutional behaviors will, therefore result in resolving social and political problems. In the Nigerian, Rwandan, and South African context ethnic conflict begins with the idea that social institutions are not beset with problems, but are, in fact, the source of the problems.

Studies on ethnic relations have developed a view that ethnicity is an inherent aspect of social change in all culturally heterogeneous societies. This view argues that neither the disappearance nor a significant amelioration of ethnic conflict is possible. It sees the stability of these societies as threatened not by communalism, but by the failure of national institutions to explicitly recognize and accommodate existing ethnic divisions and interests. It recommends political arrangements which accord to all communal groups a meaningful role in national life and which are able to keep communal conflicts within manageable bounds (Melsen and Wolpe, 1970). This view partially explains the inevitability of political instability in Rwanda, Nigeria, and South Africa.

The theory of relative deprivation began in the early 1960s with the publication of James Davies' book "Toward a Theory of Revolution."

The theory states that revolutionary events are likely when a prolonged period of rising expectations and increasing gratification is followed by a short period of sharp reversal. During this time, the gap between expectation and gratification quickly widens and becomes intolerable. This is what is also known as Davies' "J-curve" theory. One of the shortcomings of this study is the typical conclusion reached when transition to majoritarian democracy fails. In these failed transitions where ethnicity is evidently a factor in mobilizing for political change or for anticipated electoral politics, a more vivid explanation for the conflict can be found by applying the dual citizenship theory.

In Gurr's work, Why Men Rebel, he argues that "the primary causal sequence in political violence is first the development of discontent, second the politicization of that discontent, and finally its actualization in violent action against political objects and actors." Discontent is the product of relative deprivation, which is defined as a perceived discrepancy between men's values, expectations and their value capabilities (Gurr 1970, 12-13). Thus, relative deprivation from Gurr's perspective leads only to the potential for political conflict. The translation of this potential in Nigeria requires structural and cultural facilitation, organizational mobilization, and careful evaluations of the risk involved in confronting the military government.

The most dominant theme of the modernization perspective is that increased urbanization, commercialization, schooling, communication and professionalization on ethnicity will lead to the integration of diverse ethnic groups (Morrison and Stevenson, 1972). Although economic factors are usually mentioned, most modernization analysts tend to deal with them briefly and then go on to emphasize bicultural factors such as the degree of inter-ethnic racial and cultural differences, ethnocentrism, differences in institutions, the absence of value consensus, and the clarity and rigidity of group definition, or to synthesize subsets of these.

According to Sanda (1976), one major theoretical issue in many of the recent studies of ethnic conflict in Africa is the extent to which ethnic units and cultural entities coincide, or the extent to which ethnic affiliations can be said to be predictive of socio-cultural attitude and beliefs.

Richard Sklar's (1976; 1993) position on the same controversy agrees with those of Sanda, that tribalism is an instrument in the hands of political elites. According to Richard Sklar (1993), tribalism is widely supposed to be the most formidable barrier to national unity in Africa. It is less frequently recognized that tribal movements may be created and instigated to action by the new men of power in furtherance of their own special interests which time and again constitute the interests of emerging social classes. Tribalism then becomes a mark for class privilege. Donald Horowitz (1987) argues that the social psychological perspective may explain incidents of ethnic conflict and violence that are otherwise intelligible only in terms of some hypothesis – inadequate, in his view – of elite manipulation and deception. Re-interpreting the account of conflict between the Itsekeri and Urhobo ethnic groups in Nigeria, that erupted into mob violence, he writes: "A more fruitful explanation . . . lies in the disparaging evaluations of group worth to which Itsekiri and comparable groups were subject, evaluations that led them to want to do something to retrieve their self-esteem." This threat to ethnic groups is sufficient motive for mass involvement in any ethnic conflict in Nigeria, Rwanda, and South Africa. The contest for group legitimacy, for political inclusion and exclusion, merges with the quest for group worth to form a politics of ethnic entitlement (Diamond 1987; Lemarchand 1995). This constitutes the major engine of mass ethnic conflict in the three nations. Thus, as ethnic consciousness increases in scope and intensity, the socioeconomic and political atmosphere becomes charged with tension. Under these circumstances, the ethnic factor assumes a self fulfilling and self-sustaining dynamics of its own. Ethnic hostility, loyalty and identification are passed on to successive generations through the process of socialization. The family, press, private and public conservation and other agencies of socialization are infected by ethnicity. Therefore, even when the original basis of ethnicity, socio-economic competition among classes and individuals is eliminated, there remains the problem posed by the internalized dimension.

In recent times, ethnic groups have formed two types of nationalism. Geertz (1994) called this civic nationalism and ethnic nationalism. According to Michael Ignatief (1993), and Milton Esman (1994) civic nationalism is when a nation is composed of its entire people regardless of race, color, creed, gender, language, or ethnicity. Here, people possess equal political and social rights and choose to be members of a nation, along with others, regardless of ethnicity, who share broadly similar beliefs and values. Ethnic nationalism, by contrast, holds that people's allegiance is to an ethnic group or nationality into which they have been assigned, not to a larger political entity encompassing many different ethnic groups or nationalities. Here, an individual's deepest attachments are inherited, not chosen.

The dual citizenship theory provides a precise way of analyzing the relationship between ethnic identity, authority and legitimacy. On one hand, ethnic citizenship, legitimacy and authority rest on cultural practice, family, clan, extended kin, and to a community. On the other hand, individual claim to nation-state citizenship is vested in the public realm by passports, voting cards, bureaucratic and legal instruments. Ethnic legitimacy in post-colonial Nigeria begins at the clan level that provides the basic unit of solidarity and public discourse outside the family. According to Stephen Ndegwa (1997), Stewart (1995), Frost (1994), Peled (1992), ethnic identity rests on a socially, as opposed to a legally constructed definition of belonging. Belonging in the Nigerian, Rwanda, and South African societies or ethnic communities is established by birth, marriage or adoption into a family and kin that believe in shared history and values. Therefore, duality of citizenship is complicated by the fact that it is conceived differently in the nation-state of these nations and their ethnic communities. The recognition of ethnic groups as a basis of citizen formulation and the strong loyalty attached provides a powerful instrument to explain why ethnic groups are more committed to their communities than their nation-state. In the past four decades Rwanda, Nigeria, and South Africa have witnessed cases of intense ethnic conflict based on dual citizenship and ethnic nationalism – the Biafra civil war in Nigeria, genocide in Rwanda and several riots in South Africa due to white supremacy regime are examples.

Tribalism

Nigeria, like most African nations comprise of different tribes, each with a different homeland and language. The word "tribalism does not refer to this fact, however, nor to the natural affinity which individuals feel for those to whom they can talk in their mother tongue, nor the pleasure they get from the landscape, customs, food and so forth with which they have been familiar from childhood. Rather, it refers to relationships between people from different tribes, and two things are immediately clear about it.

The first is that modern tribalism is a creation of colonialism. It has little or nothing to do with pre-colonial relations between tribes. In Nigeria by October 1960, as we shall see later, the main poles of tribalism were the Hausa-Fulani, Igbo and Yoruba tribes. Before colonial rule in 1861, however, there were no enmity and scarcely any relationship at all between these tribes. What brought these tribes into relations with each other for the first time was their shared involvement in the colonial economy. The foundations for modern tribalism were laid when the various tribal modes and relations of production began to be displaced by capitalist ones, giving rise to new forms of insecurity, and obliging people to compete with each other on a national plane for work, land, and ultimately for education and other services seen as necessary for security.

Secondly, tribalism is an ideological phenomenon. Essentially it consists in the fact that people identify other exploited people as the source of their insecurity and frustrations, rather than their common exploiters. Of course this does not happen spontaneously. Colonial regimes have played an important part in fostering tribalism by their policy of trying to channel all political and economic dealings between individuals and the state through the medium of tribal authorities, and by discriminating in favor of some tribes and against others, especially in their own recruitment policies. After independence indigenous politicians started playing similar roles, by putting themselves forward as patrons capable of bringing the maximum benefits to their people, at the expense of other people whose leaders are denounced as tribalist for trying to do the same. These candidates often call for tribal unity and condemning as divisive and almost treasonous anyone who calls attention to the real causes of unemployment, landlessness and insecurity, and who tries to direct popular feeling against those who benefit from it including themselves.

To put the matter in a nutshell, tribalism is primarily a form of consciousness, like racism, whereas class is primarily a relation of production, and only under certain historical conditions it is also refereed as a form of consciousness. In neo-colonial Africa class formation and the development of tribalism accompany each other.

To see the mutual relationship of class and tribalism in Nigeria more clearly, we have first to recall the way in which the uneven development of capitalism affected the position of the Igbos. Before 1914 when the colonial rule amalgamated north and southern Nigeria into one nation, the Igbos had been expanding demographically and territorially, and had established themselves as a network of trading communities with complex relations with the Yorubas to the west and the Hausa-Fulani to the north. The other side of the coin, however, was that the Igbos were among the first people to adapt western education, social structure and capitalist mode of production. Besides learning to be wage laborers, some of the more enterprising Igbos also learned to trade with the European capitalist sector, in so far as they were allowed to, and their notables quickly learned to turn to commercial advantage the colonial chiefships which they were able to obtain, and laid the foundations of numerous petty-bourgeois family fortunes.

Pre-Independence Politics

The existence of people within the territory of what is now Nigeria can be traced back to 5,000 BC, when some groups appear to have settled and practiced agriculture. The existence of large states such as Kanem Borno Empire and the Sokoto Caliphate (Muslim Kingdom) with centralized governments beginning about the 19th century is well-known (Tamuno, 1972). Between the 11th and 15th centuries a series of Islamic Hausa states flourished in the north of Kano, Kasina, Zaria and Nupe. In the south there were empires centered at Ife, Oyo and Benin. Ife, despite a later decline in political influence, retained a spiritual and institutional importance. Its bronzes and terra-cotta sculptures are world famous. Folklore has it that descendants from Ife founded the Kingdoms of Oyo and Benin. Economically Oyo became an important trading and crafts center, and with the aid of a strong cavalry it soon forged a powerful empire. The Benin political system rested much more on a sacred monarchy and palace bureaucracy whose powers were checked by associations of titleholders. Its main period of imperial expansion was in the 14th and 15th centuries and is well illustrated in the famous bronzes produced in Benin. In the south-eastern part of Nigeria, the Igbo and other ethnic groups evolved societies that were loose federations without a strong central authority or king (Ajayi, 1965; Tamuno, 1972). In fact, out of the 250 ethnic groups in Nigeria the vast majority had their own societies based on subsistence agriculture with appropriately strong political or military establishments as their geographic proximity to others groups required.

The first European contacts date from the late 15th century, when the Portuguese had their first meetings with the kingdom of Benin (Nigerian Factfinder, 1995). Trade was initiated in peppers and later in slaves. The arrival of other Europeans furthered the rise of the slave trade: the British began to replace the Portuguese as leading traders on the coast of West Africa, and slaves rapidly became the major export (Ikime, 1969). According to Ajayi (1965) and Tamuno (1972), estimates of slaves that were exported from West Africa range between 30 and 40 million people. Many of these were Nigerians. The internal effects of the slave trade encouraged military instability and severely discouraged agriculture and economic advancement. The exported adults constituted the source of manpower for economic development in the West African region.

Biobaku (1965) asserts that the northern part of Nigeria was largely untouched by the Europeans. Trade was still conducted principally with North Africa. In the 19th century the north witnessed a series of revolutionary upheavals within the Hausa Kingdoms, initiated by Usman Dan Fodio, a Muslin leader of the Fulani ethnic group. The result was the replacement of the Hausa Kings with Fulani rulers and the establishment of the Sokoto caliphate. There was clearly a moral, intellectual, religious and reformist thrust to Jihad (holy war) exemplified in the North by Usman Dan Fodio. Under his leadership the Fulani formed a cohesive group with superior cavalry to police the whole Sokoto caliphate.

The slave trade on the coast of West Africa came to an end in the 19th century when Britain became economically ready for a changeover in trade pattern. The change was from a mercantile sugar-based trade (which centered on an exchange between slaves and sugar) to an industrial economy, which required raw materials like palm oil from West Africa and could utilize a potential market for manufactured goods there, as well (Ikime, 1969). Fearing challenges to its economic supremacy in Africa and desiring to control future economic prospects, Britain prepared to undertake direct political control (Tamuno, 1972). At the 1883 Conference of Berlin, European powers reached agreement on how they would partition Africa and Britain set about the military conquest of the Nigerian people. The decisive factor in the conquest according to Ikime (1969) was clearly the superior European military technology, but there was strong resistance in many areas, and the conquest was not achieved without the bloody and ruthless use of modern weapons, especially in Benin (Niger delta area).

The British conquest of Nigeria, one of the world's most ethnically diverse societies with its over 250 identifiable ethnic groups, led to the establishment of a colonial administration in 1900 which was not particularly sensitive to the variety or history of these groups. Before the British conquest, these ethnic groups had never been under a single administrative system. The Hausa-Fulani, Yoruba, Igbo, Kanuri, Tiv, Edo, Nupe, Ibibio, and Ijaw groups together account for almost 80 percent of the population. There are however three very large ethno-linguistic groups – the Hausa-Fulani in the north, the Yorubas in the west and the Igbos in the east. Each of these major ethnic groups are surrounded by smaller groups known as the minorities which, added together are more numerous than the major groups combined (Ajayi, 1965; Tamuno, 1972). The overwhelming majority of the northern population is Muslim, and Muslims are widely thought to comprise more than 50 percent of the total population. Christianity is strong in the south, accounting for perhaps 35 percent of Nigeria's total population, while the balance of the population practice traditional religion. The ethnic groups that have now been resurrected to constitute the component units of a confederation were different sovereign nations before the colonial era. The British overlooked the importance of this history. Larry Diamond (1983), contends that for half a century – from the time that separate protectorates were declared for Northern and Southern Nigeria in 1900 to the Constitutional Conference of 1950 – Nigeria was ruled in an essentially authoritarian fashion by the colonial power. But that fashion of ruling was not uniform across the country. The colonial government's policy was not to dissolve traditional political structures but rather to rule through the aristocracy of the conquered peoples – it was this idea that lay at the heart of the concept of "indirect rule." Even after the formal amalgamation of the two protectorates in 1914, the British continued to rule Nigeria, in effect, as two countries (Diamond, 1983).

British companies began to promote trade and support missionary work in the coastal areas of Nigeria in 1885. According to Rolf Theen and Frank Wilson (1995), the British seem to have been motivated by a European notion of "civilizing" Africa by ending the slave trade. British companies operating along the valley of the Niger River had come together to form the Royal Niger Company. In order to take proper hold (monopoly) of their trade along the Niger River valley, the British Royal Niger Company asked for the King's authority, i.e., a Charter, to administer the area. This Charter was granted to the Royal Niger Company in 1885 and withdrawn in 1900. The area came under the supervision of the colonial office in 1900. That same year the British Foreign Office changed the name of the Niger Coast Protectorate to the Protectorate of Southern Nigeria. The land formerly administered by the Royal Niger Company became the Protectorate of Northern Nigeria.

The third phase of British entry to Nigeria also involves trade. The British established an extensive market for Nigerian palm oil beginning in 1861. As their political and economic interests in Nigeria expanded, the British formally acquired control over the area. Lagos became a British colony in 1861; all Yorubaland became a British protectorate in 1888, and the Igboland was added to what was called the Niger Coast Protectorate in 1893.

Northern Nigeria resisted British penetration because they felt that the British colonial rule would destroy their well-developed political, homogenous and religious communities. It was not until the conquest of Sokoto in 1903 that the Sultans and Emirs of the north accepted British rule. The strong pre-colonial political structure in the north made the British colonial government decide to establish "indirect rule" there. Such a policy appealed to the parsimonious minds of Treasury officials as being less costly, but more importantly it provided an effective guarantee of a stable means for the extraction of economic surplus. According to William Graf (1988), the underlying motives of colonialism was thus to ensure the effective and unchallenged exploitation of the colony to the benefit of British finance and industry.

Indirect rule perpetuated inter-ethnic and inter-regional differences. This indirect rule policy practiced in the northern part of the nation, encouraged ruling through native social institutions and leaving them more or less intact along a more traditional orientation (Mayer et al. 1996). Meanwhile, the people of the south were more highly educated than the northerners in a European or Western sense, exacerbating the feelings of ethnic differences between the northern and southern tribes. Virtually all of the Nigerian elites who studied in either the United Kingdom or United States came from either the Igbo or Yoruba tribes. These Western educated Nigerians were socialized into a predominantly Christian tradition with Western values, while the Northerners either received little or no formal education or were educated into a more conservative Muslim tradition (Mayer el al. 1996). The early Christian missionaries came by the sea; thus, their contact with the indigenous population was with the Igbo and the Yoruba, who controlled the major port cities. These groups therefore became the beneficiaries of Western education and culture. Hence, the cultural and linguistic factors that prevented the development of a sense of community among Nigerians were buttresses by fundamental religious differences, creating a deeply segmented society.

During the indirect rule period the traditional authority of the rulers rested largely upon their ability to maintain ethnic-group cohesiveness, tribal customs, and their distinctiveness from adjacent groups. Indirect rule therefore, reinforced the most conservative aspects of traditional political organization, and shut out other tendencies towards multi-groups cooperation. The system worked well in the North where there was Fulani aristocracy but, in the South, things did not work so smoothly because the British did not understand the southern forms of political organization where there were no clear ruling groups as such. William Miles (1994) asserts that the irrationality of colonial-era world politics is well illustrated in the northern Nigerian case since part of Hausaland, one of the more developed pre-colonial political entities in Africa, ended up in the British colony and another part further north came under French rule in the colony eventually known as Niger.

The first error of the federal structure of Nigeria sprang from the British colonial heritage. It was characteristic of most British colonial policy making that it failed to have any long term plans, but rather extemporized and reacted to nationalist or regional pressures. Throughout this period the British government did not prepare for the time when the different geographic regions would become one nation, the largest in Africa. From 1900 to 1914, Northern and Southern Nigeria were treated as separate entities, although the British government had already recognized the confined territories by the name Nigeria. The name "Nigeria" was invented by an African correspondent of the Times of London as a convenient means of identifying the diverse West African peoples and regions that had been added to the British Empire. Nigeria was derived from the word "Niger" which is the name of the river that constitutes the most remarkable geographical feature of the country. Together with their tributaries, the Niger River and the River Benue have served as the most important means of communications linking the peoples, through whose land they flow.

In 1914, Northern and Southern Nigeria were amalgamated under the governorship of Lord Lugard. To assist him oversee the two Protectorates, lieutenant governors were appointed and stationed in Kaduna and Enugu. Kaduna and Enugu became the new capital of the Northern and Southern respectively. The Southern Protectorate was split into two in 1939 and renamed the Western and Eastern group of provinces. Ibadan became the capital of the Western Provinces and Enugu continued to be the capital of the Eastern Provinces. Lagos also retained its status as a colony. The amalgamation, however, did nothing to unite the peoples of Nigeria, and successive governors of Nigeria in Lagos had the utmost difficulty in persuading the lieutenant governors of the North to follow their policy (White,1981). The Eastern and Western groups of provinces were named Regions in 1946 and this was the setting until Nigeria attained independence on October 1, 1960.

The Northern region comprised roughly 56 percent of the population and almost three-quarters of the area of Nigeria in 1960. This was one of the reasons why Amadu Bello, the Sardauna of Sokoto and Premier of the North, assumed a powerful position most incompatible to Nigeria's unity at independence.

The South was divided into two regions in 1939, so that at independence in 1960 the new federal state of Nigeria was made up of three regions each with a political center of gravity in its major ethnic and historical group: the Hausa, Fulani and their Kanuri allies in the North, the Yoruba in the West and the Igbo in the East. Each of these majority groups comprised some two-thirds of the population of their region while the remainder consisted of a number of different minority tribes. For example, in the eastern region, there were non-Igbos such as Ijaw, Efik, Ibibio, Idomi and Ogoja people. In the North, there were the Tiv, Idoma, Igbira, Igala and Jukun peoples, together with those of the plateau area, Adamawa and Southern Zaria, and a number of Yoruba peoples in Ilorin. All of these peoples differed from the ethos of the dominant Hausa-Fulani Empire. As independence approached, the minorities became more restive, and although some identified with the regional power and accepted its patronage, others campaigned for a Middle Belt Region comprised of Non-Muslims and Non-Hausa Fulani people.

According to James Coleman (1958), despite the internal tensions in the region, the northern ethos was an attractive one to most of its inhabitants. The empathy between British administrators and Northern Nigerians was considerable and characterized by mutual respect. This is probably because of the pre-colonial well-established political system in the northern part of Nigeria. All the northern administrators were able to speak Hausa, the main language of the region, and had a considerable pride in the North and its rather conservative ethos of indirect rule, which nonetheless allowed for considerable development by native authorities in partnership with district officers who were British. At independence, Sir Abubakar Tafawa Balewa, the Federal Prime Minister, spoke of the changing relationship between the British and the Nigerians as being one "always as Friends." By this statement, he was drawing on his northern experience. The sense of Northerners extended even to the Middle Belt people who were neither Hausa nor Muslim. Okion Ojigbo (1980) asserts that creation of the Northern ethos was a thing of value but the North as a governmental unit should have been abolished and replaced by a larger number of constituent regions or states if Nigerian federal unity was to survive. The British colonial administration had its last chance to break up the large regions with the establishment of the Willink Commission of

1957-1958. Lennox Boyd, however, as the Colonial Secretary, tilted the balance against the creation of new states by saying that to do so would involve putting off independence for two more years, which nobody wanted to do (Coleman, 1958).

After World War II, Britain began making arrangements for a staged withdrawal from Nigeria. The country was in theory more or less unitary because the governor in Lagos had formal authority over all Nigeria, but in practice the degree of suspicion between regional governments was considerable. When the British colonial administration started reforming the nation, it produced a series of constitutions that ignored the obvious balances of federalism and were therefore unworkable. The first Constitution was the Clifford Constitution of 1922 to 1945. This Constitution provided for a Legislative Council for Nigeria. This Council made laws for the western and eastern protectorates, as well as for the Lagos colony. The governor-general of Nigeria was empowered to make laws for the northern group of provinces, the rationale for which is not known. The order establishing the Legislative Council in 1922 was amended in 1928 and in 1941. On each occasion the number of legislators and of Nigerians participating in the council was increased.

The second constitution, the Richards Constitution, was enacted in 1946. The constitution was named after the then governor-general of Nigeria, Governor Arthur Richards (later Lord Milverton). It provided for a central legislature for the whole of Nigeria and three Regional Houses of Assembly, one for each group of provinces, with advisory powers only in regards to legislation. The Richards Constitution made it possible for the first time in the history of the nation for representatives of the northern and southern regions to have direct contact in Lagos. The Richards Constitution failed to provide for a proper federal legislature since its members were to be co-opted from local native authorities or elected by the regional legislative councils. One very serious defect of the Richard Constitution of 1946 was that the governor-general was not required to consult with the people he was authorized to administer, according to constitutional stipulations. As a result, the constitution was widely criticized by the emerging political class as unfit for Nigerians.

The third constitution was the Macpherson Constitution, which came into effect in 1952. The constitution was named after Sir John Macpherson, the governor-general who succeeded Arthur Richard in 1951. The Macpherson Constitution created, for the first time, Council of Ministers with twelve Nigerian members. These twelve council members were chosen on regional bases. The constitution afforded increased regional autonomy and extended to Nigerians a fuller share in making policy and in the direction of executive government action.

The desire for greater regional autonomy and the need for precise assignment of functions between the center and the regional governments made it apparent that yet another constitution was required almost immediately. Conferences on a fourth constitution (the Federal Constitution) were held in London in 1953 and in Lagos in 1954 (Nigerian Year Book 1993, 78). Under the Federal Constitution, the central government had exclusive jurisdiction over such matters as aviation, census, customs, defense, exchange control, external affairs, immigration, police, shipping, mines and minerals, post and telegrams, railways and trunk roads, trade and commerce between Nigeria and other countries, and between the regions. Jurisdiction was shared between the federal and regional governments on matters relating to bankruptcy, electricity, industrial development, insurance, labor, and registration of business names, scientific and industrial research, statistics and water supply.

The obvious lack of cohesion resulting from the constitutional allocation of functions was apparent in the 1953 cabinet crisis over the proposed resolution for self-government in 1956. The Southern members of the cabinet who considered 1956 to be an appropriate time sponsored the resolution. The northern members who wished for self-government as soon as practicable rejected this resolution. The North, was outnumbered in educationally qualified persons by about ten to one and it feared close union would give control to the better educated southerners. Two explanations can be given for the difference in educational achievements between northern and southern Nigeria. The first explanation is that the British entered the country from the sea and introduced Christianity and English education in the southern territory long before their influences reached the north. The second explanation has to do with the way the British colonial administration managed the affairs of the country. They ruled Nigeria as two countries and their educational policy may well have been designed in that fashion. Therefore, the North's mistrust of strong federal power was basically a fear of losing jobs, contracts, government patronage and strong religious identity. In the latter instance, the spread of Christianity in the Islamic north was resisted given the strength of Muslim religious commitment and their belief that Islam was superior to Christianity.

Following the self-government debate in 1956, Northern ministers were harassed in Lagos and at every southern railway station on their return home. A campaign team of the Action Group, the party of the Western Region, led by Samuel Akintola, at that time a lieutenant of Awolowo, came to Kano (a Northern City) and was deliberately waylaid by thugs organized by local leaders of the Northern Peoples Congress (NPC), the ruling party of the North (Dunn 1977, 135). The resultant riots and two-day war between the traditional city of Kano where the Muslim Northerners lived and the New Town (which is called Sabo Gari) where Southerners or Christians lived caused at least thirty-five deaths, and made it clear that many in the North would react violently if they felt they were likely to be ruled by Southerners in Lagos.

Nigeria's effort to achieve independence from British rule began almost as soon as the colony was consolidated in 1914. Nationalist groups seeking home rule and later independence had begun operating as early as the 1920s. Within the independence movement was a group headed by Herbert Macauley (Tamuno, 1972). He founded the Nigerian National Democratic Party (NNDP) in 1923. The NNDP was the first Nigerian political organization to advocate independence from Britain. By the mid-1930s, a new and more militant nationalist group led by Dr. Nnamdi Azikiwe, the Nigerian Youth Movement challenged the NNDP. Although their goals were similar their timetables and their degree of militancy differed.

Regional and ethnic differences were evident in the various groups associated with the independence movement. Eventually, separate nationalist groups were formed in each area: the Igbo dominated National Council of Nigeria and the Cameroon (NCNC – Known as the National Congress of Nigerian Citizens after independence) in the southeast; the Yoruba-led Action Group (AG) was formed in the southwest, and the Northern Peoples' Congress (NPC) among the Hausa-Fulani people of the north. Even in their efforts to oppose British imperial rule and to seek independence these groups found it difficult to unite. Each nationalist group became involved in political struggles in its own region and defended regional interests in national politics.

At constitution conferences held in London in 1957 and 1958 respectively, it was agreed that the Eastern, Western and Northern regions should become self-governing by March 1959. The British government also agreed that if a resolution asking for independence was passed by the Federal Parliament early in 1960, her Majesty's Government would agree to that resolution. The British government, in pursuance of this undertaking, introduced the required Bill in Parliament to make Nigeria a fully independent country on October 1, 1960. Elections to the new House of Representatives were held in December 1959. The victories of the NPC, the AG, and the NCNC in their home regions established a close identity between the region, its political party, and its dominant ethnicity that was to heighten over the course of the 1950s.

The results of the 1959 election led to an alliance within the federal legislature between the NPC and the NCNC. When the office of federal Prime Minister was created in the late 1950s, NPC President Sir Ahmadu Bello chose to remain the premier of the North, and the party's vice president, Abubakar Tafawa Balewa, became Prime Minister. He then constructed a coalition cabinet embracing all three major political parties. Oyeleye Oyediran (1979) asserts that even though the two southern political parties had a sufficient number of seats to have formed a coalition government, the NCNC found it more expedients politically to join with the NPC in a coalition government. Tafawa Balewa, deputy the leader of the NPC, became prime minister and Nnamdi Azikiwe, president of the NCNC, was president of the Senate, and later, Nigerian governor-general. Larry Diamond (1983) contends that despite the significant anti-democratic currents in the 1959 elections, the colonial administration maintained some semblance of political order and electoral integrity, and the keen anticipation of independence produced a post-election spirit of accommodation. Although battered by the extraordinary bitterness of the campaign, the tacit pre-election alliance between the NPC and NCNC matured into a coalition government led by the former, which were only a few seats short of an absolute majority in Parliament. The alliance was facilitated not only by the NCNC's desire to bridge the North-South divide on the eve of independence, but also by both political parties' resentment of the AG's aggressive effort to mobilize ethnic minority groups in their regions. Unknown at the time was the outcome of the first elections after independence, where were to confirm the domination of the new nation by the northerners.

Post-Independence Federalism

It the meetings of the Federal Legislature in January 1960, both the Senate and the House of Representatives unanimously passed the resolution calling for independence. The British government approved this resolution and granted Nigeria the status of an independent and sovereign nation. Thus, Nigeria achieved independence on October 1, 1960, but with minimum internal cohesion. The constitution of this First Nigerian Republic was based on British parliamentary government with a Prime Minister and cabinet dependent upon the support of a majority of the parliament. William Graf (1988) contends that the sheer size and diversity of Nigeria, particularly after a half-century of indirect rule, precluded any total transference of the unitary Westminster model to the post-independence nation. The homogenous nature of British society, its consensual political culture and its advanced degree of industrialization – the latter achieved partly at the expense of the colonies at the periphery – ensured the proper operation of parliamentary government there. None of these conditions were present in post-independence Nigeria (Graf, 1988). The British, therefore, in consultation with Nigerian successor elites, superimposed on the Nigerian territories a system of federalism, which, like federalist governments elsewhere, were to permit a degree of autonomy to the different units. But binding the different ethnic groups into a voluntary association dominated by a central government was another matter. And in spite of numerous objections and protests, particularly from Nigeria's minority group representatives, the British expected the federal model to unify the various territorial sub-sections under a single government.

Post-independence experiences, however, soon demonstrated that more meaningful factors than federalism and the common colonial heritage had to be utilized in the effort to achieve that degree of national cohesion that could assure a politically developed and stable society. The problems of nationhood, revolving around the issue of power sharing, brought Nigeria to the brink of fragmentation and disintegration soon after independence. The most pressing issues of nation building, which Nigeria faced, were the questions of defining the new nation and the related issue of creating an effectively integrated polity. These issues arose because the concept of the "nation" among "Nigerians" was still very abstract. Although the various groups that composed the independence movement had shared a common goal and often acted as a common front, they did not air or resolve their disagreements. Thus, their shared identity was for independence, not for an integrated Nigerian nation.

The elimination of the British colonial administrators at independence, intensified ethnic competition. Powerful new positions and rewards came within the grasp of the new elites, and ethnic competition for these positions was intense. Added to this scramble for power was the fact that regional imbalances induced by the colonial extractive economy persisted and in most cases became more pronounced (Graf, 1988). These imbalances generally spilled over ethnic group boundaries, thus reinforcing inter-ethnic competition and creating a further source of instability. The wealthier Yoruba and Igbo (western and eastern) regions feared that the poorer northern regions that in Nigeria happened to be the most populous regions would use their political power to force a redistribution. At the same time, the poorer regions resented their status that they tended to see as the outcome of ethnic politics.

No sooner was independence achieved than Nigeria's post-independence political experience became a particularly turbulent one. Several factors contributed to political instability. These included a shaky tripartite federal structure with strong regionalism, disparity in the size and populations of the three regions, tribally sustained political parties, ambitious politicians, most of whom were unfamiliar with national politics, and a weak constitution. These were the major contributory factors to an unhealthy political development in Nigeria.

According to Adedeji Adebayo (1981) and Ladipo Adamolekun (1986), social groups maintained their independence from government control after 1960. As in the colonial period, ethnic groups exerted considerable political power, particularly over the regional governments. The Hausa-Fulani controlled the north, the Yoruba the west, and the Igbo the east. The Bini, Igbo, and Urhobo formed the three largest ethnic groups in the smaller midwestern region.

In a similar manner, religious groups maintained the political independence they had secured during the colonial period. In the north, Muslim leaders controlled the educational and judicial systems and reinforced the power of the Hausa-Fulani aristocracy. In the south, Churches played a less important political role. Even though Muslims and Christians competed for conversions among the Yoruba people, their ancestral city (family birthplace), not their religious affiliation, shaped political allegiances. Most Igbo joined Christian churches, which provided the educational opportunities needed for upward social mobility into the governmental and private business sectors.

The northern part of Nigeria was relatively insulated from Western education and influence because they mainly under the control of native emirates during British indirect rule. Therefore, the values imparted by Western education were similarly more rare in the north. Moreover, the dominant Muslim religion on the north entails a number of non-Western values, such as a hierarchic and authoritarian view of society, polygamy and the subordination of women, and the view of the state as an instrument to advance and defend the faith, as opposed to the Western concept of the separation of the church and state. Acceptance by the Muslim north of any political format that may result in Christian or any non-Muslim control of government is unthinkable, as is acceptance by the Westernized Christians of the south of continued northern domination. Hence the northern and southern parts of the nation did not just differ on some specific policy-relevant values, as between the former confederacy and the north in the United States. Rather, northern and southern Nigeria have completely irreconcilable world views that are buttresses and perpetuated by the differences in religion and language.

Post-independence occupational pluralism also characterized the first Nigerian republic. Dominant economic groups included the Fulani business elites, Hausa merchants, and Igbo and Yoruba executives. Below them in the economic stratification system came some lower-ranking professionals (doctors, lawyers, teachers), small-scale traders, and clerks. A few Nigerians worked in coal mines, textile factories, construction firms, ports, and railroad networks. Around 80 percent of the labor force farmed the land, raising for either for their subsistence needs or for the export market. Even though all these economic groups had the freedom to articulate their policy preferences, the business elites possessed the greatest organizational ability to press their claims on government officials.

Nigeria's major problem was the distribution of political power, a situation that was aggravated by the existence of several political parties and a multiplicity of ethnic groups. It was not so much that the competitors for power were too many. Rather a basis for the equitable distribution of power was either lacking or ill-defined. The major competitors for political power were the Northern Peoples Congress (NPC) and Hausa-Fulani in the North, the Action Group Party (AG) and the Yoruba in the West, and the National Convention of Nigerian Citizens (NCNC) and the Igbo in the East. Also competing were the virile but minority ethnic groups such as the Edo, Urhobo, and Isoko in the Mid-West, the Tiv and Idoma in the Middle Belt, and assorted others in the Calabar-Ogoja-River (COR) area.

Another weakness of Nigerian federalism in the First Republic (1960-66) was the fear of the South that it was being dominated by the political power of the North not only because of its tradition of assumed right to rule, but also because its share of the population (more than 50 percent), which gave it a majority of seats in the Lower House of Parliament on which executive power depended. In a federal system the

Upper House provides a way of checking the threat of majority domination by giving equal representation to states of unequal population size. Under the First Republic, the South, with its two, and later, following the creation of the Mid-West, its three regions, enjoyed a majority in the Senate. The Senate's powers however, modelled after those in the British House of Lords, was a more ceremonial body with little effect on law making.

Obafemi Awolowo's failure to become the prime minister can be regarded as the original source of the Action Group crisis of 1962 and the accompanying treason trial (Oyediran, 1979). As leader of the opposition in the federal legislature, Awolowo accused Prime Minister Abubakar Tafawa Balewa of wasting the country's resources, with giving preferences to the North, with operating a spoils system that benefited his northern constituents, and with overall mismanagement and corruption. The defense pact signed between Britain and Nigeria formed the central focus of Awolowo's attack on colonialism (Oyediran, 1979). Awolowo claimed that Britain had extorted the pact from the Nigerian government as a condition for granting independence. As Action Group parties leader, Awolowo also had differences with premier, Samuel Akintola. Their disagreement centered on Akintola's acceptance of the federal Prime Minister's idea for strengthening national unity through the three major political parties. Awolowo strongly opposed this idea and used his newspaper to criticize Akintola as well as the policies of his Western Region government. This dispute resulted in fighting in the Western Region's Parliament and it caused Balewa to declare a state of emergency. Balewa also suspended the regional legislature and executive, and sent Dr. Majekodummi, as his special administrator. But when the state of emergency was lifted, the federal government ignored Majekodummi's advice to hold regional elections and instead reinstated Akintola who obtained a majority in the Regional House with his new party, the Nigerian National Democratic Party (NNDP).

The non-Yoruba peoples of the Western Region, the Edo, Itsekiri, Isoko, Urhobo, Mid-west Igbo, Ishan, Ijaw and other peoples of the Mid-west region were likewise attracted to the regional government by ties of power and patronage. When the opportunity arose they voted overwhelmingly for the creation of their own Mid-West State in 1963.

In the Eastern Region the non-Igbo peoples, the Ibibio, Efik, Ijaw, Idomi, and Ogoja people, looked to the regional capital Enugu for patronage as long as political power was exercised from that regional capital. But when Colonel Yakubu Gowon created two states for the minority peoples of the East in 1967, they, for the most part, welcomed this dispensation and identified with the federal side in the civil war. Thus, the Nigerian case has been a great and continual pressure for the creation of new federal units. To every minority the prospect of the creation of its own state is both a chance for patronage and for government position, as well as spiritual enhancement.

Thus, the First Republic (1960-1966) failed to meet the challenges of unification and development. Regional and ethnic conflict overwhelmed efforts of parliamentary government. Corruption was widespread and the first democratic government lost its legitimacy. Moreover, in the growing political crisis, the government proved incapable of preserving domestic order as the politicians ignored the necessary tensions and spreading violence.

The 1962 census became the focal point for much of the tension and violence. The Southerners feared the census would result in the permanent dominance of the more traditional and allegedly more authoritarian northerners. On the other hand, the northerners saw the southerner complaint as a tactic aimed at their monopolizing control of the national government (Theen and Wilson 1996; Mayer et al 1996). When these conflicting perceptions could not be reconciled, tribal, regional and ethnic violence intensified. Attacks were launched against Igbos in northern cities and the Tiv uprising of 1964-1966 was a clear consequence of this disorder. Election campaigns were also accompanied by violence and the results of the elections were denounced as fraudulent or rigged. By the end of 1965, unrest and violence were common throughout Nigeria. In the Western Region, the near total breakdown of law and order provided the army with its opportunity to interpose itself between the warring parties.

During the military regime from 1966 to 1997, the dynamics of resource allocation generated divisive ethnic conflicts. Military and bureaucratic officials competed to control the allocation of revenue, jobs, and contracts. Middlemen competed for access to state officials. Foreign corporations competed by proxy through their ethnic agents. The operations of commercial triangles perpetuated nepotism, tribalism, and statism. The triangular form of commercial relations created a closed government system in the country. This led the public to resent the increasing corruption and incompetence of the military government. Thus, politicians, businessmen, and academics resented the appropriation of opportunities by small cliques of ethnic-minded military rulers and their ministries' Directors-General. They saw themselves as qualified and competent to help the nation improve economically, technologically and politically rather than a clique of ethnic elites whose self interests were above those of the nation-state.

The annulment of the June 12, 1993, presidential election by northern military generals does justify Ojukwu's prognostication made over two decades ago. Moshood Abiola, a Yoruba, was said to have won a presidential election in 1993, against a representative of the Hausa-Fulani tribes, but it was annulled. Northern dominance in Nigeria has meant nothing more than power for the Hausa-Fulani ethnic group, via the use of some upstart civilians, politicians, and military officers. Under the able scheming of the Sokoto Caliphate, northern power alternates between its civilian and military minions in an unabashedly rabid power play that reduces the entire south to a group of glorified second-class ethnic groups.

A measure of the Hausa-Fulani's grip of power has been perhaps best portrayed by the tribulations of Moshood Abiola in the 1993 presidential elections. Local and foreign authorities and, ironically, some leading spokesmen of the northern tribes pronounced the election the freest and fairest Nigeria had ever had. But General Babangida annulled the election, although, he is not from either the Hausa or the Fulani tribes. Professor Omo Omoruyi (1997), former director of the Nigerian Center for Democratic Studies critically contended that both Shahu Shagari, the emir of Sokoto, and several other northern elites influenced General Babangida to annul the election. This development intensified the polarization of the society into subnational ethnic cultures that are separated in terms of identity, loyalty, and geographical location. The only significant point of contact among these different ethnic groups is the marketplace, but inter-ethnic competition and conflict are increasingly characterizing even this. Consequently, the ethnic factor has assumed a self-fulfilling and self-sustaining dynamic of its own. The persistence and growth of ethnicity in Nigeria have become inevitable. Therefore, the issue of whether modernization erodes ethnic loyalties or whether ethnic loyalties develop or become accentuated as a result of the process of modernization is far from being resolved in the Nigerian case. Moshood Abiola was arrested and thrown in prison without a trial when he declared himself president as elected in 1994 by General Sani Abacha, a Hausa and successor of Babangida. General Abacha died in June 1998 of a heart attack, and General Abdusalam Abubakar, another northerner, became the head of state. Chief Abiola, however, died in detention on July 7, 1998, after spending four years in prison.

The implication, of the Hausa-Fulani grip of political power in Nigeria is what Geertz (1994) refers to as ethnic nationalism. The right to political control is seen as an allegiance to an ethnic group into which they have been born. An adequate solution to the ethnic problem must therefore tackle the question of dual and competing citizenship, and come to grips with individual insecurity and the internalized dimension of their ethnic sentiments. It must, however, be preceded by a detailed examination of how ethnicity has emerged, persisted, and grown in a concrete case such as Nigeria.

In 1997 the Federal Military Government headed by General Abacha decided to place a new local government headquarters in the domain of the Ijaw ethnic group in the Warri Delta State of the country. Within a one month however, government, decided to move the headquarters to the domain of another ethnic group, the Itsekiris. This decision of the federal government galvanized inter-ethnic violence between the Ijaws and the Itsekiris, which resulted in the death of several hundred citizens in the region.

The Urhobos and Itsekiris have been known to be the only two tribes warring each other in the Warri region. Over the years, the Ijaws have managed to stay out of regional ethnic wars probably owing to self-restraint. The Ijaws decided this time to fight for their plight for two possible reasons: (1) the insensitivity of the federal government to the plight of the Delta people, when the majority of the national wealth is produced in their backyard; and (2) their failure, unlike the Itsekiris to share in the "crumbs" received from the government.

It is true that the rivalry between the Ijaw, Itsekiri, and Urhobos ethnic groups of the Warri region goes back a long way. However, co-existence and inter-marriage are common features of the ethnic groups of that region. The problem, like in most parts of Nigeria, started with the arbitrary drawing of administrative boundaries, which was initiated by the British and continued by the Nigerian government after independence. What is peculiar about the ethnic conflict in the Warri region is that the ethnic groups in the region watched oil companies drilling away for about 40 years, and they do not have the political clout like the Hausa-Fulani groups to redirect resources back into their communities. The only commercial city (Warri) in the region continues to suffer from neglect from the federal government.

The ethnic conflict in the Warri region is really a microcosm of the broader dual and competing citizenship, as well as the political and economic problems facing Nigeria. The Warri ethnic problem is a case of transferred aggression. The ethnic groups are really sending out a cry for help and a plea for political and economic rewards or progress. Riots and hijacking oil company equipment and personnel are symptomatic of the deeper issues raised above. If given real political and economic rewards, ethnic group attitudes, tolerance, and patience grow and whatever administrative mechanisms exist to resolve boundary and local government headquarters problems will stand a better chance of resolving these issues. It is therefore clear from the foregoing that ethnic groups draw legitimacy and loyalty from their ability to provide for their members in time of need.

Since the elected civilian government of President Obasanjo was sworn in on May 29, 1999, there has been a handle full of disturbance caused by either ethnic or religious conflicts. On February 27, 2000, Muslim and Christians clashed in the Hausa City of Kaduna leaving over 1000 people dead and several people injured. On the following day February 28, 2000, reprisal attacked was carried out on Hausa communities in the Igbo cities of Owerri and Aba on Sharia issues. Samuel Idowu (2001) pointed out how there has been sporadic fighting between the Hausa and Yoruba communities in several states of the federation. There was some attack on Hausa communities in Ibadan in Oyo state, later this fighting spread to Shagamu in Ogun state and Lagos. Before the government could control the situation more than 300 people were killed.

During the Sharia law crisis in Kaduna and Kano reprisal action were carried out by street urchins known as "Almajiris and Yandabas." The Sharia religious issue was over politicized, leaving room for certain northerner Moslem indigenes to whip up sentiments with religious issues. Nigeria was consequently thrown into mourning sessions following killing, arson and vandalism that characterized the crashes between Muslims and Christians in some northern cities. Although, these crisis have subsided there is no guarantee that will not be stirred up in the near future. Thus, ethnic and religious conflicts in Nigeria are in a state of uncertainty. What can the government do to resolve these callous problems in the twenty-first century?

Prospect For Resolving Conflict

The general analysis of Nigeria's political history provides a systematic support for the point made by situationalists that "politicized communal contention over economic distribution issues is the prevalent form of political relevant ethnicity" (Ekeh 1976; Gurr 1993; Sklar 1993). While the above analysis suggests a clear dichotomy in citizenship and in the form it takes, the reality is less clear-cut. In Nigeria, individuals hold multiple and shifting identities and change roles depending on the situation in which they find themselves. Ethnic groups also experience liberal citizenship demands at the national level that they may not find consistent with ethnic community demands. Faced with this situation ethnic community demands will be met, and national liberal citizenship demands undermined. Ethnic conflict in Nigeria demonstrate to a great extent how dual and competitive citizenship among indigenous ethnic groups could lead to explosive, bitter and bloody confrontations. A common ground among the three nations, however, was the fact that ethnic conflict resulted due to unequal access to political and economic rewards. One important factor that comes up in this analysis is that the relative frequency of conflicts among the various ethnic groups reflects the super-imposition of colonial divide-and-rule politics, and postcolonial political competition on the primordial ethnic map of pre-colonial Africa.

Table 2.1 shows the different ethnic groups in Nigeria. Under this multi-ethnic structure co-existence in these nations is not the same as in single political community of most modern Western nation-states.

Table 2.1
Major Ethnic Groups in Nigeria

Ethnic groups	%
Hausa	21
Yoruba	21
Igbo	18
Fulani	11
Ibibio	7
Kanuri	4
Edo	3
Tiv	2
Bura	2
Ijaw	2
Nupe	1
Others	8

Source: Nigerian Fact-Finder 1995; and Keesing's Record of World Events 1997.

Ethnic groups that capture a nation's majority vote do enjoy a larger bundle of rights and undertake a greater responsibility for the nation than members of the minority ethnic groups.

Political differentials, tribalism, racial supremacy, inequality, and discrimination also caused some of the grievances in these nations under study. The military action in Nigeria could be explained in terms of ethnic mobilization. Political competition within the context of unstable multi-ethnic coalitions and rebellions are due to dissatisfaction in the distribution of economic resources and powers between the various competing ethnic groups or citizenship. Faced with this situation, what are the prospects for containing ethno-political conflict in Nigeria?

Policy Options

Nigeria could adopt a corporate pluralism policy, in which all minority ethnic groups would be expected to adopt in full the cultural ways of the majority groups. This will enhance greater tolerance toward ethnic diversity in the nation. They should also undertake sweeping measures to foster political and economic equity among ethnic groups. Specifically, these policies should be aimed at improving the social and economic standing of the long-term victims of discrimination. Accommodative and consensual approaches that accept pluralism as legitimate and permanent sharing include federalism or regional self-government, cultural pluralism, electoral coalitions, and systems of power sharing (Bates 1974; Rothchild 1981; Esman 1994; Sisk 1995). Accommodation approaches may occur separately or in combinations, an example of the latter being the carefully crafted pattern of ethnic regionalism and central power sharing that has evolved in Belgium and Switzerland.

Alternatively, these nations could adopt a melting pot or an assimilation policy. This will require the formulation of a hybrid culture whereby all present ethnic groups will converge. The implications of this policy however, is that out of the various ethnic groups in these countries, which group will be selected and what will be the criteria for selection? Although, formulation of a hybrid language was successful in Indonesia, the citizens of these nations might be suspicious of any government nursing this line of thought. The amalgamation or the intermixing of diverse ethnic groups in these nations would however, advance ethnic convergence.

Multi-culturalism as a government policy could recognize, respect and encourage the retention of ethnic cultures within the larger societies of these nations. Consociationalism and federalism would allow for smaller arenas of political practice in which to enact ethnic citizenship and for representation at the center, and they also provide institutional mechanisms at the national level to moderate elites exploiting or acting on ethnic obligations (Lijphart 1977 & 1984; Hyden and Bratton 1992; Halisi 1997). However, the extent to which multi-culturalism will be accommodated by these nations, and how these factors affect the development of a definite national identity is another issue this policy should address. Sustaining and enhancing multi-culturalism can only hinder the movement of the various ethnic groups into mainstream institutions, thus perpetuating the system of ethnic stratification. Multiethnic coalitions can insure that ethnic communities or factions within them participate in government.

In military or single-party regimes, where control of the state is decided by non-electoral processes, ruling elites should be careful to include representatives of constituent ethnic communities in decision-making roles to reassure them that their status is respected and that they share in benefits provided by the state. Such coalition arrangements require continuous delicate political management to appease mutually suspicious constituents.

Uncontrollable conflict is not inevitable, and the answer to the problems of democracy and ethnic conflict is not to redraw the maps of Nigeria. Rather, it lies in political structures that discourage the polarization of ethnic conflict and encourage trans-ethnic alignment and crosscutting cleavages. The crucial institutional variables in containing ethno-political conflicts are those pertaining to the party system and central local relations in government and party structures. The elites of the majority ethnic groups should be aware that reducing the fear of losing power need not involve abandoning either state expansion or democratization process. Milton Esman (1994), and Donald Horowitz (1990) rightfully stated that electoral systems in which politicians depend on votes only from coethnics tend to reward ethnic extremists who assert maximal demands (Kellas, 1991). Political systems in which politicians seeking election must appeal to members of more than a single ethnic community and depend on their electoral support generally produce more moderate politics and reward accommodative politicians with cross-ethnic appeals.

Political parties need stronger organization with greater input from ordinary citizens than has existed in these countries since their respective independence (Ndegwa 1997; Esman 1994; Sklar 1993; Olorunsola 1972). Such parties should encompass multi-ethnic coalitions, and should give the coalitions a greater stability by introducing effective supra-ethnic party identities, and patterns of political integration. If there is competition among parties, all need to feel that they will continue to have a fair chance to win in the future if they lose the next election. The fear that electoral competition would lead to intense conflict that would threaten the integrity of these nations was the justification most frequently given for military intervention, whose decree led to moderate decrease in non-violent protest and moderate increases in rebellion in Nigeria and Rwanda.

Redemocratization will probably rekindle non-violent ethno-political mobilization and protection to some extent. But strong parties and faith in having a fair chance to win in future should direct such mobilization into institutionalized channels, and keep it from threatening a regime's stability (Horowitz 1990; Ekeh 1976; Sklar 1993).

Delegation of power to local rather than state governments and party units needs to be both substantial and institutionalized, so that ordinary people will have an effective voice in the arena that matters most to them (van den Berghe 1975; Esman 1994; Gurr 1995). Elites in national level competition will be guaranteed the opportunity to protect their local power bases. Under these conditions both democracy and state capacity will be strengthened. There will be the sense of political security for both the leadership and the populace. This will help keep a broad multi-ethnic coalition stable and to moderate the self-perpetuating tendency of communal contention.

Institutional arrangement will make economic growth less likely to generate strong grievances (Crawford 1976; Lijphart (1977; Selassie 1992; Esman 1994; Ndegwa 1997). However, like the argument presented by the relative deprivation perspective, if economic decline is too great, of course, all political institutions will be threatened. The formation of a working class that parallels the advantaged class in drawing its membership roughly in proportion from various ethno-political groups will help to separate ethnic and class conflict.

Finally, the elimination or at least the minimization of foreign intervention will also contribute greatly to the containment of ethno-political conflict in Nigeria. Settlement thus rests on mutual agreement usually based on substantive compromise.

Conclusion

Nigeria's disunity is in part a reflection of the form and character of the governmental system and structure imposed by the British government during the period of colonial rule. The development of southern and northern Nigeria between 1898 and 1960 marked important stages in the evolution of the Nigerian state. By 1914, when Lord Lugard amalgamated Northern and Southern Nigeria, most of the 250 different ethnic groups had been forced to yield their pre-colonial sovereign powers. Many scholars have argued that the roots of Nigeria's civil war was the Lugard decision of 1914, when the British attempted to weld the disparate tribes and regions into a single political entity (Oyediran 1979; Adebayo 1981; Graf 1988; Mayer et al 1996).

Surely, there was no cultural or social basis for this decision, and it could be argued that given the geographically and defined linguistic and cultural diversities, it was never possible for a pan-national sense of community to develop in Nigeria. Nevertheless, the northern peoples, with a well-developed culture and political structure, resisted European influence. The Yoruba, the Igbos and several of the Southern ethnic groups, however, were more vulnerable to European ideas. Given these circumstances, the British colonial administration did not prepare Nigeria for a democratic system of government before granting independence. Thus, shortly after independence, politics resembled an ethnic "tug-of-war", with the different regional parties structured not along class or ideological lines, but reflecting the interests of rival ethnic groups. Among multi-ethnic societies in Africa, Nigeria has experienced constant cases of bloody conflict and inequalitarian pluralism. The distinguishing identities of the political units are also not obliterated. Individuals in the nations under study operate with dual citizenship, one in an ethnic group and the other in the nation-state The dual and competing citizenship practiced cannot be fully fudged; however, the tension inherent in their coexistence can be mitigated. In such situation, electoral laws could be enacted to respond to the reality of ethnic voting founded upon ethnic citizenship. This would offer incentives to ethnic elites and politicians to seek votes outside their ethnic groups of accountability.

Typically, federalism, consociationalism and limited electoral engineering are the policy options suggested to accommodate ethnicity problems in pluralistic societies, such as those in Nigeria. Despite the legacy of centuries of ethnic conflicts in this great African nation, power sharing may yet prove to be the way out of this impasse.

Ethnic conflict and change are inherent features of a multi-ethnic nation such as the three under study. Due to significant economic, political, and social inequality among the various ethnic groups, challenges to the dominant social order arise periodically. Also cultural and religious differences among the ethnic groups may continue to impel ethnic conflict.

By combating socio-economic insecurity, which arises from scarcity and inequality, Nigeria will move towards either equalitarian pluralism or corporate pluralistic nations. Pragmatic and appropriate policies associated with regional autonomy, assimilation, pluralism and power sharing have the potential for accommodating the essential interests of most disadvantaged and politically active ethnic groups. However, assimilation policy should be the long-term national goal. If those changes can be sustained, there is a strong reason to expect that comparative change can be achieved in other societies with severe ethnic divisions.

References

Ahmadu, Bello. (1962). My Life: Autobiography of the Sardauna. Daily Times Press Lagos, Nigeria.

Aka, S.M.O. (1994). "For My Northern Neighbor". Community Concord News-paper. Lagos, Nigeria. August 21, p.5.

Akin-Aina, Wale. (1994). "Logic in the Illogical." Newswatch News Magazine, Lagos, Nigeria. July 25, p.9.

Anderson, Benedict. (1991). Imagined Communities: Reflections on the Origin and Spread of Nationalism. New York: Verso.

Awolowo, Obafemi. (1947). Path to Nigerian Freedom, Ibadan, Nigeria: University of Ibadan Press, p.28.

Awolowo, Obafemi. (1981). Awo on the Nigerian War. Ibadan, Nigeria: Tribune Press.

Banton, Michael. (1983). Racial and Ethnic Competition. Cambridge: Cambridge University Press.

Bates, Robert H. (1974). "Ethnic Competition and Modernization in Contemporary Africa." Comparative Political Studies, Vol. 6 (January), pp 457-84.

Beinaart, William. (1994). Twentieth- Century South Africa. New York: Oxford University Press.

Bienen, Henry, and Jeffrey Herbst. (1996). "The Relationship between Political and Economic Reform in Africa." Comparative Politics,

Vol. 29 (October), pp. 23-42.

David-West, Tam. (1994). "Nigerian Federalism and The Virus of Disunity." Lagos, Nigeria: The Guardian Press. (January 2), pp. 5-6.

Davies, James C. (1962). "Towards a Theory of Revolution." American Sociological Review, pp. 5-19.

Deutsch, Karl. (1953). Nationalism and Social Communication: An Inquiry into the Foundation of Nationality. Cambridge: MIT Press.

Diamond, Larry. (1987). "Ethnicity and Ethnic Conflict." The Journal of Modern African Studies. Vol. 25, 1, pp. 117-128.

Dibie, Robert. (1994). "ECOWAS: Is Functionalism the Answer to Regional Economic Integration in West Africa." Journal of Ethno-Development, Vol. 3, pp. 34-37.

Ekeh, Peter. (1975). "Colonialism and the Two Publics in Africa: A Theoretical Statement." Comparative Studies Society and History, Vol. 17, 1, pp. 24-37.

Esman, Milton. (1994). Ethnic Politics. Ithaca, New York: Cornell University Press.

Funga, F. (1991). "Pouvoir, Ethnies et Regions" Dialogue (149) (November - December).

Geertz, Clifford. (1994). "Primordial and Civic Ties." pp 29-34 in Hutchinson and Anthony D. Smith ed., Nationalism. New York: Oxford University Press.

Glickman, Harvey, ed. (1995). Ethnic Conflict and Democratization in Africa. Atlanta, Georgia: African Studies Association.

Gordon, Milton M. (1964). Assimilation in American Life: The Role of Race, Religion, and National Origins. New York: Oxford University Press.

Grosse, S. (1994). The Roots of Conflict and State Failure in Rwanda. The Political Exacerbation of Social Cleavages in a Conteext of Growing Resources Scarcity. Ann Arbor, Michigan: Department of Population Planning and International Health, School of Public Health.

Gurr, Robert T. (1993). Minorities at Risk: A Global View of Ethnopolitical Conflict. Washington, D.C: United States Institute of Peace Press.

Gurr, Robert. (1970). Why Men Rebel. Princeton, New Jersey: Princeton University Press.

Halisi, C.R.D. (1997). "From Liberation to Citizenship: Identity and

Citizenship in Black South Africa Political Thought." Comparative Studies in Society and History Vol. 39 (January): pp. 66-85.

Horowitz, Donald. (1985). Ethnic Groups in Conflict. Los Angeles, California: University of California Press.

Horowitz, Donald. (1990). "Making Moderation Pay: The Comparative Politics of Ethnic Conflict Management." In Joseph Montvile, Conflict and Peacemaking in Multiethnic Societies. Lexington, Massachusetts, Lexington Books.

Horton, John. (1966). "Order and Conflict Theories of Social Problems." American Journal of Sociology (May/June), pp. 51-73.

Hyden, Goran and Micheal Bratton. (eds). (1992). Governance and Politics in Africa. Boulder, Colorado: Lynne Reinner Publishers.

Ignatief, Michael. (1993). Blood and Belonging: Journeys into the New Nationalism. Toronto: Penguin.

Jagun, Dokun. (1993). "Nigeria: The Basis of Union." Lagos, Nigeria: The Nigerian Guardian (April 8), pp. 3-7.

Kellas, James. (1991). The Politics of Nationalism and Ethnicity. London: Macmillan Education.

Lelyveld, Joseph. (1985). Move Your Shadow: South Africa, Black and White. New York: Penguin.

Lemarchand, Rene.(1994). Burundi: Ethnocide as Discourse and Practice. New York: Cambridge University Press.

Lemarchand, Rene. (1995). "Four Models for Resolving Ethnic Conflict." African Voices, Vol. 4 (Summer): pp. 1-37.

Lijphart, Arend. (1977). Democracy in Plural Societies: A Comparative Exploration. New Haven, Connecticut: Yale University Press.

Lijphart, Arend. (1980). "Federal, Confederal, and Consociational Options for the South African Plural Society." In Robert Rotberg and John Barrat ed. Conflict and Compromise in South Africa. Lexington, Massachusetts: Heath.

Maharaj, Gitanjali. (1999). Between Unity and Diversity. Claremont, South Africa: David Philip Publication.

Mamdani, M. (1996). Citizen and Subject. Contemporary Africa and the Legacy of Late Colonialism. Princeton, New Jersey: Princeton University Press.

Marger, Martin. (1997). Race and Ethnic Relations. New York: Wadsworth Publishing Company.

Melson, Robert and Howard Wolpe. (1970). "Modernization and the

Politics of Communalism: A Theoretical Perspective." American Political Science Review, Vol. LXIV (December).

Morrison, D.G. and H. M. Stevenson. (1972). "Cultural Pluralism, Modernization and Conflict: An Empirical Analysis of Sources of Political Instability in African Nations." Canadian Journal of Political Science. Vol. V, 1, March, p.90.

Ndegwa, Stephen. (1997). "Citizenship and Ethnicity: An Examination of Two Transition Moments in Kenyan Politics." American Political Science Review. Vol. 91, 3 (September).

Nnoli, Okwudiba. (1980). Ethnic Politics in Nigeria. Enugu, Nigeria: Fourth Dimension Publishers.

Ola, Robert and Samuel Hume. (1994). Government and Local Development in Western Nigeria, Benin City, Nigeria: Ambik Press.

Olorunsola, Victor. (1972). The Politics of Cultural Sub-Nationalism in Africa. Garden City, New York: Anchor Books.

Osifo-Whisky, Onome. (1994). "The Trouble with the North." Lagos, Nigeria: Tell Magazine (August 15), p.3.

Ottaway, Marina. (1994). Democratization and Ethnic Nationalism: African and Eastern European Experiences. Washington, DC: Overseas Development Council.

Park, Robert. (1924). "The Concept of Social Distance." Journal of Applied Sociology, Vol. 8, pp. 339-344.

Parsons, Talcott. (1975). "Some Theoretical Considerations on the Nature and Trends of Change of Ethnicity." In Nathan Glazer and Daniel Moynihan (eds). Ethnicity: Theory and Experience. Cambridge: Harvard University Press.

Peled, Yoav. (1992). "Ethnic Democracy and the Legal Construction of Citizenship: Arab Citizens of the Jewish State." American Political Science Review, Vol. 86 (June), pp. 432-43.

Prunier, G. (1995). The Rwanda Crisis: History of a Genocide. New York: Columbia University Press.

Richard, Joseph. (1987). Democratic Challenges in Africa. The Carter Center Working Papers Series. Atlanta, Georgia: Carter Center.

Ross, M.H. (1993). The Culture of Conflict. Interpretations and Interests in Comparative Perspective. New Haven, London: Yale University Press.

Rothchild, Donald. (1964). Safeguarding Nigeria's Minorities. Pittsburgh, Pennsylvania: Duquesne University Press.

Rothchild, Donald. (1981). Ethnopolitics: A Conceptual Framework. New

York: Columbia University Press.

Samuel, Idowu. (2001). "Two Years of Democracy." Ibadan, Nigeria: Nigerian Tribute Newspaper.

Sanda, A.O. (1976). Ethnic Relations in Nigeria. Ibadan, Nigeria: The Caxton Press.

Saxton, Lloyd, and Walter Kaufmann. (1971). The American Scene: Social Problems of The Seventies. Belmont, California: Wadworth, p.2.

Schermerhorn, R. A. (1970). Comparative Ethnic Relations: A Framework for Theory and Research. New York: Random House.

Selassie, Alemante G. (1992). "Ethnic Identity and Constitutional Design for Africa." Stanford Journal of International Law. Vol. 29, 1, pp. 1-56.

Sisk, Timothy. (1995). Democratization in South Africa. Princeton, New Jersey: Princeton University Press.

Sklar, Richard. (1993). "The American Frontier for Political Science." In Africa and Disciplines, edited by Robert Bates, V.Y. Mudimbe, and Jean O'Barr. Chicago: University of Chicago Press.

South African Institute of Race Relations. (1997). Race Relations Survey. Johannesburg: SAIRR.

Stewart, Angus. (1995). "Two Conceptions of Citizenship." British Journal of Sociology, Vol. 46 (March), pp. 63-78.

Thompson, Leonard. (1990). A History of South Africa. New Haven, Connecticut: Yale University Press.

Uvin, Peter. (1997). "The Prejudice, Crisis, and Genocide in Rwanda." African Studies Review, Vol. 40, 2 (September).

van den Berghe, Pierre. (1978). Race and Racism: A Comparative Perspective. 2nd ed. New York: Wiley Press.

Waters, Malcolm. (1989). "Citizenship and the Constitution of Structures Social Inequality." International Journal of Comparative Sociology, Vol. 30, 3-4, pp. 159-180.

William, Gavin and Terisa Turner. (1978). "Nigeria." In West African States: Failure and Promise. Edited by John Dun. Cambridge University Press, London.

Yinger, Milton. (1981). "Toward a Theory of Assimilation and Dissimilation." Ethnic and Racial Studies, Vol. 4, pp. 249-264.

Young, Crawford. (1976). The Politics of Cultural Pluralism. Madison, Wisconsin: University of Wisconsin Press.

3 The Public Bureaucracy

Introduction

The development of Nigeria has required major input from its public bureaucracy, and the British colonial experience played a major role in shaping Nigeria's character and, hence, its performance following independence. The bureaucracy in Nigeria after independence was in all respects similar to the British bureaucratic-authoritarian system that preceded it. Between 1954 and 1966, the bureaucracy was thoroughly "Nigerianized." The bureaucracy and administrative component of government are employers of a fairly large proportion of professional and technically trained people in Nigeria. The ministries and public enterprises whether the products of colonial administration or of long-standing independent government, these agencies are indispensable instruments for the exercise of governmental authority. If the decisions and the policies of political or military leaders are to be carried out, if the programs launched are to have any effect, it is the administrators who will do it. Otobo (1999), Adebayo Adedeji (1981), and William Graf (1988) contend that the process of transferring power to "successor elites" in the Nigerian bureaucracy produced several permanent structural deficiencies: (a) a dearth of qualified personnel at all levels; (b) a stratified and ossified bureaucratic structure not interested in popular needs and demands that, moreover, was cleft between senior and juniors and rent by rivalries between the older generalists and the emerging professional-technical cadres; (c) a bureaucratic class separated by training, education, and wealth from most of the population; (d) the nucleus of a self-interested civil servant class that was attempting to transform the political power that the class conferred into the economic power that it could buy – this of course implied the exploitation of ethnicity and sectionalism to entrench one's political power; and (e) a network of patrons and clients and, hence, a great potential for corruption. Nigeria's experience with military rule also influenced its structure and outlook. Successive military governments introduced programs to reform and reorganize the bureaucracy, the objective being a more professional corps that could work in close relationship with the military juntas. Therefore, although 70 percent of Nigeria's citizens live in rural areas, government resources have been concentrated in urban centers, and a majority of the nation's public officials live and work in the larger cities.

Ayoade (1999) contends that the predicament of equity in Nigeria started with the problem of an unequal North-South duality. Further to these North-South problem was the division of the South into two parts. Thus, the attempt to resolve the North-South regional imbalance resulted in the creation of states which further resulted in weakening the South against the North. The federal character principle became a means of resolving the imbalance in Nigeria's geo-politics. The practice of the Second Republic of Nigeria shows that the federal character principles tend to promote mediocracy in governance at the expense of meritocracy and professionalism. In contradiction to the principles of representation and national unity, federal character allows ethno-regional patrons and their clients to exploit and mismanage state resources without contributing to any meaningful development. By focusing on regional and ethnic representation, the federal character exacerbates differentiation instead of enhancing mutual trust, accommodation and national unity (Abubakar, 1999).

The current national bureaucracy in Nigeria has three components – the cabinet ministries, the independent agencies, and public corporations. The cabinet ministries employ a majority of the federal civil servants and the President appoints the heads of the ministries. There are thirty federal ministries. The independent agencies are smaller than the cabinet ministries and tend to have considerable more focused missions. For example the Federal Environmental Protection Agency (FEPA) is responsible for environmental regulations and National Agency for Food and Drug Administration Control (NAFDAC). Another example of independent agencies is the Nigerian Social Insurance Trust Fund (NSITF). Included in the independent agencies are regulatory agencies. Unlike the regulatory agencies in the United States, Nigeria's regulatory agencies do not perform judicial and legislative functions within the regulatory agencies. The third type of bureaucracy is the Government Corporation. There are several government corporations in Nigeria. Some of the major public corporations in Nigerian National Petroleum Corporation, Nigerian Railway Corporation, Nigeria Iron and Steel Corporation, Nigerian Flour Mill, Nigerian Paper Mill, National

Electric Power Corporation, Nigerian Cement Factory, Nigerian Telecommunication, Nigeria Post Office, Nigerian Airways Corporation, and Nigerian Ports Authority. Although the President appoints the directors of these corporations they are quite independent. In addition, the directors of the independent agencies are mostly from the majority party that controls the national government. Due to the high level of corruption in Nigeria, independent regulatory agency directors are deeply immersed in both behind the scene politics and often befriend the groups they are supposed to regulate.

To understand the process of policy implementation in Nigeria one must begin with an examination of the pattern of colonial administration and its role in ordering and structuring the contours of the Nigerian public bureaucracy. This chapter will also describe the Nigerian bureaucracy as it exists today. The chapter will focus on the pattern of colonial administration, the postindependence civil service, the military and administrative reform, and the administrator's role in public policy making and implementation.

Bureaucracy and Developing Nations

Max Weber (1946) studied the bureaucracy phenomenon. In his study of bureaucracy, Weber argues that the existence of a neutral bureaucracy based on hierarchy and rule is essential if a country is to become modern. In accordance with Weber's usage, bureaucrats are public officials who acquire their positions on the basis of their qualifications and skills and are primarily responsible for the implementation of public policy, not its creation. In Nigeria, the term bureaucrat generally refers to all government officials who are not elected to a legislature or to a chief executive's post, and who are not judges or soldiers. The main characteristics of a bureaucratic type of organization as envisaged by Weber are as follows:

1. Workers operate within fixed jurisdictions.
2. Authority is exercised within a firm system of hierarchy. Subordinates are clearly under the control of their superior, a fact known by subordinates and superiors alike.
3. Hierarchy also strengthens accountability, since each person is responsible to some specific boss.
4. Bureaucracy operates on the basis of written rules.
5. Bureaucrats assume their positions through expert training.

6. Bureaucrats are primarily responsible for the implementation of public policy.

To Weber, a bureaucracy or organization possessing these features is the most superior form of organization. He believed that such an organization is capable of attaining the highest degree of efficiency and utilizes the most rational means of carrying out control over human beings. It is customary to define bureaucracy in ways that associate it with large-scale and complex organizations. In their search for neutrality, some writers have gone so far as to identify bureaucracy with organization (Simon 1958; Etzioni 1968; Blau 1982). Herbert Simon (1987, 1960) presented a major challenge to Weber's understanding of bureaucracy by emphasizing the psychology of decision making and by introducing a cost calculus to test the criterion of efficiency rather than to simply assume, as Weber did, that bureaucracies are efficient. The fact that the Weberian concept of bureaucracy has been widely adopted does not mean that his ideas have not been criticized. In fact, the attack that has been mounted upon Weber's conceptualizations is formidable. Some writers have questioned the rationality of Weber's rational bureaucracy. They have particularly noted the informal organization that often develops within a bureaucracy and the dysfunctional consequences of bureaucracy, for example, its too rigid adherence to rules (Rosenbloom 1998) Other criticisms have been concerned with the cultural and political limitations of administrative rationality, or the absence in Weber's writing of the importance of values and attitudes (Friedrich 1963, 471; Rosenberg 1988). Other scholars who have been particularly interested in issues of change, especially the problems of change in developing areas, have challenged the Weberian conceptualization more seriously. Martin Albrow (1970) asserts that the degree of rationality a bureaucracy might have depends on the cultural context in which it is located (54-61). Therefore, he considers invalid for developing countries the basis on which Weber constructed his "ideal type" of bureaucracy.

Victor Thompson (1964) challenges more seriously the relevance of a Weberian-type bureaucracy to a developing country. He contends that in the Western industrialized countries, administrative practices and principles were derived from an established professional occupation and a system of accountability. As a result, administrative practices have little value for development bureaucracy where the need is for an adaptive administration, one that has to incorporate changes constantly. Other scholars argue that not only is bureaucratic organization incompatible with the sociopolitical culture of most non-Western developing countries, but that from an economic point of view bureaucratic organization is not actually an efficient model suited for development activities. They might agree with Bernard Schaffer (1969), who argues that it is likely that administration in less-developed conditions will not be bureaucratic (189). Indeed, some non-bureaucratic forms of organization are emerging in less-developed countries (Ilchman 1969, 472-526). Bernard Schaffer's argument reminds us that non-bureaucratic administration has, after all, worked and survived as much in the West as in the rest of the world. Many alternatives are possible and almost none are wholly without merit. One may also cite non-bureaucratic methods of organization in East Asia, East Africa and elsewhere that aim at placing some portion of public administration in the hands of the citizens and that now include some lower courts, some police functions, as well as some significant local roles in economic administration. These self-help ideas represent a modern more-politicized version of the older approach of community development.

Recognition of cultural variations that bear upon the operation of bureaucracies has prompted analysts to devote considerable attention to comparative public administration. It is hoped that by doing so, it will eventually be possible to analyze the effects of environmental and cultural factors on public bureaucracies. Still, these criticisms should not be taken as rendering the Weberian analysis useless. All one needs to do is to belong to an organization, or better yet, try to form one, to realize how dependent Nigerian society is on the principles of bureaucratic organization. Specialization (often by committee), hierarchy (for coordination, often by a governing board or council of some type), and formalized procedure (Robert's rules) are well-known attributes of contemporary organizations, whether they be social clubs, university departments, or governmental units.

The general ability of bureaucracies to defy change, innovation, and any other kind of leadership by the heads of organizations they serve has become a focus of study by several prominent political analysts in the past three decades. Graham Allison (1971) analyzed presidential decision making at two different levels to come up with (1) the organizational process model and (2) the bureaucratic politics model. He concludes that large bureaucracies tend to divide complex functions into a maze of small fragments, each fragment surrounded by its own sub-bureaucracy. What is often described, as "decision" at the top is little more than the sum of many small decisions made in relative isolation to other, related decisions.

Allison (1971) states that these low-level decisions are often made in ways that, first and foremost, bring comfort to the sub-bureaucracies and sometimes actually frustrate the goals sought by the overall leadership. Thus, the watchwords of small organizations within larger ones are "standard operational procedure" (SOP), the maintenance of existing programs and a general and instinctive resistance to any change. Allison argues that, even at the top levels of government, the heads of separate bureaucracies are often more intent on maintaining the importance of their particular activities than they are on arriving at some integrated policy among the sub-bureaucracies. In addition to such "turf protection," there is also the instinct for agency heads to compromise on what, professionally; they know to be the best policy. They do so in order to maintain their links to other agencies, as well as to the chief executive. Again, rational executive decision making can be undermined by such bureaucratic complexity.

The administrative bureaucracy has been the single most important arm of government in Nigeria. Some writers contend that it is appropriately so in a developing country. Dennis Rondinelli (1993) asserted that development bureaucracy is concerned with achieving national advancement. Development bureaucracy therefore, manifests it in the process of directing change toward the achievement of economic, social, and political objectives that have been authoritatively determined in one way or another. Bureaucracy is an indispensable part of the Nigerian governing process, but it also is slow, complex, and impersonal, – hence, frustrating to those dependent on its services. Most bureaucrats have the necessary self-esteem that enables them to get the job done but many are victims of their own bureaucratic complexity rather than the cause of it. As modern economic planning begins to drive the development of Nigeria, the bureaucracies as well as the military become inseparable agents of social, political, and economic change.

The problem of underdevelopment in Nigeria is due in large part to the poor governance of the nation since 1960. For more than thirty-five years the military was in control of the nation's petroleum, sugar, precious metals, or whatever a Nigeria is most apt to produce as a moneymaking crop or resource. Second, during that period the Nigerian military eliminated any possible opposition to its control. To that end it devoted a powerful military, a police force within all major municipalities, and a secret police to warn it of impending political opposition. Third, it levied taxes on the citizens with its structural adjustment policies so that it has additional sources of income and reminds the citizens of its power and its presence. Fourth, the military engaged in certain public services that were either essential to the running of a civilized society (sanitation, water, power, etc.) or even "do something for the people in the name of the government" such as building hospitals or schools or enshrine national monuments.

The citizen's responsibility, under an authoritarian government, is to pay their taxes, to obey the laws, and not to attempt to involve themselves in political decisions. Generally, as in Nigeria, citizens were not allowed to organize political parties, labor unions, or engage in too many demonstrations. A rigged election every now and then is sometimes used to help legitimized the regime. Justice, morality, and ethical conduct were at the lowest in Nigeria during the military regime. Scholars regard an authoritarian government as a rather unfortunate alternative to preserving political democracy in Nigeria. Nordlinger (1977) was right when he asserted that if the military intervene in politics the values of political equality, liberty, freedom of opposition, and constitutionalism will be tampered with. These values are realizable only where the people's supremacy is respected and civilian control is implemented democratically. More recently (in 1998), however, troubled by extensive government repression in Nigeria, political scientists and the international community have insisted that democracy, human rights, and social equity be integral parts of political development in the nation. Generally, it is believed that governments that are held accountable to the population by means of competitive elections are more likely to be efficient and honest. Similarly, a free and independent mass media helps keep governments accountable.

In a similar vein, many analysts have noted that the Asian nations that have been enjoying the most spectacular growth in recent decades – Malaysia, Singapore, South Korea, Indonesia, and Thailand – were almost all authoritarians. Many concluded from this that an authoritarian government was necessary in the early to middle stages of industrialization in order to control labor and reduce popular consumption so as to encourage heavy investment of capital (Handelman 1996). It should be noted that in 1997 and 1998 these Asian nations suffered severe financial crises. While these theories remain subject to debate, they do demonstrate that the relationship between economic and political development is complex.

Despite the various reasons for military intervention in a country's political life, all authoritarian regimes are concerned not only with political stability but also with positive economic performance. They therefore remain dependent on the administrative apparatus for the implementation of their decisions and policies. According to Oladipo Adamolekun (1999) the main elements of governance on which there is broad consensus and popular participation of the citizens of a nation would include rule of law, freedom of expression, and association, electoral legitimacy, accountability and transparency and development orientated leadership.

Pattern of Colonial Administration

The civil service in Nigeria had its origin in the British military occupation and the first public officers were military personnel drawn from the colonial regiments and occupation forces. In the early stages the civil service was mainly concerned with the collection of revenue and the maintenance of law and order. The main core of this British administrative service was composed of three branches: the provincial and district commissioners, the police, and the treasury officials. These branches of the service were closely related functionally, and they provided a countrywide administration of the services that existed. The civil service was essentially one that was constructed to further British imperial policies in Nigeria, essentially to exploit Nigeria as a source for primary commodities and as a limited market for British industries.

Nigerian public bureaucracy has its origin in 1900, the year in which the British government divided the area (now known as Nigeria) into three separate colonial territories. Different administrators directly responsible to the United Kingdom independently governed these three territories – Lagos, and the protectorates of northern and southern Nigeria. The two southern colonies were brought under a united bureaucracy in 1904. The protectorates of northern and southern Nigeria were amalgamated in January 1, 1914, to form modern Nigeria. The people of Nigeria became British subjects owing allegiance to the British sovereign, and British laws were elevated over Nigerian traditional law. Lord Frederick Lugard became the first governor-general of the country. The administrative areas of northern and southern Nigeria were, however, placed under two lieutenant governors, each with a secretariat and departmental organization of its own. Adebayo Adedeji (1968) contended that different policies regarding native land prevailed in the southern and northern bureaucracies, and the only occasions in which the higher officials of the two bureaucracies met were the annual sessions of the Legislative Council that were convened in Lagos.

The northern bureaucracy reflected somewhat the conservatism of the Islamic culture and continually agitated for the distinct and separate development of northern Nigeria. It also often suggested that the north of Nigeria should be cut from the south (Adu 1982). Lord Lugard rationalized and imposed a system of local administration known as indirect rule. The essential features of indirect rule were the preservation of traditional African political institutions and their adaptation, under the tutelage and direction of British administration, to the requirements of modern units of local government. Until the post-World War II period, when a substantial devolution of political and fiscal authority occurred, the native administrations were in effect made local extensions of the British superstructure. Traditional rulers such as emirs, obas, and elders realized that their positions and perquisites depended more upon the goodwill of British district officers, residents, and chief commissioners than upon the consent of their people. Lord Lugard centralized only those departments that were invisible or whose functions applied to the whole of Nigeria (e.g., the judiciary, military, railways, posts and telegraphs, and audit). These departments were under the control of the governor-general, and assisted by the central secretariat. The officials of the northern and southern bureaucracies spoke different official languages. In the south, because of the complex polytonic languages, English was spoken. Hausa, not English, was spoken in the north (Coleman 1958). Thus, there was a distinct and independent administrative development between the north and the south that has continued till the present day.

The 1954 constitutional changes turned Nigeria into a federation of three component parts. With this constitutional development, the Nigerian public service was split into four public services – a federal bureaucracy and three regional public services, one each for the three regions. Adebayo Adedeji (1968) asserted that the central and unitary nature of the Nigerian public service was considerably modified by the delegation to regional administration of certain powers of appointment, promotion, posting and discipline. For example the North had embarked on the establishment of a purely northern public service to keep away the southerners. If a qualified Northerner was available he/she was given priority in recruitment. If a qualified Northerner was not available, an expatriate may be recruited. A southerner was only recruited as a last resort and on contract term only pending when a qualified Northerner will be recruited. The Northern civil service recruitment policy was directed more against southern Nigerians than against expatriates. The purpose was mainly to make the Northern Nigerian civil service a representation of the cross section of the northern society (Ayoade, 1999).

In 1963, when the Mid-West Region was created out of the Western Region, it too established its own civil service. Apart from the Northern public service that discriminated against southerners the regions in the south were very liberal in their recruitment policy.

The structure of organization adopted for the Nigerian public service is similar to that of the British civil service. According to Humphrey Nwosu (1977), the structure of the regional and federal civil service is very much alike. Each service is divided into the following three broad classes:

1. General service classes comprising (a) the administrative class (b) the general executive classes (c) the secretarial/stenographic classes, and (d) clerical, messengerial and miscellaneous classes.
2. Specialist classes made up of people with a wide range of professional, scientific, and technical qualifications, including ancillary technical staff.
3. Departmental classes consisting of posts that are peculiar to particular departments, e.g., nurses, health inspectors, tax officers.

The federal and regional governments are divided into a number of ministries. The ministries are also divided into departments. The number of departments in a ministry depends on the range and variety of functions for which the ministry is responsible. Within each ministry there is a division that is primarily responsible for financial control, accounting for expenditures, stores, establishment, and organization matters. This department, which is usually called Administration and General Division, is responsible for the overall management of the individual ministries, and it relieves high-ranking professional and administrative staff of day-to-day routine administration. The other departments of the ministries are organized on a functional basis. For example, the Federal Ministry of Education has seven departments: Finance, Establishment, Education Administration, Students and Special Services, Registration Assessment, Inspectorate, and Technical Education. Each ministry is organized hierarchically, that tends to reduce administration to a routine process. Documents and memoranda are passed from subordinates to their superior officers, who in turn are content to issue orders accordingly or to forward the documents to their own superior. The result is that most programs and policies are initiated at the top echelon.

Every department is subdivided into branches, sections, and subsections. The permanent secretary is the administrative head of the ministry. He is also the accounting officer and is responsible to the minister. Thus, when the parliamentary system was adopted in 1960, the structure of the British civil bureaucracy was transferred intact to Nigeria.

Post-Independence Civil Servant

The British colonial administrative experience made a number of very powerful impressions on Nigeria's public administrators. The first impression was the tradition of (1) a strong bureaucracy with an elaborate lines organization of positions and roles and (2) a structure that assigned direction and supervision to generalists. The second impression was that the colonial administrative inheritance stressed slow, thorough, risk-avoidance, mistake-avoidance, and secretive public administration. The third impression was a strictly adhered to single-line organization from the top to the lowest level. This organization excluded staff agencies and eliminated the possibility of outside or nonorganizational influences. The fourth impression was that the colonial bureaucracy serviced executive, legislative, and judicial arms of government. It also guided and assisted local governments and agencies (parastatals) in the development of their management systems. And the fifth impression was that the colonial bureaucracy was largely anonymous, presumed to be nonpartisan, loyal, committed, and subordinate to political and administrative leadership groups (Adamolekun 1986, Adedeji 1981; Nwosu 1977).

The civil service in the First Republic was highly regionalized. As the unified colonial civil service was gradually phased out in the mid-1950s and the independence government was prepared for centrifugal federalism, the most able and experienced civil servants joined the regional bureaucracies. There, they were closely allied with the dominant political and economic elites and indeed in part merged with them. The regional governments recruited civil servants according to their ethnic affiliations, and the bureaucrats implemented policies based on their ethnic loyalties. For example, business people from the ethnic group represented by that administration received the greatest subsidies, contracts. Licenses and loans. Even within the federal government, ethnic considerations shaped personnel decisions. The quotas system for allocating military officials to the general staff, defense headquarters, and field command ensured that the north would secure 50 percent; the east, 25 percent; and before 1964 the west, 25 percent; after 1963 the west received 21 percent of appointments and the Midwest 4 percent (Adamolekun 1986). Thus, ethnic representation permeated both the federal and regional governments.

Despite the ethnic and regional affiliation, the civil service, whose existence antedated that of the other political institutions and that therefore by and large attracted the best qualified people, was stronger and better organized than the remaining subsystems, such as the parties, executives, and legislatures (Graf 1988). In the national, state, and local governments, the civil servants played key policy role. The most powerful bureaucrat in Nigeria, the secretary to the military government and the head of the civil service, unified the whole administrative structure. At both the national and state levels, permanent secretaries wielded the dominant power. The local government secretary, a civil servant, ran the town councils. All these bureaucrats performed a wide range of activities.

Given this colonial legacy the central post-independence relationship between Nigerian civil servants and its military (or) political leaders is based on the doctrine of political neutrality. Humphrey Nwosu (1977) describes the essential tenets of this doctrine:

1. Politics and policy are separate from administration. Politicians or military officers make policy decisions while public servants execute/implement the decisions.
2. Public servants are appointed and promoted on the basis of merit rather than on the basis of party affiliation or patronage.
3. Public servants do not engage in partisan political activities.
4. Public servants provide forthright and objective advice to their political masters in private and in confidence. In return, political executives protect the anonymity of public servants by publicly accepting responsibility for departmental decisions.
5. Public servants do not express publicly their personal views on government policies or administration.
6. Public servants execute policy decisions loyally and zealously irrespective of the philosophy and programs of the party in power and regardless of their personal opinions. As a result, servants enjoy security of tenure during good behavior and satisfactory performance.

The administrative structures, principles, and motivation strategies of the British colonial regime were retained after independence. Local governments were, however, encouraged to develop their distinctive administrative systems: to hire and train their staff, maintain discipline, and stimulate commitment. Similarly, government agencies designed their respective organizational structures, training programs, conditions of service, and work ethics. Ladipo Adamolekun (1983) asserts that these designed attempts were not generally modeled after the practice of the civil service of a developing nation but rather after institutions in the United Kingdom.

The merit system in civil service recruitment and advancement, however, was modified by the politicians who discovered that because of educational imbalances between the northern and southern states of Nigeria, the strict application of the merit system in recruitment and promotion would prevent some Nigerians from being recruited or promoted (Adedeji 1968). What the politicians advocated was a simple quota arrangement that would reserve 50 percent of all vacant positions and promotion posts to the north and south, respectively. Agencies responsible for recruitment and promotion in Nigeria were then expected to do the same for candidates from the northern and southern part of the country. A subsequent problem of this quota system relates to the other ethnic minority groups. These minority ethnic groups argued that the majority tribes were discriminating against them. Humphrey Nwosu (1977) contended that these developments had a negative impact on staff motivation and leadership supervision. The overriding consideration however, was that of national unity, and it was agreed that sacrifices made by the minority tribes in pursuit of this goal were worth making. Thus, regionalization of politics also necessitated some measure of trade-off of the principle of merit in favor of representatives.

For example in the process of developing the northern civil service (a less- developed region in the late 1950s and early 1960s), where the attempts failed, it attracted an influx of Igbo civil servants into the north, resulting in open ethnic hostility (Oyovbaire 1984). Public employment expanded substantially during the post-independence period. The federal public bureaucracy, shown in Table 3.1, increased from 98,877 employees in 1974 to over 213,802 in 1988. By 1990 the federal civil service employment figure had increased to over 273,392. Also, the

Table 3.1
Federal Civil Service Employment 1960-1998

Year	Number of Employees
1960	30,000
1970	45,154
1974	98,877
1988	213,802
1990	273,392
1998	200,000

Source: Federal Office of Statistics, Annual Abstract of Statistics (1997), #. 82. Abuja, Nigeria: Government Press. Otobo, E. (1999). "Nigeria" in Oladipo Adamolekun (ed.) Public Administration in Africa. Boulder, Colorado: Westview Press.

Table 3.2
Public Sector Employment 1975-1994

Govt. Levels	1975	1985	1994
Federal Bureaucracy	98,877	213,802	273,392
State Bureaucracy	167,600	255,892	423,492
Local Government	92,500	127,833	191,225
Corporations/ Universities	160,000	217,845	260,236
Teaching Services	195,000	230,189	239,993
Others	250,000	250,955	319,000
Total	963,977	1,296,516	1,707,338

Source: Federal Government of Nigeria, Office of Statistics, Annual Abstract of Statistics, 1994, Abuja, Nigeria: Government Press. pp. 85-92.

Public enterprise sector (nonagricultural) employed at least 160,000 workers, about 16 percent of public sector employment and 11 percent of the non-agricultural employment in the modern sector, as shown in Table 3.2. According to a 1995 estimate, wage employment in the Nigerian economy increased from 1.5 million in 1975 to 3 million in 1990, bringing the percentage proportion of the "wage class" in the labor force to 10 percent in 1990 (Central Bank Report 1995). A large proportion of the Nigerian labor force – 27.8 million out of 32.2 million or 90.3 percent – were self-employed workers in the agricultural sector (Federal Office of

Statistics Annual Report 1995). The absolute size of the bureaucracy has grown rapidly, especially during the military regime. Another source of the growing bureaucracy was the creation of new states in 1992. The federal government had to build its secretariat in each of the new states and deploy civil servants. Thus, the size of the bureaucracy continued to grow through the 1990s.

In a general way, the technical and planning evolution of the government bureaucracy in Nigeria tends to make public administration a more or less autonomous political force. Federal civil servants in Nigeria continue to be conscious of the general interests of the state in the struggle against individual interests as represented by political parties, pressure groups, ethnic interests, and the military.

Military and Administrative Reform

The role of the public bureaucracy in military regimes has been referred to as a coalition of soldiers and civil servants. Edward Feit (1968) contended that African armies are the apotheosis of administration, and he saw them as structuring an administrative traditional order. He also saw the military – civil service coalition as one without a consensus or basic legitimacy in which both military officers and public bureaucrats often are reluctant to assume responsibilities through direct involvement in politics even after a military and civil servant alliance has been established. The military elite use the public bureaucrat to help the former establish its legitimacy while the latter look after their own personal and institutional interests. One will therefore notice a fluctuation in the relationship between the public bureaucracy and the military in Nigeria. Over thirty-five years of military rule in Nigeria has significantly influenced the post-independence civil service. The governing coalition during this period should be viewed as composed of the military and the civil service. Jointly, the soldiers and bureaucrats made policies and laws and implemented them. In reality, the civil service has initiated a majority of the substantive policies and programs during periods of military rule. One of the most important changes made by the military, however, was the introduction of a single executive in the Nigerian public bureaucracy system. Before the advent of military rule in 1966, Nigeria had a plural or collegial executive system in which the legislature consisted of the executive and cabinet members of the federal government. Under the post-1966 single executive system (presidential system 1979-1983, and the entire military regime period), the president and state governors have their ministers or commissioners who serve as their advisers and agents, but not as colleagues with equal powers.

Associated with the single executive type of administration is the centralization of powers at the federal level. Before the first military administration, Nigeria had a federal administration in which the functions and powers of government were substantially shared between the federal and regional governments. This arrangement allowed the regions to have a wide range of powers. Once the long period of military rule began, however, military values of centralism and uniformity were inculcated in the expanding civil service. There is now a tendency to centralize most of the governmental powers at the federal level. The military government tends to control and dominate national affairs, and the civil services within the several states depend, in varying degrees, on directives from the federal government.

Another administrative imprint of the Nigerian military government is the regular use of administrative commissions. The Gowon, Mohammed/Obansajo, Buhari and Babangida military regimes, respectively, made enormous use of such expert study groups to examine important administrative problems and to make recommendations to the government. Lewis (1992) contends that during General Yakubu Gowon's regime he used bureaucrats and former politicians for important policy and linkage roles. For example, Gowon assigned strategic policy responsibilities to senior public servants who became known as the "super" permanent secretaries – more commonly, "super permsecs" (Lewis 1992). The most senior public servant in the ministries were called "super permsecs." These senior bureaucrats were responsible for government strategic planning and implementation in most of the ministries in both the federal and state governments. Their role in the economic development process of Nigeria during General Gowon's administration made them to steer the nation through a period when it was just recovering from a civil war. The civil service during this period also witnesses a change from professional goal and economic policy achievement to those of massive self enrichment.

The military regime has often used administrative panels to investigate the activities of ministries, departments, and corporations of governments, including consideration of issues raised concerning these bodies. Junior civil servants agitated for the introduction of a national minimum wage, for the abolition of the daily wage system, and for general improvement in the condition of service, thus forcing the federal government, to appoint the Morgan Commission. The commission examined the various demands and made recommendations that included a small increase in salary and a modest improvement in the condition of employment. It also identified problems in the non-salary condition of employment. Between 1964 and 1970 no further review took place in the country. The lack of attention to civil service concerns caused the formation of the Civil Servants Joint Action Committee (just after the civil war in 1970) that called on the military government to improve the civil servant's condition of service or face a nationwide strike of government employees. To defuse the explosive situation, in 1970, General Gowon set up the Adebo Commission. This commission made larger salary increase recommendations that were implemented immediately, but it failed to acknowledge the nonsalary matters (i.e., training, motivational incentives, promotion, grading and job evaluation) identified by the Morgan Commission.

The Gowon administration established a Civil Service Review Commission in 1972. The Civil Service Review Commission was headed by Chief Jerome Udoji. Adamolekun (1986) and Lewis (1992) assert that the main purpose of the Udoji Commission was to conduct a comprehensive review of standards of service and compensation in the civil service and public corporations (Public Service Review of Nigeria, 1974). The Udoji Commission conducted its' review of the nature of civil service in the early 1970s and made its' recommendation to the Gowon administration. Part of its' recommendation included an increase of public sector salaries, a unified and integrated administrative structure, the elimination of waste and the removal of deadwood/inefficient departments, and the introduction of a result-oriented civil service, that functioned on the basis of management by objective (Lewis 1992). In order to better integrate the whole public sector in Nigeria, the recommendation of the Udoji Commission especially, those aspects that has to do with job-grading and compensation policies were extended to both federal and state ministries as well as public corporations. The objective of the Gowon administration in doing this was on one hand to integrate the public service across the nation. On the second hand his administration wanted to overhaul the civil service by increasing standardization and efficiency in public corporations in such a manner that they would become customer oriented public institutions that would provide better services to the citizens of the nation. Unfortunately, the Gowon administration did not implement majority of the policies that was recommended by the Udoji Commission.

Otobo (1999) pointed out that the major goal of the Udoji reforms was to introduce modern management style, techniques, and culture to the Nigerian civil service. Unfortunately, these goals were not achieved. The Udoji Commission was better known for the salary increase it gave public servants.

In 1976, the government of General Murtala Mohammed revisited the recommendations of Udoji Commission after observing the extent to which efficiency in the public service had fallen when compared with the private sector.

Murtala Mohammed and his cohort ousted Gowon from office while he was attending an Organization of African Unity meeting in Uganda. Unfortunately for Mohammed, he was killed during a failed coup headed by Dimka less than a year in office in February 1976. After Mohammed's assassination General Olusegun Obasanjo became the head of state. The two military regimes immediately after the Gowon administration introduce new economic policies that were different from those of Gowon. As a matter of fact the two military rulers after Gowon felt that senior bureaucrats and military governors of the states during the Gowon era were responsible for the outrageous corruption and inefficiency in the civil service and public corporation. Ayida (1987) and Lewis (1992) pointed that several permanent secretaries especially those who served during the Gowon regime were fired from their position in the civil service. Murtala Mohammed also dismissed several senior and middle cadre civil servants who were found to be corrupt. There were also many public administrators who were retired from the civil service. At the end of the "housecleaning" activity of the Mohammed and Obasanjo regimes more than 10,000 civil servants were fired, retired, or forced to resign from the Nigeria civil service and public corporations. Kirk-Greene (1981) and Lewis (1992) pointed out that the Nigerian Ports Authority was also plague with outrageous corruption. As a result of this, more than 600 civil servants working in that institution were dismissed. Mohammed and Obasanjo regimes also appointed military officers to replace and manage several public institutions, including government corporations (Ayida 1987, 113 - 116). The aftermath of these actions was the insecurity and demoralization that was created in the civil service. Unfortunately, the massive dismissal and retired of civil servants in the public sector did not help to solve the problem of corruption and inefficiency in Nigeria.

General Obasanjo administration succeeded in handing over government to an elected civilian government in 1979. In 1983, General Buhari and his cohort planned a successful coup and ousted the civilian administration headed by Shehu Shagari. One of the first things Buhari's regime did was to announce a reform plan. Although his intention was well received because of the way public offices were abused during the civilian government of Shagari, General Buhari failed to offer a detailed program for cleaning up the civil service. The only meaningful housecleaning exercise that his administration carried out involved the downsizing of the civil service and the public corporations, by more than 15,000 staff (Lewis 1992). General Buhari's regime is known for carring out the most single public layoff in the history of Nigeria. This layoff exercise in the civil service did not help the Buhari regime to resolve the fiscal and budgetary problem which it inherited from the Shagari administration. Needless to say, it nonetheless helped remove corrupt and inefficient employees from the public service.

Despite the housecleaning exercise that General Buhari implemented corruption and inefficiency still persisted in the civil service. The Buhari administration was characterized with human right violation He also introduced "a war on indiscipline" policy but the declining economy galvanized some senior officers within the military government to oust General Buhari and General Idiagbon from office. The leader of the officers who ousted Buhari in a bloodless coup was General Babangida. On August 27 1985, General Ibrahim Babangida became the new President and Commander in Chief of the Armed Forces. One of the first things he promised to do was the revitalization of the civil service which has been demoralized because of actions taken against it by previous military leaders. Babangida was able to attract highly qualified professionals to his administration.

General Babangida established a Civil Service Reform Commission head by Professor Dotun Phillips in 1988. It will be recalled that before this reform the civil service at the federal and state levels was characterized by a service structure that had remained largely unchanged for seventy years. It is very important to note here, that before 1988, the Nigerian civil service had adopted the British or Westminster administrative model for over 70 years even though the culture, religion, ethnic groups, economic development priority, civil administrator's role and functions had changed significantly. The civil service in spite of the earlier attempts at downsizing was still grossly overstaffed in what were perceived to be unproductive areas, while understaffed in critical areas of economic and technological expertise. Policymaking, personnel, financial and general management practices also were too centralized. There were too many conflicts between the administrative cadre and professionals and between political appointees and career administrative officials. And as

Dotun Phillips (1990) contends, before the 1988 civil service reform appropriate and effective information and data management systems were virtually absent.

The 1988 civil service reform was meant to enhance professionalism. The new civil service rules required staff that hitherto had not specialized in their duties to now do so. Such rules applied to bureaucrats who lacked appropriate and recognized educational or technical skills for the jobs they were assigned to perform and who shuttled from one professionally distinct job to another and from one ministry to another. The new bureaucratic structure was broken down into three professional categories: assistant, officer, and director – all of different grades (Phillips 1990, 8). The assistant was a subprofessional and thus not required having a university degree or equivalent professional qualification. The officer was a full professional who was required to have a university degree or equivalent professional qualification. The director category was reserved for full professionals who had been given general management functions as heads of a branch, division, or Department. Professionalism also required regular training and retraining for all Nigerian civil servants. Staff training was made obligatory and a periodic exercise in the schedule of civil administrators. Staff deployment was henceforth based on the bureaucrat's degree of specialization and qualifications for the position.

A major consequence of the civil service reform of 1988 was that the position of permanent secretary was abolished and replaced by that of director-general of the civil services (Civil Service Reform Report 1988, 5). Appointment to the position of director-general was political and the duration of the appointment is at the pleasure of the president at the national level or the governor at the state level. Directors therefore were required to retire with the government that appointed them, but an incoming administration could request reappointment. Few weeks after President Obasanjo was sworn into office he reintroduced the position of permanent secretary in 1999.

In 1994 the military regime set up another Review Panel on the Civil Service reform. This panel was also called Ayida Panel, named after its chairperson. The Ayida Panel submitted its report in 1995. Otobo (1999) pointed that the Ayida panel revised most of the changes recommended by the 1988 Civil Service Reform. The panel recommended that the Head of Personnel Board in each ministry should be given the position of Assistant Director. It also recommended that recruitment into the civil service, especially at the entry grade of professional cadres, should as much as possible be based on a combination of merit and federal character, such that the best candidates from each state are selected on a competitive basis. The Ayida Panel also addressed the issue of pay. It recommended that the government should periodically review the pay and other incentives for civil servants in Nigeria. It argued that low pay was one of the reasons for corruption. Therefore, remuneration in the civil service should be sufficiently attractive to discourage corruption. Further the panel recommended that in order for the government to deal with the problem of corruption in the civil service, there should be strict sanctions applied against those found to have engaged in corrupt practices (Otobo, 1999).

The reforms recommended by Udoji (1972-1974), Phillips (1988) and Ayida (1994-1995) have had very important impact on local governments is Nigeria. Specifically, these reforms have refined local governments and change their orientation from field administration of the state governments to being semi-autonomous local government institutions that were responsible to their local electorate. Local governments in Nigeria are now regarded as government at local level exercised through representative's councils established by law to exercise specific powers within defined areas (Otobo, 1999; Ggoyega 1999).

The reforms also were directed toward reduction of the misuse and abuse of authority. Checks and balances and procedures to promote accountability were instituted. Bureaucrats were required to notify the accountant-general of all prepayment audit queries. Ministers also were required to be the only persons permitted to issue expenditure instructions. Various internal discipline procedures were introduced for controlling civil servants. The use of political institutions such as the presidency (military), legislature (1990-1993) and judiciary to check accountability ranged from such measures as funds cutting, investigation of abuse of office, executive power, reorganization, fiscal power, and administrative law. The Civil Service Code of Conduct also stressed what should be the appropriate behavior of the bureaucrat and included punishment for violations of the code.

Despite this strong accountability policy, the post-reformed bureaucracy has continued its corrupt practices. The most notable consequence of the accountability measures in the Nigerian public bureaucracy has not been accountability but rather the widening of the scope of abuses. Politicians and military and administrative functionaries continued to pursue, unabated, their self-enrichment activities. Military officers are themselves highly implicated in corrupt enrichment. In view of the extensive involvement of many of its members in corrupt practices, the Nigerian military has no credibility as an anti-corruption crusader. Moreover, the military's self-assigned role as the moral guardian of Nigeria is an invitation to bureaucratic and political chaos. Among other things, this role has created a situation in which every soldier, despite his dubious background, feels the urge to liberate Nigerians. Further the military is, but a coercive arm of the dominant Nigeria class. At best, in its custodian role, the can replace one fraction/faction of the dominant class for another fraction without fundamentally transforming Nigerian politics, public bureaucracy, and society. The custodian role of the military legitimizes force and violence as the most efficacious instruments for Code of Conduct in the civil service and political change. As such, the military is increasingly being transformed both into an instrument for private enrichment and as a hired gun for settling old political scores, reorganizing bureaucratic structure, and making appointments in the civil service. Adamolekun and Ayeni (1990) contend that corrupt practices in Nigeria include embezzlement, bribery, fraud, and outright theft. Peter Koehn (1990) asserts that Nigerian public servants are more concerned with self-enrichment than with government service. He raises the question as to whether the corrupt practices of the Nigerian bureaucracy ought to be cited as one of the reasons for the nation's under-development or at least for its slow development.

The Nigerian public increasingly has come to view bureaucrats as corrupt and inefficient. There is a general distrust of and public alienation from the bureaucracy. The absence of a strong commitment to professional ethical standards on the part of the public bureaucracies, together with the absence of business ethics on the part of the private sector entrepreneurs, has produced a situation in which corruption flourishes both in and out of government. Although the incumbent military government has demonstrated the will to expose and punish persons guilty of corrupt practices, it has not yet tackled the fundamental issues of rethinking the system of government contracts, setting limits to individual wealth, and imposing clearly articulated professional ethical standards on public functionaries.

With this background in place, the current government must ensure that wages, salary, and benefits meet the needs of all public employees. Good labor relations are also necessary, and the political rights of each employee must be recognized and honored. The current regime should also ensure that all levels of the civil service, including the military, are complying with the Code of Conduct policies. All heads of ministries and government agencies should be delegated as principal instruments in the execution of national accountability policy and Code of Conduct. A strong disciplinary system is also required to effectively enforce the policy. It should be noted that when government policies on accountability are clearly defined and communicated to all civil servants, and when the policies are strictly enforced, the need to invoke disciplinary procedures is greatly reduced. Unfortunately, there are many bad actors in the Nigerian government who will not respond well to the policies and procedures outlined above. Consequently, the public trust requires that the government also develop policies and procedures that protect its operations against fraud and other types of criminal behavior. The use of internal and external audits often provides this extra measure of protection. In combination with a well-developed sense of organizational unity, public entities can reach the high degrees of efficiency, economy, and effectiveness that are demanded by their ever-watchdog constituencies.

Fiscal federalism is still a salient aspect of Nigerian public administration. Since independence in 1960, the allocation of revenue to regions and later states and local governments has often been a major problem to Nigerian federalism. In an attempt to solve the problem of revenue allocation the National Revenue Mobilization, Allocation and Fiscal Commission was established in 1989 (Gboyega, 1999). This institution was required to design and effectively mobilize all sources of public sector revenue, as well as prescribe a revenue allocation formula. This formula is what is now used for sharing money among federal, state and local governments. Since 1989, the revenue allocation formula has been adjusted twice to the disadvantage of state governments. On the one hand, the state share of the national revenue decreased from 32.5 percent to 30 percent in 1990. On the order hand, the local governments share of the national revenue account increased from 10 percent to 15 percent in 1990 (Gboyega, 1999).

During Sani Abacha's regime, the state revenue steadily increased while the local governments suffered some decrease. Abacha channeled revenue that was previous given directly to local government by the federal government through the states to their local governments. This new process gave state governments more power over their local governments. Most state governments used find one reason or the other to make deductions from this revenue before they were given to their local governments.

General Abacha's administration exercises dominance in all aspects of intergovernmental relations in Nigeria. Gboyega (1999) reported how General Abacha appointed a new chief justice for Ondo State in 1996 without consultation with the state governor (military administrator) of the state. As a matter of fact, during the military administration in Nigeria, it was the Head of State who appointed the state governors. But on like other regimes before Abacha, he required states and their local governments to seek his approval before making any important appointments.

Since the introduction of democratic role in Nigeria in May of 1999, a new form of intergovernmental relations has emerged. Otobo (1999) pointed that a number of administrative consultative forums bring together senior policymakers at the federal, state and local levels. For example, conferences of accountant generals, and conferences that bring together ministers (heads of federal ministers) and commissioners (political heads of ministries at state levels) in such areas as finance, education, and agriculture. These forums have enabled public administrators from all levels of government to explore mutual interest that could lead to sustainable development in the future.

The Bureaucrats Role in Public Policy

Nigeria's bureaucracy is actively engaged in the decision-making processes. The military leadership readily works with the bureaucracy in national decision-making. The military-run political institutions must bargain with the bureaucracy in policy making and in policy implementation. Nigerian governmental bureaucracies are the repositories for the information and expertise that the federal and thirty state governments need for effective policy making. The power relationship between the higher bureaucracies and the military junta requires constant tending and involves delicate political management. While this relationship undermines Nigeria's legitimate political institutions, the bureaucracy's reservoir of talent and information provides it with extraordinary powers that it is not reluctant to use.

Policy decisions are made each day by the Nigerian government on a variety of problems. Some of the decisions take a very short time, in terms of hours or minutes to make; others require weeks and months, even years. A crucial element in the making of a decision is the policymaker, that is, the person who assembles and then processes the available information and arrives at a particular policy decision. In the Federal government of Nigeria, the policy makers are frequently the senior civil servants and professionals at the grade levels of director to director general rather than legislators or "legitimate" political leaders. The Permanent Secretary is generally regarded as the head of the ministry, if government has appointed no political head, a minister or commissioner. In the absence of a functioning national assembly, not unusual during the reign of military regimes, the Permanent Secretary or managing-director (in the case of government agencies) exerts great influence over what the government does. This is one of the reasons why the Permanent Secretary and the senior civil servants have become very powerful during the public administration and policy making processes in Nigeria. The Permanent Secretaries are still very powerful because the current lawmaking bodies (the National Assembly) are concerned with broader policy issues, not the day-to-day decisions. The Permanent Secretary is present in government ministries and departments at the national and state level.

The power and autonomy of the Nigerian public bureaucracies have expanded enormously during the years that the military has dominated the political system and since 1999 when the civilian administration was sworn in. In particular, the public administrator role in policy making has increased since the end of the civil war in 1970. In the absence of a legislature and elected representatives, the federal and state public bureaucracies have acquired wide management functions. They also play a major part in the recommendation and formulation of social, economic, educational, and political objectives. Humphrey Nwosu (1979) contends that Nigerian civil servants hold unique positions in the hierarchy of ministries, departments, corporations, and other state agencies, and these positions enable them to access a wealth of technical data. Thus, a symbiotic relationship exists between Nigeria's military rulers and its top public servants.

Nigerian senior bureaucrats provide the military rulers with ideas, policy proposals, information, and value premises for fundamental decisions. The military in exchange shields the bureaucrats and allows them to increase their power in both decision making and policy implementation. One effect of the dominance of the top bureaucrats in goal setting and decision making is that most decisions of government tend to be remote from the basic needs of Nigerians, the majority of whom live in the rural areas. It is often difficult for senior civil servants in the big commercial cities to articulate effectively the primary needs of rural Nigerians, if the former is aware of those needs at all.

Planning and Control

Planning in the Nigerian military government is closely related to the function of framing policies and their implementation. Since Nigerians are living in an era when government activities have expanded and the resources for executing them are limited, planning becomes necessary to optimize the available human and material resources for the accomplishment of social objectives. Moreover, public administrators have been closely associated with Nigeria's planning efforts since the adoption of the nation's economic and political development strategy in 1946 (Nwosu 1977, 87-133). Also, since Nigeria attained political independence in 1960, public servants have helped in the formulation of five national development plans (1962-1968, 1970-1974, 1975-1980, 1980 -1985 and 1986-1990).

According to the popular image, bureaucrats in Nigeria have devised solutions to national problems independent of the influence of interest groups and by employing their professional training and experience. Scholars from Reinhard Bendix (1945) to Theda Skocpol (1985) consider the persuasiveness of the bureaucracy in modern times as a consequence of the increasing sophistication of the bureaucrats' technocratic skills. The Nigerian bureaucracy's monopoly of government expertise has supposedly encouraged politicians in authoritarian (military) and democratic regimes alike to depend on technocrats for the development of national policies. Public servants, more than other groups of Nigerians, possess the talents and skills necessary not only to implement and coordinate the planning activities of the government but also to institutionalize social change. Bureaucratic expertise is judged to have greater importance now that Nigeria is at the crossroads of its development and is increasingly called upon induce to not only increase in the available social products but also to ensure equitable distribution of these products.

When the Nigerian military government restructured the federation in 1967, 1976, 1990, and again in 1996, the federal and state civil servants were instrumental in making the twelve, nineteen, twenty-one, thirty, and finally thirty-six state structures a reality. Without the effective contribution of the various cadres of public servants, it would have been impossible for the military junta to carry out the division of the Nigerian federation in a cost-effective and efficient manner. The successful implementation of these policies by public bureaucrats contributed immensely to the process of political integration at a time of considerable political upheaval.

The major flaws in the Nigerian bureaucracy in the post-independence era are not found in the collection of data or the identification of long-term objectives but in the shortage of qualified personnel, especially in scientific and technical fields. More significant, the shortcomings are seen in the lack of reliable census data, ineffective coordination within and outside the government and, most of all, in bureaucratic corruption. Further, the federal character principle is another flaw that contradicts the unity and representative bureaucracy that the civil service ought to promote. The first flaw of the federal character is in the area of freedom of movement. The second flaw is that of freedom from discrimination. In both cases, the expansive interpretation of movement which includes career choice and upward mobility abridges career movement and stunts self-realization in a discriminatory manner. Subjecting appointment and promotion to federal character discriminates against merit and therefore unfair to certain sectors of the Nigerian society (Ayoade, 1999). The promotion and appointment of persons to various civil service positions should be made from the best available in the group or section in the nation. Recruitment to positions which require specialist training such as medical professionals, architects, engineers, professors and pilots should be based on merit. Further, to ensure merit, efforts should be made to give equal access to education to all the citizens of Nigeria. This will help to abridge the educational disparities between North and South as well as give opportunities for further professional training. Finally, in spite of Nigeria's desire to accelerate economic development, bureaucratic accountability is still a distant goal.

Conclusion

The British colonial government played a critical role in the development of government bureaucracy in Nigeria. Apart from the deficiencies of inherited techniques and procedures, a review of public bureaucracy ineffectiveness includes the following. The first is low productivity, which is seen sometimes as the result of the pursuit of private business activities by public bureaucrats and sometimes as the result of resource-wasting rivalries between departments and interethnic group civil servants. It is also seen as the result of narrow bureaucratic perspectives that place a premium on controlling resources, particularly public expenditures, rather than on output or social and economic benefits expenditure. The second is poor policymaking or decision-making. The third is low execution or implementation capacity. The fourth is defective structures, usually a reaction to overcentralization.

The doctrine of political neutrality in the Nigeria on public bureaucracy has been discarded, and public administrators have ceased to be nonpartisan and neutral. Today's civil service is a formidable political force with a strong role in policy formulation, in the distribution of patronage, and the allocation of resources. The Nigerian public administrators have vital role in economic matters because most military and political leaders have little alternative but to rely on their advice. Unfortunately, however, Nigeria's bureaucrats have not used their power to improve the management of government but rather to satisfy their individual and collective ambition. Bureaucrats in the nation have been playing the role of informal brokers between the national government and their ethno-regions and engaged in cover politics. Ayoade (1999) contends that the only solution to the problem of integration is adherence to true federalism and a reduction in the powers of the national government. A decentralization of critical national institutions and political power will result in a relax bureaucracy, less-heated inter-ethnic relations and an efficient and accountable civil service.

A major question in Nigeria, therefore, is whether public administration in Nigeria can be transformed into a self-motivating but rationally responsible institution that is concerned with the country's modernization needs. The Structural Adjustment/Make-or-Buy technology policy was intended to begin this kind of transformation.

References

Aborishade, Oladimeji, and Robert Mundt. (1998). Politics in Nigeria. New York: Longman.

Abubakar, Dauda. (1999). "Consociationalism and Democratic Stability in Nigeria." In Federalism and Political Restructuring in Nigeria edited by Kunle Amuwo, Adigun Agbaje, Rotimi Suberu and Georges Herault. Ibadan, Nigeria: Spectrum Press. pp. 164-176.

Adamolekun, L. (1986). Politics and Administration in Nigeria. Ibadan, Nigeria: University of Ibadan Press.

Adamolekun, L. and V. Ayeni. (1990). "Nigeria." In Public Administration in Third World Nations, edited by V. Subramanian. London: Longman, pp. 120-145.

Adamolekun, Oladipo, ed. (1999). Public Administration in Africa: Main

Issues and Selected Countries Studies. Boulder, Colorado: Westview.

Adedeji, Adebayo. (1992). "Factors in the African Development Equation." African Journal of Public Administration and Management, Vol. 1, 1 (January), pp. 15-37.

Adu, A. (1982). The Civil Service in Commonwealth Africa. London: George Allen and Unwin.

Albrow, M. (1970). Bureaucracy. London: Pall Mall Press.

Allison, G. (1971). Essence of Decision-Making: The Cuban Missile Crisis. Boston: Little Brown.

Anderson, J. (1984). Public Policy-Making. New York: Holt, Rinehart, and Winston.

Ayida, A. A. (1987). "In the Public Service." In Reflections on Nigerian Development, Lagos, Nigeria: Heinmann. pp. 113-116.

Ayoade, J. A. (1999). "The Federal Character Principle and the Search for National Integration in Nigeria." In Federalism and Political Restructuring in Nigeria edited by Kunle Amuwo, Adigun Agbaje, Rotimi Suberu and Georges Herault. Ibadan, Nigeria: Spectrum Press. pp. 164-176.

Blau, P. (1956). Bureaucracy in Modern Society. New York: Random House.

Coleman, J. (1956). Nigeria: The Background to Nationalism. Berkeley: University of California Press.

Collin, Paul. (ed.) (1980). Administration for Development in Nigeria. Lagos, Nigeria: African Education Press.

Egonmwan, J. (1991). Public Policy Analysis: Concept and Application. Benin City, Nigeria: Aka and Brothers Press.

Etzioni, A. (1968). The Active Society: A Theory of Societal and Political Processes. London: Collier-Macmillan.

Falola, T. (1996). Developing Planning and Decolonization in Nigeria. Westport, Connecticut: Greenwood.

Feit, E. (1968). "Military Coups and Political Development: Some Lesson from Ghana and Nigeria." World Politics. Vol. 20.2 (January), pp. 179-193.

Friedrich, C. (1963). Man and his Government. New York: McGraw-Hill.

Gboyega, Alex. (1999). "Intergovernmental Relations in Nigeria." In Nigeria: Politics and Governance 1986-1996 edited by Oyeleye Oyediran and Adigun Agbaje. Daka, Senegal: CODESRIA.

Graf, W. (1988). The Nigerian State, Political Economy, State Class and Political System in Post-Colonial Era. Portsmouth, New

Hampshire: Heinemen Press.

Guidelines for Local Government Reform. (1976). Kaduna, Nigeria: Government Printer.

Harris, Belle. (1980). "The Reorganization of Local Government Under the Military Rule in Nigeria, 1966-1974." In Administration for Development in Nigeria, edited by Paul Collins. Lagos, Nigeria: African Education Press.

Hendelman, H. (1996). The Challenge of Third World Development. Upper Saddle River, New Jersey: Prentice-Hall.

Humes, Samuel, and Robert Ola. (1994). Government and Local Development in Western Nigeria. Benin City, Nigeria: Ambik Press.

Kirk-Greene, A. and Douglass Rimmer. (1981). Nigeria Since 1970: A Political and Ecnomic Outline. London: Hodder and Stroughton.

Lewis, P. (1992). The Political Economy of Public Enterprise in Nigeria. Ph.D. Dissertation Princeton University.

Nwosu, H. (1997). Political Authority and Nigerian Civil Service. Enugu, Nigeria: Fourth Dimension.

Olowu, Dele. (1991). Nigerian Public Administration: Past Present and Future. Ibadan, Nigeria: Shaneson C. J. Limited.

Olowu, Dele. (1999). "Accountability and Transparency." In Public Administration in Africa: Main Issues and and Selected Countries Studies edited by Oladipo Adamolekun. Boulder, Colorado: Westview.

Otobo, E. (1999). "Nigeria." In Public Administration in Africa: Main Issues and and Selected Countries Studies edited by Oladipo Adamolekun. Boulder, Colorado: Westview.

Oyeleye, Oyediran, and Adigun Agbaje. (ed.) (1999). Nigeria: Politics of Transition and Governance 1986-1996. Dakar, Senegal: CODESRIA.

Phillips, A. (1990). The 1988 Nigerian Civil Service Reforms and Their Post-1992 Prospects. Ibadan, Nigeria: NISER Publication.

Rondinelli, D.A. and H. P. Minis, Jr. (1990). "Administrative Restructuring for Economic Adjustment: Decentralization Policy in Senegal." International Review of Administrative Science, Vol. 56, 3, pp. 447-66.

Rosenbloom, D. (1998). Understanding Public Management, Public Policy and Law. Upper Saddle River, New Jersey: Prentice-Hall.

Simon, H. (1958). Administrative Behavior. 2nd Edition. New York: Macmillan.

4 Military Administration

Introduction

The Nigerian military has been the subject of a number of studies (Dent 1964; Graf 1988; Kirk-Greene 1964; Luckham 1970; Ukpabi 1972). The Nigerian military has been described, variously, as a dictatorship, a body of nation builders; an all-powerful "national watchdog," ineffective administrators; change agents; politicians in uniform; and arbitrators, or guardians, of Third World countries. During the last two decades, African scholars such as Mazrui (1986), Oyediran (1979), Diamond (1983), Ihonvbere (1994), and Theen and Wilson (1996) have characterized the Nigerian military as corrupt, arrogant, ethnic oriented, and responsible for the political decay and underdevelopment of the country. Henry Bienen (1978) and Dent (1978) have also noted the inability of the military regime to contribute to political and economic development. They contend that the expansion of the role of the military into governing has seriously impaired its professionalism. It is their opinion that military officers can indulge in politics only at the cost of their fighting skills (Bienen 1983).

Robert Jackman (1976) contends that military intervention in the politics of Third World countries has no unique bearing on social change, regardless of either the level of economic development or geographic region. Other scholars argue that the low pace of modernization and political development in a new nation is what produces military takeovers but that such intervention will eventually have beneficial consequences for the country. They believe that the military is better able to organize a Third World country's effort at modernization because of its ability to impose political order in an otherwise tumultuous setting. The military can provide discipline, organization, and hierarchical control that civilians often find elusive as they seek to govern and change their societies (Maniruzzaman 1987).

Critics of the military's role as modernizer stress that the organizational logic of the armed forces is different from that of political formation and development (Janowitz 1977). Samuel Huntington (1968) also has expressed doubt about ability of the military to develop effective political institutions, especially those institutions like political parties that organize broader citizen participation – that is, the very institutions that are needed for political development. The political skills needed for developing a viable and self-sustaining political system include, among others, ideological commitment, the capacity to respond to new challenges, and the arts of administration, negotiation, representation, and bargaining. The Nigerian military has not demonstrated the requisite political and economic skills needed in a developing country.

The purposes of this chapter are (a) to analyze the development of the Nigerian military during the colonial period (b) to examine the reasons given for the frequent intervention of the army in Nigerian politics and (c) to examine the Nigerian army's role in public management and nation building. This chapter examines the nature of the military national and state governments, and the consequences of military rule for society the Nigerian society. Although lacking in the political art of governorship, the military has been able to legitimize its political impact by engaging in a political strategy of sharing administrative functions with civilian employees while retaining ultimate control.

The Colonial Legacy

One of the prominent legacies of British Colonial Government in West Africa is the Nigerian army. Many British companies operated along the valley of the River Niger before 1850. The British, however, colonized Lagos in 1861 and the following year formed the Lagos constabulary. While this was going on in Lagos, in 1862 all the British companies along the Niger delta merged to form the Royal Niger Company. The reason for the merger was to achieve total control and promotion of trade in palm oil along the Niger valley. During this period palm oil was exported to Britain as a raw material for the soap and margarine industries. In order to take complete control of their trade along the Niger River valley, the Royal Niger Company asked the King of England to gran' it the authority to administer the area. Ukpabi (1972) contends that after the Royal Niger Company was granted a charter in 1886, it assumed administration of the Niger delta. The charter authorized the company to raise the Royal Niger Constabulary. This quasi-military power was used to enforce the authority of the British colonial administration. When the British colonial government expanded its influence into the hinterland and consequently came into conflict with the inhabitants, the government found it necessary to increase the size and improve the training of these forces. Kirk-Greene (1964) asserts that in 1892, the Niger Coast Protectorate Force numbered about 40 ordinary ranks, but by 1900 this force had risen to a strong battalion of nearly 1,000 men. This British colonial force was divided into the police and the regiment forces. While the police force was then delegated to handle civil matters and the maintenance of law and order, the regiments were deployed to deal with military matters such as the protection of the territorial boundaries of the protectorates. In 1901, the various regiments and dependencies of Great Britain along the West African coast (Nigeria, and Gold Coast – now Ghana, Sierra Leone, and Gambia) were merged to form the West African Frontier Forces (WAFF). In Nigeria the WAFF had two regiments – one in the north and the other in the south. The two WAFF regiments were merged on January 1, 1914, as a result of the amalgamation of the north and south of Nigeria. WAFF was changed to Royal West African Frontier Forces (RWAFF) in 1928. RWAFF became the Nigerian Army in 1960.

According to Ukpabi (1972) the RWAFF was administered as a truly colonial force. British officers and non-commission officers (NCOs) were deployed to serve in all units. The Nigerians in the colonial military were mostly ordinary ranks, and conditions were required for the granting of a commission (i.e., high school diploma and the age of twenty-two years). Ukpabi also contend that before 1949, there were no officers of Nigerian origin in the army. By January 1949, however, some Nigerian soldiers were selected for training as officers (Jemibewon 1978). Duke Bassey was the first Nigerian to be commissioned into the Officer Corp of the Nigerian Army in April 1949, followed by Aguiyi Ironsi and Sam Ademulegun in June 1949. Other Nigerian officers later commissioned included Ralph Sodeinde (April 1950), Babafemi Ogundipe (August 1953), Adeyinka Adebayo (December 1953), Nwawo (May 1954), and Francis Fajuyi in November 1954 (Achike 1978). David Jemibewon (1978) asserts that out of the 250 officers in the Nigerian army in 1956, only 15 were Nigerians. The General Certificate of Education (ordinary level) with an age limit of twenty-two years made it difficult to raise enough qualified Nigerians to send for training to the Royal Military Academy at Sandhurst in England, where the earlier group of officers was trained. While the officer corps had few Nigerians, the other ranks were overwhelmingly staffed with Nigerians by 1958.

During the 1940s and 1950s service in the army was unattractive for a variety of reasons. The people of Nigeria did not see the role of the military during the colonial period as promoting civilization and humanitarianism. On the contrary, they regarded the military as an instrument fashioned by an alien authority for the purpose of destroying the political independence of the various tribes and their cherished way of life (Ahmadu 1962, 23). Under the prevailing situation it was not surprising that the colonial military had a negative rather than a positive influence on the society. In many situations the army uniform was depicted as only suitable for dubious children of tribal chiefs and traditional rulers (Omojukun 1979).

The legal control of the RWAFF was firmly vested in the British government, which was represented in each of the four member states by a governor. While the governor exercised the power to deploy the local units in the state, the British Army Council reserved to itself the powers of deploying the army for international or foreign assignments (Achike 1978). Thus, the general officer commanding in each region was responsible to the governor (title Commander-in-Chief of the RWAFF unit in the state) and also to the general officer commanding-in-chief of the West African Command, who was directly responsible to the War Office in London. The RWAFF structure was transferred to the Nigerian army in 1960, and this has become the structure of the Nigerian army to the present day.

The transfer of the RWAFF military tradition was another matter, however. First, a high standard of discipline and training was maintained and was inherited mostly through the numerous administrative regulations and provisions of the British Army Act (Jemibewon 1978). The system of documentation and monitoring of accountability in the Nigerian army's administration continues to remain fashioned on the British model. It is also interesting to note that after thirty years of political independence, Nigeria still uses official British military acts like the Manual of Military Law and Queens Regulation as authority in dispensing justice in the military. Secondly, the British tradition had the characteristics of inspiring its troops with a sense of belonging to a united or monolithic force. It had been deployed in action under a national army and had won battle honors that became a source of pride in the history of the nation's force. Thirdly, the RWAFF has been a platform of interaction among the four member countries of Nigeria, Liberia, Ghana, and Sierra Leone for over ninety years. Such a long association must have contributed to the identification of similar national objectives and to military cooperation in the region.

The RWAFF units, however, were not insulated from the internal politics of their respective states. Ukpabi (1972) contends that British officers in the Nigerian Regiment played an important role in the political development of Nigeria. Long before independence, a number of army officers were appointed district commissioners, and after the consolidation of British rule many officers remained in administrative or political posts. A few examples of such officers may be relevant. Major J. H. Burdon, who was the commandant of the Royal Niger Company Constabulary in 1898-1999, was appointed the Resident of Sokoto in 1903-1906, and 1909-1910. In 1926, Major F. Jeffries was the Divisional Officer of Onitsha Division, while in 1943 Captain Glover, the first administrator of Lagos, and Frederick Lugard, the first commissioner and commandant of Northern Nigeria, were military men (Ukpabi 1972, 73).

The attainment of independence by Ghana in 1957 led to the disintegration of RWAFF, and on April 1, 1958, Nigeria assumed full budgetary responsibility for its military. Okay Achike (1978) asserts that between 1958 and 1960 the process of handing over control to the Nigerian army was gradual, and the British still made grants to augment the financial provisions of the military. Further, about 82 percent of the officer's corps was still British. However, with the assumption of ministerial control by the Prime Minister in February 1960, the transfer of the military to Nigerian administration was completed. The new Nigerian administration of 1960 began to introduce policies aimed at correcting certain defects of the military. For example, before 1958, when the Nigerian government took over the primary financial responsibility for the upkeep of the Nigerian military, the British government recruited most of the infantry from northern Nigeria while the technical units were staffed by men from southern Nigeria (Ukpabi 1972). This British colonial practice did not make for the development of a fully representative Nigerian army.

As soon as the Nigerian administration took over the control of the military in 1958, efforts were made to ensure that ordinary ranks were recruited from all parts of Nigeria. The prevailing regional recruitment quotas of 50 percent from the northern Nigeria and 25 percent from the western and eastern Nigeria were agreed upon when Nigeria took over the control of the military in 1958. Northern Nigeria was given a quota of 50 percent because it was larger in size and population than the southern regions. Policies were also enacted to ensure that each military unit was mixed – that is, each unit should contain men from several ethnic groups.

In addition, military units were not allowed to stay too long in one place lest they become engulfed in local politics.

The uniform of the colonial army that featured British emblems was changed to a new green and is composed of a long-sleeve jacket, long pants, and a peaked cap. The old RWAFF emblem of a palm tree was replaced with an eagle and a star. Efforts were also made to recruit university graduates into the military in order to raise the quality of the Nigerian officer corps and the image of the military. Ukpabi (1972) contends that this attempt to improve the image of the military and to secure its loyalty to the government in power led to large increases in army pay. It was hoped that these increases in pay would attract many people to the army, thereby giving the military the opportunity to select only the best candidates to fill the various quotas allotted to the regions. In order to further change the trends of imperial training and power and to assert the independence of the Nigerian military, Nigerian troops were sent for training to the United States, Canada, India, and Australia, thereby changing the practice during the colonial period of having such soldiers trained only in Britain.

The strength of the Nigerian army in 1958 was only 7,600. The general officer commanding of the army announced the plan to increase the size in May 1964 by about 2,900. Of the 10,500 in April 1965, only a little over 500 belonged to the officer corps – 330 of who was combatant status (Oyediran 1979). William Gutteridge (1964) has contended that three to five hundred officers in a country of forty million based mainly on five military stations, the majority of which were far from the capital, could not be regarded as a political factor of the greatest importance. The fact that this numerically small army was able to take control of the political power without much difficulty less than two years later shows Nigerian political leaders underestimated the military custodian role.

The process of building a national army for Nigeria began in 1958. The Nigerianization of the officer corps was stepped up at the same time as British officers were redeployed to the United Kingdom in anticipation of Nigeria's independence. According to Ukpabi (1972), by 1960 only 60 British noncommissioned officers remained where four years previously there had been more than 300. After 1963, all the battalions were commanded by Nigerians, and in 1965 the last British commander of the Nigerian army left the country, to be followed a month later by the last British serving officers in the Nigerian army (Miners 1971, 104; Peters 1995). The composition of the military after that time reflected an agreed-upon regional quota system. Nigerian soldiers were recruited on the basis of 50 percent from the Northern Region, and 25 percent from the Western and Eastern regions, respectively. The same quota system prevailed in the recruitment of officers. Robin Luckhan (1971) contends that Nigerian soldiers saw themselves as citizens of the nation, and as such were affected by the political circumstances challenging the nation (201). Because of the quota system, however, officers and ranks had cause to represent their individual regions, not the more abstract national state. This crisis of identity led some soldiers to develop parochial attitudes that inclined them more to regional governments and their political leaders, and less to national issues.

A review of the structure of the Nigerian military between 1958 and 1965 shows that it was divided along ethnic lines: a majority of the officers of the rank of major or above were Igbo, but most junior officers and ordinary ranks were from the middle-belt minority tribes of the Northern Region (Ostheimer 1972). The younger officers, lieutenants and captains, made attempts to redress the tribal imbalance, but those predominantly northern and western officers preferred a far slower rate of advancement. The building of a new Nigerian military after the departure of the British colonial army opened vacancies for young officers at the higher levels, which made some of them superior colonels at young ages. Once these vacancies were filled, however, the rank structure became frozen, stifling the junior ranks by the mid 1960s. The frustration and anger of the junior officers was seen in the killing of the superior Igbo officers in 1966 (Luckham, 1974).

The government of Nigeria at independence in 1960 still regarded the Queen of England as the head of state; therefore, the army was named the Royal Nigerian Army. On attainment of a republic in October 1963, the army changed its name to the Nigerian Army. Many Nigerians were trained and commissioned as officers to replace the outgoing British officers. During the transition period the British government mixed political activities with those of the military. For reasons that the British did not explain, most of the military facilities and training grounds were located in the northern part of Nigeria, especially around Zaria and Kaduna. Ukpabi (1972) contends that the location of military facilities in the north might be due to political rather than strategic reasons. In 1914, with the amalgamation of the south and north, Nigeria had four battalions. Two military battalions were stationed in the north, one in the west and the other in the east. The Nigerian administration seems to have followed this British pattern in locating military institutions after independence. The

Military School was located in Zaria (1960); the Nigerian Defense Academy (1964) in Kaduna; the Command and Staff College at Jaji (1973), near Kaduna; the Institute of Policy and Strategic Studies (1976) at Bukuru, near Jos; and the Nigerian War College (1992) in Lagos. The Nigerian War College is the only military institution in the southern part of the country. The politicization of the Nigerian army is also reflected in the pattern of recruitment, promotion, and discipline (Luckham 1974). This preferential location of facilities has led to the northern domination of the army's higher ranks for the last twenty-five years.

Post-Independence Intervention in Politics

Three major schools of thought have been developed in an attempt to explain post-independence military intervention in the politics of Nigeria. The "internal characteristics model" suggests that one can explain military intervention in politics mainly by reference to the internal organizational structure of the military (Janowitz 1964, 27 - 9). The social background of the officers, their skill, centralized command, hierarchy and career lines, internal social cohesion and cleavages, degree of professionalization, and political ideology within the military are important factors that help explain direct military intervention. Morris Janowitz stressed that intervention will also arise because of organizational decay in the military.

Samuel Huntington's (1965, 1969) custodian theory states that the military is the custodian of the nation's constitution, and, as such, it feels impelled to intervene when constitutional propriety is being violated. He asserted that the military would usually be willing to return to the barracks after a dispute has been settled. Thus, the military only acts as the guardian to check the activities of corrupt civilian administrators and to ensure political stability. Huntington (1969) stressed that the military will intervene when civilian government lacks legitimacy due to inadequate electoral support and an ineffective executive.

Thus, the praetorian army will tend to replace weak and unstable political regimes. Samuel Finer (1969) argued that the most important cause for military intervention is the low or minimal political culture of the society concerned. According to Huntington and Finer, the interpretation of military coups relates to the characteristics of the Nigerian army. Finer, more than Huntington (1969) stressed the role that corruption plays in intervention. Finer (1969) noted that in Nigeria some members of the ineffective military leadership have been found to be corrupt and inept and to pursue self-seeking ambitions. The most vehement repudiation of the "custodian thesis" is the argument made by Wole Soyinka (1972) and Julius Ihonvbere (1997) that the Nigerian military is more corrupt than other is institution. They denounced the military regime, proclaiming it to be a regime of humiliation and tyranny and a dictatorship whose tyranny imposed a travesty of justice far beyond any ills that have been witnessed in the civilian regime. Henry Bienen (1976) found similar opposition to the military among civilian politicians, though they still were willing to work under a military regime.

There are two main theses that have been used to explain the failure of the military regime to relinquish power to elected civilian government as it had promised. The first is the "hidden agenda thesis. This thesis asserts that General Babangida in 1993 and General Sani Abacha in 1998 failed to relinquish power because they never genuinely intended to transfer power to politicians (Kieh and Abgese 1996; Ihonvbere 1997; Washington Post 1998). According to this thesis, while both generals were in public posture and pretended to be earnestly preparing the nation for civil rule, secretly they had a hidden agenda, namely, that they were secretly preparing themselves for perpetual self-rule. For example, while Babangida professed a commitment to military withdrawal from politics, he later turned around to abort the relinquishment of power. Babangida used the transition program that he introduced to cause confusion and public clamor for the military to remain in power, in order to restore public order and stability. He tactically allowed civilian politicians to discredit the return to civil rule (Obansanjo 1993). In the case of General Abacha, he set up a three-year transition program in 1995 from a military to a democratically elected civilian government. In his address at the inauguration of the National Conference on Monday, June 27, 1994, General Abacha stated that "we in the present government in Nigeria are committed to ensuring that there is speedy and unimpeded transition to a civil democratic rule in which we shall not be participants." But contrary to his promise, transition program mandate, and the constitution approved by the National Electoral Commission of Nigeria (NECON), in April 1998, he ordered the five political parties that he created to nominate him as the only presidential candidate. This gesture violated the provision of the constitution that stipulates that "current members of the armed forces of the federation cannot be lawfully registered as a member of a political party." Thus, General Abacha, being a military officer could not be a candidate, since according to the law made by him as head of state, a candidate must be a member of a political party, and the same law forbids officers from being members of a political party. Decree No. 9 of 1997, also signed into law by General Sani Abacha on July 15, 1997 provides that "it shall be the duty and responsibility of all organs of government and of all authorities and persons to conform with, observe and ensure the provisions of the political programs as set out in Schedule 1 to 4 of the Decree." The deepening cynicism and apathy with which the general public now views the transition program has led to a state of unprecedented program gloom and despondency in Nigeria. The electorate in the recent national elections in 1998 manifested this gloom in the abysmal participation.

General Babangida (1991) advanced the second thesis, the "corrigible politicians" thesis. According to the corrigible politician's thesis, the military is eager to relinquish power. However, civilian politicians who continue to sabotage military disengagement have so far frustrated the military's sincere efforts by their nefarious political conduct. While the military is eager to withdraw from politics, it would not do so under unfavorable circumstances. It would not transfer power to civilian politicians who have not demonstrated their capacity to engage in political conduct devoid of maladministration, corruption, violence and human right abuse. This thesis asserts that the military will relinquish power only when political contests among civilians are free of fraud, violence, and chicanery. So long as Nigerian politicians insist on practicing unwholesome politics, the military will delay the transition program. Continued military rule will, among other things, serve as an object lesson on correct political behavior. Once that lesson is learned, the military will promptly transfer power to civilians. Therefore, the onus for military withdrawal rests not on the military, which is eager to see return of democracy in Nigeria, but on civilian politicians. Thus, the obstacle to military withdrawal is the inability of civilian politicians to rise above sordid political behaviors such as electoral rigging, inept, and so on. I will provide evidence of these theses in the rest of this chapter and other parts of the book by critically analyzing post-independence military regimes in Nigeria.

The late Major Chukwuma Nzeogwu led the first military intervention in Nigeria on January 15, 1966. The military's main argument for intervention at the time was that the civilian government's loss of legitimacy reduced its ability to deal effectively with the conditions that were destroying the country. The statements of the majors who carried out the coup demonstrated beyond doubt their deep concern with reforming Nigerian life. Because politicians were perceived by the officers to be at the center of corruption, the military decided that the politicians must go. Major Nzeogwu, the coordinator of the January 1966 coup, stated: "Our purpose was to change our country" (Schwarz 1968, 191). The coup resulted in the death of the federal Prime Minister, the finance minister, and the northern and western premiers. Other reasons given for this intervention by the military included the succession of intense political crises, the deepening polarization, the incessant political instability, and civil strife. Further reasons given included the style and tone of political behavior and conflict, the violence, the repression, and the failure to play by the rules of the game. Nigeria by the time of the intervention had passed through six years of civilian incompetence, inefficient executive leadership, gross abuse of office, corruption, and a resulting lack of economic development. The precipitating factor that galvanized the military to intervene was the violence that erupted from the two political parties headed by Awolowo and Akintola in the Western Region of Nigeria. The attempt by Major Nzeogwu and other middle – ranking officers in Lagos, Kaduna, and Ibadan to take power was unsuccessful, but it forced the civilian cabinet to hand over the administration of the country to Major-General Aguiyi Ironsi.

In the course of the first military intervention, four out of five of the northern senior officers, two out of six Yoruba senior officers, and one out of ten of the eastern senior officers also were murdered. Among civilians, the deaths were equally one-sided. Abubakar, the prime minister from the Northern Region, and Okotie-Ebor, the federal finance minister from the Mid-Western Region, were murdered in Lagos. The Sardauna of Sokoto was killed in Kaduna, and Akintola was killed in Ibadan. There was no violent coup and there were no deaths in Enugu and Benin, and the premiers of the Eastern and Mid-Western regions, who were both Igbo, survived unscathed (Dudley 1982, 79; Peters 1995). This one-sidedness may have been partly due to operational considerations, since any group from one tribe tends to associate more with its fellow tribesmen and to not regard them as potential enemies, but the effects were catastrophic to the northerners. Major-General Ironsi escaped the coup in Lagos and put himself at the head of the northern NCOs who had rallied with northern officers to put down the coup. General Ironsi later emerged as the new leader of Nigeria after the federal cabinet handed power to him in an effort to restore order.

The demise of the First Republic was a severe blow to Nigeria's political system. Reactions to events differed profoundly between the

Eastern and Northern Regions. The distrust arising among northerners and some westerners, and the failure of General Ironsi, himself an Igbo, to try the Igbo conspirators who had murdered fellow officers and political leaders made it almost impossible to reform the federal system. William Graf (1988) contends that the ease with which the military was able to assume political power is astounding. A relatively small army (10,500 men in 1965), lacking in experience (80 percent had no more than four years in service), poorly educated (66 percent of combat and non-combat officers had no more than secondary education before being commissioned), and extremely young (62 percent were between twenty and twenty-four years old), had destroyed the First Republic, eliminated many of its most prominent leaders, and assumed the power to lead the nation (Dudley 1976, 36; Mayer et al. 1996).

Rotimi Suberu and Adigun Agbaje (1999) contend that military regimes in Nigeria had two phases. The first phase was between 1966 and 1979. In this phase military rulers, especially state governors were allowed to exercise most of the powers assigned to the regions under the suspended democratic constitution. Military governors were allowed to incorporate several credible and notable civilian professionals and ethno-regional elites into the structure of their administration. They also redesigned the structure of Nigerian federalism and initiated as well as implemented a fairly successful program of redemocratization which culminated in the inauguration of the Second Republic in October 1979.

The second phase of military role was between 1984 and 1999. This period was characterized by excessive personalization and concentration of state authority in the military head of state. The military leaders became more repressive in managing state affairs, ethnic conflict and religious bigotry, as well as societies inter-relationship. During this period, the military also foster the willful frustration and abortion of the nation's democratic aspiration. Suberu and Agbaje (1999) pointed out that the over centralization of the military during the second phase includes: the complete subordination of constituent state governments to the unified military command system through the center's appointment and frequent redeployment of relatively junior military officers as state administrators. The military head of state was also involved in the organization and reorganization of local government council in a federal political system in which state and local governments were expected to be autonomous. The military conducted a systematic and unchallengeable manipulation of statutory intergovernmental revenue sharing arrangement in manner that reinforced the financial hegemony of the national government and the fiscal emasculation of state and local governments.

In spite of the carnage, the army was a popular institution, and it initially won over the Nigerian public. With its rigid discipline, austere nature, ability to get things done, devotion to duty, and seemingly more selfless attitude, the army was regarded as the savior of the country. After the coup, many things were said and done to discredit the former politicians and some Nigerians prayed for many years of military rule. According to Ladipo Adamolekun (1985), the federal military government under General Ironsi as head of state and supreme commander of the armed forces moved from the federal model to an extreme centralization of power. All legislation was by decree, and noncompliance to an order was subject to strict penalties. Decree Number One proclaimed the doctrine of unitary government, which was strongly supported by radicals and by most Igbos who stood to gain from what was perceived to be an open job market. General Ironsi declared the military government was only a "custodian regime" (Finer 1969), but that extreme measures were needed to correct problems in the Nigerian political system. One such problem, he noted, was the regionalism that threatened national unity. He therefore appointed military governors in each of the four regions. All regional governors were expected to be men under authority obedient to their superior officers in Lagos.

In order to fulfill its task of creating greater unity in Nigeria, the military government needed a common purpose and a climate of trust among Nigerians. Neither purposes nor trust existed among the people neither as a whole nor in the army where the bulk of the combatant soldiers, the NCOs, and the ordinary ranks were northerners.

The initial impetus of the military regime to rule decisively was soon dissipated, and the Federal Supreme Military Council did not use its powers under Decree Number One to legislate for the regions. Every issue was to be interpreted in regional and tribal terms, thereby creating a continuing struggle for power. General Ironsi proved less perceptive by appointing an Igbo to investigate the prospects for rapid unification of the four regions and federal civil services. Since control over the regional civil service was cherished by northerners as a safeguard against Igbo infiltration and domination, northerners disliked his plan. Popular support for some of the government's moves, such as investigations into the corruption of politicians, was undermined by the sudden accumulation of wealth by elements of the military officer corps (Ohonbamu, 1970). The most important factor in General Ironsi's loss of popular support, however, was his haste in proclaiming a new Unitary Constitution (Decree No. 34 of

May 24, 1966) even before the commission directed to study a new constitutional arrangement could turn in their report. This decree galvanized people to riot in the northern Region, and the riot quickly became an attack against Igbo sectors of northern cities, where an estimated three thousand people were killed. Whatever the Ironsi regime had done to legitimate military intervention could not overcome the suspicion that tarnished it. As a result, the distrust, riots, and bloodshed that took place in various parts of the country led to a counter-coup organized by northern officers in July 1966.

General Ironsi's regime was short-lived. He and the then western Region military governor, Colonel Francis Fajuyi, were kidnapped and killed by mutinous troops in late July 1966. After several days of anarchy, Colonel (later General) Yakubu Gowon, an officer from the middle belt of northern Nigeria, emerged as the new head of state. He promptly prepared a decree that restored the federal structure and promised an early return to civilian rule as soon as a constitutional conference could meet and agree upon a design for a new system of government. Gowon rebuked the murderous soldiers of the May 1966 riots and slowly reestablished discipline and control, but the basis of trust for his military regime had been fatally undermined.

During riots in September and October 1966, 30,000 Igbos were killed in the North, in a slaughter far beyond the scale of previous riots in May of the same year (Ostheimer 1973). The Hausa-Fulani were still incensed at the earlier assassinations of their leadership, and the presence of thousands of Igbo traders, businessmen, and civil servants living in the northern Region presented a constant reminder of this communal bitterness. The mass killings forced easterners from all over the federation to migrate in search of refuge (Oyediran, 1979). With close to a million Igbo refugees fleeing south, it became clear that the Igbo-dominated Eastern region was considering secession under the leadership of Lieutenant Colonel Odumegwu Ojukwu. A constitutional conference was called to discuss the political predicaments facing the nation, but no consensus was reached because the various regions and ethnic groups demanded too much political power for themselves. On October 3, 1966, the constitutional conference was adjourned. Economic sanctions were placed on the Eastern Region when its leaders refused to participate in further dialogue concerning the political impasse. Non-easterners, other than Mid-western Igbos, were expelled from the Eastern Region. Colonel Ojukwu announced that the constitutional arrangements of the national government of Nigeria no longer represented a guarantee to the military government of the Eastern Region. Igbo lives and property could not be protected. The Igbos had lost confidence in a federated Nigeria and had no illusions about the chances of welding Nigerians into a single nation. Therefore, secession of the Eastern Region became inevitable.

In May 1967, Gowon tried to prevent the secession of the Igbos by appointing a National Reconciliation Committee that allowed Colonel Ojukwu to express his concerns. Gowon therefore accepted the committee's recommendation to end economic sanctions against the Eastern Region. His government divided Nigeria into twelve states, which included breaking up the North into six different states. The changes however came too late. The Igbos had seceded, and the consequence was a bloody and costly civil war that lasted thirty months, from July 1967 to January 15, 1970, and resulted in the defeat of the Igbo secessionists. The war was called the Biafra civil war. The word Biafra was derived from the region's location on that section of the Atlantic Ocean called the Bight of Biafra.

Between 1967 and 1970 General Gowon directed the attention of the federal military government toward winning the Biafra civil war. In this process the size of the Nigerian military increased from its prewar level of about 8,000 to more than 250,000 men by 1970 (Ukpabi 1972). Such an increase was bound to affect not only the influence of the military in the country but also its performance and general standing.

Ever since independence, strenuous efforts were made by successive governments to weld the various ethnic groups together. These effects included definite steps to shift the main power base from the regions, and later from the states, to the center by increasing the number of regions or states so that each would become more similar in size and area to the others. In 1963, the First Republic increased the number of regions by one, making them four. In 1967, these four regions were broken into twelve states. In 1975, the number of states was again increased, this time to nineteen. The total number of states in 1996 was thirty-six. Given this multiplicity of states, the power base has definitely tilted in favor of the central government. No state now can hold the entire country to ransom, as the Eastern Region was able to do during the thirty-month civil war (1967-1970). Other steps taken to hold Nigeria together as a nation have included the deliberate whittling down of the powers of the states. The 1979 constitution, for instance, made the states dependent on the federal government for their revenue, and with the local government reform of the early 1990s, state government powers have been further circumscribed. Thus, Gowon's regime was instrumental in breaking down the preindependence ethnic and regional powers and in widening the platform for integration among the various groups in Nigeria.

General Gowon was a capable and generally well regarded leader, who did much to patch up the wounds caused by the Biafra war and who in 1970 set out to oversee a return to civilian government (Oyediran 1979). In the eyes of his critics, he moved too slowly, however, and did too little to curb corruption, inflation, and economic mismanagement. Much of the profit from Nigeria's oil boom of the early 1970s was squandered or stolen, and the return to civilian government was delayed.

The concerned with these mismanagement and with the damage being done to the reputation of the military, reform-minded senior officers seized power in a coup on July 29, 1975, the ninth anniversary of the original coup that brought it to power. The government of General Gowon was overthrown without bloodshed while he was attending an Organization of African Unity (OAU) summit in Kampala, Uganda. This coup was met with widespread manifestations of relief and elation. Only one military commander took steps to support Gowon, but his efforts came too late. Brigadier Murtala Mohammed, with Brigadier Olusegun Obansajo as chief of staff, supreme headquarters and Brigadier Theophilus Danjuma as army chief of staff headed the new regime.

The coup makers of failing to fulfill his promise to hand over the government to a democratically elected civilian regime accused Gowon. General Murtala Mohammed, a Hausa-Fulani officer and head of the new military regime, began drafting a new constitution for a civilian government. He removed all state governors from power, purged the army, and announced a four-year timetable for the return to civilian rule. Within two months of assuming office, he dismissed 150 military officers and 10,000 civil servants that were found guilty of corruption and abuse of office. Mohammed increased the number of states from twelve to nineteen (see map in Appendix A), and decided to move the federal capital from Lagos to Abuja. The fast-moving programs of General Mohammed caught the imagination of the public at large, but it they stirred foreboding and resentment among those whose positions had been disturbed. As a result, a group of army officers who feared for their own position attempted a coup on February 13, 1976. The attempt was unsuccessful, but General Mohammed was killed. His chief of staff, General Olusegun Obasanjo, a Yoruba, assumed power. This was the first time that Nigeria had a Yoruba head of state. As head of state, Obasanjo continued in the spirit of his predecessor.

The reasons for organizing a coup given by Major Nzeogwu, and those given by General Gowon, Mohammed, and Obasanjo, reflect the schools of thought described earlier. For instance, the 1966 coup was motivated by ethnic rivalries and civil disorder, while other coups either were the result of rivalries within the military or were a measure to correct the corrupt practices of government. The Nigerian military, in order to justify its ascension to power through coups, sought legitimacy by virtue of its avowed allegiance to the nation and its commitment to nationalistic objectives. This is the notion of Samuel Huntington's custodian and praetorian theories, which postulate that the military might serve as the guardian of the constitution of a country. The major speeches and decrees issued by key military officers after they assumed control also used this rationale that reflects Huntington's thinking.

The periodic incursions of the Nigerian military into the political leadership not only was a lust for power but also was a product of the conflict, riddled with intrigue and conspiracy, between the two major elite groups that emerged in the Nigerian military. At the close of the civil war in 1970, the military leadership was divided into two groups, the northern faction, led by the "Kuduna Mafia," and the middle belt wing, led by the "Langtang faction" (Ihonvbere 1994; Mayer et al 1996). The major military coups in Nigeria have emanated from one or the other of these two factions. For instance, while the Gowon-led counter-coup of July 1966 was meant to reassert northern control of the nation, Gowon, a middle belt Christian was never accepted by the mainstream Hausa-Fulani oligarchy of northern Nigeria. Hence, the Murtala Mohammed coup of August 1975 was intended to remove any lingering ambivalence about northern control. The failed Dimka-Bisalla coup of February 1976, which led to the death of Mohammed, may be seen as a desperate attempt by the military wing of the Langtang faction to reassert lost control of the military and of the country as a whole. Gowon, who was implicated in the coup, was exiled to Britain, and Lieutenant Colonel Dimka, Major-General Bisalla, Police Commissioner David Gomwalk, and other military leaders from the middle-belt Langtang faction did not recovered from this decimation of the langtang leadership.

The Buhari-Idiagbon regime that came to power in December 1983 seemed to be an exception to the usual military escapade into national politics in that it made some attempt to address the rampant corruption and ineptitude of the Shagari regime that it overthrew. The northern-abased Kaduna faction feared, however, that the Buhari regime threatened northern control of the nation and engineered the Babangida coup that overthrew Buhari in August 1985.

During the Babangida regime, a new "progressive faction" emerged within the Nigerian military made up of fringe elements from Kaduna faction, non-commissioned (NCOs) officers from the middle belt (Plateau and Benue states), and an ideological group from the Mid-west (the Edo clan). This faction twice attempted to overthrow the Babangida regime, first in December 1985, under General Mamman Vatsa, and the second in April 1990, under Major Gideon Orkar. Both coup attempts failed and resulted in the execution of their leaders. Thus, history will show that the Nigerian military has been one of its own worst enemies with a high propensity for self-destruction. Ethnic loyalty and numerous coups in Nigeria, more than any other factors, have depleted the nation of its finest military talents.

In October 1979, the military regime of General Obasanjo stepped down and ushered in a new democratically elected civilian government, called the Second Republic. Shehu Shagari was elected president of Nigeria. His government, however, collapsed within a few years due to corruption, persistent strikes, and rampant tribalism. New elections were held in August – September 1983. Whereas the 1979 elections had been generally accepted as fair, the 1983 ballot met with numerous accusations of vote rigging and violence. This weakened the legitimacy of the government. Julius Ihonvbere (1994) contends that corruption reached its height during Shagari's administration. Millions of Naira (the Nigerian currency) was misappropriated by government officials and high levels party members who were responsible for the Abuja (the new federal capital) projects. This drained the country's wealth, causing many ambitious development projects to suffer.

On December 31, 1983, still another coup was staged by senior army officers, which brought the Second Nigerian Republic to an end. Major-General Mohammed Buhari became head of state and ruled through a Supreme Military Council (SMC). General Buhari's reasons for the military intervention included rigged elections, the inability of the Second Nigerian Republic to cultivate financial discipline and, to manage economic development, and the ever-present corrupt leadership (African Press 1984). Table 5.1 shows the trend of military intervention in Nigeria's politics between 1960-1997.

General Buhari's regime instituted a "War Against Indiscipline Policy" and emphasized prudent housekeeping in its economic management. Buhari set an objective to save the country from economic and political collapse. Buhari's regime also promised to put into place measures to eliminate massive waste in economy caused by corruption within and outside the government, reduce the need for the state to borrow money from external sources, and ameliorate degrading domestic conditions. From such a vantage point, Buhari's intervention could be perceived as a guardian factor that could have been used to correct the situation. His fellow senior officers, however, overthrew General Buhari. Generals' Babangida, Abacha, Diya, Kontagora, and Dogoyaro declared that Buhari's rule was too harsh and too slow in moving to restore democratic civilian rule. General Ibrahim Babangida replaced Buhari in August 1985. Taking the title of President, which is unusual for a military ruler, Babangida retained almost all of the members of the Supreme Military Council, but he renamed it the AFRC. He also added officers of lieutenant-colonel rank. Babangida set up a Political Bureau composed of academics and professionals, who was asked to prepare a timetable for the restoration of democratic rule.

The regime of General Babangida ruled Nigeria from 1985 to 1993, despite a failed coup attempt by Major Gideon Orkar in April 1990. Having experienced so many coup attempts in their short history, ordinary people greeted Major Orkar's assault on the Dodan Barracks with remarkable indifference, going about their personal business in the city much as if nothing unusual was happening. In the wake of the failed coup, Orkar and over seventy of his fellow conspirators were executed in the summer of 1990.

Major Orkar's coup was another example of the resurgent tribalism from which Nigerian apparently cannot escape. Orkar claimed his coup was on behalf of the middle belt and southern Nigeria (Keih and Agbese 1996; Mayer et al. 1996). Orkar, who came from the middle belt, had proposed to expel the five northern states from the federation, illustrating that his operation was another manifestation of middle belt (Tiv, Igala, Idoma people), southeastern (Igbo, Efik, Ijaw people), and/or southwestern (Yoruba, Edo, Uhrobo, Isoko people) resentment of the perennial northern domination. Ironically, the mostly Christian middle belt had sided with the northern Nigeria in the civil war; however, more recently these regions have been increasingly siding with the southeastern and western Nigeria. Muslim northern Nigeria, fearful of being dominated by the more-educated and more-modern Igbo and Yoruba to the south, has continually insisted upon being guaranteed a dominating position in the government of the federation that they initially opposed because of that same fear. The Yoruba and the Igbo populations look down upon the military that was domination by less educated and less-modern northerners. Thus, the problem of changing loyalty from one's tribal, ethnic, and linguistic group to a broader sense of Nigerian community and back to the ethnic group also prevailed in the Nigeria military as well as during Babangida's administration.

When General Ibrahim Babangida came to power in 1985, he promised to relinquish power as soon as necessary political arrangements had been made for a qualitative and visionary political leadership to emerge in Nigeria. Like the Murtala/Obansanjo regime 1975 - 1979, the Babangida regime enumerated a number of tasks that had to be accomplished as a prelude to military disengagement from politics. Many of these tasks involved several forms of political engineering in the body politics of Nigeria. A Political Bureau was appointed to canvass the country and ascertain the views of Nigerians on the optimum political system for Nigeria. After the bureau submitted its report, a Constitution Review Committee (CRC) was appointed to draw up a new constitution from the framework of the 1979 Constitution. The new constitution was promulgated into law in 1989. With the promulgation of the new constitution, the ban imposed on political activities after the 1983 military coup was lifted. Under the 1989 constitution, no more than two political parties could operate in Nigeria.

The hand over power to a democratically elected civilian government was later postponed to 1993 on the grounds that the initial deadline would not have given the authorities enough time to lay the foundation for the transition. Several measures were taken by the Babangida regime to prevent "bad" Nigerians from participating in politics or holding any position of public responsibility. These measures included (1) a decree that bans politicians of the First and Second Republics and any other person found guilty of corruption or abuse of office from contesting elections or participating in political party activity. The military hoped that by preventing Nigerians who espouse radical economic or political views from capturing state power, Nigeria's national cohesion and stability would be assured, (2) the creation of a Code of Conduct Bureau and a Code of Conduct Tribunal to try public officers charged with corruption or abuse of office, (3) the unilateral The target date of 1990 when Babangida's regime promised to establishment of two political parties (i.e., the National Republican Convention (NRC) and the Social Democratic Party (SDP)), (4) public financing of political parties, and (5) the privatization of government enterprises in order to reduce the scope of state economic activities.

Table 4.1
Nigeria's Trend of Military Intervention in Government 1960-2002

President/Head of Government	Period	Type of Government
Azikiwe/Tafawa Balewa	Oct. 1960 - Jan. 1966	Civilian govt.
General Ironsi	Jan. 1966 - Jul. 1966	Military regime
General Gowon	Jul. 1966 - Jul. 1975	Military regime
General Mohammed	Jul. 1975 - Feb. 1976	Military regime
General Obasanjo	Feb. 1976 - Oct. 1979	Military regime
Shehu Shagari	Oct. 1979 - Dec. 1983	Civilian govt.
General Buhari	Dec. 1983 - Aug. 1985	Military regime
General Babangida	Aug. 1985 - Aug. 1993	Military regime
Ernest Shonekan	Aug. 1993 - Nov. 1993	Interim/mixed govt.
General Abacha	Nov. 1993 - Jun. 1998	Military regime
General Abubakar	Jun. 1998 - May 1999	Military regime
President Obasanjo	May 1999 - Present	Civilian govt.

Although national and state elections were held, Babangida annulled the June 12, 1993 presidential election, arguing that the elections were rigged. As point of fact, the military leaders did not trust Moshood Abiola, the winner of the presidential election. Moshood Abiola was a Yoruba and a Muslim as well as the presidential candidate of the SDP. ABIOS did not do well as a candidate in northern Nigeria's who largely favored Basher Toffee (a Hausa-Fulani), the presidential candidate of the NRC. Abiola also faced opposition in south Nigeria from Christians and Igbos who did not want to be ruled by a Yoruba. The fundamental problem of electing a president through the democratic process is the fear shared by Nigeria's 250 different ethnic groups of domination by one ethnic group. Unfortunately, these fears were exploited by the AFRC.

In the face of mounting opposition, however, General Babangida resigned his office and turned power over to a civilian interim government headed by Ernest Shonekan. Chief Shonekan's government, however, was unable to stabilize the political scene, and the protests and demonstrations continued. This social unrest set the stage for General Sani Abacha to intervene. General Sani Abacha's coup took place in November 1993 when civil disturbances, rising ethnic and religious tensions, economic collapse, and widespread riots plunged the country into near chaos.

Moreover, the situation worsened between 1993 and 1997.

When Abacha became head of state, internal purges were launched to weed out Babangida loyalists, purges that heavily hit the Langtang faction from the middle belt. Officers either retired under pressure or were reassigned abroad or to low-responsibility posts. The frequent coups and counter-coups have only widened the ethnic and tribal differences in Nigeria. Human rights violations have increased, including the killing, torture, and imprisonment of citizens who protest against the military government. Furthermore, General Abacha's regime strained its relationship with the Western countries when it hanged nine Ogoni minority rights activists in November 1995, despite an almost worldwide appeal for clemency. The Ogoni activists had been arrested for protesting against the social and environmental effects of drilling by the Royal Dutch, and Shell Oil companies. The activists demanded a share of the country's oil revenues when the drilling destroyed their land and fishing rivers. Nigeria was suspended from the commonwealth nations (Britain and its formal colonies) and threatened with expulsion if the government failed to restore democracy within a period of two years. Later in October 1995, the European Community reaffirmed its commitment to existing sanctions that had been imposed in 1993 (notably an embargo on the export of armaments and military equipment to Nigeria) and extended visa restrictions to civilian members of the administration; the European Commission also announced the suspension of development cooperation with Nigeria. The governments of the United States, Canada, South Africa, and the European Community member nations recalled their diplomatic representatives from Nigeria in protest against the executions.

General Sani Abacha ordered the arrest of more than 150 top military officers in 1995, apparently in response to widespread disaffection within the armed forces. His administration subsequently confirmed reports of a conspiracy to overthrow the government. However, opponents of Abacha's regime claimed that the government had fabricated a coup attempt. The arrest of the former head of state, General Olusegun Obasanjo, and Major General (retired) Shehu Yar Adua, together with other prominent Abacha's critics of his regime, prompted international protest. Those arrested were accused of planning the fabricated coup. Unfortunately, Shehu Yar Adua died in prison in 1997. General Abacha also used this strategy of fabricated coup attempt to arrest his second in command, General Diya, in 1997. Several military officers from the Yoruba ethnic group were associated with this coup and were condemned to death along with General Diya in early 1998.

The three-year transition program that Abacha announced in October of 1995 is scheduled to end on October 1, 1998, when a new president is to be inaugurated, after elections at the local, state and national level. New constitutional provisions, which were largely in accordance with recommendations of the National Constitution Conference, were adopted. Abacha installed five political parties and divided the nation into six regions to facilitate the allocation and rotation of the presidency and other principal executive and legislative offices for thirty years. Abacha's transition to civil rule was anchored on the assumption that the only way to assure a stable future civilian government is to sanitize the political system by precluding pathologically corrupt and fraudulent Nigerians from capturing state power. No sooner had Abacha announced the good intentions of his transition program than his regime's ambivalence to corruption was demonstrated by the fact that, while it attempted to exclude some corrupt Nigerians from political participation, it gave pride of place to some public officers found guilty of corruption. The regime not only appoint to public offices former military governors found guilty of corruption, but it also allowed some of those appointees to serve in the National Constitution Conference, an institution that created new laws for the nation. If nothing else, this practice sends a double message about the stance of the Abacha regime on corruption and the establishment of political legitimacy. In April 1998, Abacha and his close aide where said to have ordered the five political parties to nominate him as the sole presidential candidate, despite laws and decrees that prohibited members of the armed forces from becoming members of any political party (Washington Post 1998). This new move by General Abacha supports the hidden agenda thesis, namely, that all along his regime had a plan to continue to stay in power either as a military or civilian leader. The way in which he has tampered with the transition process has rendered the whole program a sham.

On June 8, 1998 General Abacha died of heart attack, and he was replaced by General Abdulsalam Abubakar a Muslim from the north. Abubakar immediately canceled all the elections held during Abacha's tenure, and dissolve the five political parties that were handpicked by the formal regime. General Abubakar, further, introduced his own transition program that would end on May 29, 1999. Before that date, he promised to have new political parties registered, conduct new elections and formally hand-over power to a democratically elected president and national legislature.

The democratic upsurge in Africa reinvigorated popular

communities and constituencies. While many of the new democratic tendencies remain fragile, even uncertain, the African political landscape has witnessed the emergence of hundreds of new political parties, civil liberties associations, prodemocracy movements, and new activists. In fact, many die-hard despots, even military leaders, have been forced to accommodate democratic demands. In West Africa, the civilization of military juntas is becoming the norm. If nothing else, this is open acknowledgment of the irreversibility of the democratic enterprise in the continent. Even in military-ruled Nigeria, there is on going speculation as to General Abubakar plans for another northerner to take over from him on May 29, 1999. Of course, such a development, which seems the more possible by the day, will introduce novel developments and calculations into Nigeria's political equation and the contest for dominance within and between power blocs and constituencies. Finally, while Abacha's regime is said to be the most corrupt of any on record, General Abubakar's regime has attempted to revive the nation from a politically delay system to a pragmatic and legitimate political system that respect human rights. The undulating political turmoil of the past makes it very difficult for us to envisage the basis for a stable democratic political system in Nigeria even in the twenty-first century.

When General Abdulsalam Abubakar assumed power in June 1998, he systematically took measures to defuse tension that Abacha left behind after his death. Of the many political associations that sprouted and sought registration as political parties under Abubakar's transition plan, only three were eventually registered based on their performance in the local government election of December 1998: The People's Democratic party (PDP), the All People's Party (APP), and the Alliance for Democracy (AD).

General Obasanjo was a relatively late entrant into the PDP, and the party performed woefully in his home state, not even winning at his own polling station. In addition, the mainstream pan-Yoruba organization rebuffed the general, solidly supporting Falae (the presidential candidate for APP and AD alliance) instead. Why, then did the PDP nominate Obasanjo, and how can his victory in the party nomination and the presidential poll is explained? Three explanations stand out.

First, the single most important factor in Obasanjo's triumph was the support of his fellow retired generals, including Babangida. Obasanjo's retired generals' friends and supporter were the source of the donation that he gave to the party and were well represented at the occasion at which 400 million naira was raised for his campaign. The general's camp was also alleged to have funded the candidacy of Chief Jim Nwobodo, an Igbo, in order to discomfit Dr. Alex Ekwueme and divide his support base among the Igbos. All candidates used money to win delegates votes. Therefore, it was not hard to imagine that the candidates with the most resources enjoyed an advantage.

Second, unlike its rival, the PDP remained united after the party nominated Obasanjo. The defeated Ekwueme not only remained a loyal party member but also was active in Obasnajo's campaign. He chaired the general's fund-raising dinner and was always in Obasanjo's entourage during his campaign in the East.

Third, the feared Igbo protest vote did not materialize. The call by the Ohaneze for Igbos to vote APP was largely ignored. General Obasanjo, for instance, won 76 percent of the votes in Ekwueme's home state of Anambra. Igbo political leaders in the PDP may have felt reluctant to risk their investment in the PDP for an uncertain welcome in the AD/APP alliance.

General Olusegun Obasanjo emerged victorious even though he was rebuffed and resisted by Afenifere, the mainstream umbrella organization of his Yoruba ethnic group. Indeed, the four states – Lagos, Ondo, Osun, and Oyo – in which he failed to score the mandatory 25 percent are his entire home zone. The solidarity and support Obasanjo received from Nigeria's military elites in reserve facilitated his victory. His election signals the emergence of the military in retirements as the most potent political force in Nigeria, based on its massive fortunes accumulated, and social networks established, during its long stay in power. There can be no doubt that these retired military generals have their own agenda and will seek to wield influence in the new administration of President Obasanjo.

Military and Economic Decay

Between 1966 and 1999 when the military was involved in the politics of Nigeria, their involvement has cost some amount of lost in professional preparedness and economic growth to the nation. According to Lewis et al (1998) there has been evidence of discord within the armed forces in recent years includes three successful military coups. These coups include those of Buhari, Babangida, and Abacha. Apart from these three successful coups, there have been two other coup attempts, in 1985 and 1990, and two other plots alleged by the Abacha regime, in 1995 and 1997 (66). There has also been grapevine of attempted coups that circulate constantly in Nigeria. During the Babangida, Abacha and Abubakar regimes the Nigerian army experienced constant purges, reshuffles, trials, and executions. These drastic actions have shaken the officer corps. Lewis et al. contend that the most notorious episodes after the abortive Vasta coup of 1985 were the failed revolt in 1990, and the alleged conspiracy of 1995. These purported episodes galvanized the execution of more than ninety officers and jail terms for several officers. Some Nigerian scholars have noted that the Nigeria army has dismissed more than 350 officers since 1995. Among these officers are also those who forced to retire. Among the fired officers are sixty-four air force officers sacked in mid-1997. The chiefs of army and naval staff were dismissed in 1995, and the following year military administrators in the thirty-six states were relived of the position (Lewis et al. 1998). After the nation must have spent more than 2 million dollars to train each of its senior army officers, these officers are then retired at their young age of between 40 and 45 years old. In most cases these well-trained military officers are perceived as threat to any ruling regime. The phenomenon of retiring professional trained military officers has led to decay in the military readiness as well as lost of funds to the Nigeria economy. These monies could have used in the sustainable development of the economy. If you know that you are going to retire an officer after some expensive training in the United States, Britain, and Indian and so on, why should the government bother to send them at all?

According to Lewis et al. (1992) several senior military officers had taken early retirement, some reportedly under duress, and others were sidelined to obscure postings (67). The environment in the Nigerian army seems to be characterized with distrust among officers. Some officers are also hungry to be posted to political positions so that they could accumulate wealth to satisfy their personal desire. The personal interest syndrome that has now engulfed the army officers cadre has consequences eroded their professionalism. As a matter of fact, it is common knowledge now that all retired army generals are self proclaimed millionaires and owners of big private businesses around the nation.

During General Abacha's regime some Nigerian scholars contend that he did not trust any other army unit. The only unit he trusted was his presidential guard. The highest level of distrust was proclaimed when Abacha ordered the arrest of Lieutenant General Oladipo Diya, his deputy head of state on December 21, 1997 (Lewis et al. 1998). The arrest of Diya and several other Yoruba senior officers was viewed by many as a conspiracy by Abacha to get rid of Yoruba officers that he did not trust. Another school of though contend that Abacha's arrest of Diya and other Yoruba senior officers was a plan for Diya not to succeed him. At that time Abacha was suffering from chronic heart decease and he knew that his end was getting nearer. One cannot tell the reasons he had for arresting Diya but distrust the thesis help to explain why certain actions were taken. An interesting phenomenon that occurred however is that the due process of law was never followed when army officers or civilians were arrested. As a matter of fact, senior military officers were known to be above the law during the military rule. When Diya was arrested the Abacha regime was very slow in producing evidence in support of its allegations that Diya and others were planning to topple his regime. It was reported that groups of northern traditional rulers and foreign diplomats were privately presented with some videotape confessions of Diya and others under detention but the public had several reasons to doubt Abacha (Lewis et al. 1998). General Abacha was reported to have personally selected the members of the military tribunal who tried Diya and his cohort in prison. The closed military tribunal handed its' judgment on April 28, 1998. As in all cases of military coup in Nigeria, the tribunal sentenced Diya and five other senior officers to death. Ten other defendants were sentenced to long prisons terms. The tribunal also acquitted thirteen defendants. Lewis et al. (1992) contend that whether or not these charges were valid, they indicate deep divisions within the Nigerian Army and the chronic insecurity of the leaders of the military (67).

The Nigerian army has now become an institution were officers raise money to seek political positions. The military has become a recruitment ground for federal ministers and state military administrators or governors. Several young men have joined the army as a means to become rich. In another development, if a senior officer becomes to surf and professional he could be viewed as somebody who might plan a coup. As a result, such offices were identified as target for retirement. That was simply the nature of the Nigerian army during Abacha's regime. After the military handed power to a democratically elected government head by President Obasanjo in 1999, Obasanjo started to unfold his plan for the army. Just barely few weeks in office, Obasanjo retired more than 100 senior military and police officers that had held political positions in previous regimes. The new president actions indicated that he too did not trust the military that were to protect him during his administration. President Obasanjo's actions also reveal the undulating and uncertain path that the Nigerian army officers have been passing through at the expense of their professionalism.

A critical review of the development process during the military regime regimes would reveal that they have not been good public managers. Oyejide and Soyibo (1993) and Adedoyin Soyibo (1999) present some performance indicators by regimes in Table 4.2.

Table 4.2
Performance Indicators by Regimes 1960-1998

Regime/ Period	Growth Rate of Real GDP %	Inflation Rate %	Money Supply Growth Rate %	Fiscal Deficit/ GDP Ratio %	Exchange Rate Premium (N1/US$
Balewa 1960-1965	5.2	3.2	9.8	-	0.03
Ironsi/ Gowon 1966-1975	9.4	7.5	20.9	-0.9	0.64
Mohammed/ Obasanjo 1976-1979	2.2	18.3	36.9	2.4	0.43
Shagari 1980-1983	-2.2	13.4	19.4	5.1	1.18
Buhari 1984-1985	2.2	26.6	10.9	3.8	2.81
Babangida 1986-1992	5.3	26.0	29.5	8.9	3.38

Source: Adedoyin, Soyibo (1999). "The Economy" in Oyeleye Oyediran and Adigun Agbaje edited Nigeria: Politics of Transition and Governance. Dakar, Senegal: CODESRIA.

The Nigeria premiums widen more than 8 per dollar between January and March of 1992. Deficit that was virtually unknown in Nigeria 1960 and 1980 increased when General Babangida became the Head of State. The fiscal deficit increased as a ratio of GDP from 5.3 percent in 1987 to 12.4 percent in 1991. The growth rate of money supply ranged between 2.3 percent in 1986 and 57.0 percent in 1992. During this same period the money supply average at about 29.5 percent (Soyibo, 1999). The inflation rate also grew worst during the military regimes. The inflation rate increased from 5.4 percent in 1986 to 49.5 percent in 1992. The inflation rate steadily maintained an average rate of 26.0 percent during the military regimes. The official exchange rate of the naira (Nigerian currency) to the United State dollar dropped from 10.56 percent in 1993 to 41.3 in 1995.

Table 4.2 shows that the military regime demonstrated the worse way of managing the finance of the Nigerian government. During the military regimes, the fiscal deficit of the nation increased uncontrollably, causing inflation. Poverty, unemployment, poor health and diseases increased in Nigeria than ever before. With the introduction of the structural adjustment came reduction of funding to hospitals, schools as well as the decline of municipal services like provision of water.

The military management style was such that they would use the nation's money to buy off members of the armed forces who were potential rivals as well as the civil elites who would otherwise be clamoring for early return to civil rule (Soyibo, 1999). Nusakhare Isekhure (1998) nicely describes the Babangida and Abacha regimes as those that used the most brilliant scholars to write speech using philosophical prose which the head of state themselves did not understand. In fact the Babangida and Abacha regimes could both be classified as periods of intellectual fraud, with characteristics of intellectual criminality. Their public management style was such that their respective government told the people of Nigeria, the opposite of what the government has in mind. Doing this actually killed the essence of good public management and pragmatic governance.

According to Suberu and Agbaje (1999) most attempts to restructure and restructure Nigerian federalism have been initiated by the various military authoritarian regimes. These regimes act extract constitutionally without guidelines or constitution to breach. Examples of such initiatives are the annulment of the 1993 election results and General Abacha's marked out repressive leadership style. Thus, the increasing investment in personal rule in the Abacha's regime has generally further advanced the project of de-institutionalization and capture of the state by private centers of power already noticeable in the preceding Babangida's administration. The consequences of personal role of both Babangida and Abacha have equally been reflected at almost all levels of government institutions and structures. These personal leadership styles were characterized by hegemonic repression and continued investment in and the strengthening of institutions of coercion. The aftermath was however, the weakening of public institutions and the structure for effective and efficient governance in Nigeria (Seberu and Agbaje, 1999).

Delegates from President Obasanjo's Administration recently signed a contract with the United States military to help harmonize the Nigeria military into a more professional force that would respect the ongoing democratic process in the nation. The United States Military Professional Resource Initiative (MPRI) a private consultancy organization manned by retired U.S. senior military officers has been mandated by the United States government to re-orientates and reorganized the Nigerian military following the return to democracy in 1999.

Conclusion

The problem of corruption, bribery, nepotism, tribalism, incompetence and lack of accountability are all evidence of the dilemma of military intervention in Nigeria's politics. The contradictions created by military rule in Nigeria militate against soldiers transforming the political system to a better system than the one they inherited from civilian politicians. The Nigerian military seem to be part of the corrupt political system against which it professes to be fighting. The military, when it assumed power in Nigeria, called itself a corrective regime. From interviews with government officials in 1995 and 1997, it seems that the military's concept of development is simply the maintenance of law and order, an increase in the production of goods, and the amassing of personal wealth. Although occasionally announcing economic development plans, the military's forte has not improved economic development. Neither has it prepared citizens for democratic participation. The military rules in an arbitrary manner, perhaps even more so than did the British colonial government. The military relies essentially on civil administrators for advice. It will be recalled that these are the same public officers who are immersed in the almost constant struggle for power. Moreover, interviews conducted among key military officers, federal public servants, foreign mission officials, and development program coordinators in Nigeria show that resources have not been equitably distributed among the various groups in the country.

As an institution, the military has become a haven for corruption, graft, and other methods of looting societal resources in Nigeria. Since access to state wealth constitutes one of the most lucrative avenues for private capital accumulation and the military has monopolized political power for more than three decades merely to achieve personal wealth. Nigerian military officers have over the years amassed huge private fortunes. Retired and active military officers now dominate many of the most lucrative sectors of the Nigerian economy, such as banking, agriculture and real estate (Ihonvbere 1994). It has become the ambition of many military officers to acquire their choice of political posts in order to enhance capital accumulations.

The question then is what did the military regime in Nigeria correct between 1966 and 1999? The failure of economic projects, the poor quality of life, the high inflation rate, soaring unemployment, the breakdown of law and order, the gross violation of human rights, the uneven development of the country, the decay of towns and villages, the ever-increasing incidence of robbery, and unbridled corruption. All these unethical problems facing the nation clearly indicate the failure of Nigeria's successive military governments. In the pursuit of political acumen, the Nigerian military has somewhat lacked troop readiness, reliability, discipline, modern weapons, presence of special forces, sound intelligence, force structure and leadership, domestic weapon production, and appropriate troop training.

References

Aborisade, O. and R. Mundt. (1998). Politics in Nigeria. New York: Longman.

Achike, Okay. (1990). Groundwork of Military Law and Rule in Ibadan, Nigeria: Ibadan University Press.

Bienen, Henry. (1971). The Military and Modernization. Princeton, New Jersey: Princeton University Press.

Bienen, Henry. (1978). Armies and Parties in Africa. New York: Africana Publishing Company.

Collier, David. (1979). The New Authoritarianism in Latin America. Princeton, New Jersey: Princeton University Press.

Dent, M. (1978). "Corrective Government: Military Rule in Perspective." In Soldiers and Oil: The Political Transformation of Nigeria edited by Keith Panter-Brick. London: Frank Cass Press, pp. 101-137.

Dent, M. J. (1975). "The Third Military Coup in Nigeria." World Today. (September Issue).

Diamond, Larry. (1993). "Nigeria in Search of Democracy." Foreign Affairs (Spring).

Duddley, B. (1982). An Introduction to Nigerian Government and Politics. Bloomington: Indiana University Press.

Finer, Samuel. (1969). The Man on HorseBack: The Role of the Military in Politics. London: Pall Mall Press.

Graf, William. (1988). The Nigerian State, Political Economy, State Class and Political System in Post-Colonial Era. Portsmouth: Heinemann Press.

Huntington, Samuel. (1965). "Political Development and Political Decay." World Politics. Vol.7, 3, pp. 386-430.

Huntington, Samuel. (1969). Political Order in Changing Societies. New Haven: Yale University Press.

Ihonvbere, Julius O. (1994). Nigeria: The Politics of Adjustment and Democracy. New Brunswick: Transaction Publisher.

Isekhure, Nosakhare. (1998). 201 Solutions to Vission 2001. Benin City, Nigeria: Oduna Communications.

Jackman, Robert. (1976). "Politicians in Uniform: Military Governments and Social Change in Third World." American Political Science Review. Vol. 70. (December).

Janowitz, Morris. (1964). The Military in the Development of New Nations. Chicago: University of Chicago Press.

Janowitz, Morris. (1977). Military Institutions and Coercion in Developing Nations. Chicago: University of Chicago Press.

Jemibewon, David. (1978). A Combatant in Government. Ibadan, Nigeria: Heineman.

Lewis, P., P. Robinson, and B. Bubin. (1998). Stabilizing Nigeria. New York: The Century Foundation Press.

Luckham, R. A. (1971). The Nigerian Military: A Sociological Study of Authority and Revolt. London: Longman.

Miners, N. J. (1971). The Nigerian Army 1956-1966. London: Methuen.

Ostheimer, J. (1972). Nigeria Politics. New York: Harper & Row Publishers.

Peters, J. (1995). The Nigerian Military and the State. African Series Books. London: Tauris I. B. Company.

Soyibo, A. (1999). "The Economy." In Nigeria: Politics of Transition and Governance edited by Oyeleye Oyediran and Adigun Agbaje. Dakar, Senegal: CODESRIA.

Suberu, T. and Adigun Agbaje. (1999). "The Future of Nigeria's Federalism." In Federalism and Political Restructuring in Nigeria edited by Kunle Amuwo, Adigun Agbaje, Rotimi Suberu and Georges Herault. Ibadan, Nigeria: Spectrum Press. pp. 335-347.

Ukpabi, S.C. (1972). Military Involvement in Nigerian Politics. Ibadan, Nigeria: University of Ibadan Press.

Part II

Public Administration Operations

5 Teaching of Public Administration

Introduction

What exists in the minds of students and practitioners of Nigerian public administration is a conception of British or American public service and how they should best imitate these foreign models. This fault is not wholly that of students or practitioners of public administration. The fault could be placed on the political instability that Nigeria has faced the nation since 1960. Apart from the political instability there are two aspects of the Nigerian public sector that have not been properly articulated by public administration scholars in spite of the tremendous opportunities they have to do so. These aspects are on the one hand, the northern style of public management and on the other hand, the southern model. The northern civil servant form a formidable political force with almost a monopoly of power in policy formulation, the dispensation of patronage, and the allocation of resources. Thus, the northern states public administrators were not politically neutral. For instance, in 1966 the northern civil servants helped to organized resistance against the General Ironsi's unification decree. The civil service model in the south was different in such way that public administrators were forbidden to use their administrative powers to influence the outcome of an election in favor of competing parties. Public administrators in the south like the British model were expected to serve as an impartial referee.

The development of public Administration in Nigeria started between 1902 and 1905 during the British colonial rule. The genesis of the subject started with the writings of Fredrick Lugard's Political Memoranda in 1906. This Political Memorandum by Lugard was described as the District Officers' "Bible" during the British colonial rule in Nigeria (Adamolekun 1985; Oluwo 1991). The second public administration manual, which was used in Nigeria, was written by Donald Cameron in 1934 and entitled "Principles of Native Administration and their

Application." Adamolekun (1985) and Olowu (1991) contend that after Lugard and Cameroon was a set of expatriate writings in public administration. These scholars include Crooker (1936), Margery Perham (132), Heussler (1963, 1968), Kirk-Greens (1965) and Nicolson (1969). Another group of colonial administrators also wrote about procedures in the civil service. These scholars include Hall (1931), Cameron (1939), Perham (1956, 1960), Lugard and Smith (1968) and Sharwood and Smith (1969).

According to Adamolekun (1985) and Oluwo (1991) the first indigenous writing in public administration started in the early 1970s. Most of the indigenous writings emerged from conference proceedings and book chapters. Nigerian public administrators have used such opportunities to freely and frankly expressed themselves as they see it in a new independent nation. The first indigenous public administration scholars in Nigeria include Asiodu in Oyediran (1979), Awoniyi and Oyinloye in Tukur (1972), Ayida and Asabia in Adedeji (1968), Atta (1979) and Ayida (1973, 1976). Oladakpo Adamolekun's volume emerge out of his conference on twenty years of Nigerian public administration seems to have succeeded in getting some of the senior administrative officers to speak of their experiences both from federal and state government perspectives (Adamolekun, 1985).

By the 1980s the field of public administration in Nigeria had built a strong connection between professional administration and professional academics in the study of public administration in the nation. As a result of this link or close collaboration between students and practitioners of the subject, the students of Nigerian public administration have exercise a lot of influence on the direction of the practice and reform of Nigerian public administration although disproportional to their members. Towards the ending of the 1980s and early 1990s the study of public administration started to attract the attention of other academic disciplines, such as law, finance, history, economics and so on. Today the study of public administration in Nigeria is now a multidisciplinary subject.

During the military regime the training of civil servants were not taken seriously. Adamolekun (1985) pointed out that while the military regime often sent it's officers for training outside the nation and sometimes within Nigeria, there was no systematic and comprehensive training program for civil servants. Training of public administrators were ill planned and uncoordinated, and no appraisals of training results were made. In short the military regime did not attach much value to the training of public servants between 1966-1999.

The study of public administration in Nigeria faces a number of problems. First, there is a problem of the conception of the Nigerian public service both in terms of its political and philosophical understandings and in terms of its central values. Second, there is the problem of the increasing centralization of the public service (especially during the long military regime) for a nation with a highly diverse and geographically disperse population as Nigeria. Thirdly, there is the problem of public sector inefficiency, a point that has lead to call for major reform of the civil service in Nigeria. Fourthly, The administrative implication of Nigeria's economic liberalism is yet to be fully articulated beyond the agenda set generally for all African nations by the World Bank (1981). Unfortunately, as the 1988 civil service reforms demonstrated, the preference of policy advisor and politicians is for the overhead democracy model, when in reality the challenge before a nation with an underdeveloped political class. Furthermore, a highly federal society should dictate that Nigerians explore the opportunities in the democratic administration model that President Olusegun Obasanjo has introduced since 1999. The poor fit between recommended administrative models and the Nigerian social is bound to continue to be one of the worrisome aspects of Nigerian public administration.

This chapter examines the teaching of public administration in Nigeria. It explores two models of public administration. The Obafemi Awolowo University Ife and Ahmadu Bello University Zaria models. The study argues that public administration in Nigeria follow the concept of either the British or American model, however, the poor fit between these models and the political environment where they are practiced have been very worrisome to Nigerian practitioners. This chapter analyzes the views of Nigerian Public Administrators about Public Administration education and training in the nation. Some suggestions are given on how to improve the study of public administration in Nigeria in future.

Teaching of Public Administration: Two Models in Nigeria

There are varying definitions of literacy. These definitions range from one which stipulates that literacy is fixed, quantified and measurable, to a more relativist and explicitly political definition (Chowdhury, 1997). The definition adopted here is that literacy is a conscientization process of developing skills in reading the world not just the word (Freire, 1973; Freire & Macedo, 1987; Chowdhury, 1997). In addition, literacy is one of the key indicators of a country's education status and level of social development.

Illiteracy and lack of education is a form of censorship that prevents people from exercising their human rights. Those who are otherwise knowledgeable are unable to share the information effectively because of rural isolation, communication problems, illiteracy, colonial legacy, and unavailability of resources and infrastructure to disseminate knowledge to a wider population base. Literacy campaigns by states like Nigeria have yielded disappointing results (Grainger, 1987). The overall enrollments in educational institutions grew rapidly between 1980 and 1992 worldwide.

The proposed continental model of education aims at the following: (1) developing relevant skills; (2) providing for participation and involvement of the masses in education and development; (3) providing equal educational opportunity and accessibility by all people at any age; (4) improving management and planning; (5) emphasizing rural development for rural needs; and (6) encouraging mutual interdependence and relationships (World Bank, 2000).

Education policy in Nigeria would have to benefit the people at the grassroots level for it to be regarded as education for social development. This education for social development should also aim at influencing changes in policies for admission to educational institutions, promotion policies at places of work, and the current value system about rewards based on formal education. Knowledge in public administration would have to be translated into skills so that the school "dropouts," unemployed, and underemployed will have jobs. Viable networks should be able to combat any social, political, economic or health problems.

After independence it was the wish of the Nigerian government to use education as an instrument for individual and societal development. This objective was started through the provision of a universal basic education in a variety of forms to meet the needs of all citizens. The desire to diversify and restructure the education system from those inherited from the British colonial regime 6+5+2+3 model (six years in primary school, five years in secondary school, two years in high school and three year in the university) led to the introduction of a new 6+3+3+4 system (six years in primary school, three years in junior secondary school, another three years in senior secondary school and four year in the university) of formal education in 1986. This system was designed to provide compulsory prevocational core subjects at the junior secondary school level along with the arts and sciences (Ehiametalor and Oduaran, 1991), with a view to developing technicians and local technology instead of importing or depending on its transfer.

The federal and state governments are responsible for higher education, and in 1998 there were 133 universities and polytechnics/college of technologies. Among the 133 higher education institutions the federal government is responsible for 90 and the rest are administered by the state in which they are located. In 1993, 383,488 students were enrolled in the 133 higher education institutions (i.e., Universities, Polytechnics and Colleges of Education). Estimated expenditure on education by the Federal Government of Nigeria in 1995 was N12, 172 million, equivalent to 5.4 percent of expenditure in the federal budget.

The quality of higher education is low and possibly declining in Nigeria. One reason for this is the brain drain syndrome, where scientists, professional and technicians migrate to other nations because they are either under utilized or discontented with the political instability and high rate of corruption in the nation. The immediate consequences are that academic standards of many graduates are unacceptably low. Despite the various anti-illiteracy campaigns, initiated since 1960, the official estimated adult literacy rate published in 1995 shows 56 percent.

Four decades after independence as a nation, Nigeria policy makers can not boast of a solid public administration, rural, adult and community education. This shows that Nigeria is yet to appreciate the need to equalize the formal and non-formal education system. There is, at present, an over-emphasis on the formal education to the extent that almost all aspects of adult and community education in Nigeria are under-funded and haphazardly provided (Oduaran 1991). It is true that Nigerian adult and community education have in the last ten years witnessed some phenomenal growth in terms of structures. This is clear from the number of national commissions and state agencies that have so far been established to provide mass education. At the national level, there is the National Commission for Mass Literacy, Adult and Non-Formal Education, the National Commission for Women Affairs, and the National Commission for Nomadic Education. But the establishment is yet to be matched with commensurate funding and appropriate staffing (Oduaran, 1991).

There are two major models of the teaching of public administration in Nigeria. From the beginning, the Institutes of public administration were established in two regional universities. Ahmadu Bello University (ABU), Zaria and Ife (later renamed Obafemi Awolowo University (OAU) were the pioneers in the field of public administration. The two universities have virtually dominated the scene until the most recent times when the federal government of Nigeria established the Administrative Staff College of Nigeria (ASCON) in Badagry, Lagos State to change the hegemony. Since then a number of other administrations centers have emerged in the federal universities located at Nsukka, Lagos, Ilorin, Jos, Ibadan, usually as part of political science departments.

The Obafemi Awolowo University Ife, management training center was established in 1963 following the report of a committee that was earlier set up by the then Western Nigerian Regional Government on the matter in 1962. The committee recommended that an Institute of Administration is established, but this should be located in the Regional University that was then also taken off. The Obafemi Awolowo University Ife public administration programs offer courses that lead to the following degrees as shown in Table 5.1.

Table 5.1
PA Model 1: Public Administration Degree Programs at Ife

Public Administration Degree Programs	Year Estab.	Dept.
Certificate in Tax Administration	1964	Pub. Admin.
Certificate in Local Government Administration	1968	Pub. Admin.
Certificate in Public Administration	1971	Pub. Admin.
Certificate in Management Studies	1971	Pub. Admin.
Certificate in University Administration	1972	Pub. Admin.
Certificate in Project Analysis and Management	1972	Pub. Admin.
Certificate in Administrative Management Techniques	1972	Pub. Admin.
Diploma in Public Financial Management	1972	Pub. Admin.
Post-Graduate Diploma in International Affairs	1971	Pub. Admin.
Post-Graduate Diploma in Development Economics	1971	Pub. Admin.
Post-Graduate Diploma in Tax Administration	1972	Pub. Admin.
Higher Diploma in Local Govt. Administration and Mgt.	1973	Pub. Admin.
Bachelor of Public Administration	1964	Pub. Admin.
Master of Philosophy in Public Administration	1966	Pub. Admin.
Master of Public Administration	1968	Pub. Admin.
Master of Public Admin. (Development Economics)	1973	PA & Econs.
Master of Public Admin. (International Affairs)	1973	PA & Pol Sci
Doctor of Philosophy (Ph.D.) in Pub. Admin.	1980	Pub. Admin.

Source: Interview and Notes from Field Research in Nigeria 2002.

Most of the certificate programs in public administration were introduced in late 1960s and early 1970s. The bachelor degree program also introduced during this period. Thus, apart from the undergraduate programs that was introduced in the 1980s, it is correct to say that the main elements of the structure of courses and degree programs in the Faculty of Administration today emerged essentially in the 1960s.

Currently, the Obafemi Awolowo University Ife's Master of Philosophy (M. Phil) and Doctor of Philosophy (Ph.D.) programs are based entirely on thesis work. All course work was expected to have been completed at the M.Sc./MBA/MPA level. The difficulty student's encounter with thesis writing has exposed this arrangement as unsatisfactory. There is now a definite move to introduce complementary course work at the M.Phil. and Ph.D. Levels. The new university postgraduate regulations provide that only masters with thesis degree holders will qualify to pursue the Ph.D. degree in public administration at Ife. The Obafemi Awolowo University Ife, School of Public of Public Administration has produced a total number of 4,000 graduates, including 11 Ph.D.s and 5 M.Phil.s over the past twenty-five years. Table 5.2 will show details of the degree programs offered by Ahmadu Bello University Zaria.

Table 5.2
PA Model 2: Public Administration Degree Programs at Zaria

Degree Programs in Public Administration	**Year Estab.**	**Dept.**
Ph.D. in Public Administration	1985	Pub. Admin.
Master of Public Administration	1970	Pub. Admin.
Master of Science in Local Govt. Administration	1986	Local Govt.
Bachelor of Public Administration	1962	Pub. Admin.
Bachelor of Science in Political Science	1981	Pol. Sci.
Post-Graduate Diploma in Public Administration	1988	Pub. Admin.
Post-Graduate Diploma in Local Government	1975	Local Govt.
Higher Diploma in Local Govt. Administration	1970	Local Govt.
Advanced Diploma in Local Government	1985	Local Govt.
Advance Diploma in Public Administration	1986	Pub. Admin.
Diploma in Local Government	1980	Local Govt.
Certificate in Middle Management	1975	Pub. Admin.

The Ahmadu Bello University Zaria designed the second public Administration model in Nigeria. This institution was first established in 1947 as the Institute of Administration, for the training of clerical staff in Northern Nigeria. The Institute of Administration was integrated into Ahmadu Bello University in 1962.

The Ahmadu Bello University Zaria unlike the Ife model offers courses those leads to the following degrees in public administration. Three academic departments jointly offer degree programs in public administration. These academic departments include (1) Department of Local Government; (2) Department of Public Administration; and (3) Department of Political Science.

Table 5.2 shows that two departments share the undergraduate specialization in public administration at Ahmadu Bello University Zaria. Although, the teaching of public administration occurs at both the sub-degree as well as post graduate levels and this is shared by three major departments, Political Science, Public Administration and Local Government Studies (Olowu, 1991). Table 5.3 shows the type of degrees offered by universities that have public administration departments.

Table 5.3
Degrees Offered by Public Administration Department in Nigerian Universities

Universities	Ph.D. in PA	MPA	DPA	B.A.	Dip.	Cert
Ahmadu Bello University Zaria	X	X	X	X	X	X
Obafemi Awolowo University, Ife	X	X	X	X	X	X
University of Abuja	X	X	-	X	-	-
University of Benin	X	X	X	X	X	X
University of Calabar	-	X	-	Pol	X	-
Enugu State University, Enugu		X	-	Pol	-	-
University of Maiduguri	X	X	-	Pol	-	-
University of Nigeria, Nsukka	X	X	X	X	X	-
Namdi Azikiwe University, Akwa	X	X	X	-	-	-
University of Port-Harcourt	X	X	X	-	-	-
University of Uyo	-	X	X	-	-	-

#11: X = Offer PA Program; - = Do not offer program.

Source: Interview and Notes from Field Research in Nigeria 2002.

Over the past ten years the teaching of public administration in Zaria has experienced several problems. These problems include; inadequate skills needed to teach many of the subjects offered, lack of incentive for faculty members in public administration and limited supportive services that accompany teaching. Another major managerial problem is the inadequate resources to finance research and the purchase of equipment such as duplicating machines and relevant literature.

Table 5.4
Degrees Offered by Political Science Department in Nigerian Universities

Universities	Ph.D. in PS	MPA	MA	B.A.	Dip. in PA	Cert
Ahmadu Bello University Zaria	X	X	X	X	X	-
Obafemi Awolowo University, Ife	X	X	X	X	X	-
University of Abuja	-	X	-	X	-	-
University of Benin	X	X	X	X	X	-
University of Calabar	-	X	-	X	X	-
Enugu State University		X	-	X	-	-
Bagauda University, Kano	-	-	X	X	-	-
Abia State University, Uturu	PA	X	X	X	-	-
Bayero University, Kano	X	-	X	X	-	-
Delta State University, Abraka	-	-	X	X	-	-
Edo State University, Ekpoma	-	-	X	X	-	-
University of Ibadan	X/PA	-	X	X	-	-
University of Ilorin	-	-	X	X	-	-
Imo State University, Owerri	-	-	X	X	-	-
University of Lagos	X	X	X	X	-	-
University of Jos	-	-	X	X	-	-
Lagos State University, Lagos	-	X	-	X	-	-
Ogun State University	-	-	X	X	-	-
Ondo State University, Ado Ekiti	-	-	X	X	-	-
Usman Danfodio University, Sokoto	X	-	X	X	-	-
University of Nigeria, Nsukka	X	X	X	X	X	-

#21: X = Offer program; - = Do not offer program.
Source: Interview and Notes from Field Research in Nigeria 2002.

Apart from the Ife and Zaria universities covered above Nigeria have 35 other universities. The State governments own seventeen of the universities, while the Federal government owns 20. Generally, Nigerian universities adopt either the Ife model or Zaria model of teaching public administration. Table 5.4 shows the universities that have a political science department as well the type of degrees they offer.

Research Method

This study analyzes the teaching of public administration and the views of Nigerian Public Administrators about Public Administration education and training in the nation. The field research was conducted in Nigeria, and sponsored by the Indiana University Research Council grant. The data for this study was collected through a survey administered personally by the author of the study in Nigeria in summer of 2000. 300 questionnaire were administered to senior public administrators in the national, state, and local governments. 100 questionnaires were administered to each level of the Nigerian government structure. 165 responses where received out of the 300 originally administered. The data collected from the 165 response were analyzed using the SSPS computer program.

The following specific research questions provided the basis of this present research:

1. What are the different types of Public administration degree programs offered by Nigerian universities?
2. What is the level of importance of various components of public courses, as perceived by practicing public administrators?

Data Analysis and Discussion

Table 5.5 shows the profile of the respondents to this survey. The total number of respondents was 165. 109 of them were male, while 50 were female, and the sample had six missing variables. This is typically the ratio of gender in the work force of Nigeria. The culture of the nation is most favorable to male and they occupy majority of the senior positions in both the public and private sectors of the nation. The profile had three male and three female directors. Assistant directors were 15 in number, nine men and five females. The managerial position had respondents, 24 men and eight women. The supervisory level constituted the largest number of the respondent. 44 of them were men, while 28 were female.

The surveyed public managers had five male professors who were conducting research for the government in two of the ministries visited. There were about six respondents who did not indicate their position in the survey.

Table 5.5
Profile of Nigeria's Public Administrators that Responded

Position Title in Organization	Gender			Total
	Male	Female	Missing Variables	
Director	3	3		6
Asst. Director	9	5	1	15
Manager	24	8	1	33
Asst. Manager	14	5		19
Supervisor	44	28	1	73
Professor	5	-	-	5
Others	8	-	-	8
Missing Variable	2	1	3	6
	109	50	6	165

Table 5.6 provides a detail profile of the educational qualification. The table shows the type of general education that the respondent had and the specific type of public administration training they had received. The National Certificate of Education (NCE) is held by 7.9 percent of the respondent, while approximately 10.9 percent of them hold either the Ordinary National Diploma (OND) or the Higher National Diploma (HND). The OND and HND are the type of degrees/diplomas awarded by polytechnics in Britain and Nigeria. The HND is equivalent to a Bachelor degree, while the OND is equal to an Associate degree in the United States. Majority of the respondents (about 26.7 of them) holds a Bachelor degree. While 34 or 18.8 percent of the respondents hold a master degree, only 14 or 8.4 percent of them holds a master degree in public administration or a related area. Only 3 or 1.8 percent of the respondent holds a Doctorate degree. It is, however, interesting to note that 32 or 19.4 percent of the respondent did not indicate their public administration qualifications.

Table 5.6 shows that although Nigeria's public managers have fairly good educational qualifications and background, majority of those interviewed was not trained public administrators. Thus, a lot of Nigeria's public managers do work in areas that they were not trained for. This explains while they are not motivated, unproductive and highly inefficient.

This deficiency breeds corruption in the civil service.

Table 5.6
Educational Profile of Public Managers

3. General Education	Frequency	Percentage	4. Public Admin. Education	Frequency	%
NCE	13	7.9	ONC/OND	6	3.6
ONC/OND	3	1.8	HNC/HND	7	4.2
HNC/HND	15	9.1	BA/BS	17	10.3
BA or LLB	44	26.7	Graduate Dip.	2	1.2
Graduate	11	6.7	MA/MPA	8	4.8
Dip.	31	18.8	Masters	6	3.6
Masters	4	2.4	Ph.D.	3	1.8
Ph.D.	29	17.6	Others	32	19.4
Others	15	9.1	Missing Variab.	84	50.9
Total	165	100.0	Total	165	100.0

Table 5.7 shows Nigeria Public Administrators' perception of public administration courses. The survey analysis showed that 104 male and 48 female participants responded to the survey questions. The survey has a variation of between 10 and 14 missing variables. Data were collected from 168 respondents. Out of this number, 77 respondents indicated that administrative law was very important, while only one candidate felt it not important. Administrative Theories was another public administration course that received very favorable scores from the respondents. Out of 152 respondents, 68 indicated that it was very important, while others indicated that it was somewhat important. The gender chi-square statistics that was run indicated that male felt it was significant (.000), while female indicated that it was not that significant (.203).

Seventy-one respondents indicated that Budgeting and Financial Management was very important, while the rest of the respondents felt that it was somewhat important. It is very interesting to note that 36 out of 150 respondents indicated that marketing was not an important course. While on the one hand 73 and 77 respondents indicated that management studies and personnel management were very important respectively, on the other

Table 5.7
Public Administrators' Perception of Public Administration Courses

Courses in Public Administration	Not Important	A little Important	Important	Very Important	Extremely Important	Male	Female	Total	Chi-Square Test Gender	
									M	F
Administrative Law	1	4	43	77	27	104	48	152	.002	.166
Administrative Theories	-	12	49	68	23	105	47	152	.000	.203
Nigerian Government and Politics	-	3	44	36	69	104	48	152	.044	.164
Budgeting and Financial Mgt.	-	6	22	71	55	106	48	154	.003	.592
Business Studies	2	24	70	34	22	104	48	152	.000	.257
Comparative PA and Policy	9	16	39	59	29	105	47	152	.001	.499
Development Administration	1	22	40	66	22	103	48	151	.000	.233
Environmental Studies	2	26	90	15	18	104	47	151	.006	.727
Information Technology	1	2	46	56	48	103	49	152	.053	.065
Local Government Politics	2	15	60	54	30	104	47	151	.024	.034
Management Studies	-	7	34	73	41	106	49	155	.093	.179
Organizational Behavior	2	12	26	63	50	104	49	153	.000	.090
Personnel Management	-	3	11	77	63	104	49	153	.010	.302
Public Policy Analysis	-	-	54	63	35	104	48	152	.000	.014
Public Finance	-	4	49	61	38	105	47	152	.004	.116
Public Policy Making	-	1	46	64	43	106	48	154	.003	.049
Public Sector Ethics	1	3	37	77	35	105	48	153	.000	.056
Public Sector Management	-	11	49	49	44	104	49	153	.000	.225
Research Methods	13	22	75	31	10	104	47	151	.000	.000
Sandwich Placement in Public Agencies	4	59	31	40	17	93	48	131	.000	.006
Social Policy	12	14	70	51	9	101	45	146	.000	.006

hand Environmental Studies and Public Sector Ethics were considered to be one of the most important courses offered in public administration programs across Nigerian universities. Although 13 respondents indicated that Research Methods is not important, another 75 respondents thought it was important. Similarly while 12 respondents indicated that Social Policy, as a public administration course is not important, another 70 respondents indicated that it is.

It must be pointed out that courses in African Politics are not perceived as very important to male or female respondents. This is probably because they are Nigerians and do not consider politics around Africa to be relevant in performing public administration duties for their nation. Ironically, they indicated that courses in Nigerian Government and Politics were very important and significant for male respondents.

An interesting finding that resulted from the analysis of the survey data shows that the chi-square test produce male and female significance in subject areas such as Information Technology, Local Government Administration, Organizational Behavior, Public Policy Analysis, Pressure Group/Parties and Media, Research Methods, Sandwich Placement in Public Agencies, Social Policy and Gender and Society. Thus, these subjects are generally accepted by gender in respective of the usefulness of courses offered by the public administration programs in the nation. Apart from these findings, another set of courses was rated as either very important or extremely important. These rating is based on the combined percentages of both very important and extremely important. They include: Nigerian Government and Politics (65%), Budgeting and Financial Management (76%), Development Administration (55%), Public Policy Analysis (60%), Management Studies (86.1%), Information Technology (58%), Organizational Behavior (70%), Personnel Management (86%), Public Policy Making (66%), Public sector Ethics (69%), and Public Sector Management (57%). It appears that based on the valid percentages, personnel management is the perceived as being the most important course offered by the public administration programs in Nigerian universities. These findings should therefore serve as a guide to Public Administration/Political Science Departments in Nigerian Universities; as to what courses they should offer in the future.

Public Administration Training and Improved Performance in the Future

What can the new civilian administration do to increase performance in the public sector in order to improve Nigeria's national development in the twenty-first century? The need for public administrators in Nigeria to receive solid training in public management cannot be emphasized enough. Moses Kiggudu (1989) makes the point very clear that "the gift of public management knowledge also has far more lasting effects and is far more closely relevant to the concept of development." Give a man a fish, as the saying goes, and you are helping him a little but for a very short while; teach him the art of fishing and he can help himself all his life. On a higher level, supply him with a fishing tackle; this will cost you a good deal of money, and the result remains doubtful; but even if fruitful, the man's continuing livelihood will still be dependent upon you for replacements. But teach him to make his own fishing tackle and you have helped him to become not only self-supporting, but also self reliant and independent" (Balogun and Mutahaba, 1999).

The findings of this study show that, although the numbers of universities and polytechnics in Nigeria has increased over the past twenty years the supply of graduates in public administration has fallen short of the demand required in the public sector. On one hand, the university system has failed to meet the ever-growing demand of the society for higher education due to financial and manpower constraints that militate against the desirable expansion of programs. On the other hand, the military administration was unable to effectively address the needs of university faculty and staff. Nigeria universities are known for having the highest number of strikes in sub-Saharan Africa. Therefore, concerted efforts should be made by both the national and state governments, and the universities to expand the supply of high-level manpower significantly so that the nation can cope with the rapid pace of socio and sustainable advancement.

In respect to the financial problems that emerged in the universities as a result of the cuts in budgets, the National Universities Commission should seek a consensus with the national government on how to resolve the problem. In the twenty-first century one would hope that the national government would evolve a new strategy for the financing of Nigeria University education. Further, universities and polytechnics should also tackle the financial problem on their own by engaging in activities that would generate funding. Universities should also involve themselves in raising funds from the private sector.

Several authors have focused on the use of citizens/government comment loop as a means to improve government performance. For example, Carter (1989), Johnson and Lewin (1990), and Johan Holmberg (1992) have proposed that state and local government are required to publish an annual report to their residents similar to the annual report published by corporations for their shareholders. They argue that the various constituents of the state and local jurisdiction have a legitimate need for information about the activities of their government. The rational for requiring state and local governments to publish an annual report is based on the need to provide state and local investors with information equivalent to that received by their corporate counterparts and on the need to achieve greater accountability of them to their public.

Conclusion

This study examines Nigerian's public administrators' perception of Public Administration courses and how the training of public managers could affect future performance in Nigeria's public sector. It adopts the perspective that if more public managers are trained in public administration oriented programs, there is the possibility that accountability and performance monitoring would improve considerably in Nigeria's public sector. Appropriate public administration courses in Nigerian universities would serve as one of the most fruitful way for correcting the problems of maladministration and corruption in the public sector of the nation. The study argues that effective performance monitoring is essential for the achievement of public policy goals in Nigeria. It noted that although previous military leaders in Nigeria have pushed for better performance information as part of their reform efforts, such exercise was not pursued with adequate vigor and common sense, taking into account organizational and situational contingencies.

The recommendations suggested in this study are based on the research findings. The study demonstrates that the civil service that provides consumer-oriented services to the citizens of a nation would better address the needs of national development. Providing staff development and performance standards that emphasize courteous treatment and involving recipients in case planning are important first steps. Likewise, the provision of on-time information to workers and streamlined organizational reporting should be considered in the re-engineering of public services during the new civilian administration of president Obasanjo. Addressing these concerns through performance standards and quality service indicators may result in better service delivery and outcomes in the public service of Nigeria. Indeed, these changes would improve consumer satisfaction ratings and redirect client worker efforts into more constructive areas.

The Nigerian government needs to develop a good manpower plan for the twenty-first century. Manpower planning is the process of determining and furthering those objectives, policies, and programs that develop, utilize and distribute manpower resources with a view to achieving economic and other goals (Adamolekun, 1999).

The World Bank (2000) annual report contended that appropriate intervention by the government of Nigeria should vary according to the problem to be addressed. In education, for example, both the national and state governments should be involve in removing barriers to access and providing books, materials, and trained and motivated university faculty. Government commitment at the highest level should also be complemented with multiple partnerships at all levels with civil society and the private sector. This chapter also found out that scholars and public administration practitioners in Nigeria generally criticized the corrupting influence of the new civilian administration on bureaucratic activity. They implicitly hope for the elimination of politics from program development and proposed public administration solutions in the form of more communication, better training to cure bureaucrats of the poor performance ills.

Public administration training in Nigeria in the future need to incorporate new courses in data analysis, data collection, computing methods, ethics, management of ethnic diversity, financial management, budgeting and other relevant measures to improve government performance. These measures will help to shape accountability and redefine the limits of public sector performance in the new civilian administration so that Nigeria can be in the path of national development in the twenty-first century.

Future service delivery and sustainable development efforts in Nigeria should be measured in terms of public administrator's capability rather than by economic indicators. The product of the proposed design and approach will help to improve (1) the quality of public management as a profession in Nigeria; (2) the quality of service delivery and life of all people; (3) the conditions of living of all people, and (4) intra-societal and inter-society relations, as the basic concept in the model spreads throughout Sub-Saharan African countries and possibly other developing countries.

Despite the problem of inadequate public management training program, mismanagement, and corruption in Nigeria, there is a persistent interest in, and recognition of the need for effective performance monitoring as a major component of government administrative reform. Performance monitoring is not a new idea, but success has often proven illusive.

References

Aborishade, Oladimeji, and Robert Mundt. (1998). Politics in Nigeria. New York: Longman.

Adamolekun, Ladipo. (1982). Public Administration: A Nigerian and Comparative Perspective. London: Longman.

Adamolekun, Ladipo. (1985). Nigerian Public Administration 1960-1980: Perspectives and Prospects. Ibadan, Nigeria Heinemann.

Adamolekun, Ladipo. (1999). Public Administration in Africa. Boulder, Colorado: Westview.

Adamolekun, Ladipo and Victor Ayeni. (1994). "Nigeria" in V. Subramaniam (ed). Public Administration in the Third World. London: Longman.

Adamu, S. (1978). The Nigerian Statistical System. Ibadan, Nigeria: University of Ibadan Press.

Adedeji, Ajayi. (1992). "Factors in the African Development Equation." African Journal of Public Administration and Management. Vol.1, 1, pp. 15-37 (January).

Adu, A. (1969). The Civil Service in Commonwealth Africa: Development and Transition. London: George Allen and Unwin.

Aminu, Jubril and Egonmwan. (1992). "Education and Public Policy in Nigeria." In Towards Education in Nigeria for the 21st Century, edited by S. O. Oriafor, and U. Gbenedio. Benin City, Nigeria: Institute of Education, University of Benin.

Balogun, Jide, and Gelase Mutahaba. (1999). "Redynamizing the African Civil Service for the Twenty-first Century: Prospects for a Non-bureaucratic Structure." In Bureaucracy and the Alternatives in World Perspective, edited by Keith Henderson and P. Dwivedi. New York: St. Martins.

Barzelay, Michael. (2000). The New Public Management: Improving

Research and Policy Dialogue. Berkeley, California: University of California Press.

Biersteker, Thomas. (1983). "Indigenization in Nigeria: Renationalization or Denationalization." In The Political Economy of Nigeria edited by William Zartman. New York: Praeger.

Biobaku, S. (1980). Education Evolution in Nigeria: Growth without Development. Ibadan: Ibadan University Press.

Carter, N. (1989). "Performance Indicators: Backseat Driving or Hands off Control?" Policy and Politics Vol. XVII, 2, pp. 13-38.

Chowdhury, K. P. (1996). "Literacy and Primary Education." Working Papers. Human Capital Development and Operations Policy, pp. 1-19.

Cooper, T. L. (1990). The Responsible Administrator: An Approach to Ethics for the Administrative Role (3rd ed.). San Francisco: Jossey-Bass.

Dunn, John. (1978). "Conclusion." In West Africa States: Failure and Promise. Cambridge: Cambridge University Press.

Ehiametalor, E. T. and Oduran. (1994). "A. Fundamentals of Adult Education." Benin City, Nigeria: Nigerian Educational Research Association, pp. 88-100.

Esman, Milton. (1991). Management Dimensions of Development: Perspectives and Strategies. West Hartford, Connecticut: Kumarian Press.

Fafunwa, A. B. (1974). History of Education in Nigeria. London. George Allen and Unwin.

Falola, T. (1996). Developing Planning and Decolonization in Nigeria. Westport, Connecticut: Greenwood.

Farazmand, Ali. (1991). Handbook of Comparative and Development Public Administration. New York: Marcel Dekker.

Federal Republic of Nigeria. (1990). Guidelines for the National Rolling Plan 1990 - 1992. Lagos, Nigeria: Government Press.

Forrest, Tom. (1995). Politics and Economic Development in Nigeria. Boulder, Colorado: Westview.

Freire, P. and D. Macedo. (1987). Literacy: Reading the World and Otherworld. South Hadley, Massachusetts: Bergin and Garvey.

Friedreich, Carl. (1968). Constitutional Government and Democracy. Fourth ed. Boston: Blaisdell Publishing Company.

Government of the Federal Republic of Nigeria. (1986). National Education Policy. Lagos: Government Printing Press.

Graf, William. (1988). The Nigerian State, Political Economy, State Class and Political System in the Post-Colonial Era. Portsmouth, N.H.: Heinemann.

Grainger, I.P. (1987). The Literacy Campaign in Zimbabwe. Journal of Social Development in Africa, Vol. 2, 2, pp. 49-58.

Holmberg, Johan. (1992). Making Development Sustainable. Washington D.C.: Island Press.

Horwitz, Frank and Mark Neville. (1996). "Organization Design for Service Excellence: A Review of the Literature." Human Resource Management, Vol. 35, pp. 471-492 (winter).

Johnson, R. and A. Lewin. (1990). "Management and Accountability Models of Public Sector Performance." In Public Management: The Essential Readings edited by S. Ott, A. Hyde and J. Shafritz, Chicago, Illinois: Nelson-Hall.

Kiggundu, Moses. (1989). Managing Organization in Developing Countries: An Operational and Strategic Approach. West Hartford, Connecticut: Kumarian Press.

Koehn, Peter. (1990). Public Policy and Administration in Africa: Lesson from Nigeria. Boulder Colorado: Westview Press.

Mayne, John and Eduardo Zapico-Goni. (1997). Monitoring Performance in the Public Sector. New Brunswick: Transaction Press.

Metcalfe, L. and S. Richards. (1990). Improving Public Management. London: Sage.

Mohapatra, Manindra. (1996). Management Training and Public Service Education as Correlates of Orientations towards Public Service Professionalism among State Administrators in the Fifty States. Eric Documents No. ED 388204.

Mordi, O. (1998). "General Problems in Data Collection in Nigeria." Journal of Nigerian Statistical Association, Vol. 1, 1, pp. 5-17.

Myers, R. and R. Lacey. (1996). Consumers Satisfaction, Performance and Accountability in the Public Sector. International Review of Administrative Science, Vol. 62, pp. 331-350.

Oduaran, Akpovire. (1991). "Developing Nigerian Adult and Community Education from the Position of Strength". Journal of Nigerian Educational Research. Vol. 12, 2, pp. 1-15.

Olaleye, Y. (1992). The Problems of Data Collection in State Statistical Surveys in Nigeria. Ibadan, Nigeria: NISER.

Olowu, Dele. (1991). Nigerian Public Administration: Past, Present and the Future. Ibadan, Nigeria: Shaneson C. J. Limited.

Otobo, E. (1999). "Nigeria." In Public Administration in Africa edited by Oladipo Adamolekun. Boulder, Colorado: Westview Press.

Peters, Guy. (2000). "Policy Instruments and Public Management: Bridging the Gap." Journal of Public Administration Research and Theory, Vol.10, 1, pp. 34-47.

Phillips, A. and E. Ajakaiye. (1993). Nigerian Economic and Society: Economic Policy and Development. Ibadan, Nigeria: NISER Publication.

Riggs, Fred. (1984). Administration in Developing Countries: The Theory of Pristimative Society. Boston: Haughton Mifflin Publishers.

Rodinelli, D. (1987). Development Administration and U.S. Foreign Aid Policy. Boulder, Colorado: Lynne Reinner Press.

Rodinelli, Dennis. (1993). Development Projects as Policy Experiments: An Adaptive Approach to Development Administration. New York: Routledge.

Turner, M. and David Hulme. (1999). Governance, Administration and Development. West Hartford, Connecticut: Kumarian Press.

Umeh, Joseph. (1992). "Capacity Building and Development Administration in Southern African Countries." International Review of Administrative Science, Vol. 58, 1, pp. 87-104.

World Bank. (1981). World Development Report. New York: Oxford University Press.

World Bank. (2000). World Development Report. New York: Oxford University Press.

6 Public Administrators' Perception of the Importance of Managerial Skills

Introduction

Nigeria is classified as one the poorest nations of the world. One of the reasons given for Nigeria's underdevelopment is the inefficiency of its public sector. The public servants of the nation have been accused of failing to provide politicians with sound advice on public policy. The civil servants of Nigeria have sometimes been referred to as agents of mismanagement and waste of public funds. Another common weakness of the Nigerian government has been the lack of balanced emphasis between public and private sectors. During the past four decades in Nigeria, national and some state government plans dealt almost exclusively with the public sector and the discretionary authority the public placed in the hands of elected officials and public administrators were often abused. Public resources are sometimes utilized to serve the personal interest of senior public managers. Too often we have seen this abuse at virtually every level of government in Nigeria. The few ethical public administrators in Nigeria have questioned how the country has arrived at a point that there is no much unethical, immoral, and illegal activity in government. During the thirty-five years of military rule, the government often failed to recognize that policies and services to foster a favorable climate for capital formation, external investment, and industry and trade, are as essential in a nation's development plan as are public undertaking and enterprises.

A close survey of Nigeria reveals that the nation has developed far more resourcefulness in the formulation of comprehensive plans than in the design and execution of the policies and projects contemplated under the plans. Development plans have also suffered because they did not come to grips with the real substance of social and economic change. Between 1985 and 1999, Nigeria's development plans consisted of little more than a compilation of projects, which the military and public managers found appealing, for example, roads, airports, army barracks, public corporations such as breweries, banks, flour mills, cement plants and so on. These were often unrelated to resources and to fiscal realities.

This chapter analyzes Nigerian public managers' perception of the importance of managerial skills and management principles. The study presents the argument that national and state governments in Nigeria should use management principles to "steer, not row" their respective societies. It outlines some of the major steps required to create a dynamic public management and governmental machinery capable of both the planning and execution of comprehensive development programs in the future. The chapter addresses the question: How can Nigeria's government extract management resources from its society and deploy them to create and support a coercive and innovative administration? It further suggests reasons why public management in Nigeria needs to be reformed to play a more developmental and accountable role in the future. New public management principles are also utilized in evaluating how the reform can be accomplished.

Government Organization and Sustainable Management

Government organizations serve a variety of development purposes. The setting of objectives or goals to be achieved, the resolution of policies, the formulation of plans and their translation into programs and projects, the preparation and administration of budgets for programs implementation, and the mobilization and utilization of a nation's resources in the execution of programs.

Manindra Mohapatra's (1996) study views schools and public sector organizations such as ministry or departments as professional socialization agencies of any nation's public administrators. The socialization of public administrators points out the importance of dealing with the various expectations surrounding public administration career and degree programs. Professional socialization in the civil service, therefore, includes civil service college, professional organizations, continuing education delivery agencies, students, current employers, potential employers, organizations of academics, university administrators, competing agencies and so on.

It is axiomatic that public organizations in Nigeria should be designed specifically for the purposes to be served. Different purposes require different types of organizations. One of the great obstacles to sustainable development and implementation is the failure of the government to revamp and transform for new purposes the government and practices evolved over the years to perform traditional functions. According to Rodinelli (1993) and Esman (1991) the administration of development is a radically different function than the maintenance of law and the conduct of routine public tasks. Sustainable development and public management tasks are concerned with producing change. The machinery of public management in Nigeria in the future must therefore be designed to execute pragmatic change.

Management principles such as setting goals or objectives, strategic planning, cost benefit analysis, program evaluation and accountability have become commonly accepted values in most societies, just as rationality, neutrality, scientific management are to public administration. Rational administration according to David Rosenbloom (1998) involves running government in the image of business; using cost-benefit analysis, rapid computerized information feedback loops, systems analysis, and quantitative models. The main contention of a good administration is that certain fundamental management principles and practices exit in all-governmental operations in order to obtain efficiency, accountability and economy. Rational administration is also epitomized by Luther Gulick's famous acronym POSDCORB (1937), and Max Weber's idealized organization form bureaucracy (1922). "Bureaucracy is the means of transforming social action into rationally organized action" (Weber, 1968; cited in Rosenbloom 1998). The views associated with these scholars also stress the objective of efficiency and the technical problems of specialization of functions and division of labor.

According to Carl Friedreich (1968) and Ferrel Heady (1991) administration is the core of modern government. That is, no nation can do what a government does without some apparatus to carry out decisions and enforce laws. The recent analysis of Herbert Simon (1987) focuses on administrative activity as the interrelationship of people in organizations, and how they pursue the problems of decision-making and of behavior within those organizations. Charles Goodsell (1988), Moses Kiggundu (1989), Milton Esman (1991), David Rosenbloom (1998) and Guy Peters (2000) have argued that all organizations are systems of coordinated activities in which cooperating people perform formal functions to fulfill a common purpose and communicate that purpose to all concerned, and are also associated in patterns of informal behavior that maintain the common values in which they believe. The task of public administrators is thus to provide the system of communication among the members of any government organization as well as to implement the purposes and objectives of the agency.

According to Meyer (1985), rational administration is not a means to an end but rather an end itself. Charles Lindbloom and David Brayrooke (1970) have pointed out that administrative decision making is generally not preceded by the establishment of precise goals, while the pressures of limited time and a large volume of information prevent the administrator from attending to all the facts and choices available. The public administrator must simplify the relevant data to make it comprehensible and may often act, in Herbert Simon's word, as a "satisficer," seeking a satisfactory decision rather than the best possible one.

Marshall Meyers (1985) and Balogun and Mutahaba (1999) central purpose in writing "Limits to Bureaucratic Growth" is to connect the idea of rational administration with the fact of bureaucratic growth. The fundamental tenets of organizations "command hierarchy, the positive functions of management, and the imperative of efficiency," were first advocated by classical organization theorists, such as Frederick Taylor, Max Weber, Henri Fayol, Luther Gulick, and Woodrow Wilson and were intended to promote organizational efficiency and hierarchical accountability.

Nils Brunsson (1985), John Mayne et al (1997) and Guy Peters (2000) propose an important but unusual argument that, irrationality in decision-making is not a dysfunction in public organization rather it is a necessity for action and change. Decision rationality and action rationality are opposing forces. Decision rationality leads to action, while action rationality might lead to non-action or, at best, minimal incremental change. On the other hand, decision rationality can yield innovative action, when the consequences of the environment are analyzed or alterations of the environment are central to a public organization's effectiveness and decision.

The characteristics of administrative systems in Western societies are not necessarily desirable in Nigeria or any other developing nations. According to Fred Riggs (1984), Ladipo Adamolekun (1982), William Graf (1988), Adebayo Adedeji (1992), Peter Koehn (1990) and Ferrel Heady (1991) administration in African nations has been a formidable burden since the colonial governments of Europe rarely prepared these countries for independence and self-government. Experience from the newly independent African countries show that since former colonial powers withdrew their political and administrative organization, most developing nations have been faced with the dilemma of a society whose industries are undeveloped and whose economy cannot yet support a good educational structure. Several African nations still contain a largely uneducated people and thus have a small source from which administrators can be drawn. The civil services are obliged to compete with industrial, commercial, and educational institutions for skilled individuals from that small source. The dilemma is intensified where the society lacks a common language. Nepotism, favoritism and patronage have been the major means of recruitment of public administrators. Furthermore, there is often an uneasy relationship between public administrators and the political executive concerning their respective spheres of competence. At the same time the shortage of competent administrative personnel and the poor lines of internal communication have led to excessive centralization in many sub-Saharan African nations, with consequent delays in decision making, inefficient operation, and deleterious effect on expression of differing opinion.

In some sub-Saharan African nations' public service was a relic of either the British or French colonial administration. It is the general feeling in developing nations that if their public service is to meet the challenge of development, there needs to be transformation that would revitalize the administrative machinery of government, to make them more responsive and rational to the needs of rapid changes taking place in within them. The irony of the situation, however, is that civil servants in the nation are underpaid, lack motivation, and sometimes have no sense of direction or purpose. In some state and local governments, government employees are used to receiving their salaries late or not at all for several months. Thus, the civil service in some Nigerian states can be best described as corrupt, deplorable, ineffective, sloppy and wasteful. These factors in turn affect the instruments used by national and state various governments to influence the economy of their society. Working under deplorable conditions in Nigeria has caused a differential impact on the success of public policy programs.

Data Source

This chapter seeks to analyze Nigerian public administrators' perception of the importance of managerial skills and management principles. The field research in Nigeria was sponsored by an Indiana State University Research Council grant. The data for this study was collected through a survey administered in Nigeria during the summer of 2000. 300 questionnaires were administered to senior public administrators in the national, state, and local governments. 100 questionnaires were administered to each level of the Nigerian government structure. 165 responses were received out of the 300 originally administered. Data collected from the 165 responses were analyzed using the Statistical Package for Social Scientists (SPSS) computer program.

This chapter reports the views of senior public manager of Nigeria about managerial knowledge, skills and values that are considered as important for public administrators in order for Nigeria to meet training needs more effectively and efficiently and attain sustainable development in the twenty-first century.

The following specific research questions have provided the basis of this present research:

1. What is the level of importance of various managerial skills as perceived by Nigerian Public Administrators?
2. What are some of the core beliefs the Nigerian Public Administrators have about management principles?
3. What managerial skills and competencies are considered to be important by public administration practitioners in Nigeria?
4. What can be done to improve Nigeria's public managers' performance in the future?

Data Analysis and Discussion

Table 6.1
Profile of Nigeria's Public Administrators that Responded

Position Title in Organization	Gender			Total
	Male	Female	Missing Variables	
Director	3	3	-	6
Asst. Director	9	5	1	15
Manager	24	8	1	33
Asst. Manager	14	5	-	19
Supervisor	44	28	1	73
Professor	5	-	-	5
Others	8	-	-	8
Missing Variable	2	1	3	6
	109	50	6	165

Table 6.1 shows the profile of Nigerian public managers that responded to the questionnaire. The total number of respondents was 165. 109 of the respondents were male and 50 were female. There were a total of six missing variables. Males occupy the majority of the senior public management positions in Nigeria; hence the differences in aggregation shown in Table 6.2.

Table 6.2 shows Nigeria's public administrators perception of managerial skills. To help us accomplish the goal of analyzing this data, twenty-two managerial skills were examined in our survey. Respondents gave their opinion about these managerial skills on the bases of a scale 1-5, one being extremely not important and five being extremely important.

One hundred and fifty-two (98%) respondents indicated that Conceptual Skills were somewhat very important to public management in Nigeria. Out of this number, 50 were female and 105 male. Further, while 7.7% of the respondents indicated that Public Sector Ethics was not an important skill, more than 92.3% felt that such skill were either very important or extremely important. Similarly, while 17.3% of the respondents felt that Decision-Making Skills were not important, 82.7% of them were in favor of such skills in the public sector. Further, while 38.6% of the respondents indicated that Managing Cultural Diversity was not an important skill for public administrators, 61.4% of the respondents indicated that it was very important. About 13.6% of the respondents rated Mentoring Career Development as an unimportant managerial skill. Despite this negative rating, 86.4% of the respondents indicated that Mentoring Career Development was important. It was surprising to note that in this age of information technology 1.9% of the respondents felt that information technology skills were not important for public managers in Nigeria to do their job. Apart from this observation, about 98.1% of the respondents indicated the importance of information technology skills in the nation's civil service.

The study, shows that Nigerian public administrators felt that most of their peers should have extremely high skills in the following areas: Teamwork Building skills, Problem-Solving skills, Disciplining of Employees, Program Evaluation, Financial Management skills, Evaluating Employees Productivity skills, Time Management skills, Efficiency and effectiveness skills, and Managing Conflict skills.

Table 6.2
Nigeria's Public Administrators' Perception of Managerial Skills

Managerial Skills	Extremely Not Important	Partially Not important	Important	Very Important	Extremely Important	Male	Female	Total	Chi-square Test Gender	
									M	F
Conceptual Skills	-	3	35	67	50	105	50	155	.000	.481
Numerical Skills	3	50	52	40	10	105	50	155	.000	.409
Problem Solving Skills	-	12	19	42	79	105	50	155	.000	.262
Assertiveness Skills	-	6	50	58	24	91	47	138	.001	.117
Democratic Values	3	5	39	54	54	105	50	155	.000	.299
Public Sector Ethics	11	1	50	58	34	105	50	155	.000	.613
Disciplining Employees	1	1	35	57	60	105	49	154	.000	.799
Efficiency and Effectiveness	1	-	8	68	79	106	50	156	.000	.619
Program Evaluation Skills	3	7	48	51	41	106	50	156	.001	.079
Evaluating Employee Productivity	2	3	16	70	64	106	49	155	.088	.009
Financial Skills	1	8	41	46	57	105	48	153	.001	.011
Information Techno. Skills	1	2	56	46	48	104	49	153	.017	.000
Interpersonal Communication Skills	-	3	58	56	38	105	50	155	.045	.436
Administrative Law	2	33	71	42	6	104	50	154	.000	.214
Decision Making Skills	11	16	31	51	47	106	50	156	.000	.160
Managing Conflict	-	13	31	72	40	106	50	156	.001	.096
Managing Cultural Diversity	23	36	28	50	16	103	50	153	.000	.786
Mentoring Career Development	12	9	58	56	19	105	49	154	.000	.123
Time Management Skills	-	9	43	55	47	104	50	154	.002	.478
Teamwork Building Skills	-	4	15	60	76	106	49	155	.205	.358

The chi-square test of statistical significance indicates that there was a statistically significant relationship between gender and managerial skills such as: Financial skills, Information technology skills, Influencing Superiors and Peers skills, and Program Evaluation skills. There were, however, 19 managerial skill areas where the male respondent's data showed major significance and those of the female respondent did not.

Although this study shows that Nigeria's public managers have a great deal of positive perception of managerial skills, their productivity and labor turnout is still very low. To be effective, public managers in Nigeria need to possess technical, human, conceptual, diagnostic, and political skills. Experience is as important as formal education in forming effective public managers. The issue is not whether education or experience is the best teacher. It is what combination of the two is most beneficial for a particular individual in a particular situation. Public managers in Nigeria who climb the ladder in the civil service usually have both education and experience in management techniques. One difference between the new and old breed managers, however, is that the former integrate the use of computers into their work smoothly.

Future Strategies to Reform the Public Sector

Management transformation of the public sector over the past several years has generated an immense number of alternative techniques designed to make government perform better. New public management strategies in Nigeria should be closely associated with innovative economic planning capabilities. The public management strategies suggested in this study to help Nigeria move forward were based on the findings of this research. The strategies should be guided by lessons from previous efforts at induced administrative reforms and from judgements of what might be effective, pragmatic and feasible in each nation's economic development programs. Drawing on the works of Peters (2000), Riggs (1984), Graf (1988), Rodinelli (1993) and Dibie (1996), among others, have advanced the notion of development administration as a panacea for what is described as the Nigerian bureaucratic pathologies.

Development administration begins with the goal of effecting change in any developing society for the twenty-first century. This kind of administration is different from the conventional type, which aims merely at changing procedures. Development administration for the 21st century should be regarded as government activities that would promote economic growth, improve human and organizational capabilities, promote equality in the distribution of opportunities, income and power, and involves deliberate attempts at social and behavioral changes. The instruments required for public management reform are also very important for service quality.

In order for public management to be effective in Nigeria the national and state governments would have to move their public organizations towards the empowerment administration strategy. This involves establishing an organizational strategy that is aligned with its structures, systems, human resources practices and employee skills. At the heart of service excellence is the extent to which core values or beliefs about excellence form an intrinsic part of public management strategy and culture.

The nature in which top management communicates or practices these values by providing leadership in implementing service excellence are very vital to the achievement of development goals. Although information technology has become an important factor in improving an organization's competitiveness, technology is replicable by competitors. Skills, work motivation, and organizational commitment are variable and much more difficult to replicate. Table 6.3 shows the fixed and variable organizational characteristics that Nigeria public sector could adopt for service excellence in the future.

A new style of public administration (which is different from the colonial one) means adopting innovative management techniques in the public sector, which would enable Nigeria to cope with the challenges of economic development in the new millennial and beyond. The present situation, impelled the adoption of first: a new conception of management, providing a more production or results-oriented approach to public service and concentrating attention and resources on the purposes for which public institutions are created, as servants of society.

Second, Nigeria should not underscore the need for a public service that will recruit and train specialized personnel and use scientific knowledge to a much greater extent than present. In essence, their public administration must draw upon the resources of research and educational institutions, and the experience of the private sector within African nations and abroad. In this perspective, Nigeria need a new style of public administration that has potential to manage their human resources in such a way as to motivate them to achieve definite goals, serve as team members, and engage in common enterprises for the public good.

Table 6.3
Fixed and Variable Organization Characteristics for Excellent Performance

	Organization Characteristics	
Organization Dimension	**Fixed**	**Variable**
Structure	Few levels between contact personnel, top management	•Specialization vs. integration of labor •Unit size •Decentralization of power
Strategy	•Focus on customers as top priority •Formal process of setting service quality goals •Employee/job fit	•Evaluation and compensation system
Human resources strategies	•Importance of socialization process •All level accountable and responsible •Clear liaison devices	•Extent of team work
Communication	•High level of interaction between management and customers; management and contact employees •Top management attention to service issues •External orientation of admin. systems •High level of communication between contact and operations departments •Consistent policies and procedures	•Formality of planning and control systems •Standardization of tasks
Systems	•Management commitment to service quality Organization focus on key attributes Continuous improvement	•Degree of perceived control among contact personnel
Core Values and Skills/technology	•Technology/job fit	•Appropriateness of training

Source: Adopted from Horwitz Frank, and Mark Neville. 1996. "Organization Design for Service Excellence: A Review of the Literature." Human Resource Management, Vol. 35, 471-492 (Winter).

According to Guy Peters (2000), and Benveniste (1989), the new style public administrator should not be interested in pushing a file or writing a memo, as in the old colonial tradition. Public managers must work to achieve results. Public administrators for the 21st century in

Nigeria should not merely administer the established order by processing matters that come before them, they should manage and make things happen by organizing people, money and materials in order to achieve the particular objectives of their ministries or agencies within time targets.

Third, inducing administrative reform is basically an institution building activity. Institution building has three main program implications: (a) Major reforms occur in and through formal organizations. Therefore new organizations must be built or older ones remodeled with the capacity to protect and promote innovations in their environment. (b) Building indigenous capabilities – individuals and organizations – which have the capacity to sustain innovations and to continue operational results. This implies a high priority to staff development and to investing in the organization. The emphasis of foreign advisers should therefore be on developing capabilities and commitments among local staff rather than on the organization's immediate outputs. This is required to build new local administrative expertise. (c) Every program of action should involve good relationships with other government agencies whose behaviors and tenets are required to follow innovative lines.

The ability to control depends on an appropriate management strategy to identify and understand the cost and benefit between activities and results: the ability to determine events and outcomes. Foreign experts (especially in high technology areas) should train indigenous public administrators so that they can develop the necessary skills to be innovative in managing accurately. Public administrators must satisfy the conditions needed for the establishment of effective control systems i.e., goals, purposes, standards needed for timely measurement of outputs, and means for information feedback. Control of the new style public service in Nigeria should also require near perfect or absolute faith. Stout (1980) argues that organizational control requires specific rules and regulations that permit administrators to accurately predict responses in given situations. Thus, control in Nigeria's public sector should give considerable promise for helping public managers learn how to assess an organization's environment.

One dimension of primary concern in Nigeria is the question of the inherent ability of employee to do the work in question. Some problem employees in the public sector are incapable of performing their duties; while others are quite able to do good work. In addition to the question of ability, these problem civil servants also differ in their willingness to change the behavior shown to be detrimental to government goals and objectives. Taken in combination, there are those who are unwilling to change their behavior, although they are capable of performing their work; those who are willing to perform their jobs; and those who are both willing to change and able to do their work.

Table 6.4
Approaches for Managing Poor Performance

Factor	Attitude toward	Change of behavior
Ability to do the work	Unwilling to change	Motivation required
Unable to do the work required	The candidate for discipline	The candidate training
Able to do the work required	The candidate for coaching	The candidate for mentoring
DISCIPLINE = use of a combination of negative and positive sanctions to change behavior.		
TRAINING = use of focused learning experiences to impact new job-related skills.		
COACHING = use of intensive supervisory attention to develop appropriate attitudes towards job performance.		
MENTORING = use of senior, experienced employees to help junior or problem employees to acquire good management and judgement skills on the job.		

Sources: Adopted from Barzelay, Michael (2000). The New Public Management: Improving Research and Policy Dialogue. Berkeley, California: University of California Press. Ban, Carolyn and Norma Riccucci (1997). Public Personnel Management: Current Concerns, Future Challenges. New York: Longman.

Different strategies are presented on how to manage each of these four combinations in the public sector of Nigeria. Table 6.4 shows a recommended course of action for administrators in the twenty-first century. For example, the "really nice person" is a good candidate for training; that is, such a person is very likely to express a willingness to change, but he/she lacks the ability to perform at higher levels. The value of that employee to an agency would be enhanced if he/she were provided training that is specifically designed to improve present performance or teach new and necessary tasks that others in the public management of Nigeria have not mastered.

Another example is that of problem employees in the twenty-first century who can not do their jobs and are willing to change their inappropriate behavior – for example, indecisive employees – may respond to mentoring. Carolyn Ban and Norma Rccucci (1997), and David Rosenbloom (1998) contend that mentoring would encourage professional maturation by passing on lessons acquired from experience. The intention is to help someone who lacks judgement develop it in his/her own work. The mentor should be a superior officer who possesses the reputation of exercising good judgement in his own job.

The flexible worker is often able to perform tasks and is often willing to change. When these kinds of employees are identified, they should be matched with a highly respected and well placed senior executive who can give such a flexible employee a good sense of how to balance the need for personal dedication with the need for public management success.

When a problem employee is able to do work but is unwilling to change, coaching is probably a fruitful approach to management of the activities of such employees in the twenty-first century in Nigeria. In the case of such an employee, coaching that often nets benefits entails the purposeful assignment of responsibility. David Rosenbloom (1998) asserts that external criticism may be the appropriate way to enhance change and control for success in this kind of candidate.

In those most difficult cases, when problem employees are incapable of doing their job and are also unwilling to admit the need for change, the recommendation for management to deal with such employee should be the progressive discipline approach. For example, excuse makers would eventually find out that their views are no longer given credibility, even when they actually deserve respect. Progressive discipline should begin with a reprimand and, if such behavior is repeated, the employee should be provided counseling, suspension without pay may follow after another repeat. Reassignment, demotion, and eventual discharge should be implemented incrementally as the offense is repeated. Penalties may be specified in the management policy of Nigeria, so those would be offenders know in advance the consequences of their actions. Ineffective discipline may encourage repeat of unacceptable behavior in the public sector. On the other hand, prompt and decisive disciplinary action may resolve a problem and may relieve the employer of liability.

A cherished part of the political tradition in Nigeria is that there should be a separation between politicians who make policy and the administrators who implement the policies (politics/administration dichotomy). This separation is very critical for Nigeria to achieve and kind of efficiency in the public sector. In the 21st century, good working relationships between political leaders and professional bureaucrats would generally help in attaining the economic development goals for the respective countries. With few exceptions, there is common agreement transcending differences in political ideology, culture and style that

Nigeria's bureaucracy should adopt in its operation. Public administrators should serve as change agents and not as masters.

Another major objective of the reform in Nigeria's civil service is to enhance professionalism. Under this reform, staff should henceforth perform duties in which they have recognized professional and technical competence. Development of educational and training programs, which concentrate on the preparation of personnel for critical development tasks, is greatly needed. This should include assigning to specialists or professional administrators and supervisors the responsibility of training and ensuring that their staffs are provided the knowledge and skills required for their position. Staff who hitherto had not specialized in their duties (that is, staff who lack appropriate and recognized education, qualification, training and technical skills for the jobs they are assigned to perform) should be identified and sent for training.

There is also the need for the creation of a modern human resources system which (a) classifies positions, (b) attracts and recruits the best talent, (c) screens out persons of second-rate quality, (d) makes possible rapid advancement of persons of outstanding competence while preventing the promotion of the less fit, (e) sets equitable salary scales with sufficient compensation to enable employees to live modestly without having to engage in other employment, (f) provides good working conditions, and (g) protects honest employees from political reprisals or favoritism Initiation of a comprehensive and sustained program of management improvement in the operation of ministries and agencies in order to overcome inadequacies in planning, organizing, and carrying out development activities is also crucial for the 21st century.

The horizontal internal structure of each "Ministry" should be professionalized, such that the maximum of eight departments in each ministry would reflect on the operations and major functions of the ministry. Thus, the breakdown of the former administrative functions into professional components should comprise Personnel Management, Finance, Supplies, Planning, Research and Development, and Information Management.

One crucial concern in the public sector management in Nigeria is public choice and accountability. Many of the techniques that the new public management postulates raise important concerns about how government in the sub-region can be held accountable when there is such limited direct control over outcomes.

Table 6.5
Tools that would Facilitate Accountability in Public Management

Ends to enhance accountability in the public sector	Means of achieving accountability in the public sector
Legitimacy of Decision-makers	Constitutions; electoral systems for governments and decision-making bodies; bureaucratic systems of representation; Royal prerogative; legislation; letters of appointment; formal delegation of authority; standing orders.
Moral Conduct	Societal values; concepts of social justice and public interest; professional values; training/induction programs.
Responsiveness	Public participation and consultation; debates; advisory bodies; public meetings; freedom of speech.
Openness	Parliamentary question times; public information services; freedom of information laws; public hearings; green and white papers; annual reports.
Optimal resource utilization	Budgets; financial procedures; rules of virulent; parliamentary public accounts committees; auditing; public inquiries and participation; formal planning systems.
Improving efficiency and effectiveness	Information systems; value for money audits setting objectives and standings; program guidelines; appraisal; feedback from public.

Source: Adopted from Hayllar, M.R. (1991). "Accountability: Ends, Means and Resources." Asian Review of Public Administration, Vol. 3 (2), pp. 10-22. Turner, M. and David Hulme. 1999. Governance, Administration and Development. West Hartford, CT: Kumarian Press.

Accountability is very crucial in respect to attributes of the market entity over which individual civil servant or government units have control. Therefore, governments in Nigeria should conduct performance evaluations according to the tasks and attributes that they provide. This practice should involve measurement, evaluation, and rewarding of service attributes for which each employee is responsible. Public organization leaders should be careful not hold individuals accountable for attributes over which they have no control, because it could be counterproductive. Future civil service compensation systems should reward the type of service behavior that the government seeks to promote.

Table 6.5 shows a variety of tools that are available to make public servants in Nigeria accountable. The factors in the table demonstrate that particular tools are designed to suit particular purposes.

In order to achieve accountability, it is desirable that Nigeria adopts a combination of tools. One critical point of contention is that the adoption or the existence of a particular tool does not necessarily mean that it is effectively been used. National governments should ensure that these tools are appropriately used to enhance accountability.

Enhanced professionalism, decentralization and delegation are all critical aspects of the proposed reforms, which would make for the general modernization of the Nigerian' civil service. But another major aspect, which is aimed at general modernization, is the creation in every ministry, a Department of Planning, Research and Development. With the creation of this department in all ministries, the major weakness in the civil service would be considerably solved. Not only would short, rolling, medium and perspective planning become routinized, ministries would also have timely, regular and full data and information about sectors of the society over which they have jurisdiction, and about the internal operations and management conditions of the ministries themselves.

In addition to the development of this department in each ministry, top officials in the civil service should also be active in facilitating the durability and sustainability of the reforms. They should always read and distribute government documents to their subordinates. Basically because of relative inaction by top officials in these two aspects, many junior public administrators might not understand some governmental guidelines and regulations. Therefore, top officials need to significantly enhance their knowledge and actively disseminate the details of the reforms. While the organizational arrangements to carry out these tasks may vary from one of Nigeria's state and local government to another, two requirements are important. First, the organizations need to be related closely to the leadership role of the chief executive so that it could receive unwavering support. Secondly, the organizations should be sufficiently related to the budget and planning agencies, so that essential coordination and teamwork could be engendered in driving forward to fulfill the nation's development goals.

The civil service in Nigeria should introduce appropriate technology in the service delivery systems. The use of new technology to achieve the task in hand is vital if the reliability and assurance elements of customer expectations are to be satisfied. Automation should be employed wherever it can add value for the customer, leaving employees to concentrate on the value adding attributes that cannot be automated. These principles hold regardless of the types of political systems in the nation. Thus, the nature of technology employed in the future should determine the type of training and skills that new employees would be required to have before joining the civil service. There is also the need for the respective governments in the sub-region to conduct on-the-job training frequently.

Finally, there is the need for new programs in schools, new ways to provide training and technology skills. While, it is important to encourage innovation in addressing Nigeria's problems and opportunities, public management reform would provide the innovative objectives and strategies required to develop the respective nations. Thus, civil servants, planners and senior public officials should ensure that an environment is provided in which innovative ideas are not just permitted, but encouraged and nurtured, through a new professionalized civil service. As long as the behaviors of public administrators in Nigeria are consistent with moral or ethical rules, regulations, and the pursuit of objectives that serve the interest of the public, one can say that the trust placed in the hands of these public officials is been satisfied.

Conclusion

This chapter has examined the perception of public managers about managerial skills and administrative problems in the public sector of Nigeria. It argues that economic and societal development is dependent on effective management principles within a favorable political environment. Societies such as Nigeria that are stagnant do reflect the lack of dynamic political and public organizations. It contends that development cannot be successful without a sustaining philosophy of the doctrine, political action of a dramatic order, and effective organization for the mobilization of popular support. Therefore the future structure of the Nigerian government should be of a character that encourages responsible political action and facilitates the involvement of a wide cross section of the citizens in the sustainable development process of the nation. The public management strategies suggested in this research, if implemented, should facilitate the process of reform.

The study also demonstrated that the application of innovative management skills and principles requires planners (professionalized and well-trained civil service personnel) and ethical administrators to view social problem solving as a pragmatic process for social interaction and learning. Such an approach requires an institutional culture quite different from that practiced in the nation between 1960 and 2000. For Nigeria to foster economic development, it must among other things, implement substantial amounts of strategic and professionalized organizational design.

Dealing effectively and respectively with development problems on a large scale in the 21st century will depend on the ability of planners and administrators to use more effectively the political, social, and economic mechanisms of authority, exchange, and persuasion which we think are the fundamental means of influencing behavior. Public planners and administrators in Sub-Saharan African governments must not only understand this mechanism better but also learn how to combine them in new ways to cope with complexity and uncertainty.

Modern public administration requires skilled people who can act as catalysts, that would mobilize the support or commitment needed to make innovative programs and projects appropriate, and successful. It demands administrators who can respond creatively to the needs of intended beneficiaries and quickly to change in conditions which affect the success of development activities. It requires people who are willing and able to seek out and correct mistakes as they are discovered, and who can plan and manage simultaneously. It requires administrators who view themselves as leaders rather than as bureaucrats. It calls for administrative systems that allow good managers time to manage, and that rewards them for their efforts and results.

Finally, future plans and public management programs for development capable of bringing about a substantial improvement of conditions for the entire nation would require the elimination of special privileges for the few. These plans should involve the dismemberment of large land holdings, and the creation of greater social responsibilities on the part of private enterprise. A considerable degree of coercion may be required to subject antagonistic and privileged elements to these changes, and also to produce, through progressive taxation, the capital essential for infrastructure and productive public enterprises.

References

Adamolekun, Ladipo. (1982). Public Administration: A Nigerian and Comparative Perspective. London: Longman.

Adamolekun, Ladipo and Victor Ayeni. (1994). "Nigeria." In Public Administration in the Third World, edited by V. Subramaniam. London: Longman.

Adedeji, Ajayi. (1992). "Factors in the African Development Equation." African Journal of Public Administration and Management, Vol. 1, 1, pp. 15-37 (January).

Adu, A. (1969). The Civil Service in Commonwealth Africa: Development and Transition. London: George Allen and Unwin.

Aucoin, Peter. (1995). The New Public Management: Canada in Comparative Perspective. Quebec: Institute for Research on Public Policy.

Balogun, Jide, and Gelase Mutahaba. (1999). " Redynamizing the African Civil Service for the Twenty-first Century: Prospects for a Non-Bureaucratic Structure." In Bureaucracy and the Alternatives in World Perspective, edited by Keith Henderson and P. Dwivedi. New York: St. Martin's Press.

Ban, Carolyn and Norma Riccucci. (1997). Public Personnel Management: Current Concerns, Future Challenges. New York: Longman.

Barzelay, Michael. (2000). The New Public Management: Improving Research and Policy Dialogue. Berkeley, California: University of California Press.

Benveniste, G. (1989). Mastering the Politics of Planning. San Francisco, California: Jossey Bass.

Braybrooke, David and Charles Lindbloom. (1970). A Strategy of Decision. New York: The Free Press.

Brusson, Nils. (1985). The Irrational Organization: Irrationality as a Basis for Organization Action and Change. Chichester, United Kingdom: Wiley and Sons.

Esman, Milton. (1991). Management Dimensions of Development: Perspectives and Strategies. West Hartford, Connecticut: Kumarian Press.

Farazmand, Ali. (1991). Handbook of Comparative and Development Public Administration. New York: Marcel Dekker.

Friedreich, Carl. (1968). Constitutional Government and Democracy. Fourth ed. Boston: Blaisdell Publishing Company.

Goodsell, Charles. (1988). The Case for Bureaucracy. Hatham: New

Jersey: Chatham House Publishers.

Graf, William. (1988). The Nigerian State, Political Economy, State Class and Political System in the Post-Colonial Era. Portsmouth, New Hampshire: Heinemann.

Hayllar, M.R. (1991). "Accountability: Ends, Means and Resources." Asian Review of Public Administration, Vol. 3, 2, pp. 10-22.

Heady, Farrel. (1991). Public Administration: A Comparative Perspective. New York: Marcell Dekler Inc.

Heady, Farrel. (1993). Development Projects as Policy Experiments: An Adaptive Approach to Development Administration. New York: Routledge.

Hirschman, A. (1989). The Strategy of Economic Development: New Haven Connecticut: Yale University Press.

Horwitz, Frank and Mark Neville. (1996). "Organization Design for Service Excellence: A Review of the Literature." Human Resource Management, Vol. 35, pp. 471-492 (Winter).

James, Williams, Naya Seiji and Gerald Meier. (1989). Asian Development: Economic Success and Policy Lessons. University of Wisconsin Press.

Katz, S. (1979). Exploring a System Approach to Development Administration, Durham, North Carolina: Duke University Press, pp. 109-36.

Kiggundu, Moses. (1989). Managing Organization in Developing Countries: An Operational and Strategic Approach. West Hartford, Connecticut: Kumarian Press.

Koehn, Peter. (1990). Public Policy and Administration in Africa: Lesson from Nigeria. Boulder Colorado: Westview Press.

LaPorte, R. Jr. (1970). "Administrative, Political and Social Constraints on Economic Development in Deylon." International Review of Administrative Science, Vol. 35, pp. 158-79.

Mawhood, P. (1983). Local Government in the Third World: Experience of Tropical Africa. New York: Wiley.

Mayne, John and Eduardo Zapico-Goni. (1997). Monitoring Performance in the Public Sector. New Brunswick: Transaction Press.

McCaffery, J.L. (1989). Making the most of Strategic Planning and Management. San Francisco, California: Jossey Bass.

Meyer, Marshall. (1985). The Concept of Rational Administration. Berlin: Walter de Gruyter.

Mohapatra, Manindra. (1996). Management Training and Public Service Education as Correlates of Orientations towards Public Service

Professionalism among State Administrators in the Fifty-State. Eric Document No. ED 388204.

Nelberg, B. (1989). "Review of Public Sector Management Issues in Structural Adjustment Lending." Washington: World Bank.

Pearson, L. (1993). Partners in Development (The Pearson Commission) New York: Praeger.

Peters, Guy. (2000). "Policy Instruments and Public Management: Bridging the Gap." In Journal of Public Administration Research and Theory, Vol.10, 1, pp. 34-47.

Riggs, Fred. (1971). Frontiers of Development Administration. Durham, North Carolina: Duke University Press.

Riggs, Fred. (1984). Administration in Developing Countries: The Theory of Pristimative Society. Boston: Haughton Mifflin Publishers.

Rodinelli, D. (1982). "The Dilemma of Developmental Administration: Uncertainty and Complexity in Control Oriented Bureaucracies." World Politics, Vol. 35, 1, pp. 43-72.

Rodinelli, D. (1987). Development Administration and U.S. Foreign Aid Policy, Boulder, Colorado: Lynne Reinner Press.

Rodinelli, Dennis. (1993). Development Projects as Policy Experiments: An Adaptive Approach to Development Administration. New York: Routledge.

Rosenbloom, David. (1998). Public Administration: Understanding Management, Politics, and Law in the Public Sector. (4th ed.) New York: McGraw-Hill.

Rowat, Donald. (1988). Public Administration in Developed Democracies: A Comparative Study. New York: Marcel Deker Inc.

Simon, H. (1987). Administrative Behavior. (First ed.) New York: Knof.

Stout, R. Jr. (1980). Management or Control? The Organizational Challenge. Bloomington, Indiana: Indiana University Press.

Subramainian, V. (1990). Public Administration in Third World: An International Handbook. Westport, Connecticut: Greenwood Press.

Turner, M. and David Hulme. (1999). Governance, Administration and Development. West Hartford, Connecticut: Kumarian Press.

7 Administrators and Correcting Government Failures

Introduction

Nigeria became an independent nation on October 1st, 1960. Since this date the expanding role of the government has required the citizens of the nation to demand more services from the government. At independent, the civil service inherited the Westminster model from Britain, but over the past forty years it has metamorphosed into being a Nigerian oriented civil service. The current civil service in Nigeria continues to remain competent in the discharge of routine services, however, the attitudes of public servants and their operational capabilities are not adequate. Civil servants in Nigeria have distance themselves from the act of governance by refusing to accept responsibility, by share lack of competence to generate policies, innovative ideas and by being lazy couple with the notion that they have secured jobs. Nosakhare Isekhure (1998) contends those government officials during the military regime in Nigeria; tacitly colluded with soldiers to destroy credibility and accountability at all cost. Jide Balogun and Gelase Mutahaba (1999) pointed that the civil service in Africa (especially Nigeria) has been involved in various forms of ethical violation and buccaneering that have resulted in the distortion of internal rules and procedures. They further describe this notion as a localized form of corruption, one that takes place within the organization, as against other forms involving the external clients of the organization.

The methods of planning analysis and management which were introduced between 1960s and 1990s and which continues to dominate the procedures of most government departments were primarily concern with flexibility and extraction of government resources for personal gain. Most public managers in Nigeria behave as though government is "no man's business" because according to them government is nobody, and as such its properties nor interests do not need to be protected. Ironically, one wonders if these public officials were trained with the orientation that government interests equals public interests and authority. The courteous relationship that ought to exist between public servants and the citizens is absent. For example the Nigerian Police that ought to be the friends to the public are usually perceived as enemies of the citizens, untrustworthy, corrupted and some times act as an accomplice in crime. Further, if Nigerian Telecommunication (NITEL) staffs are not tossing your telephone lines just to extort money from the citizens, they would be opening up citizens telephone lines to others to call Europe and North America, and at the end of the month the subscriber would be sent bills which must be paid otherwise the phone would either be disconnected or recovered. Thus, if Nigerian public administrators' perception of the importance of managerial skills and management principles are re-oriented positively, they will know better not to treat citizens and the delivery of public service in this manner. Another general problem in Nigeria's Public administration is related to the fact most of the government functions are too centralized. Olowu (1991) pointed to the fact that perhaps the long military rule in the nation might have caused an increasingly centralized public administration. He further noted, that a nation that has about seventy percent of its citizens in the rural area still spend most of its public resources in the urban areas. This might be one area where Nigeria has departed from the norms of development administration or sustainable administration and adopted the legacy of colonial administration.

Phillips (1990) analysis of the Nigerian 1988 Civil Reform noted that the public service of the nation has been denied things that would have enable it to fulfil its mission, particularly at the crucial period in the nation's history. The shortcomings facing the Nigerian public administration include a good public image, clearly articulated job description, performance standard, competitive salaries, sustained opportunities for training and retraining and a commitment to the research of critical public issues in Nigeria.

In respect of training of public servants in Nigeria, even though the Civil Service reform of 1988 address the need for mandatory training, just like the Udoji reform did in the 1970s, no such policy has been articulated or well implemented. There is, therefore, for the development and identification of institutions that will be responsible for the training and retraining as well as professional improvement of public administrators in Nigeria. Without this in place, the practitioners of

Nigerian public administration and the government will continue to fail the citizens. Further, the complex overlapping jurisdiction, economy of scale, and growth and decay of cities and towns mean that tax collection and public policy coordination of services are difficult. Generally, each problem is significant and helps explain the challenge of public policy, market, and government failures in Nigeria.

This chapter analyzes the symbolic relationship between the study of public administration in Nigeria and why government policy implementation fails in the nation, based on Tables 5.7 and 6.2. It examines the question: What administrative Framework can help Nigeria to correct its problem efficiency and Government's Failures? The chapter argues that the gap between the study of public administration and its practice in Nigeria is one of the main reasons for government failure in the nation. The final section suggests ways to correct public management and government failures in Nigeria.

Public Administrators and their Role in Managing Public Good

The literature on development administration made a distinction between changes as a result of emulating colonial administration and change as a result of innovation. The former concept applies to nations and how they respond to the demands of change, emerging from colonial regimes after independence (Turner and Hulme, 1997). Innovation in development Administration is an adoption process that brings in new ideas on how to formulate and implement sustainable development policies in a developing nation. It represents a change in administrative processes and the ways in which developing nations relate to their environment. A variety of public management issues result from this focus: (1) market failure; (2) government failures; and (3) how to correct market and government failures.

According to Jide Balogun and Gelase Mutahaba (1999), there are two ways of viewing the developmental role of the bureaucracy. First, it may be assumed that the legal-rational momentum of classic bureaucracy is strong enough to overcome the dysfunctional effects and thus propel the bureaucratizing systems to growth and help in the sustainable development process of a nation. Second, the classic bureaucracy may be seen as containing the seed of its own destruction, that by its very nature, the Weberian bureaucracy is incapable of pioneering change or bringing about substantial development.

The traditional market failures – public goods, externalities, natural monopolies, and information asymmetries – provide widely accepted rationales for such public policies as the provision of goods and the regulation of markets by government agencies. The term public or collective goods is frequently used in the literature. It refers to the goods that are collectively owned by a community, state, or nation. The presence of non-competition, non-excludability, or congestion can lead to the failure of markets to achieve Pareto efficiency (Weimer and Vining 1992). Market failure, therefore, indicate the possibilities for action to be taken in order to improve the efficiency of market outcomes through collective activities of public administrators and the private sector. This call for action commonly advances the rationale for sustainable public policies.

No nation or political system is completely successful in accomplishing what it wishes. This is certainly the case of most developing nations such as Nigeria. Most individual choices expressed through participation in markets and other voluntary exchanges, further such social values as efficiency and liberty. But some individual choices, like those that arise in situations I identify as market failures, detract from social values in predictable ways. Collective choice exercised through governmental structures offers at least the possibility for correcting the perceived deficiencies of individual choice. But just as individual choice sometimes fails to promote social values in desired and predictable ways, so too does government choice. When this happens, it is called government failure. Therefore, public administrators should be informed and trained to have an understanding not only of market failure but of government failure as well.

Public administrators' behavior and their perception of managerial skills in a particular nation help us to understand if they know what is required to implementing collective decisions in centralized and decentralized systems of government and of using public agencies to produce and distribute goods (Adamolekun 1986; Turner and Hulme 1997; Nafziger 1997). Together, the insights from these fields help us to realize that even governments blessed with the most intelligent, honest, and dedicated public officials cannot be expected to promise social good in all circumstances. Grindle (1991) and Joseph Umeh (1992) argued that two factors greatly influence the way public administrators actually behave. First, they have their own private interests. It would be naive to believe that they do not consider their own well being and that of their families. Second, individuals must incur costs to monitor the behavior of their representatives. Given financial and time constraints, individuals will usually not find it in their private interest to articulate policy preferences or to monitor the actions of their representatives closely. More generally, however, analysts find allies among public administrators whose private interests happen to lead them to what they believe to be good policy.

Government often establishes public organizations to deal with perceived market failures. However, the extent to which public organizations continued existence contributes to aggregate social welfare depends greatly upon the diligence and motivations of the public administrator who determine their budgets and oversee their operations (Nafziger 1997; Adedeji 1992). Threatening budget cuts and badgering agency executives may not be very effective ways of influencing behavior by the employees at the lowest level of the bureau who, in most cases, actually deal with the public. Again, separation between politics and administration limits the capability of public agencies to meet consumer wants effectively. Therefore, government, like markets, sometimes fails to promote the social good. Consequently, a broad perception of managerial skills, training and management principles are required by public administrators in Nigeria in order to link market, government and stakeholder objectives with broader organizational goals.

Framework for Correcting Public Management and Government Failures

In this section our focus will be on policy solutions towards correcting public management and government failures in the twenty-first century in Nigeria. The various types of actions that the Nigerian government can take to deal with perceived policy problems in the twenty-first century will be referred to as pragmatic policies. These pragmatic policies represent a range of general strategies. Since policy problems are usually complex and always contextual, pragmatic policies must be tailored to specific circumstances to produce viable policy alternatives. Nevertheless, familiarity with pragmatic policies encourages a broad perspective that helps policy-makers craft specific solutions. We must note, however, those policy problems rarely have perfect solution, and that some policies are better when others are. A primary task of the policymaker is to identify those policies that have the best prospects for improving social conditions. To facilitate this task, we indicate the market failures, government failures, or equity concern that each pragmatic policy most appropriately address, as well as the most common limitations and undesirable consequences associated with the use of each. In order to prepare you to examine further the issues relating to pragmatic policy, they have been grouped into five general categories: (1) freeing, facilitating, and simulating markets; (2) using taxes and subsidies to alter incentives; (3) establishing rules; (4) supplying goods through nonmarket mechanisms; and (5) providing insurance and cushions or economic protection.

Freeing regulated markets should be considered in situations where an effective market can be expected to reemerge with relatively minor efficiency distortions - in other words, where there is no inherent market failure. When the complete withdrawal of government may be neither feasible nor desirable, there may be opportunities to stimulate markets via various auction processes. Deregulation, legalization, and privatization are the major means of freeing markets. Historically, the federal government of Nigeria and many state governments have engaged in price, entry, and exit regulations of competitive markets. Whatever the putative rationale for regulation, deregulation almost inevitably involves complex efficiency and distribution issues. Consequently, successful deregulation often requires vigorous advocacy that details the failures of the regulatory regime and allays fears about distribution effects.

Legalization refers to freeing a market by removing criminal sanction. The impetus for legalization often stems from changing social attitudes. Sometimes decriminalization is advocated as a partial form of legalization: Criminal penalties are replaced with civil fines. Decriminalization lessens the stigma and punishment associated with previous criminal actions but does not fully sanction the actions as socially acceptable.

Another means of freeing markets is privatization. The word privatization is used in several different ways: (1) switching from agency subventions to user fees; (2) contracting out of the provision of a good that was previously produced by a government bureau or agency; (3) denationalization, or selling off of state-owned enterprises to the private sector; and (4) demonopolization, the process by which the government relaxes or eliminates restrictions that prevent private firms from competing with government agencies or state-owned enterprises (Rhoads, 1993). Only these latter two types of privatization are directly related to the freeing of markets. The World Bank and the IMF have recommended a major trend toward privatization, or partial privatization, to African nations as a condition for obtaining loans from these financial institutions.

In situations where efficient markets cannot operate, it may be possible for the government to simulate market processes. Weimer and

Vining (1992) assert that the right to provide the good can be sold through an auction. A more efficient approach to auction is to require bidders to submit the lowest retail price at which they will supply customers. An auction could be used in the allocation of rights for the exploitation of publicly owned natural resources. An auction also has an advantage relative to setting a fixed price for the exploitation rights. Auctions may be useful allocative tools in situations where governments must allocate any scarce resource. The Central Bank of Nigeria now fixes the foreign exchange rate based on the highest bidding by commercial financial institutions. Auction might be usefully employed in other areas as well.

Subsidies and taxes are market-compatible forms of direct government intervention. Our primary concern is with the use of taxes and subsidies in situations where the intention is to correct market failures or achieve redistribution. In general, taxes and subsidies can have one of three possible impacts on efficiency. First, where taxes and subsidies are aimed at correcting for externalities in particular markets, their impact may enhance efficiency. Second, where the objective of taxes and subsidies is purely to redistribute, there is inevitably some net deadweight loss. Third, taxes may be used in an attempt to extract scarcity rents such as those that arise in the extraction of natural resources such as petroleum. In theory, such taxes can be designed to transfer rents without losses in efficiency; in practice, limited information about the magnitude of rents generally leads to market distortions.

Government uses rules to coerce, rather than induce, certain behaviors. Either criminal or civil sanctions may enforce compliance. Establishing rules may provide the most efficient method for dealing with market failures in some contexts. Rules can be divided into two major categories: (1) framework rules, encompassing both civil and criminal law, and (2) regulation, including restrictions on price, quantity, quality, and information, as well as more indirect controls relating to registration, certification, and licensing of market participation. Contract law, tort law, commercial law, labor law, and antitrust law can all be thought of as a framework of rules. One of government's goals regarding the most basic of public goods is the establishment and enforcement of property rights, including the rights to health and safety. Contract law can also be formulated to reduce the consequences of information asymmetry. For example, insurance law places the burden of informing the insured of the nature and extent of coverage on the insurer. Further, antitrust law, which can be designed to employ either criminal or civil procedures, seeks to prevent firms from realizing rents through collusive efforts to restrict competition. Framework rules can also be used to counter some of the problems associated with government failures. For example, individual rights given as constitutional guarantees can protect minorities from the tyranny of the majority under direct democracy. Similarly, restrictions on gifts and perquisites that can be given to representatives may help avoid the most blatant abuses of rent seeking. While on the one hand, framework rules facilitate private choice in competitive markets; on the other hand, regulations seek to alter choices that producers and consumers would otherwise make in these markets. Regulations generally operate through command and control: directives are given, compliance is monitored, and noncompliance is punished. For example, price regulation could be used as a method of preventing monopolies from charging rent-maximizing prices.

Supplying goods through non-market mechanisms is another means of correcting both government and market failures. Indeed, the choice between government provision and other pragmatic policies is one of the least well-understood policy issues. Perhaps the reason is that while there is a convincing theory of market failure and government failure, there is no overreaching theory that delineates the efficiency trade-off between market failure and government failure (Rhoads 1993; Gillis et al. 1992; Nafziger 1997). Generally, market failure provides a rationale for government intervention, rather than specifically for direct provision by government. For example, consider the possible responses to natural monopoly: auctions to take advantage of competition for markets, subsidies to facilitate marginal cost pricing, and direct regulation. These approaches are alternatives to government ownership of monopoly. Once a decision has been made to supply goods publicly, governments can do so either directly or indirectly. Direct supply involves production and distribution of goods by government agencies/institutions.

The means of indirect supply are independent agencies, usually government corporations or special districts or various forms of contracting-out. According to Otobo (1999), Nigerian government domestic production can be divided into ten functional areas: (1) supporting internal administrative needs; (2) laws and justice; (3) facilitating commerce; (4) health care and social services; (5) managing public lands; (6) technical assistance; (7) education and training; (8) marketing; (9) research and testing; and (10) contracting public works and managing real property. An analysis of these government functions suggests that some market failure or re-distributive rationale could justify all. This, however, does not address the question of whether these goods could be efficiently provided by other pragmatic policies or provided indirectly by government. Clearly, some of these goods can be supplied using other policies; for example, elements of health care can be variously provided in free markets, through market incentives, and other rules.

Some government interventions provide shields against risks. The essence of insurance is the reduction of individual risk through pooling. Insurance can be purchased in private markets to indemnify against loss of life, damage of property, cost of health care, and liability for damages caused to others. Government can use its authority to mandate universal participation in insurance plans to prevent adverse selection from operating. Mandatory insurance may be used to privatize regulation. Rather than mandating insurance, the government can provide it at subsidized premiums when myopia, miscalculation, or other factors appear to be contributing to underconsumption. Fairness should serve as a rationale for subsidizing premiums. Rather than pay the subsidies directly,

Table 7.1
Alternative Policy Solutions

Problems	**Market Mechanism**	**Incentives**	**Rules**	**Non-market Supply**
Market failures				
Public goods	S	S	S	P
Externalities	S	P	P	S
Natural monopoly	S	S	P	S
Information asymmetry	-	-	P	S
Government failures				
Direct democracy	-	-	P	-
Representative government	P	-	P	-
Bureaucratic supply	P	S	S	S
Decentralization	S	P	-	S

P = Primary source of policy solutions. S = Secondary source of policy solutions.

governments should force private insurers to write subsidized policies in proportion to their total premiums. Whereas insurance schemes reduce the variance in outcomes by spreading risk, cushions reduce the variance in outcomes through a centralized mechanism. The key difference is that, with insurance, individuals make ex ante preparations for the possibility of unfavorable outcome, while with cushions they receive ex-post compensation for unfavorable outcomes.

Table 7.1 shows the pragmatic policy area's that are most likely to provide appropriate solutions for each of the major market failures, government failures, and distribution concerns. In many cases, more than one pragmatic policy could provide potential solutions for the same problem. The solutions are never perfect and must be tailored to the specifics of the situation and evaluated in terms of the relevant goals.

The framing of problems in terms of market and government failures often leads directly to models linking policy variables to the conditions of concern. However, understanding the problem involves investigating the symptoms that can also prompt client interest, framing the undesirable conditions in terms of market and government failures, and developing behavioral models that relate the conditions of concern to variables that can be manipulated by public policy. Each of these three tasks, especially modeling, can be done professionally at the outset of an analysis.

The third stage is policy formulation. Policy formulation is the stage where steps are developed and plans are made to remedy a problem. The expected result of policy formulation is a solution to the problem. The fourth stage is policy adoption. This is the stage where some person or group that has the power and authority to make decisions accepts the proposed solution. Policy adoption may occur through the legislatures, courts, or directly by the chief executive. Budgeting is the fifth stage. To achieve the policy goals, programs require funding. Implementation is the sixth stage. It involves carrying out or executing a policy that has been adopted through legislation or by executive or judicial order.

Jones (1984) argues that implementation involves three activities: organization, interpretation, and application. Policy implementation is the stage of policymaking between the establishment of a policy – such as the passage of a legislative act, the issuing of an executive order, the handing down of a judicial decision, or the promulgation of a regulatory rule – and the consequences of the policy for the people whom it affects. Without effective implementation the decisions of policymakers cannot be successfully carried out (Ripley, 1991). The seventh stage is policy evaluation. The evaluation of policies is carried out by government agencies, outside consultants, the press, and the public. The essence of evaluation is to find out the impact of the policy. If the results are favorable the policy might continue; if not, it might be terminated or modified to effectively solve the problem. In describing these processes, it is important to remember that the activities of the various political actors are greatly constrained by political, cultural, and socioeconomic conditions.

The Nigerian government should start to emphasize the importance of performance evaluation. The policies implemented by public administrators and services provided by civil servants will suffer a terrible set back if the government underscore the values of performance evaluation. As Blunt and Popoola (1990, 108) contended, the problem of appraisal should be limited to the intrinsic nature of the job in question. Bunt and Popoola also pointed out that for most part, the practicalities of public organizational appraisal process in Nigeria as well as most African nations are rarely straightforward. Some of the factors that might militate against straightforward performance evaluation include ethnicity, religion, gender, kinship, corruption, economic factors and political issues. It is therefore, a necessary requirement that public administrators at the national, state and local governments are made to follow established guidelines to restore trust and confidence in the system. This requirement would be a major step towards enhancing the legitimacy of the nation's governance system. This is necessary because lack of legitimacy may lead to the civil society being reluctant or refusing to pay taxes, and if it degenerates to such a low level, the nation would not be able to attain sustainable development.

Trust and accountability are major factors of instilling confidence in any public and private organization. Thus, any public organization that lacks a good system of accountability will hardly contribute to the nation's sustainable development goals. It is therefore very important that some public administrators have to answer or held accountable for the failure or success of a government ministry, agency or program.

Apart from the economic strategies to correcting government failures mentioned above, there are a lot of new public management approaches that need to be taken by the Nigerian government in order for the nation to meet the challenges of the twenty-first century. These approaches include positive administrative values, efficiency performance, productivity evaluation, controls and sanctions, program evaluation, and accountability. Basically, the public administration of the new century should be one that is citizen oriented rather than self-serving. It should be innovative rather than rule-bound. It should be capable of forging constructive partnership with outside groups rather then being patronage or corruption ridden. Obviously, the new public administration must operate within the limits set by the law rather than resorting to legalism.

Table 7.2
Model toward Balancing Public Administration Study and Practice

Government Action

1. Focus on the Citizens.
2. See Problems from Broader Socio-political angles.
3. Maintain the highest professional standards in the management of human, material, financial and information resources.
4. Respect the rule of law but not hide behind legalism. Substitute Management accountability for routine hierarchical control.
5. Integrate the needs of individuals and informal groups with formal organizational designs.
6. Training and retraining of public bureaucracy, as well as adequate provision of administrative materials and hardware to operate with.

Source: Adopted from Balogun, Jide and Gelase Mutahaba. 1999. "Redynamising the African Civil Service for the Twenty-first Century: Prospect for a Non-bureaucratic Structure." in *Bureaucracy and the Alternatives in World Perspective* edited by Keith Henderson and P. Dwivedi. New York: St. Martin's Press.

Balogun and Mutahaba (1999) and Adedeji (1992) contend that the public bureaucracy of the twenty-first century in Nigeria should enlist information in the service of policy and program implementation. Public managers should also be truly purposive, results-oriented, time and cost conscious institutions. They should not be involved in constantly slowing down the processes of policy implementation by hierarchy, protocol, cynical interpretations and application of rules. The new public management of the twenty-first in Nigeria should strengthen management accountability rather than act as a device for stiffing initiative and creativity. Olowu (1991) pointed Nigerian public servants have suffered from wage compression due to inflation and devaluation, yet everybody wants them to perform more than before.

The onus is, therefore, on the government to address the problem of wage erosion, if they want public servants to be highly motivated.

Further the government should clearly articulate job description, performance standards and ensure more drastic reduction of excess staff. Mandatory training and retraining programs for public servants should also be established. There is a major need for the Nigerian government to appropriate funds to research important aspects of public administration. Such research would provide further insights for resolving some the problem areas in the practice of public administration in the nation. Table five shows the major areas that the Nigerian government needs to take action in the twenty-first century. These actions are necessary for the nation to balance both study of public administration and the practice of it for sustainable growth and development.

It does not matter whether it is private or public organization; usually the underlying policies applied are the same. When evaluating the impact of planned change interventions based on policy change that viewed the process of change as occurring generally speaking on three phases. First, planned change interventions create changes in characteristics of the public sector itself. Second, because the public organization provides the context or work setting with which public administrators behave, appropriate change in this context will lead public administrators to change their behavior. Third, because the behavior of public organization members is a key determinant of public servants outcomes, behavior change will have an impact on the nature of these outcomes. Government action should require public organization work settings to be composed of four major interrelated subsystems. (1) Organizing arrangements – the formal elements of the organization that provide the coordination and control necessary for public service delivery and policy implementation. (2) Social factors – the characteristics of the public servants in government institutions, their patterns and processes of interaction, and culture. (3) Technology, the function directly associated with the transformation of public sector inputs to outputs. (4) Physical setting – the characteristic of the physical space in which organizational elements comprising each of the public subsystem. Public administrator's behavior is a primary determinant of two categories of government institution outcomes, namely the level of policy performance and the level of public servants development. Changes in behavior should have an impact either or both of these two categories of outcomes. Finally, the twenty-first century public sector in Nigeria must change frequently to keep up with rapid changes in the world around them and the people within them.

Conclusion

The purpose of this study has been to examine the symbolic relationship between the study of public administration in Nigeria and public administrators' perception of the importance of managerial skills and management principles in the nation. The study observed that both the study of public administration and it practice have tend to move in the reverse direction where the external stimuli of action is lacking.

In order for Nigeria to transform it present public bureaucracy into an inward-looking and possibly self-serving organization, it is very essential that each and every management functions is redefined with the clients, customers and consumers orientation in perspective. The remedies to both market and government failures are also extensively covered. The observations about insurance markets and individual responses to risk suggest that public policies may have potential for increasing economic efficiency in Nigeria in the twenty-first century. There is future need for performance high standards, competitive salaries and sustained opportunities for training and the retraining of public servants as well a strong commitment by the government to conduct research in critical issues concerning public administration and the citizens of Nigeria in general. Public assessments of risks, for example, may be an appropriate response when individuals make important systematic errors in their private assessments, and public insurance may be justified when private coverage is significantly incomplete. However, policies that do not find a basis in one of these market failures must be justified by values other than efficiency. Different policies can be used to address market and government failures. In many cases, more than one pragmatic policy can provide potential solutions for the same problem. But the solutions are never perfect. They must be tailored to the specifics of the situation and evaluated in terms of the relevant goals. Generally, market and government failures help us to understand the nature of public policy problems. Being aware of policies and their consequences helps us to begin our search for solutions to Nigerian specific policy problems in the twenty-first century.

References

Aborishade, Oladimeji, and Robert Mundt. (1998). Politics in Nigeria. New York: Longman.

Adamolekun, L. (1986). Politics and Administration in Nigeria. Ibadan, Nigeria: University of Ibadan Press.

Adedeji, Adebayo. (1992). "Factors in the African Development Equation." African Journal of Public Administration and Management, Vol. 1, 1 (January), pp. 15-37.

Allison, G. (1971). Essence of Decision-Making: The Cuban Missile Crisis. Boston: Little Brown.

Anderson, J. (1984). Public Policy-Making. New York: Holt, Rinehart, and Winston.

Balogun, Jide and Gelase Mutahaba. (1999). "Redynamising the African Civil Service for the Twenty-first Century: Prospect for a Non-bureaucratic Structure." In Bureaucracy and the Alternatives in World Perspective edited by Keith Henderson and P. Dwivedi. New York: St. Martin's Press.

Bienen, H. (1978). Armies and Parties in Africa. New York: Africana Publishing Company.

Blunt, P. and Popoola. (1990). Personnel Management in Africa. London: Longman.

Brams, S. (1975). Games Theory and Politics. New York: The Free Press.

Braybrooke, D. and C. Lindblom (1963). A Strategy of Decision. New York: The Free Press.

Cohen, M., J. March and J. P. Olsen (1972). "A Garbage Can Model of Organizational Choice." Administrative Science Quarterly, Vol. 17, 2, pp. 1-25.

Collier, D. (1979). The New Authoritarianism in Latin America. Princeton New Jersey: Princeton University Press.

Dye, T. (1976). Policy Analysis. What Governments Do Why They Do It and What Difference It Makes: Birmingham, Alabama: University of Alabama Press.

Dye, T. (1997). Understanding Public Policy. 5th Edition. New Jersey: Prentice-Hall.

Dye, T. and H. Zeigler (1981). The Irony of Democracy. 5th Edition. Monterey, California: Brooks Cole.

Easton, David. (1965). A Framework for Political System Analysis: Chicago: University of Chicago Press.

Edwards, G. and I. Sharkansky. (1978). The Policy Predicament. San Francisco: Freeman.

Egonmwan, J. (1991). Public Policy Analysis: Concept and Application. Benin City, Nigeria: Aka and Brothers Press.

Etzioni, A. (1968). The Active Society: A Theory of Societal and Political Processes. London: Collier-Macmillan.

Gillis M., D. Perkins, M. Roemer, and D. Snodgrass. (1992). Economics of Development. Third Edition. New York: W. Norton and Company.

Grindle, H. (1986). Civil-Military Relations and Budgetary Politics in Latin America. Armed Forces and Society, Boston: M.I.T. Press.

Grindle, M. S. (1991). "The New Political Economy: Positive Economics and Negative Politics," Perspectives on the New Political Economy. San Francisco: ICS Press, pp. 41-67.

Grindle, M. and Thomas, J. (1991). Public Choice and Policy Change: The Political Economy of Reform in Developing Countries. Baltimore: The John Hopkins University Press.

Halperin, M. (1974). Bureaucratic Politics and Foreign Policy. Washington D.C.: Brookings Institute.

Isekhure, Nosakhare. (1998). 201 Solutions to Vision 2010. Benin City, Nigeria: Oduna Communications Press.

Jones, C. (1984). Introduction to the Study of Public Policy. 3rd Edition. Pacific Grove, California: Brooks/Cole.

Kingdom, J. (1984). Agenda, Alternatives and Public Policies. Boston: Little Brown.

Lindblom, C. (1993). The Science of Muddling Through. In Classical Readings in American Politics. edited by Nivola and D. Rosebloom New York: St.Martin's Press.

March, J. (1978). Bounded Rationality, Ambiguity and the Engineering of Choice. Bell Journal of Economics. Vol. 9, 3, pp. 587-608.

Moe, T. (1984). The new Economics of Organization. American Journal of Poitical Science. Vol. 28, 4 (November), pp. 739-777.

Mueller, D. (1979). Public Choice. Cambridge, New York: Cambridge University Press.

Nafziger, W. (1997). The Economics of Developing Countries. Upper Saddle River New Jersey: Prentice-Hall.

O'Donnell, G. (1973). Modernization and Bureaucratic-Authoritarian Studies in South American Politics. Berkeley: University of California Press.

Olowu, Dele. (1991). Nigerian Public Administration: Past Present and Future. Ibadan, Nigeria: Shaneson C. J. Limited.

Olson, Mancur. (1982). The Rise and Decline of Nations. New Haven, Connecticut: Yale University Press.

Otobo, E. (1999). "Nigeria." In Oladipo Adamolekun Public Administration in Africa. Boulder, Colorado: Westview.

Oyeleye, O. and Adigun Agbaje. (1999). Nigeria: Politics of Transition and Governance. Dakar, Senegal: CODESRIA.

Phillips, A. (1990). The 1988. Nigerian Civil Service Reforms and Their Post-1992 Prospects. Ibadan, Nigeria: NISER Publication.

Rhoads, S. (1993). Modern Economics Analysis. Upper Saddle River, New Jersey: Prentice-Hall.

Ripley, Randall. (1985). Policy Analysis in Political Science. Chicago: Nelson Hall.

Rondinelli, D.A. and H. P. Minis Jr. (1990). "Administrative Restructuring for Economic Adjustment: Decentralization Policy in Senegal." International Review of Administrative Science, Vol. 56, 3, pp. 447-66.

Simon, H. (1958). Administrative Behavior. 2nd Edition. New York: Macmillan.

Stepan, Alfred. (1986). The New Professionalism of International Warfare and Military Role Expansion. In Armies and Politics in Latin America. Edited by J. Lowenthal New York: Holmes and Meir.

Turner, Mark, and David Hulme. (1997). Governance, Administration and Development: Making the State Work. West Hartford, Connecticut: Kumarian Press.

Umeh, O. Joseph. (1992). "Capacity Building and Development Administration in Southern African Countries." International Review of Administrative Science, Vol. 58, 1, pp. 97-104.

Weimer, David and Aiadan Vining (1992). Policy Analysis: Concept and Practice. Englewood Cliffs, New Jersey: Prentice-Hall.

Wildavsky, Aaron. (1992). The New Politics of the Budgetary Process. New York: Harper Collins.

8 Assessment of Local Government Public Servants

Introduction

The formation of local government in Nigeria dates back to the early nineteenth century. A review of the history of local government shows that local governments have a long episode of trial and error. During its history, local governments have attempted to reconcile participation of indigenous people in their own administration with the needs for an efficient delivery of external services.

Local governments in Nigeria became an out growth of the indirect rule system the British colonial administration introduced. Reform in the local government started just after the end of the World War II (in 1945), when the British colonial administration attempted to democratize the system as a basis for social and economic development. This shift in local government responsibility stimulated the desire to bring the government closer to the people as well as involving the participation of the indigenous people at the grass root in the administration and development of their areas.

Oladikpo Adamolekun (1999) asserts that the most significant feature of local government reform was the recognition of that institution by the national government of Nigeria as the third level of government. The Nigerian guideline for local government reform (1976) stipulates the following functions for it: (1) To make appropriate services and development activities responsive to local wishes and initiatives by devolving or delegating them to local representatives; (2) to facilitate the excise of democratic self-government close to the local levels of Nigerian societies, and to encourage initiative and leadership potential; (3) to mobilize human and material resources through the involvement of members of the public in their local development; (4) to provide a two-way channel of communication between local communities and government (Guideline for Local Government, 1976; Udoji Commission Report 1974).

The guidelines for local government reform also separated the functions of state and the national governments from those of local governments (Udoji Commission Report 1974). Belle Harris (1980) contends that the general plea of the Udoji Commission was that the allocation of responsibilities should be considered with the resources and abilities of the level of governments. The other structural aspect of local government is that of choosing an appropriate unit.

Between 1974 and present times local governments in Nigeria have declined in relations to state and national governments. Local governments' financial positions have deteriorated in the sense that they have not been adequately accountable. Further, local governments have also lost a lot of staff to state and the national governments. The creation of more states by both Babangida and Abacha's regime galvanized a lot of local government public servants to seek positions in the newly established state governments. However, one of the major problems of local government is its inability to attract suitable and professional staff. Therefore, in an atmosphere of declining confidence in local government, reform factors have caused a virtual abolition of the notion of independent local government in Nigeria's federal system. This view is buttressed in the sense that local governments was expected to be democratically elected institutions with executive, legislative, taxation and spending powers. Unfortunately, some local governments in Nigeria have subordinated this role to their state government spelling out the distinction between the three levels of governments in the nation's federal system. During the military regimes (1966-1979) and (1983-1999) the Udoji Commissions recommendation for the democratization of local governments was rejected by the armed forces ruling council. Instead, the military preferred the national government to handle the distribution of powers and resources between levels of government (national, state and local). In other word, the military regimes' policy makes preferred technical and administrative solutions rather than to deal with political decentralization matters.

The most ominous change that took place at the local government level during the military regimes includes functions such as water supply, prisons, and education. Other activities were considered for transfer from either local government to their respective states, or to the national military government (Humes and Ola, 1994). The number of roads and medical clinics maintained by local governments was significantly reduced.

Revenue and expenditure, resources and staff decreased during the military regime. While the military opinion has been that this reduction of functions would free local government to concentrate its activities on community development, it became more difficult for local governments to develop community interest and support for functions that were wholly state responsibilities. Hulmes and Ola (1994) pointed out that the tax riots that took place in the Western State of Nigeria during the military were due to dissatisfaction over taxation and local administration.

The creation of more states by the military regimes of Babangida and Abacha in the 1980s and1990s to conform to the major ethnic groups in Nigeria was considered a positive step toward a democratically elected civilian government. However, the creation of more states did not help to solve the local government problems. General Abacha's regime also increased the number of local governments. There were thirty-six states and 589 local governments in 1996. The number of local governments was increased to 774 in January of 1997, excluding the mayoralty of Abuja, which has two mayoral districts. Today, Nigeria has 776 local governments. This has been the way the military regime restructured the federal system periodically since 1966, when they took control from the civilian politicians. Since 1996, the local governments through out Nigeria are now organized in an identical way. The new arrangement calls for a single tier-system with 776 local governments. The structure provides for not only an elected chairperson but also elected councilors with portfolios (that are councilor charged with specific policy responsibility i.e., education, finance, health, works, etc). What is particularly significant about this development is that it demonstrates the extent to which the new national government intended to be involved in local affairs. It would appear that states will no longer act as autonomously as they have in the past with regards to either the system or the functions of local government. On the one hand, this trend is significant for economic development in local governments. On the other hand, federal impact is also felt in terms of financial assistance and constitutional guarantee as never before in Nigeria's history. In this view, local governments' activities in Nigeria should not only involve policy making, implementation, and proactive public administrators. Public administration at the local government level in Nigeria should be construed not only as a managerial tool but also as a legitimate means for advancing the broader public concerns of equity and ethics.

This chapter assesses the training needs of public administrators at the local government's level in Nigeria. It traced the development of local governments in Nigeria from 1945 to present times. It argues that the shift in the critical decision-making powers and functions of local government requires its public administrators to be more trained professionals. The chapter addressed the following questions: What is the status of staff training in local governments in Nigeria? Do local government public administrators in Nigeria need training? Are there opportunities for training provided by administrative leadership? The question of interests in this chapter is how public administration at the local government level can better serve Nigeria's communities and in so doing develop authentic relationship with, and equitable representation of, the majority of the people.

The chapter contends that the new direct link between the federal and local governments is an ideal intergovernmental relations system that needs to be explored further for economic development at the grass root. The final section of the chapter suggests areas of training needs for local government public administrators and how Nigeria can best achieve development at the community and grass root levels.

Local Government and Intergovernmental Relations

One thing that is missing in local government reforms in Nigeria is the fact that the citizens do not have any input in the local decision-making and implementation process. What participatory role do the citizens play in the public affairs of local governments? In the context of the local public affairs in Nigeria, citizens are partially involved in voting, whose results are often rigged. Even then, voting is only one element of citizen participation. Voting is perhaps one of the less significant forms of citizen participation. Elaine Sharp (1990) provided four guidelines for citizens participation in the public affairs of local government as: (1) Open government policies like public hearings requirements and open meetings laws that pave the way for direct monitoring, oversight, and input into public decision-making by citizens; (2) Information gleaning devices such as citizen surveys and government units for handling citizens complaints about individual concerns; (3) Neighborhood organization activity; and (4) Co-production strategies that brings the citizens into collaborative operations for services delivery along the side of public service professionals.

A critical analysis of intergovernmental relations in Nigeria will show a contradiction between populist notion of citizen involvement and actual patterns of local government practices. The evolution of local governments from the colonial era to the post-military state also reveals that citizen's participation efforts have often been limited and trivial. Thus, from the 1900s to the 1990s the core of colonial bureaucratic institutions has not only remained intact but has also been reinforced through contemporary management practices. Alex Gboyega (1999) and Olowu (1999) contend that a real federal system and the form of intergovernmental structure that the system requires would seem in compatible with the uniform command structure of the armed forces. Therefore, like the colonial administration, the military was bound to establish a centralized control system that discourages citizens from participation in the public affairs of local governments.

The evolution of local governments in Nigeria has had long-term effects of eroding local autonomy. Local government functions have eroded over the years because citizens do not participate in the decisions that define the new role of the lower level of Nigeria's federal system. Adamolekun (1999) pointed that the highly centralized military regime has weaken the general-purpose local government in Nigeria. In the state and local government relations, a long-term centralization process that was established by the military regime also has eroded much of local government autonomy.

The evolution of local governments in Nigeria has been that of continuous reform. Between the 1890 and 1990s the British colonial administration headed by Mc'Callum and MacGregor instituted reforms because they were dissatisfied with the protectorate kingdoms. When Lord Lugard was posted to head the colonial administration in 1910, he too changed the local government structure that Mc'Callum and MacGregor had created. Lugard established the Native Authorities. Continued concerned and dissatisfaction with the performance of local governments led British Governor-Generals such as Clifford in the 1920s, Cameroon in the 1930s, and MacPherson in the 1940s to established a British-style system of local government (Humes and Ola, 1994). Dismay with the British system led to the transformation of local governments in the 1960s. Local governments were emasculated in the 1970s by indigenous commissions who were set up by the federal military government to investigate and recommend measures that would helped improve the performance of local governments in Nigeria. Thus, the method of reform decisions in Nigeria has been from the top-down approach.

The outcome of the top-down decisions and reform of local governments in Nigeria during the military regime was based on the Udoji

Report in 1974. The civil service reform in 1987 partially followed the Udoji pattern. The report raised major issues of administrative reform at the local government level. Unfortunately, the Federal military government rejected many of its recommendations. This action of the government contradicts the endorsement by newspapers, community organizations, and partisan groups.

The history of local government in Nigeria shows that there has been minimal election turnout at the rural areas of the nation. This low turnout and the limited research interpreting local voting patterns and the lack of distinctive theory of rural voting in West Africa suggest that electoral involvement cannot be a key focus in a discussion of citizen participation in local affairs. Further, there have been major contradictions between Nigeria's expectation of citizen involvement in democracy and actual levels of citizen involvement in complex, technical decision or heavily bureaucratized and strongly professionalized service delivery operations.

From this viewpoint, Adamolekun (1999) and Olowu (1999) contend that public sector managers in Africa have the responsibility of enhancing citizen's interest in local government. In a democratic setting, authentic public administration is said to require such responsibility for nurturing of civic involvement. Before local government public administrators would be able to perform these functions in Nigeria, they must be adequately trained.

Studies on local government employees in Nigeria suggest that public administrators often begin their new job at the local government with the expectation that they will receive sufficient training and information to learn the ropes and quickly become productive, successful members of the government. Many public administrators, however, show up on the first day of work and do not receive adequate formal instruction or assistance from colleague for dealing with their new assignments. Likewise, many longtime public administrators at the local government need to re-skill because of technological improvements, mandated changes, or new ways of conducting business. The leaders of Nigeria's local government administrators, which underestimate the learning challenges required, often insufficiently support such extensive and difficult changes. Why do local governments invest so little in the training of their public administrators?

Data Source

This chapter assesses the training needs of public administrators at the local government's level in Nigeria. The field research in Nigeria was sponsored by the California University Fresno Affirmative Research Grant. The data for this study was collected through a survey administered personally by the author in Nigeria during the Summer of 2001. Although, the principal investigator of the research is aware that Nigeria has 776 local governments, he divided the nation into three regions and randomly selected 50 local governments from each region. Ten questionnaires were administered to public administrators in each of the 50 local governments. Thus, 1,500 questionnaires were administered in 150 local governments selected around Nigeria. That is, 500 questionnaire per region. 1, 350 responses were received out of the 1,500 originally administered. 450 responses were received from local administrator in the West. 470 responses were received from the local government administrators in the East. 430 responses were received from local government administrators in the North. The data collected from the 1,350 response were analyzed using the SSPS computer program.

The following specific research questions have provided the basis of this present research:

1. What is the administrative profile of the survey respondents?
2. How much training dose public administrators in Nigeria's local government have in public management?
3. What are the training needs of local government administrators in Nigerium?
4. How can the civil servants at the local government level of Nigeria better serve their communities?

Findings, Data Analysis and Discussion

Table 8.1
Profile of Local Government Public Administrators that Responded

Position Title in Organization	Gender								Total
	M	F	Training Received						
			Ph.D	MA	BA	Dip	NCE	ExArmy	
LG Chair	150	0	1	3	80	10	6	50	150
Councilors	350	15	-	2	160	88	25	90	365
Director of Personnel Mgt.	140	10	-	55	95	-	-	-	150
Treasurer	131	19	-	12	130	8	-	-	150
Engineer	148	2	-	-	145	5	-	-	150
Secretary to LG	149	1	-	2	128	20	-	-	150
Other LG Staff	200	35	-	-	100	90	15	30	235
Total	1268	52	1	74	838	213	46	170	1350

Table 8.1 shows the profile of local government public administrators that was interviewed. A total of 1350 out of 1500 local government administrators responded to the questionnaire administered. Out of the 1350 local public administrators that responded, 1153 were male, while 197 were female. Among the respondents 150 were local government chairperson (Mayor in America); another 365 were council members (Councilors). The head of the civil servants at the local government level in Nigeria is called "Head of Personnel Management." 150 head of personnel management responded, and out of that number ten were female. Among the local government engineers that responded 148 were men, while only two were female. The treasury department respondent (treasurers) constituted 131 male and 19 female, thus making a total of 150. It is interesting to note that the treasurer position was the only senior management position that has more than 15 female. Among the 150 secretary to local government that responded 149 were male while only one was a female.

Table 8.1 also shows that 80 out the 150 local government chairpersons had a bachelor degree. Other local government chairpersons either had a diploma or were ex-army officers. Majority of the councilors who responded either held a Bachelor degree or a diploma or was ex-military officers. The most qualified group at the local government was the head of personnel Management. 55 of them had a mater degree, while 95 of them hold only a bachelor degree. The engineers generally held a bachelor degree in either civil or mechanical engineering. Only five engineers held Higher National Diploma from polytechnic in Nigeria. One interesting findings of this study is that although the military regime handed over power to an elected civilian administration in 1999, retired military officers are still actively involve in the administration of public affairs in Nigeria.

Table 8.2 shows the training received by local government public administrator in Nigeria. The table also shows the number of local governments that provide staff training for both new and old staff. This study asked the 1350 respondents if they had received formal training in any of the fourteen Public Management courses listed. 590 respondents out 1350 indicated that they received training in Management Studies. 413 respondents also indicated that they received formal training in Research Methods. Among the 1350 respondents 438 indicated that they received training in local government administration. It is interesting to note that 225 respectively received training in Administrative Theories, Budgeting and Financial Management, Organizational Behavior, Personnel Management, and Public Finance. Only 223 of the respondents indicated that they have received training in Development Administration. Although, there were no computer installed or displayed in any of the offices of the 150 local government surveyed, 375 respondents indicated that they had received training in Information Technology.

An average of 150 respondents indicated that they have received training in Public Policy Analysis, Program Evaluation and Administrative Law respectively. The survey result also shows that non-of the 1350 local government public administrators had received training in Public Policy Making. All they do is to muddle through the process. Another interesting finding of this survey is that, although, Nigeria is rated as one of the most corrupted nations in the world, nothing is done to train local government employees the importance of public ethics. Only 36 respondents out of 1350 indicated that they had received some training in Public Sector Ethics.

This chapter was also interested in finding the number of local government that conduct training for both new and old staffs. Table 8.2 shows that only ten out 150 local governments' conduct training in administrative law and procedure for new employees. Five local governments also provide an on going training for their staff in administrative procedures. Two local governments indicated that they provided training in Personnel management for their new employees, while 37 local governments confirmed that they provided in service training for old staff on personnel management related issues. Further, twenty-seven local governments indicated that they send their junior staff to their State Civil Service Training School annually for training in Local Government Administration. Eleven out of these 27 local governments also indicated that they do send some of their senior staff to workshop and seminars organized by either the local universities or private training institutes.

Although local government chairpersons and head of personnel management, and councilors emphasizes the importance of training and development for sustainable growth, non-of them budget money for the purpose. The survey finding shows that local governments in Nigeria do not train their public administrators. Another paradox is that there is no evidence that training and development has taken place. In some local governments where training of staff has taken place, there is no evidence that training and development has experienced an increase in resources or attention. In fact, the survey evidence seems to suggest that many local governments are reducing such resources.

Table 8.2
Training Received by Local Government Staff in Public Management

Courses in Public Administration	Yes	No	# of LG that Conduct Training for New Staff (150)	# of LG that Conduct Training for Old Staff (150)	Total
Administrative Law	145	1205	10	5	1350
Administrative Theories	255	1125	0	0	1350
Budgeting & Financial Mgt.	225	1125	0	0	1350
Development Administration	223	1127	0	0	1350
Information Technology	375	977	0	0	1350
Local Government Administration	438	912	27	11	1350
Management Studies	590	760	5	5	1350
Program Evaluation	150	1200	0	0	1350
Organizational Behavior	225	1125	0	0	1350
Personnel Management	225	1125	2	37	1350
Public Policy Analysis	150	1200	0	0	1350
Public Finance	225	1125	0	0	1350
Public Policy Making	0	1350	0	0	1350
Public Sector Ethics	36	1314	0	0	1350
Research Methods	413	937	0	150	1350

Source: Analysis of Field Survey data from Nigeria by Author.

For sustainable development to take place at the local government level in Nigeria, basic technical skills, organizational operations skills, public ethics and general supervisory skills have to be very essential. It is essential for all local governments in Nigeria to increasingly start to apply new technology and new management philosophies. The study recommends not just basic training for local government staff but also advance forms of learning.

This chapter also found out that although, local governments provided jobs for these public administrator, the respondents do not think well of the administration and local public services. Majority of the public administrators gave negative ratings to their local government. Variations across regions were minimal and the local government's negative ratings were similar in the 150 local governments surveyed.

Although, respondents indicated that they would like to see improve service delivery system, non-of them called for performance measurement so that their local government and staffs can know how well they are really doing. The reality, then, in Nigeria's local governments, is that both states and their local governments are susceptible to becoming intolerable sweatshop, trying to use old-fashioned mass production methods even though citizens demand more customization and employees require more empowerment. Evan Berman et al. (2001) pointed out that lack of training and development in any public sector often because of crush of immediate needs, means that current work environment needs for cross-training, job expansion, re-skilling, problem solving, team skill an so on will go unmet.

Dynamics for Sustainable Growth in Local Government

The survey results covered in the preceding sections have explored several distinctive modes of citizen participation in local government affairs. Having made this exploration; are there any overall, summative recommendations that we can give to improve local government performance and citizen's participation in local public affairs?

First, these research results are complicated by the different goals of the 150 local governments and the various forms of citizen participation required. As the preceding section suggests, different outcomes are expected from different formats. The level of citizen participation in local government affairs also reflects different understandings of what participatory democracy is all about. This further complicated in Nigeria because the nation was under military regime for a long time. The citizens still do not understand the details of participatory democracy. Having said this, it will be nice to be optimistic and stress the view points as well as suggest that Nigeria's local governments need the following: (1) a viewpoint that stress the educative value of political participation for citizens; (2) a viewpoint that emphasizes the capacity of citizens participation in programs to force greater government responsiveness and accountability to citizens interests; and (3) a viewpoint that expect citizens participation to be a helpful tool for public administrators. These factors will serve as a means for gaining citizens cooperation and support (Sharp, 1990).

The history of local government in Nigeria shows that both colonial and post-independence administrative reform has pursued straight and narrow paths. These reforms have focused attention on efficiency and effectiveness at the expense of other public concern such as morality; ethics and equity demand a new approach to sustainable development in the twenty-first century. Sadel (1996) offers a view of democratic citizenship in which individual look beyond self-interest to a concern for the whole and moral bond with their communities.

According to Peter Haruna (2001) Nigeria's local governments need to introduce policy that is crafted on the assumption that the responsibility of the government is to promote citizenship and public discourse. Further, the public interest will require a democratic public administration that invites participation from and collaboration with citizens. Haruna (2001) contends that there is no doubt that dialogue among scholars, practitioners, and citizens will not only help to bridge the gap between theory and practice, but also to explore and test new possibilities for a better understanding of public administration as a field of study in Nigeria.

A local government should have a bottom line: the revenue side of the budget, which is finite. As taxes decline or the demand for more constricts. Often a local government has decreasing revenues at the same time it must increase its levels of service. When a need arise for newer or better ways of doing things. This need drives innovative thinking. That is the introduction of new ideas or methods, or new ways of approaching old problems. At the local government's levels in Nigeria, the need for new programs in schools, new ways to provide training or new ways to build roads represent opportunities for innovative solutions. In the local government strategic plan, it is important to encourage innovation in addressing the problems and opportunities identified in the environmental scan. The objectives and strategies are areas in which innovative methods can be developed. Public sector planners and senior public administrators in local governments should ensure that an environment is provided in which innovative ideas are not just permitted, but encouraged and nurtured.

Local governments in Nigeria should not shy away from need assessments. Needs assessments are systematic efforts used to identify training and development necessities. Although some assessments are little more than quick managerial assertion many need assessment that will help to shaped the objectives of training and development programs in local governments. Evan Berman et al. (2001) contend that at the local government level, needs assessments often can help units identify and receive adequate training and development, ensuring that they meet their staffing qualifications and program objectives. Further, local government in Nigeria should conduct needs assessments prior to undertaking work process improvements. Local governments should reengineer their service delivery process to make them more citizens oriented and to take advantage of new information technology capabilities. Local government should also involve employee in need assessment. By involving employees, it may be possible to identify those who are eager to learn new skills and to train at an early stage.

Senior public administrators at the local government, especially those that are not political appointees should regularly ask their employees about their training and development needs. This proactive orientation would demonstrate commitment to employees. In most cases the resulting training and development activity would likely increase employees contribution to unit objectives. The survey results show the immediate need for senior local government administrators to start to ask their employees whether they have any skill areas that they would like to improve on. Depending on the financial situation of the local government, there might be the need for cost sharing with employees' expenses in acquiring the needed training. Most State governments in Nigeria, however, have very liberal training and development budgets and offer public administrators almost unlimited education opportunities.

The objectives in extending microeconomic reform to the local governments in Nigeria are explicit and in themselves not controversial. Greater accountability, increase effectiveness, improved efficiency and preventing capture of program funding by sectional interests are generally supported. What is debated, especially with the new legislative institution of the Nigerian government, are the means or strategies to achieve these objectives. Thus, what can the new civilian administration do to increase performance in the public sector in order to improve Nigeria's national development in the twenty-first century? Several authors have focused on the use of citizens/government comment loop as a means to improve government performance. For example, Carter (1989), Johnson and Lewin (1990), and Johan Holmberg (1992) have proposed that state and local government are required to publish an annual report to their residents similar to the annual report published by corporations for their shareholders. They argue that the various constituents of the state and local jurisdiction have a legitimate need for information about the activities of their government. The rational for requiring state and local governments to publish an annual report is based on the need to provide state and local investors with information equivalent to that received by their corporate counterparts and on the need to achieve greater accountability of them to their public.

Quality standards and performance indicators for all aspects of the public sector need to be defined and valid consumer satisfaction measures developed. Qualitative research methods have been proposed as solutions to these measurements concerns. Avis, Metcalfe and Richards (1990) used in depth interviews and qualitative analysis to determine the relationship between patient expectations and their satisfaction with the health care service. They concluded that those expectations alone were not an adequate model for understanding patient satisfaction. They observe that the way in which patients evaluate care changed with additional contact, and that ultimately satisfaction was based on how well the practitioner assisted them. They suggested that qualitative approach to customer evaluation and the process of "surveying through customer's stories" provide invaluable information about the function of public service delivery.

As the local governments continue to experience widespread change, many administrators struggle with the problem of how to maintain or improve service quality. Developing appropriate quality indicators is a good place to start. Specially, the change in the public Electricity and water systems with their current change in mission- provide an opportunity for comprehensive organization re-engineering. These efforts would be well served by beginning with the understanding of consumer's perspective on service delivery.

As for people's rights, the commitment of governments and development agencies to popular participation as a necessary ingredient of sustainable development and accountability has been enshrined in the Arusha Declaration on Popular Participation in Development (1990) and the Manila Declaration on People's Participation and Sustainable Development (1989). Over and above these factors, there are arguments that are more fundamental for people now to be demanding their voice in the future. Both have to do with the physical limits to expansionism, which has historically been at the core of human development and which has provided an escape-valve when pressures have threatened to explore a society's stability (Holmberg, 1992).

The independent audit of local government's performance offers another strategy based on the public disclosure mechanism to achieve accountability, efficiency, and effectiveness on the part of governmental systems. In Nigeria, these audits should be designed to examine all phases of management activities with respect to financial compliance, economy and efficiency, effectiveness of results, and propriety of goals and means to achieve these goals (Henry, 1999; Mayne 1994; Metcalfe 1993). Financial compliance should involve a determination of whether (1) financial operations are properly conducted; (2) the financial reports of the audited entity are presented fairly, and (3) the entity has complied with applicable laws and regulations.

A separation of policy and operations will help local governments to improve performance. This implies that objectives are clearly defined within firm policy frameworks, and are based on neutral, non-conflicting values which would provide unquestionable and fixed standards for public managers to work towards. Their duty should be to execute the decisions of others. According to many current administrative reforms in the United States, Canada and France, Nigeria's local government public administrators should be expected to focus on achieving specific results and their performances should be assessed in relation to anticipated values of economy, efficiency, and effectiveness under a fixed framework of reference (Metcalfe and Richards, 1990). The assumption is that policy and objectives are given parameters transmitted to public managers from political levels. In this view, effective performance from public managers requires effort in both achieving and defining goals: the relevance and feasibility of anticipated achievements is also the responsibility of public managers. Officials formally influence outcomes through policy advice. This influence along with other sorts of informal influence on political levels helps to define goals.

Senior local government public administrator's active

participation in policy formulation is as important as the work they do on execution. Their role in reality should not just be to execute programs but also to help redesign them. Good performance might require redefining rather than achieving objectives. While this does not reduce the central role of politicians in setting policy direction and defining policy objectives, it ensures that they are assisted in this process by public sector managers.

Current administrative reform to improve performance in the local government should pay attention to value diversity. Designing performance monitoring and accountability systems in Nigeria's public sector cannot neglect the existence of multiple, and often conflicting, sources of performance legitimacy. Whose expectations should public managers respond to? Trends in administrative reform should highlight the importance of client's type accountability from public managers to citizens, as consumers or users of public services (Metcafe and Richards 1990:45). The notion that civil servant should be political neutral, anonymous and powerless agents of government ought to be removed from the facts of contemporary administrative life. Further, it will be better for Nigeria to cling to the concept of a neutral and anonymous public servant or the need to have an involved, but still professional, public servant.

Local government public administrators should also be encouraged to provide a stable environment in their various ministries or agencies. It should be clear that policies are built today within a very dynamic and uncertain framework. Public managers in Nigeria's local governments should therefore be concerned with designing and applying responses to new challenges. They should be responsible for improving the organizational capacity for adaptation: to do new things and work in different ways. Whether they realize it or not, they are finally responsible both for redefining problems they confront and for identifying the most relevant issues to be addressed, for example choosing priorities.

Finally, although most local government public administrators need to play the roles of administrator, producer, innovator, and integrator, the role they should be concerned with at each point in time should reflect the specific circumstances faced rather than be dictated by history or training. Performance monitoring and accountability in Nigeria in the twenty-first century for national development should be consistent and compatible with the public manager's roles and circumstances. Further improvements will depend on overcoming resistance to implementation within and outside public institutions, and adapting performance monitoring to accommodate organizational conditions, culture, and inter-organizational relations.

Institutional infrastructure needs to cover a wide range of requirements, such as finance, training, development of quality standards, generation of necessary information, promotion of performance monitoring and development of applied research in appropriate fields for industrial development. (1) Government should take steps to prescribe stiff penalties for individual and corporate entities that conceal information or refuse to respond to data request from the federal office of statistics. (2) The federal office of statistics needs to reorganize its data collecting and analysis methods in order to overcome the problem of substantial lags both in published data and time of their release. (3) Activities and programs of the various statistical agencies and research institutions should be properly coordinated. This will minimize duplication of efforts, ensure optimal utilization of scarce statistical manpower and material resources, and evolve nationally accepted standards of data collection, analysis and presentation to facilitate meaningful aggregation of state and local government statistics into a national data bank. (4) The federal office of statistics and other data collection agencies in Nigeria should be provided with adequate funding to conduct their essential field surveys and purchase facilities such as up-dated computers to process their data.

Conclusions

This chapter assesses the training needs of public administrators at the local government's level in Nigeria. It presents an argument that local government's public administrator need to be effectively trained in order for Nigeria to attain sustainable development. It further contends that incremental improvements in citizen participation in the local government public affairs would simply buttress a system that will stimulate the emergence of true participatory democracy. The chapter adopts the perspective of accountability and performance monitoring as the most fruitful way to correct the problems of maladministration and corruption in the public sector of Nigeria. The study argues that effective performance monitoring is essential to the achievement of public policy goals in Nigeria. We noted that although previous military leaders in Nigeria have pushed for better performance information as part of their reform efforts, such exercise was not pursued with adequate vigor and common sense, taking into account organizational and situational contingencies. Thus, local governments in Nigeria cannot contribute to sustainable development without effective rule of law in the nation.

The study suggests that local governments change that creates a culture of consumer-oriented service will go a long way in addressing the more egregious of recipient concerns of citizens. Providing staff training, development and performance standards that emphasize courteous treatment and involving recipients in case planning are important first steps. Likewise, the provision of on-time information to workers and streamlined organizational reporting should be considered in the re-engineering of public services during the new civilian administration of president Obasanjo. Addressing these concerns through performance standards and quality service indicators may result in better service delivery and outcomes in the public service of Nigeria. Indeed, these changes would improve consumer satisfaction ratings and redirect client worker efforts into more constructive areas.

The unsuccessful implementation of various policies and programs in Nigeria depend on the political will of the leaders and the encouragement of skilled manpower among Nigerians to execute the policy objectives. We realize that there are other prerequisites to effective public sector reform in the twenty-first century. Such prerequisites include political will, strong leadership, and a realistic strategy. In addition, we argue that without effective performance monitoring, public sector reform as it is envisaged today will not succeed. Finally, the study suggests the need to explore new data collection, analysis and computing methods and other relevant measures to improve government performance. These measures will help to shape accountability and redefine the limits of public sector performance in the new civilian administration so that Nigeria can be in the path of national development in the twenty-first century.

References

Aborishade, Oladimeji, and Robert Mundt. (1998). Politics in Nigeria. New York: Longman.

Adamolekun, L. (1986). Politics and Administration in Nigeria. Ibadan, Nigeria: University of Ibadan Press.

Adamolekun, Oladipo. (ed.) (1999). Public Administration in Africa: Main Issues and and Selected Countries Studies. Boulder, Colorado: Westview.

Adedeji, Adebayo. (1992). "Factors in the African Development Equation." African Journal of Public Administration and Management, Vol. 1, 1, (January), pp. 15-37.

Balogun, Jide and Gelase Mutahaba. (1999). "Redynamising the African Civil Service for the Twenty-first Century: Prospect for a Non-bureaucratic Structure." In Bureaucracy and the Alternatives in World Perspective edited by Keith Henderson and P. Dwivedi. New York: St. Martin's Press.

Berman, Evan, James Bowman, Jonathan West, Montgomery Van Wart. (2001). Human Resources Management in Public Service. Thousand Oaks, California: Sage.

Carter, N. (1989). "Performance Indicators: Backseat Driving or Hands off Control?" Policy and Politics. Vol. XVII, 2, pp. 13-38.

Egonmwan, J. (1991). Public Policy Analysis: Concept and Application. Benin City, Nigeria: Aka and Brothers Press.

Falola, T. (1996). Developing Planning and Decolonization in Nigeria. Westport, Connecticut: Greenwood.

Gboyega, Alex. (1999). "Intergovernmental Relations in Nigeria." In Nigeria: Politics and Governance 1986-1996 edited by Oyeleye Oyediran and Adigun Agbaje. Daka, Senegal: CODESRIA.

Guidelines for Local Government Reform. (1976). Government Printer, Kaduna, Nigeria.

Halperin, M. (1974). Bureaucratic Politics and Foreign Policy. Washington D.C. Brookings Institute.

Harris, Belle. (1980). "The Reorganization of Local Government Under the Military Rule in Nigeria, 1966-1974." In Administration for Development in Nigeria, edited by Paul Collins. Lagos, Nigeria: African Education Press.

Haruna, Peter. (2001). "Reflective Public Administration Reform: Building Relationships Bridging Gap in Ghana." African Studies Review, Vol. 44, 1, pp. 37-57.

Henry, N. (1999). Public Administration and Public Affairs. Upper Saddle River, New Jersey: Prentice-Hall.

Holmberg, Johan. (1992). Making Development Sustainable. Washington D.C.: Island Press.

Hulmes, Samuel, and Robert Ola. (1994). Government and Local Development in Western Nigeria. Benin City, Nigeria: Ambik Press.

Iyayi, Festus. (1986). "The Primitive Accumulation of Capital in a Neo-Colony: The Nigerian Case." Review of African Political

Economy. Vol. 35, pp. 36-51.

Johnson, R. and A. Lewin. (1990). "Management and Accountability Models of Public Sector Performance." In Public Management: The Essential Readings edited by S. Ott, A. Hyde and J. Shafritz. Chicago, Illinois: Nelson-Hall.

Mayne, J. (1994). "Utilizing Evaluation in Organizations: The Balancing Act." In Can Governments Learn? Comparative Perspectives on Evaluation & Organizational Learning edited by F. L. Leeuw, R. Rist and R. C. Sonnichsen. New Brunswick, New Jersey: Transaction.

Metcalfe, L. (1993). Public Management: From Imitation to Innovation. In Modern Government ed. by J. Kooiman, San Francisco, California: Sage.

Metcalfe, L. and S. Richards. (1990). Improving Public Management. London: Sage.

Olowu, Dele. (1991). Nigerian Public Administration: Past Present and Future. Ibadan, Nigeria: Shaneson C. J. Limited.

Olowu, Dele. (1999). "Public Service Delivery." In Public Administration in Africa: Main Issues and and Selected Countries Studies edited by Adamolekun, Oladipo, Boulder, Colorado: Westview.

Oyeleye, Oyediran, and Adigun Agbaje. (ed.) (1999). Nigeria: Politics of Transition and Governance 1986-1996. Dakar, Senegal: CODESRIA.

Sandel, Michael. (1996). Democracy's Discontent. Cambridge, Massachusetts: Belknap Press.

Sharp, Elaine. (1990). Urban Politics and Administration: From Service Delivery to Economic Development. New York: Longman.

Turner, Mark, and David Hulme. (1997). Governance, Administration and Development: Making the State Work. West Hartford, Connecticut: Kumarian Press.

Umeh, O. Joseph. (1992). "Capacity Building and Development Administration in Southern African Countries." International Review of Administrative Science, Vol. 58, 1, pp. 97-104.

Part III

Enhancing Public Management Capacities

9 Management of Local Raw Materials

Introduction

At the time of independence in 1960 there was great expectation of rapid economic and social growth in Nigeria. Four decades later these expectations have not been realized. There is a consensus among Nigeria scholars that the present economic development crisis in Nigeria resulted from the development policies in the 1960s, 1970s and 1980s. The development policies in the above three decades were centered on import substitution strategies rather than development industrials that could used the raw materials available in Nigeria.

The premise of attaining development is innovation. Such innovation should reflect changes in culture, organizational procedures, attitudes and beliefs. Felix Edoho (2001) and Al-Ali (1991) pointed out that more complex the innovation or technology, the more intricate the adjustment that are necessary to make a change or bring about technology development in a nation. Many industrialized nations have achieved development by technological breakthroughs and new markets, and innovative forms of organization have spurred growth and helped enhance the quality of life. What makes this possible? Most would agree that institutions and structures of governance play an important role. The quality of laws and political institutions in large measure determines whether innovators and their ideas are allowed into the marketplace, whether they can expect to gain from their labors, and whether they in turn can be expected to treat competitors and customers fairly. Political choices, embodied in constitutions, laws, politics, and conventions, set the rules of the game and empower their arbiters. The making and implementation of this choice is the labor of democracy, which is absolutely, absent in Nigeria. Further, if these choices are not contested and adjusted over time, or if they are subverted by corruption, innovation – and hence development

– grinds to a halt in favor of military regime and protected interests opposed to change.

In the early 1970s, a lot of effort was made to acquire technology through the importation of turn-key large scale projects like the petrochemicals, motor vehicle assembly, fertilizers, chemicals, cement production, iron and steel rolling industries. These industries were established for the purpose of technology development and utilization of the abundant raw materials among others.

Unfortunately, technologies have not been acquired as anticipated. Most of the industries still depend on imported inputs while capacity utilization is still low. For the last 10 years capacity utilization of these heavy industries have rarely gone beyond 40%, while the contribution of the manufacturing sector to the GDP has continued to decrease. Between 1970 and 1975, the growth rate in GDP was about 12%, by 1975 to 1980; it had dropped to just about 5%. Between 1980 and 1985, the rate dropped further to 2.5%. These were very unfortunate developments; something had to be done to control the trend.

Nigeria introduced some neoclassical economist policies in the mid-1980s to improve on its sustainable development growth rate. These policies were called of the Structural Adjustment/Make-or-Buy Policy in Nigeria. The objectives of the policy are those of technology development, economic reconstruction, and self-reliance. But Nigeria cannot achieve these goals because it failed to transfer technology without first establishing a domestic technological base. The major drain on the nation's foreign exchange and the cause of its foreign debt is still the importation of equipment, spare parts and raw materials. That situation has not altered since 1986. Nigeria is still dependent on imported technology. What the nation therefore needs is a political stability (democracy) and, Nigerian technologies that utilize locally available raw materials and resources to produce products that will satisfy its needs.

Appropriate technology for Nigeria should entail a shift in emphasis from imported machinery materials and spare parts to the production of equipment that can be made and used domestically from its own available raw materials. An appropriate technology would involve the use of the mineral resources (iron, tin, gold, columbite, limestone, and petroleum) that are abundantly available in Nigeria, as well as the countries skilled and unskilled labor force. It should avoid products that require scare resources and capital. Thus, an appropriate technology for Nigeria would be totally concerned with more local than foreign inputs.

The development of new technologies requires experience in the production of machine tools and other capital goods. It requires design and creative skills as well as applied research. An appropriate technology for Nigeria, however, also must be cost effective. This is because Nigeria is a very poor nation with a per capita income of hardly $250 a year. An appropriate technology for Nigeria must use local resources, must save foreign exchange, must be labor intensive must involve capital saving must and produce low-cost products.

Sustainable resource-based investments and technology development form part of the foundation of industrialization in any nation. To be industrialized and become self-sufficient in the production of some of its strategic needs, a country must be able to utilize its available human and material resources for the development of an appropriate technology base. One of the most realistic approaches for the development of technology base is the acquisition adaptation and development of technology. Once an appropriate technology base has been developed, technologies developed can be therefore utilized for both civil and military applications.

In order to develop an appropriate technology base for this country. The concept of establishing small-scale resource-based industries through indigenous fabrication and installation of process equipment, commercialization of research inventions, through the establishment of pilot projects and guided development of the nation's raw materials base must be given adequate attention.

In this chapter Nigeria's major raw material resources are highlighted. In particular the possible uses of some of these raw materials by the Nigeria industries are briefly discussed. Some brief comments are also made on development programs that aimed at formulating and implementing strategies for the eventual industrialization of Nigeria. The government in particular has a very important role to play in the formulation and implementing the program. The chapter also stresses that Nigeria, as in most developed countries, would have introduced programs of technological development in the private sector. It is the private sector that was utilized by most developed nations as their foundation for industrialization. I believe that such a norm cannot be different in Nigeria, the government and indeed the private sector in Nigeria can be the pivot of technological development.

Raw Materials and Sustainable Development

The high price of imported raw materials can justify the research for local raw materials and the improvement of production techniques in order to protect the primary commodity. Substitution effects depend also on the nature of primary commodities whether they are agricultural or mining, are used as intermediate products or directly as final products. When the primary commodity is used as intermediate product in a process of transformation or manufacture, it is the market price that determines conditions of substitution either in the level of technology of manufacture or in the change of consumer behavior. If the product price is sufficiently high, it will justify the cost of the technological research that will end in marketing of a product whose relative price will be competitive.

For a country with Nigeria's level of raw material endowments, its strategies for industrial development must be grounded in the utilization of local raw materials. Efficient utilization of these raw materials will impact positively on the industrial development of our country. It is therefore expedient to discuss at this forum, the raw materials available in Nigeria. It is therefore expedient to discuss at this forum, the raw materials available in Nigeria.

The raw material resources available in the country can be classified into agricultural and mineral raw materials.

Agricultural Raw Materials

Agriculture accounts for about 70% of total employment in Nigeria. The country's varying vegetation from the rain forest to sub-Sahara and semi-arid allows for cultivation of numerous agricultural commodities, which have, extensive industrial uses to meet their national demand. They are grouped as follows: (1) Cereals (2) Legumes (3) Roots and Tubers (4) Fruits and Vegetables (5) Tree crops (6) Industrial crops (7) Forest and shrubs (8) Livestock and fisheries. All the crops and animal products indicated could be utilized as industrial raw materials. The ultimate product obtained is a function of the processing method adopted. In addition to these crops, wood is also discussed as one of the major raw materials obtained from Nigeria's forests. The country's high forest reserve in the rain forest zone contains timber species of high commercial value.

Livestock and fisheries constitute another major agricultural produce. They comprise cattle, rabbits, pigs, sheep, goat, fishes, shrimps, etc. The country can indeed produce a variety of agricultural commodities, which can support the establishment and operation of various manufacturing industries. The task of processing the country's food crops to diets acceptable to the people must be borne by the private sector.

The locally cultivated crops with investment opportunities are cocoa, rubber, sorghum, ginger, benniseed (sesame), sheanut, cassava, yam, cashew, coffee, cotton, sugar cane, and fruits. These crops have found application as raw materials (inputs) in the following sectors: (1) Chemicals and Pharmaceutical (2) Food, Beverage and Tobacco (3) Wood and Wood Product (4) Pulp, Paper and Paper Products, Printing and Publishing (5) Textiles, Wearing Apparel, Leather and Leather Products, and (6) Motor Vehicles and Miscellaneous Assembly.

Some of these agricultural commodities should be accorded attention in the consideration of self-sufficiency for the food needs of the country. These commodities can indeed contribute significantly to the country's economic development.

Mineral Raw Materials

Records available reveal strong indications of the occurrence in Nigeria of a variety of minerals of strategic importance and in commercial quantities. These mineral raw materials can be sub-divided into non-metallic, metallic, precious retails, gemstones and decorative stones, energy and fuel minerals.

Non-Metallic Minerals

Many industrial minerals have been reported in various parts of the country. These include:

Limestone, dolomite, kaolin, barytes, feldspar, salt, bentonite, phosphate, marble, soda ash, diatomite, quartz and silica sand, gypsum, talc, sillimanite, kyanite, etc. Even though a lot of work is being undertaken to develop the industrial mineral deposits, local demand far outstrips supply for minerals such as (a) Limestone/Marble (b) Kaolin (c) Barytes (d) Bentonite (e) Salt, and (f) Phosphate.

Salt

Crude salt is dominantly composed of the chloride of sodium and it is probably the most widely used industrial chemical. Common salt is used in the dairy and pickling industries, preservation of meat and fish, water treatment, and production of chemicals.

In Nigeria, the possible sources of crude salt are the brine springs and lakes. The concentration of salt in these springs has been estimated at 15 to 30 parts per thousand. The saline springs occur within the narrow belt, which extends in an NNS-SSW direction from Gombe to Afikpo, along the plains of the Benue and Cross River drainage system. Most of the brines contain high proportions of sodium chloride, with subsidiary amounts of sulphate, nitrates and bicarbonates. A total reserve of about 1.5 billion tonnes has been estimated. The average national demand is about 500,000 tonnes per annum.

Based on geophysical survey by the Nigeria Mining Corporation, the Benue Trough is also an attractive area for exploration of sedimentary salt deposits. This was confirmed in the northwest of Makurdi (Oku Lake) where a lenticular saline structure of about 600m thick has been explored. Previous investigations have revealed that there are also prospects along the Nigeria coastline with high concentrations of salt, especially in the Badagry area.

Geographically, the brine occurrences in Nigeria can be divided into two broad groups:

1. North of River Benue: the Lafia salt areas include:-
   - A. The Azara-Afri-Ribi salt springs and the Awe-Keana-Kange salt springs;
   - B. The Mutum Daya, Gyakan, Todi and Ayaba salt springs in Adamawa and Taraba States.
2. South of River Benue: the Abakaliki-Okposi salt areas include:-
   - A. Enyigba, Ameri, Ameka, Ikwo-Abakaliki in /Enugu state;
   - B. Okpoma, Gabu, Ijebu, Onyi near Ogoja, Cross River state;
   - C. Akwana, Arufu and Takum in Taraba state; and
   - D. Uburu Ugwaneke, Afikpo in Imo state.

Phosphate

Phosphate is a major fertilizer mineral of great significance to plant food. Phosphate rock refers to a mineral assemblage that occurs naturally with an exceptionally high concentration of phosphate minerals. Occurrences of phosphate rock are known in Sokoto, Abia, and Ogun states. The deposits of phosphatic beds in the Sokoto embayment represent Southwards extension of the deposits in the Niger Republic, which occur in an area within the geological feature termed the Illummeden Basin.

The deposit of phosphate in Sokoto State was reported in 1948. It occurs in the Sokoto Group of sediments, which consist of the Dange, Kalambaisa and Gamba formation. The specific areas of concentration of phosphate modules in Sokoto basin include Dange, Gidan, Bauchi, Illela, Gada, Wurno, and Gwadabawa. Recent pitting and experimental mining in Sokoto basin carried out by Nigeria Mining Corporation, in Zorno, Shagari, and Gwadabawa areas yielded average weight % P2O5 of 34.50 and 36.25%. This compares favorably with the phosphate at Hahotoe, Togo with 36.6%.

The occurrence of phosphatic beds around Ifo and Karo in Ogun State was first reported in 1921 and since then most of the exploratory activity has been conducted by the Geological surveys of Nigeria (GSN). Three types of phosphate-granular, nodular and vesicular forms are reported to occur with an average weight P2O5 percent of 34.00 percent. Very little work has been done on the deposits reported to occur in Abia State and Ifon, Ondo State. Other minor deposits occur around Akpet central and Ugep, Northwest of Calabar and in Lokoja. The actual reserves of the phosphate deposits in the country have not been fully established.

The phosphate processing plant established by RMRDC, which is located in Sokoto State, has an installed capacity of about 15,000 tones per year. The national demand of the processed phosphate by the local industries is about 200,000 tones per year, and to meet this demand, fourteen of such industries are required to be established in the country. Investors are therefore encouraged to set up similar plants to process phosphate for fertilizer production.

Metallic Minerals

Usually the sources of metals are the mineral ores, some of which are known to occur in commercial quantities in Nigeria. These include iron ore, tin ore (cassiterite) lead ore (galena), zinc ore (sphalerite), copper ore (chalcopyrite), tungsten ore (wolframite), molybdenum ore (molybdenite), etc. The reserves of most of these minerals are not yet known. However, it is important to state that these metals have a variety of industrial uses. They are extensively used in metallurgy, casting, smelting, alloying, coinage, building, fabrication, and hardware industries. Nigerian deposit of such metals in (a) Lead/Zinc (b) Iron ore (c) Cassiterite (tin ore) (d) Columbite, and (e) limestone.

Columbine

Columbine is one of the ferro-alloy minerals added to molten iron to obtain specific properties in steel. Columbite, tantalite, ilmerite and zircon are found associated in nature with tin ore (cassiterite). They are known to have large reserves. Nigeria was once accounting for 90% of the world production of columbite while the exploration of zircon and ilmenite as main products has not really commenced.

Gemstones

Among the gemstones found in Nigeria are emeralds, sapphire, aquamarine, amethyst, ruby, Flour-span, garnet, topaz, tourmaline, and rock crystals. These minerals occur mostly in Bauchi, Kaduna, Plateau, Kwara, Kogi, Ondo, Ekiti, Osun, Oyo, Taraba and Borno States. Gemstones are currently mined in the country but almost all of the raw output is imported. The Nigeria varieties of ruby, aquamarine, sapphire, emerald, green tourmaline and red garnet have been classified to be among the world's best. The prevalence of illegal mining and exploitation makes it almost impossible to assess the production of these gemstones. Since there are very few lapidaries (gemstone cutting and polishing factories) in Nigeria, almost all the mined gemstones are exported, and in most cases, in the raw form.

There is the dire need for private investors to establish lapidaries in order to add value to the gemstones before exportation. The local market for polished gemstones is also sizeable.

Precious Metals

Deposits of gold have been reported in various parts of the country. Gold mining activities started in Niger State area since the early part of this century. It is one of the major gold area producing areas of North-western Nigeria. The mining activity is restricted to the Chanchanga area to the South of Minna. Recently, the Nigeria Mining Corporation (NMC) carried out a systematic exploration for gold in an area of 200,000 sq. km of the schist belt of Western half of Nigeria. The results indicated that areas, which were thought to have been mined out, still contain some good quantities of gold. Also, some areas, which were thought to be non-mineralized, were found to contain gold. Investors are invited to undertake surveys in areas of known occurrences and commence exploitation thereafter.

Decorative Stones

The potentials for the occurrences of abundant assemblages of crystalline solid rocks with appropriate characteristics for the establishment of variable rock-polishing industry have been reported within the crystalline basement terrain in Nigeria. The rock units include large deposits of granites of different compositions, charnockites, diorites, quantzites, granodiorites, pegmatites, sysnites, gabbros, dolerites, nignabites, phorphyrites, gneisses, and amphibolites. These materials possess color and structure that impact a particular aesthetic appearance to these stones when polished. Crushed stones and aggregates of these rocks are also used in the building construction and civil engineering projects. The lithological characteristics usually considered include textural and petrographic features and other physical parameters like strength, porosity, abrasiveness, durability and lustre. Considerable reserves of up to several hundreds of millions of tonnes of raw materials could be exploited from the available discrete rock deposits within the country. These deposits of rock are commonly blasted indiscriminately to provide construction materials without given adequate attention to rock polishing. Most of the decorative stones and items used in Nigeria are currently supplied through importation. The need for relevant evaluation of the crystalline rocks in the country, especially, in the area of rock polishing is considered exceeding worthwhile and desirable. With available relevant manpower locally, government and private entrepreneurs to develop and sustain a viable rock-polishing industry in Ondo State and other parts of the country where resources abound are making efforts.

Industrial Specification for Raw Materials

One critical factor in the consideration of suitability of raw materials for use by industries is the quality or the extent to which a batch of raw material meet the preferences of the particular industry. It is a factor that has been taken for granted by suppliers but which has a strong determinant in the decision by the user to project or accepts a supply or sample of raw materials.

This represents a communication gap between the user and the supplier of raw materials. It is a gap that must be filled in order to ensure that manufacturers on one hand utilize local raw materials, while suppliers of the raw materials also try to meet the requirements of specific industries. This was another challenge, which RMRDC took up. The council's effort in the direction is already making impact on the industry.

The council responded to the problem by undertaking a survey to determine the specific needs of the quality of the raw materials. The data collected was compiled and published as a book titled "Handbook on Specification for Raw Materials by Nigeria's Industries".

Raw Materials Research and Development

Felix Edoho (2000) and Zeleny (1986) desegregated technology into functional categories: hardware (physical components and logical layout); software (know-how of tasks to achieve goals and objective); brainware (application and justification of hardware/software deployment, the know-what and know-why of technology – what to employ, how, when and why); and support net (complex network that supports the proper use and functioning of a given hardware – the unity of hardware, software, and brainwave. Also, Felix Edoho (2000) identified four components of technology: technoware, (object-embodied); humanware (person-embodied); inforware (information-based); and orgaware (institution-embodied). A major factor that would make all these types of technology possible in Nigeria is research and development. The Nigerian Raw Materials Research and Development Council (RMRDC) were established in the late 1980s. It has the sole aim of stimulating industrial development through the utilization of local raw materials. To achieve this objective, the council embarked on various programs, some of which included the following: (1) Techno-economic surveys; (2) Research and development; (3) Pilot plant projects; (4) Investment promotion; (5) Model factories; and (6) National Science and Technology Data Bank.

The Nigerian government should develop and implement policies that will strengthen its science and engineering process through international cooperation. Although, the Nigerian raw material research and development council is main focus of R & D center in the nation, the nation could form joint ventures with other developed nations in the process of world class R & D. This should be aimed at achieving or sustaining economic advantage. Research alliances can coexist with the growing technological competition, but the outlook for enduring scientific success must be guarded unless governments smooth the search for shared benefits. A high priority should be placed on assuring the uninhibited flow of scientific information and skilled professionals in Nigeria.

Techno-Economic Surveys

The first program executed by the council at inception was the Techno-economic survey of Nigeria's raw materials. The survey covered the ten industrial sectors in accordance with the classification of the Manufacturers Association of Nigeria (MAN). The survey, which was updated in 1991, is again being updated in 1996. The purpose of the survey was to obtain up-to-date information on the available raw materials, the quality specification required by industry, problems associated with local sourcing, their level of utilization.

The surveys afforded users the opportunity of identifying the various types of raw materials in the country, the traditional uses, processing technologies, requisite machinery and equipment and market opportunities.

Research and development (R & D) is very crucial for the utilization of local raw materials. RMRDC promotes innovative and applied R & D that will facilitate efficient and rapid production of goods and services based on local resources. The council has sponsored many R & D projects over the past eight years. Some of the sponsored projects have been commercialized while many others have been upgraded to the pilot plant stage. At this stage, the technical feasibility and economic viability of the projects would be established. The projects are thereafter promoted among investors.

The council embarked on the pilot plant program for the commercialization of research results. The commercialization of R & D results did not appear to have been accorded adequate attention in the nation's development plan. Much of the results of both basic and applied research from our institutes, higher institutions and private individuals, though very valuable, have been left on the shelf for years without being commercialized. It thus became imperative that a program approach be adopted to facilitate the adoption or commercialization of locally developed technologies. The council's response to this challenge was the establishment of pilot plants with the aim of demonstration the technical feasibility and economic viability of the projects. The following pilot plant projects have so far been established: (1) Full-fat Soya bean extrusion; (2) Castor oil production; (3) Sorghum malting; (4) Organo-mineral fertilizer production; (5) Smoked-fish production; (6) Coal briquetting and carbonization; and (7) Benniseed oil.

This is a program designed by the council to stimulate private investment in resource-based projects. Through the joint venture program, the council is able to assist companies by:

1. Taking equity in the venture to cover such aspects as equipment procurement;
2. Securing steady supply of raw materials for production;
3. Liaising with funding agencies to secure working capital;
4. Brokering the procurement equipment for the owners of projects, and;
5. Seeking private equity shareholders in projects, which require capital injection.

Private Sector and Local Raw Materials Development

The private sector in Nigeria perform several types of international operations spanning high-technology manufacturing, sophisticated engineering service, science-intensive training, foreign investment, development cooperation, and exchanges of executives. Naturally, thousands of businesses, universities, and nonprofit agencies could not and should not be "managed" by any single part of the government. But their goals and ideas could be surveyed and assessed more perceptively by the government agencies such as the trade ministry or the raw material R & D council that clearly have the leading role in each field. Private actions will inevitably be the leading edge of Nigeria's foreign relations during its sustainable development process. Freer market will open, newer technologies will move more quickly, and the already rising mobility of people will increase further. The Nigerian government has a crucial role to play in facilitating these trends: encouraging cooperation between the nation's public and private sectors. The government also has to foster reciprocal access by the private sector to other countries, and smoothing out the inevitable inconsistencies among international standards and regulations.

At the present time private sector involvement is the development of local raw materials in Nigeria has been very low over the years. Whereas a good number of manufacturing companies are involved in industrial activities which inevitably require most of the raw materials available in Nigeria as basic inputs, few of the companies are directly involved in he processing/development of these raw materials to the required stage. The attitude of the private sector towards local raw material processing in Nigeria is affected by a number of factors. Ranging from lack of infrastructure, high cost of investment, lack of appropriate processing technology, non-availability of the required steel products to facilitate local fabrication of machinery/equipment, lack of funding and high cost of funds, to preference for imported mineral raw materials.

The private sector should adopt a policy aimed at discouraging the importation of processed raw materials in order to encourage the processing of the available local raw materials. It is only by an expressed willingness of the private sector to tackle the teething problems that any government policy in this direction would work.

Government Policies and Raw Materials

The current government policy supports both private and government participation in local raw material processing. There is the need for close co-operation between Federal and State agencies, and other interested parties involved in local raw material processing in order to ensure optional utilization of the local raw material resources. Beside raw materials, plant and machinery, and market, the development and processing of raw materials can be facilitated by the provision of adequate and efficient infrastructure facilities such as roads, electricity, water supply, telephone etc. Various tiers of government need to provide improved infrastructure support services in order to stimulate investor's interest and to facilitate the development of local raw materials for industries.

The president of Nigeria and the various ministries and government agencies should also encourage mainstreaming of international science and technology issues in the programs and budgets of the mission agencies. A first step could be a directive to head of ministries and agencies to focus on technology development that would use existing raw materials in the nation. Such a Presidential statement could call on each ministry and agency to review:

1. The adequacy of the international office in the agency to handle technical issues.
2. The sensitivity of relevant parts of the ministry to international developments and issues.
3. The quality of ongoing coordination with state Science and technology projects, and other agencies and universities, taking major past cases as illustrations of problems and opportunities.
4. The adequacy of the government's technical personnel abroad to serve the agency's needs.
5. The resources and barriers along the path to strengthened performance linking the agency's science and technology missions with Nigeria's international activities and foreign policy.

Conclusion

This chapter has examined the nature of raw material development in Nigeria. It argues that good organization in the process of technology development does not insure successful policy, nor does poor organization preclude it. But steadily and powerfully, the organizational patterns of the executive branch of government should be able to influence and effectively encourage both the public and private sectors to use the raw materials within the nation first in their bit for future technology development.

Among the major political and economic crisis examined in this chapter, four things stand out: (1) the chronic political instability in the country (2) the high rate of inflation and the serious banking problems (3) the continuing dependence on external raw materials and technology, and (4) the increasing burden of an ever-expanding foreign and public debt. In sum, Nigeria suffers from extreme political, economic and social distress. One question raised by this crisis is how can Nigeria begin to rectify its many faults? The nation cannot build a self-reliant economy or a resilient, integrated society in the absence of a stable, people-centered government. Nor is it helpful to blame the British and the colonial legacy for the contemporary predicament. Nigeria's record over the past thirty years is a wretched one, and its future prospects are not promising.

What can be done, knowing that the military and bureaucratic elites that bear major responsibility for the dislocation and prevailing malaise will continue to dominate the country's policy and decision-making processes?

It can be hypothesized that economic development and social change, for example, providing for the nation's well-being as well as reconciling tribal and ethnic differences, cannot wait for political modernization to precede them. Denied other options or alternatives, Nigeria is forced to utilize its existing political and administrative institutions in the quest for a healthier economy and balanced social order.

Given the realities of Nigerian political life, it seems appropriate and useful to examine aspects of the country's Structural Adjustment/Make-or-Buy Policy. Such an examination can perhaps inform the observer as to whether or not the higher civil-military decision-making apparatus can unify its capabilities and, thereby, direct the nation along a more positive path.

Given the nature of the Nigerian dilemma described in this study, do the Structural Adjustment/Make-or-Buy Policy provide a vehicle wherein Nigeria's army junta and professional bureaucracy can, at a minimum, reverse the country's economic slide into deeper economic depression? Nigeria has the necessary elements in skilled and energetic people as well as natural resources, to again begin the process of national renewal and reconstruction. The Structural Adjustment/Make-or-Buy Policy offers insight into the leadership's ability to properly utilize those resources, and hence, to steer a course that not only promotes civil-military cooperation, but also promises a way out of a deepening national problem.

Accountability must be strengthened in Nigeria. Laws and ethics codes have proved insufficient because of lack of appropriate institutions to implement them. Moral awakenings do occur, but seldom by the current design of public leaders in Nigeria. If the nation cannot engineer incorruptible officials and citizens, Nigeria can nonetheless foster competition, change incentives, enhances accountability: in short, fix the systems that breed corruption. This is not easy. But three points deserve emphasis. First, successful examples do exist of reducing corruption, at the level of firms, cities, projects, ministries, and entire nations. Second, many of these success stories contain common themes. Third, the fight against corruption can be the leading edge to much broader and deeper reforms of government.

The raw materials resource endowments of Nigeria are such that should launch the country into the elite group of industrialized countries. In order to realize this dream, there are basic requirements such as the flow of information, international collaboration and active participation of local and foreign investors in the country's economy.

The country needs to share in the experience of other countries and promote trade and investments. It must be emphasized that a larger proportion of the country's resources is yet to be exploited. The challenges of development are one, which calls for discipline, dedication and a judicious use of the resource endowments. It is a challenge, which both the public and private sectors of the economy must take up with great determination for success.

Finally, the government ministries, agencies, universities and the private sector must draw upon Nigeria's strengths consistently, and understand its weakness analytically in order to correct them constructively. These public and private sectors must help Nigeria deal with fields in which it choices not to be the leader.

References

Adubifa, Akin. (1990). Technology Policy in Nigeria. Nigeria, Ibadan: NISER Publication.

Al-Ali, S. (1991). "Technological Dependence in Developing Countries: A Case Study of Kuwait." Technology in Society, Vol. 13, pp. 267-277.

Biggs, T., M. Shah and P. Srivastava. (1995). "Technological Capability and Learning in Africa Enterprises." World Bank Technical paper. No. 288, Washington DC: World Bank.

Crane, Alan and Joy Dunkerley. (1994). "The Role of Technology Transfer in the Transition of Sustainability." In Depth, A Journal for Values and Public Policy, Vol. 4, 5, pp. 85-104.

Dibie, Robert. (1997). "Business-Government Relations and Technology Development in Nigeria." Journal of Developing Societies. Vol 13, 2, pp. 195-207.

Dike, Enwere. (1994). Economic Transformation in Nigeria: Growth, Accumulation and Technology. Zaria, Nigeria: Amadu Bello University Press.

Edoho, Felix. (2000). "Transferring Management Technology to Sub-Saharan Africa." Proceedings of the Global Challenge of African Business and Economic Development. International Conference April 11-14, pp. 120-125.

Evans, Donald. (1984). "Appropriate Technology and its Role in Development." In Appropriate Technology in Third World

Development, Edited by Pradip K.Ghosh Connecticut: Greenwood Press.

Fadahunsi, Akin, and B. U. N. Igwe (1989). Capital Goods and Technological Change and Accumulation in Nigeria. Senegal, Dakar: CODESRIA.

Fransman, Martin. (1985). "The Role of Science in Technology Transfer." Research Policy, Vol. 12, 5, October Issue, pp. 287-96.

Girvan, N. P., and G. Marcell. (1990). Overcoming Technological Dependecy: The Case of Electric in Jamaica Limited. World Development Vol. 18, pp. 91-107.

Ihonvbere, Julius O. (1994). Nigeria: The Politics of Adjustment and Democracy. New Brunswick: Transaction Publishers.

Jequier, N. (1976). Appropriate Technology Problems and Promises. Paris: Organization for Economic Cooperation and Development Publication.

Kaplinsky, Raphael. (1990). The Economies of Small: Appropriate Technology in a Changing World. Washington DC: Appropriate Technology International.

Lall, S. et al. (1994). Technology and Enterprise Development: Ghana under Structural Adjustment. New York: St. Martin's Press.

Lall, S. et al. (1998). Opening Up: The technological Response to Import Liberialization in Sub-Saharan Africa, London: Macmillan.

Lall, S. and S. Wangwe. (1998). "Industrial Policy and Industrialization in Sub-Saharan Africa." Journal of African Economics, Vol. 7, Supplement 1. (June), pp. 70-107.

Lipumba, Nupguyuru. (1994). Africa Beyond Structural Adjustment. Washington DC: Oversea Development Council.

Maravcsik, Michael. (1983). "The Role of Science in Technology Transfer." Research Policy, Vol. 12, 5, October Issue, pp. 287-96.

Myint, Hla. (1971). Economic Theory and Undeveloped Countries. London: Oxford University Press.

Obasanjo, Olusegun, and Akin Mabogimje. (1991). Elements of Development in Nigeria. Lagos, Nigeria: C & A Publishers.

OECD. (1992). Technology and the Economy: The Key Relationships. Paris: OECD.

Olukoshi, Adebayo. (1992). The Politics of Structural Adjustment in Nigeria. London: James Carrey Publishers.

Onimode, Bade. (1991). Alternative Development Strategies for Africa. London: Institute for African Alternatives.

Phillips, Adedotun, and Eddy Ndekwu. (1992). Structural Adjustment Program in a Developing Economy: The Case of Nigeria. Ibadan, Nigeria: Okley Limited.

Picard, Louis. (1994). Policy Reform for Sustainable Development in Africa. The Institute Imperative. Boulder, Colorado: Lynne Rienner Publishers.

Sachs, Ignacy. (1979). "Controlling Technology for Development." Development Dialogue, Vol. 1 (April) Issue.

Sahn, David. 1994. Adjusting to Policy Failure in Africa Economies. Ithaca, New York: Cornell University Press.

Sandbrook, Richard. (1993). The Politics of African's Recovery. New York: Cambridge University Press.

Scapple, Karrin. (1998). "Cooperation and Conflict over Natural Resources." In Introducing Global Issues, edited by Michael Snarr and Neil Snarr. Boulder, Colorado: Lynne Rienner Press.

Stewart, F. and G. Ranis. (1990). "Macro-Policies for Appropriate Technology: Synthesis of Findings." In Appropriate Technology edited by F. Stewart and G. Ranis. New York: Cambridge University Press.

Wangwe, S. M. (1995). Exporting Africa: Technology, Trade and Industrialization in Sub-Saharan Africa, UNU/INTECH studies in New technology and Development, London: Routledge.

World Bank. (1999). Human Development Index. New York: Oxford University Press.

World Bank. (1999). World Development Report. New York: Oxford University Press, p. 296.

Yannkey, G. S. (1987). International Patents and Technology Transfer to Less Developed Countries. Brookfield, Vermont: Gower.

Zeleny, M. (1989). High Technology Management. Human Systems Management. Vol. 6, pp. 109-120.

10 Technology Policy and Sustainable Development

Introduction

In the twenty-first century technology will be very important to the people of Nigeria. The term technology covers not only technical subjects taught in universities and equipment developed using those disciplines, but also the expertise necessary to perform most functions in a modern enterprise. To fully understand technology, one requires the knowledge of technology itself. This knowledge includes technical skills, ideas, and equipment that organizations apply to manufacture and market goods, or deliver services. Technology is arguably the single most profound influence on people and society. The daily lives of the people in Nigeria are largely defined by the technologies used for housing, transportation, office and factory work, health, entertainment, and communications. Industrial development was expected by Nigeria's policy makers to lead the transformation out of low technology, productivity and slow growth economies into those that were dynamic and modern. But this is yet to happen in the sub-region.

The logic of exporting technology from those who have it to others who do not have it is appealing. Most Nigerian leaders think that the rise of manufacturing activity bring about modern technology and new skills to production and management. They thought technology would transform the structure of comparative advantage like in other regions, which have used the process to gain structural change and sustainable growth. Past industrial programs have tended to concentrate on expanding manufacturing capacity without building an institutional setup and expanding local capabilities to effectively utilize the capacity created. Most of the industries developed in Nigeria after independence have been capital-intensive, established as turnkey projects by foreign firms with little or no export of technological capacity to local managers and technicians.

One of the major problems confronting research in Nigeria, is the dearth of reliable data, statistics and documentation on practically all aspects of national life. Despite these shortcomings it is ironic that the public institutions whose work suffers considerably from this, and which continue to acknowledge and advocate this fact, nonetheless make so little effort to correct the situation. In the past, industrialization policies and strategies in Nigeria have discriminated against small and medium size industries, and as a result they have lacked access to credit and foreign exchange.

Nigeria is gradually beginning to recognize the vital role of science and technology as the primary vehicle for promoting development. But this recognition has not been matched with investment in the necessary resources, both human and material. Funding of science and technology in the nation has never attracted any significant priority, and has often occurred as a result of external intervention rather than a conviction of its appropriateness and need. Further, science and technology has remained mostly in the public domain where it is largely perceived in terms of establishment of institutions for research or for development of technical manpower. In the latter case, emphasis is usually placed on formal technical training rather than on skill formation, practical experience and innovation. Unfortunately, policy makers in Nigeria continue to have a hazy conception of this role of science and technology and have thus failed to optimize its use for national development planning. As a result of this problem, many African scholars have concluded that there is an evident lack of political consciousness and commitment to the development of science and technology (Adubifa 1990; Edoho 2000; Lall and Wangwe 1998).

Improved technology is one of the critical factors needed for Nigeria to become industrialized, a goal that virtually all seem to share. However, the structure of industrial activity in the sub-region remains underdeveloped. The nation is dominated by the processing of local natural resources and simple consumer goods industries, unlike those in Asia and Latin America that have broadened and deepened into a range of more complex activities. Therefore, industries in the nation have failed to achieve structural transformation, export dynamism or technical efficiency, producing little of the growth and externalities that were expected of it.

Some scholars are concerned that Nigeria is on a collision course with re-source constraints and environmental degradation. This concern has led to the concept of sustainability, to ensure that future generations in Nigeria are not deprived of a critical part of their heritage. However, sustainability is a complex and ambiguous concept that is difficult to translate into actual practice (Lipumba, 1994).

This chapter examines the problem of technology development in Nigeria. It argues that in the process of seeking technology; the Nigerian governments should endeavor to balance industrial promotion and environmental conditions in order to achieve sustainability. The chapter is more concerned with technology that is neither indigenous nor self-starting. Exporting appropriate technology will provide Nigeria with the requisite level of skills to make rational investment decisions and further lead to sustainable growth and development. Suggestions are made on how Nigeria can improve its technology in the twenty-first century.

Sustainability and Technology Development

Technology generally refers to various elements of productive knowledge, which help to transform materials into goods, create new and improved products, and develop better and efficient ways of providing services. The evolution of technology in Nigeria has elements of history and natural endowment, elements of culture and national discipline. It also has factors of environment and collective national aspiration, elements of knowledge and resourcefulness, and factors of politics and ideology. Thus technology can be seen as the interaction of science and society. On the other hand, sustainability, or sustainable development, is "a process of change in which the exploitation of resources, direction of investments, the orientation of technological development and institutional change are all in harmony and enhance both current and future potential to meet human needs and aspirations" (Biggs et al. 1995; Lall et al. 1998). In developing nations, sustainable development means finding alternatives to many of the development techniques that are currently depleting their resources. Karrin Scapple (1998) pointed out that sustainable development in the developed nations simply means reducing consumption. This would require developing plans for more efficient use of the current resources, as well as exploiting more fully, solar, wind, and thermal energy sources. Both Nigeria and western industrial nations could cooperate to develop policies that are more efficient and that ensure the provisions of basic human needs around the world.

Sustainability may appear to some, particularly in Nigeria, to be an abstract concept, of interest primarily to industrialized countries that can afford to worry about such things. They may feel that the first order of business is to develop, then to clean up later. However, the problems that have led to interest in sustainable development apply to all countries. Polluted air and water can significantly slow development for example, by causing health problems or reducing agricultural production. In addition, global warming is likely to hurt Nigeria at least as much as others because highly stressed and barely adequate agricultural systems will have great difficulty adapting to climate changes. Therefore, Nigeria's government has an interest in positioning its development in accordance with sustainability.

The "missing component" model is predicated on the idea that development can be effected by identifying the critically weak or missing element in developing a country's assets and by subsequently providing this component (Myint, 1971). Such missing elements typically are identified as domestic saving, foreign exchange, education and technology. The capacity of technology to transform nature in Nigeria for the purpose of development is such that the question of who controls technology is central to who controls development (Edoho, 2000: 120).

The problem with a development strategy that emphasizes the acquisition of foreign exchange is that it leads to foreign monetary control and over capitalization at the expense of a more balanced use of domestic resources in sub-Saharan Africa. Resulting negative effects may include excess production of labor as a substitute for capital. This latter condition is the basis for much of the argument supporting the appropriate technology concept. The efficacy of technology in the drive for development is of paramount, importance. Ultimately, it will prove to be the means by which developing nation like in sub-Saharan Africa can lift them from under development and achieve the goals that are exemplified in the basic human need strategy.

According to Lall et al. (1994), the successful transfer of new technology to developing nations has to include major elements of capacity building; simply improving equipment and operating instructions, patents, designs or blueprints does not ensure that the technology will be properly used. Lall et al. (1994) and Crane and Dunkerley (1994) pointed out that three functional categories of technological capacities are very important for developing nations to successfully transfer technology. The functional categories include Investment capability (the skills and information needed to identify and determine feasible investment); production capability (the skills, knowledge and experience imperative for running an operation and improving the plant); and linkage capabilities (skills needed to establish, maintain and produce technological links with other firms and institutions).

The use of any particular technology is not an end in itself. The criterion for an appropriate technological choice must be found in the essential goals and processes of development in Nigeria. Jequier (1976), and Crane and Dunkerley (1994) contend that in describing the situations in which technology is applied defines the private and public aspects. Private technology is that which is utilized in a small, domestically owned enterprise. It is related to the production of consumer goods, and its introduction is largely a decision by the individual entrepreneur. "Public technologies" are represented by the large industrial firms that produce consumer goods or capital equipment and by the national institutions that supply basic services, such as railway transportation, flood control and irrigation systems, power grids, higher education and banking and credit systems. Thus, the concept of technological progress in Nigeria implies new techniques that are at a higher level than the existing national standards, but need not represent the world's peak. This is because Nigeria is just beginning its stages of industrial and agricultural modernization.

According to Yarkey (1987) and Girvan and Marcelle (1990) sub-Saharan African nations have embraced technology transfer strategy as a principal means of incorporating technical change into their productive structure. Technological change, however, is a multidimensional phenomenon: it involves changes in the socio-cultural, cognitive, and managerial attributes of the society.

Converting changes in socio-cultural, cognitive and managerial attributes of the sub-Saharan African societies into the concept of sustainability of policy raises important questions about how the global social capital or patrimony should be divided between present and future generations. This capital consists of four components: man-made capital such as roads and factories, scientific and technical knowledge, natural capital such as fossil fuels and mineral deposits, and environmental assets such as clean air and water and a diverse biological base.

There is typically little concern over the first two. It is assumed in line with historical experience at least over the past three or four centuries, that each generation will be able to hand down to future generations an improved stock of both technological knowledge and manmade capital. This concern was also addressed by the World Bank and IMF structural adjustment policies prescription to developing nations in the 1980s and 1990s.

Nguyuru Lipumba (1994) pointed out that protecting the environment was not the original objective of the structural adjustment programs that were prescribed by the World Bank and IMF in the 1980s and adopted by African nations. The aftermath of this program was that the impact of adjustment on the environment was previously ignored. The promotion of certain exports such as tropical wood and flue-cured tobacco, which was under taken in some areas as part of the adjustment effort, could result in deforestation. On the balance, there is no good evidence that adjustment policies have had either a positive or negative impact on the environment. Rapid population growth rate and overgrazing are more formidable threats to the environment than adjustment. Overall, the policy challenge for sub-Saharan Africa is to maintain the delicate balance between population growth and agricultural and technological development on the one hand, and protection of the environment on the other.

The Evolution and the Quest for Technology Transfer

The evolution of technology transfer in Nigeria can be best explained by looking back at the performance of the early colonial officers with respect to their responsibilities for national planning and the circumstances under which they operated. One can then trace the relationship between the colonial legacy and the indigenous civil service after independence and the subsequent development and modification based upon the colonial foundation. The colonial civil service that administered Nigeria before 1960 was never intended to create or manage industries or the production system. It was simply meant to preserve law and order in the colonial government interest and promote trade and acquisition of raw materials. During the pre-independence period in Nigeria, there was no clear policy for science and technology. The only policy that was in place was an industrialization plan. This plan was only implicit in nature because the concern of the European colonial authorities was mostly commercial (Adubifa, 1990). The colonial administration's goal was to promote the development and transfer of agricultural commodities as raw materials for Europe.

The colonial civil service did not directly establish industries rather they were instrumental to the penetration of multinational corporations into Nigeria. First, the multinational corporations engaged mostly in commerce and transport, collecting and shipping away raw material from the sub-region for the industries of the developed countries. Second, the multinational corporations also brought finished goods, especially textiles and processed food, for the sub-Saharan African market. Third, at a later stage, the multinational corporations brought in the import-substitution strategy that became the first process of industrialization to be practiced locally in Nigeria (Adubifa 1990;Wangwe 1995). From the onset, it could therefore, be argued that the colonial administration was not concerned with the setting-up of industrialization or the provision of infrastructure. The colonial administration also did not create any formal mechanism for participation in the production system as a function of government.

At independence Nigeria started to recognize the importance of industrialization as a major vehicle for national development. Unlike other developing countries which had successfully utilized appropriate strategies for their own purpose, the Nigerian government strategy for industrialization was initially that of total reliance on foreign private investment supported by generous tax rebate and pioneer incentives. Import-substitute was the primary objective.

The issues above therefore point to a certain pattern of technological development that was inappropriate and resulted from policy failures in development planning. By failing to establish a centralized coordination of technological activities, the nation achieved a high cost assortment of desirable and undesirable technological inputs.

At present, Nigeria remains underdeveloped, dependent, and technologically backward economy (Bigg et al. 1995; Ake, 1995; Picard 1994; Ihonvbere, 1994). In the context of Africa, however, the structures of the Nigerian economy appear relatively developed, but when viewed on a worldwide basis, they are less so. The fact remains that foreign interests dominate Nigeria's economy and the society is characterized by lack of discipline, corruption, political instability, ethnic, religious and regional cleavages and a general absence of basic human needs for the vast majority.

The World Bank has reported a decline in technology development Activities for the years following the introduction of the structural adjustment programs. This was reflected in the drop in the aggregate index of industrial production estimated at 22.8 percent in the fourth quarter of 1999 (1985 being 100%). Similarly, declines of 5.0 and 5.1 percent were recorded in 1994 and 1995, respectively. The contraction in industrial production is traceable to the manufacturing and mining sub-sectors where output fell by 8.3 and 9.8 percent in 1996 and first quarter of 1997. This decline was also observed in the third quarter of 1998 when the index fell by 15.7 percent owing largely to the lingering political crisis in most sub-Saharan African nations and the problem of access to foreign exchange for import of raw materials and machinery spare parts (World Bank, 1999).

Lall and Wangwe (1998) pointed out that formal education is one way of creating human resources for efficient transfer of technology. Training by industrial firms is equally, often more important. While comparable data on this is not available, anecdotal evidence suggests those sub-Saharan African nations (especially Nigeria) also lag in vocational and technical training of its citizens. Most industrial firms invest little or nothing in employee training, providing only the basic on the training needed to operate given technologies. The nature and extent of demand for industrial skills is, moreover, changing rapidly, with new technologies and organizational forms, in the direction of multi-skilling teamwork, reliability and flexibility, and continuous education. The gap between Nigeria and other industrialized nations is increasing rather than closing.

Table 10.1
Educational Enrollment at all Levels in Vocational and Technical Subjects at Universities (Latest Available Year)

Country	Vocational training		Enrollment in Technical Field	
Africa	**Number**	**% of Population**	**Number**	**% of Population**
Ghana	22,578	0.15	712	0.00
Kenya	7,8401	0.04	1,046	0.00
S. Africa	47,801	0.15	19,958	0.06
Zimbabwe	0	0.0	4,718	0.04
Asia				
Korea	1,483,198	3.33	437,537	0.98
Taiwan	513,700	2.46	179,094	0.86
Singapore	9,391	0.32	13,029	0.47
Malaysia	90,079	0.48	12,693	0.07
Philippines	NA	0	201,701	0.29
Thailand	545,791	0.92	51,949	0.09
Latin America				
Chile	277,226	1.98	85,483	0.61
Mexico	835,079	1.03	221,867	0.27
Argentina	1,084,531	3.22	96,205	0.29
Brazil	1,480,997	0.99	149,660	0.10

Source: Lall, S. and S. Wangwe. 1998. "Industrial Policy and Industrialization in Sub-Saharan Africa." Journal of African Economics, Vol. 7, Supplement 1: (June), pp.70-107.

Table 10.1 shows enrollment rates in vocational and technical subjects in universities in some Sub-Saharan African countries in comparison with nations in Asia and Latin America. Vocational and technical training are the means by which high-level human capital for technological transfer and industrial development can be achieved. The table shows that Latin American and Asian countries are much better in the level of technical and vocational training that they provide for their citizens. The table provides data for South Africa as well as the three relatively advanced less-developed economies, Ghana, Kenya and Zimbabwe. The other sub-Saharan African countries (including Nigeria) are very much further behind. South Africa is clearly in front among sub-Saharan African nations, and it has approached the levels reached in some relatively advanced Asian or Latin American nations.

All the expenditures on research and development (R & D) fell 0.9 percent in 1995 and 26.6 percent in 1996 from 100 percent in 1985. As in previous years, the expenditure on R & D continued to account for a dismal fraction (1.7 percent) of total investment expenditure in sub-Saharan Africa (Human Development Index 1999). The performance of public and private sectors deteriorated further at the ending of 1998 reflecting decline in the levels of output and low overall capacity utilization rates. This unsatisfactory performance was attributed largely to the poor implementation of the structural adjustment programs, inadequate funding especially working capital; foreign exchange constraints to procure essential raw materials and spare parts; high cost of operations; frequent breakdown of equipment and spate political instability.

Finally, technology in Nigeria continues to be pervasive, as all sectors of the economy use it and are influenced and affected by it. Technology also acts as an interface between the production and employment, between economic system and ecosystem. It follows, therefore, that effective public-private control over technology has been necessary for realizing the development strategy. To steer the development process, Nigeria must be able to choose appropriate products and technologies and ensure their supply. Sachs (1979), contend that suppliers may be obtained by means of an indigenous design and development effort or by purchase from abroad, followed by adaptation and modification to suit local conditions.

The harmonization of technological, social, economic and environmental objectives can be achieved only by a careful redefinition of the goals (the demand side) and means (the supply side) of Nigeria. Technology weighs on both sides through the appropriate production processes. This requires that Nigeria not only limits its consideration of technology to its capital and labors aspects, but also treats it as a multidimensional entity between the public and private sectors.

Exporting Technology for Sustainability

Sanjaya Lall (1996), Lall and Wangwe (1998) and Crane and Dunkerley (1994) identified four components of technology transfer policy for sub-Saharan Africa (including Nigeria) in the twenty-first century. These policies include importing technology, upgrading the capabilities of small and medium-size enterprises, improving the technology infrastructure and raising the level of technological efforts of large enterprises (see figure 10.1).

Technology exported into Nigeria has largely taken the form of import capital goods. It is essential to encourage technology imports, especially via foreign direct investment, to improve and deepen the industrial structure, and to induce domestic firms to upgrade their skills and capabilities by absorbing the beneficial spillovers from the firms.

Individuals in Nigeria in a matter should direct industrial policy that it will provide strong technical support to small and medium size enterprises. Providing agency services for technology transfer and development, supporting training and information search efforts and providing support for management and constancy services would foster greater technology transfer.

Further more, industrial policy should be enacted to improve technology infrastructure to meet the technological demands of a more open and competitive environment. The quality and spread of technology infrastructure services could be very important in improving quality, undertaking successful innovations and breaking new export markets in the twenty-first century.

The Nigeria government need to introduce policies that would help promote R & D (Dibie, 1997). As industry moves into more complex technologies, an R & D capability becomes essentially simply to absorb foreign technologies. Industrial policy should, therefore, be designed to stimulate investments in R & D over the longer term, and to start to build the base of skills needed.

Lall et al. (1994) and Felix Edoho (2000) contend that investment, production and linkage capabilities are very important for sub-Saharan African (including Nigerian) institutions to develop sustainable growth (see figure 10.1). Investment capabilities are the skills and information Nigeria requires to locate and purchase suitable technologies, design and engineer the plant, and manage the construction commissioning, and starting up the production process. Edoho (2000) pointed out that in most cases this task is contracted out to international consultants. As a result the opportunity for developing the investment capabilities are lost.

The Nigerian government also needs the production capabilities in the form of knowledge and experience. This is very imperative for them to run an operation and improve the production plants. Nigeria would go a long way if they could develop the basic production capabilities such as quality control, maintenance, scheduling, and so on.

Linkage capabilities have to do with the elaborate networks of cooperative relationships with suppliers, buyers, and governments. It also requires Nigeria to have managers with the requisite level of skills to make rational investment decisions and improve upon their core managerial functions. Building administrative and managerial capacity as an essential step in carrying out needed transfer of technology effectively. The formulation and implementation of science and technology policies is still hindered in Nigeria by poor management capacity, as well as by weak institutional and administrative structure. The civil service is often too large and too underpaid to be efficient and to respond promptly to changing circumstances. As a critical element of capacity building efforts should therefore be developed of a learned, better-trained, and motivated civil service with a performance based remuneration system. Coupled with increased decentralization and delegation of responsibilities, the efficiently and cost effectively. Capacity building should therefore also extend to the private sector through the development of appropriate institutions, including measures to promote the role of non-governmental organizations and to enable women to participate fully in the technology transformation and sustainable growth process. Thus, upgrading management know-how among men and women, as well as in both the public and private sectors will provide the needed impetus for economic growth and sustainable progress in Nigeria. Appropriate technology transfer and sustainability in Nigeria will mean that renewable resources must replace depletable ones. Sustainability of technology also implies improving the efficiency with which energy is used, educing the environmental degradation caused by conventional energy production and use, and moving towards greater reliance on sources that do not produce carbon dioxide. Although, this is will be an ambitious program for Nigeria, that will involve many changes in policies and institutions, much of the technology is already available or close to commercial readiness (Crane and Dunkerley, 1994). Great strides have been made in these technologies over the last twenty years around the world. Nations such as those in Nigeria that lack well developed energy networks are most likely to find the adoption of renewables to be advantageous. Crane and Dunerley (1994) pointed out that it will be of everyone's interest to ensure that renewables are used whenever practical because that helps reduce emissions of carbon dioxide, lower costs, builds market, improves energy reliability, and actual technologies, some important countries may benefit from policy advice to allow renewables to compete on more equal terms. Figure 10.1 shows two approaches to sustainable technology development in Nigeria.

Figure 10.1
Approaches to Sustainable Technology Transfer

Sustainable Technology Transfer and Development

•Education in Vocational, Technical and Managerial Skills	•Upgrade small and medium size enterprises
•Investment Capabilities	•Import Technology
•Production Capabilities	•Improving the Technology Infrastructure
•Linkages Capabilities	•Policies to Promote Research and Development
•Political Will and Diplomatic Expertise	•Use Renewable Resources

Entrepreneurs need a stable business environment before they invest or increase their production in technology. Involving representative associations in the policy making process is the first step toward reducing entrepreneurial uncertainty and confirming the stability of regulatory and institutional reforms. This dialogue requires a change of attitude from all sides. Policy-makers need to acknowledge the critical role of the private sector and to avoid arbitrary actions that disrupt its activities. Structural adjustment policies should support broad-based dialogue that encourages associations to participate in the process of regulatory and institutional reform. For their part entrepreneurs must learn to operate on a level playing field on which the ability to compete and produce efficiently, not privilege or evasion, is the key to long-term success.

Other policies by the government should include not only efforts to promote new entrepreneurs but also efforts to retain existing economic activity and encourage the expansion of innovative firms. Policies to deal with the land use aspect of economic development should involve channeling economic growth into some areas (Zartman 1983; Falola 1996; Dibie 1997). Should the state or community decide to play a direct entrepreneurial role, for example, the plan would also include elements pertaining to site acquisition and development. Sub-Saharan African nations should consider subsiding and fostering entrepreneurs in the high technology industries.

Excessive bureaucratic interference breeds lawlessness in sub-Saharan Africa. It encourages entrepreneurs to find shortcuts around the rules and causes those that comply to lose their competitive edge. Removing burdensome regulations would help to eliminate the hidden costs that many entrepreneurs must pay to obtain licenses and register their enterprises. Bribes are only one sort of cost; long delays and complicated procedures inflict further costs in lost efficiency and competitiveness. If the emergence of small-scale entrepreneurs is to be encouraged, licensing and other regulations need to be rigorously scrutinized, and retained only if there is compelling justification.

Protecting infant entrepreneurship from foreign competition through tariffs might not be a healthy thing to do; rather the government should restrict foreign investment in certain sectors. Importing from technologically advanced economies will improve Nigeria's industrial efficiency. The government should, however, encourage indigenous engineers and technicians to import a foreign machine, tear it apart, learn how it was put together, and modify it to fit local circumstances. The product-cycle approach suggests that technological borrowing can proceed from imported product to a copy, usually inferior in quality, to slow improvement, with finer grades and specialties, which come with experience and improved endowment of human and physical capital. Future research might also attempt to find a means by which more entrepreneurial behavior might become more desirable to the economic development of Nigeria. This approach will help change Nigeria's comparative advantage.

Technology export is primarily an information process among people. It provides information for improving designs or the production of goods and services. It need not involve the sale of equipment, but sales can incorporate technology transfer in the form of training and additional information to give the recipient new capabilities. Education is an important form, as attested to by the thousands of Chinese students studying technical subjects in American universities.

Companies clone most technology export from the United States because it is often a prerequisite for sales. In addition to training, it can involve licensing for production, joint ventures, co-production, and other forms. The United States government transfers technology through access to information, assistance with regulation and other activities, development assistance, and educational programs. These efforts are seen as being in the United States' national interest because they are effective ways to promote development and cultivate political and economic ties.

Significant progress toward sustainability will be made only when appropriate technologies discussed in the previous section are widely available, well understood, and advantageous compared to alternatives. To be affordable, much of the equipment must be produced in developing countries, and much of the technology is well within their capabilities. China has been a world leader in the production of small hydropower equipment. Other technologies will require technology transfer for developing countries to assimilate designs and achieve adequate quality control. In addition to the physical equipment, transfer of technical and political expertise may be necessary to create adequate environmental and energy institutions, so that appropriate selections of technology can be made. A wide variety of companies are involved with technologies appropriate for sustainability. Large, international companies are well acquainted with technology transfer. For example, the nuclear industry originated in the United States, and the technology was deliberately transferred abroad.

Conclusion

This study has examined the means of exporting technology for sustainable development in Nigeria. It stresses the importance of technology as the prime factor for economic and structural transformation in Nigeria. It explored the problem of technology development in Nigeria. It argues that in the process of seeking technology, sub-Saharan governments should endeavor to balance industrial promotion and environmental conditions in order to achieve sustainability. The delay in the attainment of a strong technological base in Nigeria is traced to pre-independent colonial administration that structured the economy around extracting raw materials for European industries and private foreign interest.

Foreign investors operating in Nigeria are neither humanitarian nor generous in their economic dealings. They have been egoistic, egocentric, and prefer to give their interest more priority than any appeal to sentimentally or morally help develop a sustainable economy for Nigeria.

With particular reference to the interplay of public and private investment in technology, the crucial problem lies in the persistent drain or the siphoning by foreign investors of resources away from Nigeria. The point being made here is that imported private technology has done little to promote technological progress in Nigeria. Another observation is that Nigeria has been unable to exploit the already imported advanced technology to develop an appropriate technological system for them.

Two approaches to technological transfer and sustainable development are proposed in this study. On one hand, education in vocational, technical and managerial skills, investment, production and linkages capabilities, use of renewables and political will and diplomatic expertise are required for Nigeria to acquire appropriate technologies. On the other hand, import technology, upgrading small and medium size enterprises, improving the technology infrastructure, policies to promote research and development and the use of renewables resources are all important factors that would enable the sub region to attain technological transfer and sustainable development.

It is very important that the Nigeria governments endeavor to balance technological development, industrial promotion and environmental conditions in order to achieve sustainability. Enterprises begin with people; therefore, the governments in the sub-region should provide technical and vocational training for its citizens. Future development strategies should recognize that although governments can facilitate progress, people make things happen. The Nigerian government also need a healthy business environment, one that would enable them to plan for the future, that rewards achievement, and that encourages entrepreneurs to invest in themselves and their enterprises. They need financial and information systems that will give them access to resources, infrastructure that supports links with the rest of the economy, and institutions that promote the full development of human resources. By working with governments and local associations to improve businesses and to support entrepreneurial capabilities, donors can make a valuable contribution to this effort. In addition to the physical equipment, transfer of technology and political expertise may be necessary to create adequate environmental policies and institutions, so that appropriate selections of technology can be made in the future.

References

Adubifa, Akin. (1990). Technology Policy in Nigeria. Nigeria, Ibadan: NISER Publication.

Biggs, T., M. Shah and P. Srivastava. (1995). "Technological Capability and Learning in Africa Enterprises." World Bank Technical paper. No. 288, Washington DC: World Bank.

Crane, Alan and Joy, Dunkerley. (1994). "The Role of Technology Transfer in the Transition of Sustainability." In Depth, A Journal for Values and Public Policy, Vol. 4, no.5, pp. 85-104.

Dibie, Robert. (1997). "Business-Government Relations and Technology Development in Nigeria." Journal of Developing Societies. Vol 13, 2, pp. 195-207.

Dike, Enwere. (1994). Economic Transformation in Nigeria: Growth, Accumulation and Technology. Nigeria, Zaria: Amadu Bello University Press.

Edoho, Felix. (2000). "Transferring Management Technology to Sub-Saharan Africa." Proceedings of the Global Challenge of African Business and Economic Development. International Conference April 11-14, pp. 120-125.

Evans, Donald. (1984). "Appropriate Technology and its Role in Development." In Appropriate Technology in Third World Development, Edited by Pradip Ghosh K. Connecticut: Greenwood Press.

Fadahunsi, Akin, and Igwe B. U. N. (1989). Capital Goods and Technological Change and Accumulation in Nigeria. Senegal, Dakar: CODESRIA.

Fransman, Martin. (1985). "The Role of Science in Technology Transfer." Research Policy, Vol. 12, 5, October Issue, pp. 287-96.

Girvan, N. P., and G. Marcell. (1990). Overcoming Technological Dependecy: The Case of Electric in Jamaica Limited. World Development Vol. 18, pp. 91-107.

Ihonvbere, Julius O. (1994). Nigeria: The Politics of Adjustment and Democracy. New Brunswick: Transaction Publishers.

Jequier, N. (1976). Appropriate Technology Problems and Promises. Paris: Organization for Economic Cooperation and Development Publication.

Kaplinsky, Raphael. (1990). The Economies of Small: Appropriate Technology in a Changing World. Washington DC: Appropriate Technology International.

Lall, S. et al. (1994). Technology and Enterprise Development: Ghana under Structural Adjustment. New York: St. Martin's Press.

Lall, S. et al. (1998). Opening Up: The technological Response ti Import Liberialization in Sub-Saharan Africa, London: Macmillan.

Lall, S. and S. Wangwe. (1998). "Industrial Policy and Industrialization in Sub-Saharan Africa." Journal of African Economics, Vol. 7, Supplement 1: (June), pp.70-107.

Lipumba, Nupguyuru. (1994). Africa Beyond Structural Adjustment. Washington DC: Oversea Development Council.

Maravcsik, Michael. (1983). "The Role of Science in Technology Transfer." Research Policy, Vol. 12, 5, October Issue, pp. 287-96.

Myint, Hla. (1971). Economic Theory and Undeveloped Countries. London: Oxford University Press.

Obasanjo, Oluscgun, and Akin Mabogimje. (1991). Elements of Development in Nigeria. Lagos: C & A Publishers.

OECD. (1992). Technology and the Economy: The Key Relationships, Paris, OECD.

Onimode, Bade. (1991). Alternative Development Strategies for Africa. London: Institute for African Alternatives.

Phillips, Adedotun, and Eddy Ndekwu. (1992). Structural Adjustment Program in a Developing Economy: The Case of Nigeria. Ibadan: Okley Limited.

Picard, Louis. (1994). Policy Reform for Sustainable Development in Africa. The Institute Imperative. Boulder Rienner Publishers.

Sachs, Ignacy. (1979). "Controlling Technology for Development." Development Dialogue, Vol. 1 (April) Issue.

Sahn, David. (1994). Adjusting to Policy Failure in Africa Economies. Ithaca: Cornell University Press.

Sandbrook, Richard. (1993). The Politics of Africa's Recovery. New York: Cambridge University Press.

Stewart, F. and Ranis G. (1990). Macro-Policies for Appropriate Technology: Synthesis of Findings in Stewart et al edited.

Summers, Lawrence and Vinod Thomas. (1993). "Recent Lessons of Development." The World Bank Research Observer. 1998. (July Issue), p. 249.

Wangwe, S. M. (1995). Exporting Africa: Technology, Trade and Industrialization in Sub-Saharan Africa, UNU/INTECH studies in New technology and Development, London: Routledge.

World Bank. (1999). Human Development Index. New York: Oxford University Press.

World Bank. (1999). World Development Report. New York: Oxford University Press, p. 296.

Yannkey, G. S. (1987). International Patents and Technology Transfer to Less Developed Countries. Brookfield, Vermont: Gower.

11 Public Policy Making and Implementation

Introduction

The magnitude of economic problems Nigeria faced in the past three decades stimulated its leaders to look for solutions. These national predicaments were due to increasing balance of payment deficits, rising inflation rates, low technological base, maladministration of resources, growing foreign debt burden, lower agricultural growth rates and an oil glut on the world market and declining oil revenue. Petroleum had been the major source of revenue for this fledgling nation since its independence. Under pressure from the World Bank and the International Monetary Fund (IMF) the military government adopted a series of structural adjustment programs (SAP). Among the policies was one directed specifically toward the development of indigenous technology in the private sector? It is this policy that the military government called the SAP/Make-or-Buy policy.

This chapter examines the relationship between the Nigerian higher military and bureaucracy in decision making and decisions implementation, using the SAP/Make-or-Buy policy as a case study. The study presents data with respect to the economic consequences of the implementation of the SAP/Make-or-Buy policy. The chapter also explores the utility of the hybrid political system model in explaining the decision making process in Nigeria and especially the different responses of the federal ministries and agencies to the SAP/Make-or-Buy Policy. The making of the policy, its official proclamation and implementation is based primarily on government documents, which have been analyzed extensively. Two other types of data have also been used to assess the behavior of the federal ministries during the policy implementation stage: interviews and financial data. The interviews are examined first followed by the financial data, which are presented in table form so that the reader can compare the ministries to one another. The interviews conducted in 1995-1996, reveal intra and inter-ministerial conflict as the policy passes through an "interpretation" phase. The findings from the interviews illustrate the different mandates in each ministry, and how this perception of their distinct mandates affects their compliance with the policy. The financial data shows similar reaction and behaviors. An effort has been made here to evaluate policy performance after nine years of trial and error, notably in the creation of new technology and in the improvement of the national economy.

The central research question of this study is: What is the relationship between the Nigerian military junta and the country's bureaucracy in the decision making and implementation processes, and how has that relationship shaped the implementation of SAP/Make-or-Buy policy? The central research question is operationalized by the following specific hypotheses: (1) Does lack of consultation with the implementers in a bureaucratic-authoritarian system produce different degrees of resistance or support in the implementation of development policy? (2) What circumstances in the political/economic environment of Nigeria – (a) internationally, and (b) domestically – prompted the development of the Structural Adjustment/Make-or-Buy policy? (3) To what extent did instability in the political/economic environment constitute pressure on the nation's leadership to examine and re-evaluate its policies? (4) What decision-making procedures did the Nigerian military government follows in enacting the Structural Adjustment/Make-or-Buy policy? (5) What was the policy? What was it intended to accomplish? Why did the military government expect this policy would achieve its stated purpose? (6) Did the individual ministries view the SAP/Make-or-Buy policy as consistent with the mandate of their particular ministry? Why and how did the ministries support or resist the policy? What does the financial data reveal about the various ministries' implementation of the policy? (7) After nine years of implementation have any new technologies emerged to justify the development and execution of the SAP/Make-or-Buy policy? (8) Has the national economy improved due to development of the SAP/Make-or-Buy policy? (9) If the purpose of the SAP/Make-or-Buy policy is the economic development of Nigeria, has it succeeded in (a) the public sectors, and (b) the private sectors?

Theoretical Framework

The bureaucratic-authoritarian decision model focuses on the interaction between the military and the civilian administrators. A bureaucratic-authoritarian regime will arise when a military government decides to adopt technocratic and bureaucratic approaches to policy-making. The military regime will, therefore, oppose any political approach through which policies are shaped by economic and political demands from different sectors of society, expressed through such channels as election, legislatures, political parties, and labor unions. Increasing and intimate communication between the military leaders and higher civilian technocrats, couple with their growing frustrations with political and economic conditions encourage the "coup" mentality that results in repressive bureaucratic-authoritarian systems. According to Alfred Stepan (1988) and Guillerno O'Donnell (1973) military-bureaucracies have shaped the sustained policies of Brazil, Argentina, Chile, Uruguay, Ghana, Nigeria, Egypt and Indonesian governments.

Under the bureaucratic-authoritarian model, bureaucrats supply the administrative framework that enables a ruling military junta to maintain its power and direct economic change. In the bureaucratic-authoritarian system, however, the state exerts more centralized power. Army officers and civilian administrators dominate both central and regional government and they often try to coordinate the policy process (Bienen, 1971). Although families, churches, universities, the media, and especially large-scale domestic private business enterprises and multinational corporations retain some autonomy, the civil-military institution regulates their actions. In Nigeria as well as in many Latin America and Asian nations, the military, the civil servants, the police, and the technocrats from large-scale domestic private firms and multinational corporations influence the policy making process. The underlying concern of this chapter is whether or not such centralized military-bureaucratic systems can effectively describe the relationship between the Nigerian military and the traditional bureaucracy in the process of decision making and implementation.

Policy Process in Nigeria

The dominant feature of decision making in Nigeria is the principle of federal supremacy as defined in the 1979 Constitution. Under the constitution, the federal government is expected to provide the overall direction and leadership in the planning process from the formulation stage through the implementation and evaluation stages (Adamolekun and

Ayeni, 1990). The decision making process under the federal supremacy principle requires the National Economic Council to advise the President concerning the economic affairs of the federation. The National Economic Council also coordinates the economic planning efforts or the economic development programs of the various state governments of Nigeria. The Vice-President of the nation is the chairperson of the National Economic Council. Figure 11.1 shows key governmental agencies and institutions that are involved in the national decision make process. These include the Ministries of Finance and National Planning (Adamolekun and Ayeni, 1990).

Policy inputs come from the various ministries and departments of the Ministry of National Planning. Here policy alternatives are examined and evaluated and then translated into programs within the financial parameters stated by the Ministry of Finance. The key agency in the Ministry Try of National Planning is the National Planning Office, which is divided into four directorates, each headed by a director who is responsible to the director general (as the permanent secretary is now called) of the ministry. Besides the National Planning Office, there are two other offices or boards that report to the Ministry of National Planning: (1) the National Manpower Board (NMB) and (2) the Federal Office of Statistics (FOS). The function of NMB consists of determining personnel needs and formulating programs for personnel development. The FOS is the national agency responsible for collecting social and economic data throughout the federation. A number of other interdepartmental and intergovernmental agencies and institutions also participate in the decision making process. The most notable among them are (a) the Joint Planning Board (JPB) and (b) the Conference of Ministers and Commissioners for National and Economic Planning.

The JPB consists of the leading planning officers of the federal and state governments. The JPS meets periodically, usually in advance of the conference of commissioners of economic planning. It serves as a clearinghouse and coordinating institution for policy proposals emanating from the states. The institutional framework for planning at the state level differs from that described above in one major respect. The policy inputs that come to each state Ministry of Economic Development also includes inputs from the top bureaucrats of the local governments and is directed through the State Ministry of Local Government. Decision-making concerning the SAP/Make-or-Buy policy appears to not have followed the normal policy making process, as the study which follows will reveal. While the policy making process that led to the SAP/Make-or-Buy policy is different; it illustrates the basic dilemmas of Nigerian policy formulation procedure. In addition, it is important to note that while the policy making process was different, the bureaucratic processes and difficulties in implementing the policy were normal. Thus, the overall case study represents a good example of all the various cross pressures between the military junta and the traditional bureaucracy.

A Study of the SAP/Make-or-Buy Policy

The SAP/Make-or-Buy policy was announced by General Babangida's administration in July of 1986. The sequence of events and the decision making process utilized in the making and approval of the SAP/Make-or-Buy policy is unique and thus differs from the typical policy making procedures in Nigeria described above. It is unique because the military has never before called for a national debate on any issue or problem facing the country prior to when decisions were made. The sole decision makers in the SAP/Make-or-Buy policy were the members of the Armed Forces Ruling Council. The AFRC decision, however, was influenced by a number of domestic and international institutions. In any decision making process the existence of awareness stage occupies a prominent position. The debt crisis, the lack of domestically created technology and the possibility of the total collapse of the Nigerian economy provided the need and produced the awareness, as previously described in chapter seven, for some kind of policy to be developed. The decision making stages followed by the Armed Forces Ruling Council are the following:

Step 1: The Armed Forces Ruling Council was aware of the debt crisis and the failing economy. It was further aware in the mid-1980s of an inadequate national technological base. The AFRC articulated concerns that in the absence of a modern national technological capability, existing intensive labor practices meant output and productivity would continue to decline hence would fail to meet the needs of a growing population, or to produce marketable items for export.

Step 2: There were pressures from Nigerian politicians, and from various intra-societal associations representing economists and manufacturers for the military government to either do something to improve the economic situation or to hand over power to a civilian government. Various kinds of citizen groups representing their regional, religious, and ethnic interests made similar demands. These groups marched and demonstrated in the major cities of the country. The pressures exerted by these groups forced the AFRC to announce publicly to the nation that some kind of speedy action would be taken.

Step 3: The AFRC contacted the IMF and the World Bank to obtain loans to finance development projects around the country, including the creation of modern technology where appropriate. It was hoped that an infusion of money into the economy would at least temporarily quiet the protestors and stimulate development.

Figure 11.1
Decision-Making Process and the Relationship Between the Military and Public Administrators in Decision-Making in Nigeria

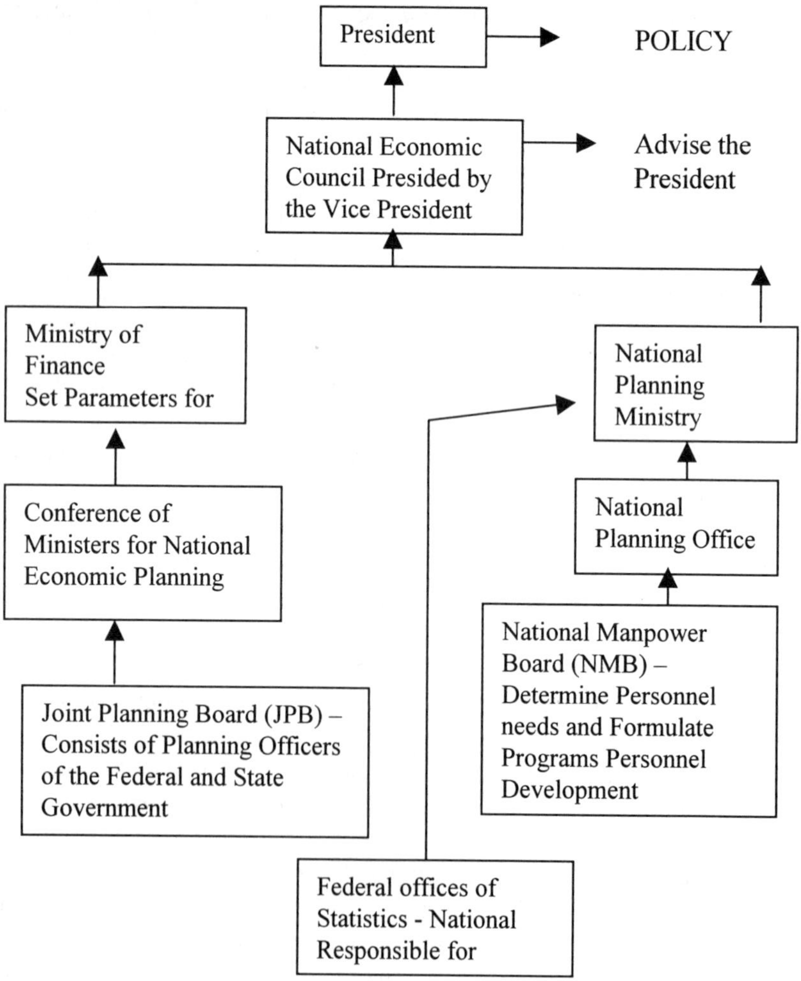

In response, the international financial institutions agreed to offer loans to Nigeria. This loans were, however, based only if the government agreed to a set of severe structural adjustment conditions, including the devaluation of the Naira, the removal of the petroleum subsidy, the liberalization of trade, the reduction of government expenditures and the privatization of government enterprises.

Figure 11.2
Dynamics of Structural Adjustment/Make-or-Buy Policy, and the Relationship between Decision-Makers and Public Administrators

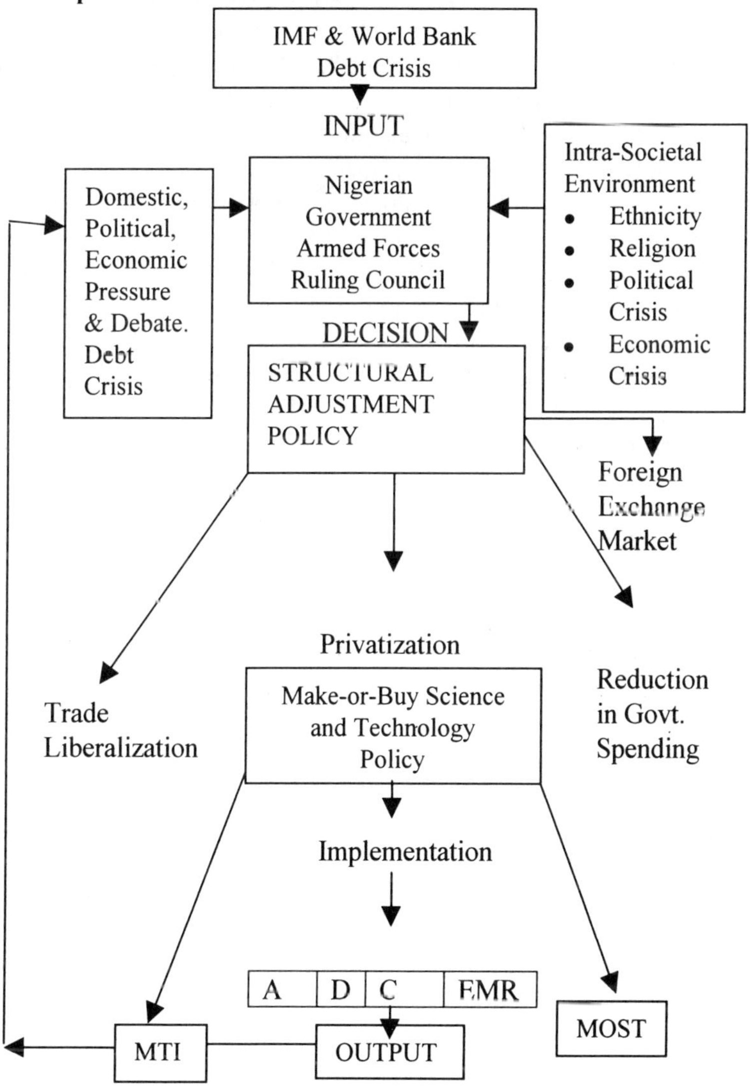

Step 4: In order to gain legitimacy for their action, the AFRC informed the nation about these structural adjustment conditions proposed by the IMF and the World Bank and called for a national debate on how to solve the Nigerian predicament. A wide range of citizens, representing different areas of Nigerian life responded. They included the bureaucracy, who opposed several of the conditions, specifically the reduction of government expenditures, which would result in layoffs of career bureaucrats, the removal of the oil subsidy, and the devaluation of the Naira. Political legitimacy had declined in Nigeria because the military regime could not adequately cope with the economic predicament plaguing the country. Therefore, to establish the belief that his regime was the most appropriate for the nation, and ever mindful of his shaky power base, General Babangida sought to maintain his support in government circle and especially in the armed forces.

Step 5: The AFRC attempted to negotiate with the IMF and the World Bank to reduce the structural adjustment conditions. Their request to reduce the conditions failed because the IMF and the World Bank felt that Nigeria might not be able to pay back the loan if it did not follow all of the conditions strictly.

Step 6: General Babangida and members of the AFRC abandoned their request for the loans from the IMF and the World Bank, but recognizing that important measures to improve the economy were called for, they decided to introduce many of the structural adjustments that had been recommended. These adjustments included trade liberalization, privatization of government corporations and operations, devaluation of the Nigerian currency, regulation of the foreign exchange market, and a sharp reduction in government expenditures. The SAP/Make-or-Buy policy was developed and announced as one of these social structural adjustments, namely the privatization of R & D activities.

Step 7: General Babangida the chairperson of the AFRC announced the SAP/Make-or-Buy Policy in July 1986 and issued the guidelines for its implementation. He asserted that Nigerians were being battered by a high rate of inflation, unemployment, underdevelopment, and reduced Living standard. This made it necessary tc give the Nigerian economy an entirely new structure because its old economic structure was near collapse.

In order to answer the central research question a hybrid system decision-making model has been developed (figure 11.2) for an analysis of the Nigerian SAP/Make-or-Buy policy. The model draws attention to the relationship between the decision and its environment, and it views that relationship purely in terms of a feedback loop that is based on sequential (output-feedback-input) type of coalition. Simply examining the larger institutional network cannot capture the relationship between higher bureaucrats and the Nigerian military junta; it must also account for the influences working in the Nigerian environment. That environment in this paper means: (a) Nigeria's political instability, economic pressures, debt crisis, ethnicity dilemmas and religious divisions; and (b) the international environment such as the World Bank, the International Monetary Fund, the London and Paris clubs. Such an approach is based on awareness that the Nigerian environment influences the political system. The hybrid model focuses attention on important and salient input considerations by Nigeria's military decision-makers whose strategies are directed at reducing their margin of uncertainty.

Goals of the SAP/Make-or-Buy Policy

The major goal of the SAP/Make-or-Buy policy was to stabilize Nigeria's economy and set it on the path of social, economic and technological growth. This radical reform policy was designed to restructure the economy, expand non-oil exports, reduce the import content of locally manufactured goods, achieve self-sufficiency in food, and give a larger role in the development of the economy to the private sector. Accompanying this policy were several other specific, but major, reforms, notably the abolition of import licenses (with reliance placed on the foreign exchange auctions to allocate scarce foreign resources). The reduction and realignment of import duties (designed to reduce protection of local industries and force manufacturers to reduce import dependence). The abolition of export duties, the introduction of tough demand management policies to ward off the inflationary dangers of large scale devaluation, and the progressive privatization of numerous parastatal companies. The government also re-structured the Nigerian companies in virtually all sectors of the economy. The SAP/Make-or-Buy policy reserved the lion's share of industrial and economic activities for Nigerian businesses, allowing only 40 percent equity participation by foreign investors in those businesses utilizing high technology and needing substantial R & D or heavy capital investment.

The SAP/Make-or-Buy Policy specifically mandates the transfer of new research and development work from the government laboratories to the private sector (Buy) with the hope that this enlarged arena for R & D would help generate sufficient technology for the development of the country's industry. There are two objectives of the Make-or-Buy Policy, a short-run objective and a long-run objective. The short-run objective is to ensure those federal ministries and agencies contract out to industry all *new* research and development (R & D) requirements. These requirements were not intended to remove the ministries from all R & D activities since they were allowed to continue their R & D projects already underway, and even to undertake new ones (Make).

The long-run objective of the Make-or-Buy policy was the development of a sophisticated technological capability in Nigeria and the modernization of the entire economy of the country. In order to achieve the objectives of the policy the Armed Forces Ruling Council (AFRC), in January 1987, issued a list of implementation guidelines that were to be followed by the various ministries and agencies which were required to develop the various R & D contracts with the private sector firms. Responsibility for the supervision and evaluation of the policy fell mainly on two ministries: The Ministry of Science and Technology (MOST) and the Ministry of Trade and Industry (MTI).

MOST's chief concern involved assuring the overall effectiveness of the policy and the periodic review of procedures for its implementation. MTI was assigned responsibility for contracting out R & D activities and setting patterns of delegation for other federal ministries and agencies (Federal Government of Nigeria, 1987).

The SAP/Make-or-Buy industrial policy also was intended to facilitate investment through the establishment of the Industrial Development Coordination Committee (IDCC). The committee comprised the Ministers for Industries, Finance, Trade, Science and Technology, Agriculture, Defense, Communication, Employment, Labor, and Internal Affairs, and was given principal responsibility for (a) approving new industry applications; (b) approving tax incentives for qualifying firms; and (c) granting expatriate quotas for qualifying new foreign firms. Other functions of the IDCC included approving pre-investment technology transfer agreements as they relate to feasibility studies, assistance in producing machinery, plants, equipment and components, engineering design services, plant installation, and plant commissioning. IDCC also was assigned the tasks of advising on the administration of government industrial incentives and of making recommendations on pertinent policies including tariffs and various measures aimed at ensuring the industrial development of Nigeria.

The seven steps in the development of this policy described earlier in the chapter reveal that the Armed Forces Ruling Council responded to the oil crisis, the technology deficit, and the overall failure of the economy by adopting many of the structural adjustment conditions recommended by the IMF and the World Bank, even in spite of their political unpopularity. The SAP/Make-or-Buy Policy was linked with the developments to promote Research and Development (R & D) and to boost Nigeria's quest for modern technology. The interviews conducted for this study indicate that the various ministries and even the planning bodies that were normally involved in the development of new policies were not invited to participate in the decision making process that led to the Make-or-Buy policy, although a few did have representation on the AFRC. Given this shift in the decision making process the SAP/Make-or-Buy policy was not taken seriously when it was first announced in 1986. Moreover, several federal ministries ignored the policy even after the guidelines were issued in 1987.

Implementation and Consequences of the Policy

Four ministries of the national government were studied with respect to the implementation of SAP/Make-or-Buy policy: the Ministry of Agriculture, the Ministry of Communication, the Ministry of Defense, and the Ministry of Energy, Mines and Resources. These four ministries were selected because they represent the major federal government ministries involved in research and development activities in Nigeria. The ministries were also selected because they represent a good cross section of the SAP/Make-or-Buy policy arena as well as bureaucratic power in Nigeria. The responsibilities of each of these ministries will be presented first. Then, they will be grouped based on their responses to the policy as revealed by the interviews. The two ministries charged with administrative responsibilities will be examined for their particular coordinate and supervisory roles with respect to the policy. They are the Ministry of Science and Technology (MOST) and the Ministry of Trade and Industry (MTI).

In the third part of this section, the financial data will be presented and analyzed. This consists primarily of the contracting-out data published by the Ministry of Science and Technology (MOST) for the fiscal years 1987 to 1994 inclusive.

Finally, the political system model will be evaluated with respect to its utility to account for the implementation phase of the SAP/Make-or-Buy policy.

Findings from Interviews

This study was conducted in Lagos and Abuja, Nigeria. It involved the administering of questionnaires and the conduction of both structured and unstructured interviews to 300 senior military officers and civilian bureaucrats. These senior officials are charged with the implementation of the SAP/Make-or-Buy Policy. Table 11.1 shows the findings of interviews conducted, and it is based on the rate of support given by each ministry to the policy.

Table 11.1
Interview Findings

Ministry	Support	Do Not Support
Agriculture	3%	97%
Communications	95%	5%
Defense	99%	1%
Energy, Mines & Resources	8%	92%

Ministries with Minimum or no Conflict with the Policy

Interviews were conducted with a number of officials in agencies charged with implementing the SAP/Make-or-Buy policy. Interviews with senior members of the Ministry of Defense July 3, 1995, and Ministry of Communications July 11, 1995, yielded the following generally results. The Ministries of Defense officials gave ninety-nine percent (99%) of their support to the policy, while the officials from the Ministry of Communications gave ninety-five percent (95%) support. Both ministries tended to perceive only minimal conflict between their ministries' mandates and the Make-or-Buy requirement to contract out their R & D requirements. Where conflict was perceived, there were three general concerns. First, these ministries did not appreciate the unusual confidence shown by the AFRC in industry as a performer of R & D. Second, scientists conducting R & D within the ministries were not consulted and they were skeptical about the policy's chances of success in the implementation phase. And third, despite the contracting concessions offered by the Armed Forces Ruling Council guidelines, the involvement of the Ministry of Trade and Industry in the administration of the contract process confused its role with that of the Defense and the Communications ministry which already had a practice of making private sector contracts.

A second factor which encouraged the Ministries of Defense and Communications to be supportive of the Make-or-Buy policy was the fact that these Ministries were generally in pursuit of major goals to which the contracting-out requirements did not pose a threat. The Ministry of Communications for example, had committed itself to the development of a sophisticated communications industry in Nigeria. Therefore, whether the associated R & D were done in-house or in-industry was not an overriding concern. SAP/Make-or-Buy was seen as a legitimate vehicle for achieving ministry goals rather than an obstacle to the progress of communications technology. Similarly, R & D managers within the Ministry of Defense (interviewed July 4, 1995) were committed to the development of a strong R & D capability within the Nigerian armaments industry and they did not envisage SAP/Make-or-Buy impeding their mission. Senior officials interviewed in the Ministry of Communications stressed that, A fundamental shift in government policy and a further demonstration of the military government's confidence in the private sector's ability to create new products, processes and services, is due to the present economic climate. The emphasis on this kind of R & D contract to industry is basically due to the fact that it will in turn create new jobs for Nigerians.

Both ministries actively encouraged the contracting out of R & D requirements. The interview response of the Ministry of Defense and that of the Ministry of Communications reflects those of the bureaucratic-authoritarian argument in the literature. The argument contends that when a military government decide to adopt technocratic and bureaucratic approaches to policy-making, it will form a coalition with the high-level civilian bureaucracy.

Ministries Perceiving Policy Conflict

Interview results indicate that the Ministry of Agriculture had three percent (3%) Support and the Ministry of Energy, Mines and Resources (EMR) gave only eight percent (8%) of their support to the policy. Both ministries perceived a higher level of conflict between their individual mandates and the objectives of the Make-or-Buy policy than did the Ministries of Defense and Communications. Several important factors account for this difference in perception.

First, interviews with senior officials in the Ministries of

Agriculture and Energy, Mines and Resources (July 13 and 14, 1995) indicate that they viewed their ministries primarily as research institutes with a tradition of scientific excellence which they believed could not be matched by the private sector. One of the senior officials in the Ministry of Agriculture stated, The essential need for economic development is not necessarily extensive indigenous technological output, but rather a capacity to use technology effectively, whether it is domestic or foreign. Therefore, they interpreted the SAP/Make-or-Buy requirement to contract out as a direct threat to their work and they opposed the policy on these grounds. The Ministry of Agriculture objected to the requirement to contract out, especially in the area of regulatory R & D, because, in several circumstances, the only institutions in the private sector capable of performing the required R & D were those that had been appropriately regulated.

The Ministries of Agriculture and of Energy, Mines and Resources believed the private sector lacked the expertise for R & D in matters of concern them. Officials within the Ministry of Agriculture argued that the pervasive importance of agriculture to the Nigerian economy demanded that related R & D work remain the responsibility of the Government. According to these senior officials:

> ...Even when a portion of the research and development is contracted out to the private sector, it is coordinated with the research of the entire international organizations, directed from the home base, and thus not necessarily fitted into the productive capacity of the Nigerian environment (Statement made by Public Servants in Nigeria, 1995).

The senior officials contend that the vigorous promotion of the free-market model by Western governments, IMF and World Bank, often as a condition for extending desperately needed financial assistance, seemed to be designed to shift power in Nigeria to the private sector, foreign as well as indigenous, and to align local business interests with foreign interference in national sovereignty, a form of neo-imperialism. Moreover, given the high capital cost of agricultural research, and the inability of the country's farmers to pay the cost of R & D activity, the ministries believed that the private sector could not measure up to the task.

Another factor, which generated resistance to the SAP/Make-or-Buy policy, was the apparent conflict of interest between the mission of the Ministry of Agriculture and the Ministry of Energy, Mines and Resources and the rationale and requirements of the SAP/Make-or-Buy

Policy. The ministers and directors interviewed expressed their disbelief that the transfer of R & D from government laboratories to the private sector would actually generate the technological spin-offs in the areas of their responsibility. They argued that it was not the absence of basic research within the private sector, which accounted for Nigeria's technological underdevelopment, but the lack of developmental R & D. They called upon industry to take advantage of the research contributions their ministries had already made. In other words, industry should be concerned with commercial viability, thus leaving the government agencies to continue with their basic research. In this way, in-house based R & D would continue uninterrupted and industry would benefit from the application of research in commercially appropriate situations. In conclusion, the resisting ministries agreed that the SAP/Make-or-Buy policy, whose objective was the transfer of basic research as well as general R & D responsibilities from the government laboratories to the private sector, was not needed. Senior officials of the Ministry of Energy, Mines and Resources argued that:

> ...While the availability of foreign technology has, in general, clearly been essential for the Nigerian economy, largely the objectives and interests of the foreign proprietor have typically dictated the method of transfer. Nothing in Nigerian environment militates against this procedure (Statement made by Public Servants, 1995).

Finally, the Ministries of Agriculture and Energy, Mines and Resources were critical of the policy because its specified procedures seemed to complicate the traditional contracting-out process by requiring the involvement of other agencies. The policy guidelines directed MOST and MTI to oversee how the Policy will be implemented by the various ministries. The ministers and directors interviewed asserted that the involvement of MOST and MTI would lead to the loss of their traditional control over contracts, and decrease the likelihood that contract specifications would be satisfied on time, if at all.

Though the interviews indicated that the Ministry of Energy, Mines and Resources would resist the Make-or-Buy Policy, officials readily admitted that their primary objection was not against the requirement to contract out as much as it was against the designation of MOST and MTI as the watchdog of the Policy. The Ministry of Energy, Mines and Resources contained a small R & D establishment, although its responsibilities in the area of mine regulation were considerable.

Contracting out was not unknown to the ministry and on numerous occasions it had sought external research assistance. The ministry's concern therefore lay not in out-souring work but in seeing its power diminished by the policy. Therefore, loss of direct control over an important and growing area of the ministry's operations was the principal concern. Additional comments concerning the roles of MTI and MOST appear below.

The SAP/Make-or-Buy policy and its guidelines evoked a different response from that of the Ministries of Defense and Communications as described earlier. The Ministries of Agriculture and Energy, Mines and Resources were generally unsupportive of the SAP/Make-or-Buy policy and this study reveals six basic reasons. First, the ministries viewed the policy as a direct threat to the continued existence of their R & D establishments. Second, they perceived it to be a major impediment to the accomplishment of their organizational mandates. Third, they understood that support for the Policy required them to transfer control over the R & D contractual process to the private sector. Fourth, they disagreed with the basic rationale of the SAP/Make-or-Buy Policy, that the transfer of government R & D work to the private sector would lead inevitably to the development of indigenous technology that would be useful for Nigerian industries. Fifth, they resented not being allowed to participate in the formulation and adoption of the policy. According to senior officials from the Ministry of Agriculture Six, they opposed giving the management role to MTI and the evaluation role to MOST.

> ...The Nigerian Government could have been more successful in establishing coherent and efficient decentralized machinery for economic and technology policies than the isolated action of the AFRC in 1986 (Statement made by Public Servants, 1995).

The non-support by the Ministry of Agriculture and the Ministry of Energy, Mines and Resources reflects the major weaknesses of the bureaucratic – authoritarian regimes. Although the dominant group of a bureaucratic- authoritarian coalition is senior military juntas, they can only impose decisions, however, when it comes to the implementation of those policies, they will have to depend on the civilian bureaucracy. Thus, only the civilian bureaucrats can provide the administrative framework that will enable a ruling military junta to maintain legitimacy and power.

Financial Data

Three tables have been developed from Ministry of Science and Technology Report that was published in November 1996. The report is an evaluation of the SAP/Make-or-Buy Policy and includes data for the period 1987-1996. These data cover the period of implementation which proceeds the period (1996-7) during which the interviews described above were conducted. The Ministry of Trade and Industry, the Ministry of Finance and Economic Development, and the Central Bank also provided additional data for analysis.

Table 11.1 and 11.2 show the mission-oriented R & D contracts and funds awarded by the Ministry of Trade and Industry for the period 1987 to 1994 on behalf the four contracting line ministries under study. The data in Table 11.2 reveals that in 1987, the Ministry of Agriculture awarded neither contracts nor funds to the private sector. It began to do so in 1989 and by 1996 had awarded 13 contracts including 3 in 1996. The Ministry of Energy, Mines and Resources contracted-out a total of 84 R & D contracts for the eight years under study. In 1987, it awarded six contracts; the number was increased to 14 the following year, but decreased to 10 and 8 in the subsequent three years. In 1992 and 1993, the ministry increased its R & D contracts to 12 and 15, respectively, however, the number decreased to 11 in 1996. The Ministry of Communications awarded a fairly higher number of R & D contracts when compared with the above mentioned ministries, namely 351 over the eight year period. It awarded 47 in 1987, 53 in 1989 and 31 in 1990. Between 1991 and 1993 the ministry maintained a constant 43 R & D contract awards each year, however, it increased the number of contracts awarded to 50 in 1996. The Ministry of Defense awarded the greatest number of R & D contracts, a total of 412 contracts between 1987 and 1996. In each year except 1987 and 1991, they awarded the largest number of contracts of the four ministries studied.

The money spent on R & D contracts by the Ministry of Agriculture as reported in Table 3 ranges from N131, 000 in 1989 to N618 million in 1996, and for a total of N941.98 million for the eight years. The Ministry of Energy, Mines for definitive conclusions regarding the compliance of the policy spent a total of N555.1 million on R & D contracts for the eight years. It spent N2.8 million in 1987 and increased its spending gradually to N233.2 million in 1996. The

Ministry of Defense spent N178.1 million in 1987 and increased the amount to N199.1 million in 1988. In 1989 and 1990 the amount decreased to N162.5 and N152 million, respectively.

Table 11.2
Number of Private Sector R & D Contracts Awarded by the Four Ministries under Study

Ministry	1987	1988	1989	1990	1991	1992	1994	1996	Total
Agriculture	0	0	2	2	2	0	4	3	13
Energy, Mines and Resources	6	14	10	8	8	12	15	11	84
Communi-cations	47	53	31	41	43	43	43	50	351
Defense	45	67	45	48	39	52	60	56	412

Sources: Data provided by the Ministry of Science and Technology, and Central Bank of Nigeria, Lagos, 1995.

The Defense Ministry began to increase its spending beginning in 1991 and by 1996 had spent a total of N3600.7 million on R & D contracts over the eight years. The Ministry of Communications spent a total of N3486.4 million on R & D contracts between 1987 and 1996. Ministry of Communication spending increased steadily from 1987 to 1996 but experienced a slight decrease in 1991 and again in 1996.

From Table 11.3 it can be seen that all the ministries tended to increase the volume of R & D funds which they contracted out over the eight-year period. These data also show the amount of money available for R & D purposes in the budget of each ministry from which the contracts were awarded. However, it does not reveal how these funds were allocated between in-house and extra-mural (contracted out) research. Therefore, caution is necessary in using these data when arguing

Table 11.3
Funds Contracted Out to the Private Sector by Federal Ministries and Estimate of Total R & D Budget of Each Ministry Under Study for the Period 1987-1996 (N. in Millions)

Ministry	1987	%	1990	%	%	%	1996	%	Total	%
Agriculture *R&D Budget Amount Spent	 442 0	 0	 598.2 92.7	 15	 20	 5	 1178 618	 52	 6377.1 941.98	 15
Energy, Mine & Resources *R&D Budget Amount Spent	 508 2.8	 1	 903.9 28.1	 3	 22	 10	 2320 233.2	 10	 7724.1 555.1	 7
Defense *R&D Budget Amount Spent	 272 178.1	 49	 524.7 152	 29	 10 0	 71	 1402 939	 67	 5850.3 38007	 65
Communication *R&D Budget Amount Spent	 343 125.3	 50	 456.9 451.8	 99	 95	 90	 1070 672.5	 63	 4830.3 3586.4	 74

Sources: Calculated from Financial data Provided by Federal Ministry of Finance; and the Central Bank of Nigeria, Lagos, 1997.
Note: In 1987 the Official Exchange Rate was $1=N5.50. In 1993-1996 $1=N80.
In 1996 the Ministry of Agriculture contracted out 42% of its R&D Budget to Supply Fertilizer and Agro-Chemicals to Farmers.
*Total R&D Budget for the Fiscal Year.

for compliance with the SAP/Make-or-Buy policy. It is important to note that the number of contracts and the amount of money may reflect opportunity, i.e., availability of grant monies, and little more. The Ministries of Defense and Communications budgets for R & D were lower than those of the Ministries of Agriculture and Energy, Mines and Resources yet they awarded more contracts than the latter. The increases in number of contracts and monies awarded, however, appear to be substantial for all of the ministries over the eight-year period of implementation.

There are several other criticisms, which can be made of the report itself. The first of these criticisms relates to the way in which unsolicited funds are represented. The report acknowledges that the data compiled about the SAP/Make-or-Buy policy reflects salary increases and may not represent a growth in funds allocated by the Federal Government for R &

D purposes. The report does not stress that the figures may also include unsolicited funds, which represent a form of bridge financing and are not provided on a long-term basis. The report also contends that:

> ...Ministries maintain the contracting funds from year to year for that purpose, and that they contract in-house during the next year (Statement made by Public Servants, 1995).

The report does not say however, how the Government knows or can tell when a new R & D project which had been approved in the B-Budget and contracted out in another year, continues to be contracted out in subsequent years when it is not new, but has become part of the A-Budget. Finally, the report attempts to evaluate adequate in-house capability as a policy objective but does so only in a very narrow way. For example, in the report, the in-house capability required of a ministry seems to be only minimally sufficient to administer and evaluate R & D contracts with the private sector, and not to perform research.

This is a very narrow definition of what in-house capability means, because what is needed in some ministries is the capability not just to manage contracts, but to actually do the research in areas where the research is mandated by the policy, and cannot be contracted out to a party being regulated. Thus, the report does not contemplate the possibility that some ministries with growing regulatory responsibilities will have good reasons, within the intent and scope of the SAP/Make-or-Buy Policy, to increase the proportion of their in-house research and the capability to perform it.

From the foregoing analysis, it can be seen that there are several shortcomings in the total data published on the SAP/Make-or-Buy Policy in the MOST Report. These shortcomings present severe difficulties for the analysis of the actual (not just the reported) response to the policy by the contracting line federal ministries charged with the policy's implementation. In order to identify accurately the ministries, which did not support the policy in practice, it is necessary to know the proportion of R & D contracts they awarded each year from the annual federal government contracts.

Using the most detailed data provided by MOST for each ministry's, an attempt has been made to calculate the number of contracts that they awarded yearly in percentage. These data are presented in Table 4. The percentages have been calculated for all ministries charged with the implementation of the policy, not just the four that are of concern to this research. The data in Table 11.3 reveal that in 1987 and 1988, the Ministry of Agriculture did not award any contracts, however, the Ministry of Communication did. The latter awarded 45.4 percent in 1987 and 40.1 percent in 1988, of the total R & D contracts awarded by the Federal Government of Nigeria.

Similarly, the Ministry of Defense awarded 20.7 percent in 1987 and 17.3 percent in 1988. The Ministry of Energy, Mines and Resources awarded 5.6 percent in 1987 and 7.7 percent in 1988. This trend of R & D contract awards continued until 1996. In 1996, the Ministry of Agriculture awarded only 1.2 percent of the total R & D contracts for that year.

Table 11.4
Percentage by Ministry of the Number of R & D Contracts Awarded by Federal Government Ministries – Based on Rate of Support for the SAP/Make-or-Buy Policy Each Year Under Study 1987-1996

Ministries	1987	1988	1989	1990	1991	1992	1994	1996
Agriculture	0	0	0.04	.2	1.2	1.2	1.2	1.2
Communications	45.4	40.1	38.2	34.8	35.5	34.0	34.0	35.0
Defense	20.7	17.3	19.3	25.2	25.2	26.5	26.0	25.0
Energy, Mines & Resources	5.6	7.7	4.4	5.3	5.0	4.5	4.8	4.0
Environment	1.3	4.1	4.6	5.2	5.0	5.0	5.0	5.2
Transport	14.3	16.5	12.2	16.7	16.0	18.0	18.2	20.2
Nat. Research Council	8.2	10.9	11.9	10.2	10.0	9.3	9.0	10.5
Others	4.5	3.4	9.4	2.4	7.1	1.5	1.8	0.9

Source: Derived from data provided by the Ministry of Science and Technology, Lagos, Nigeria.

The Ministry of Energy, Mines and Resources recorded a 4.0 percent award. The Ministry of Agriculture and the Ministry of Energy, Mines and Resources jointly awarded a total of 5.2 percent of all the R & D contracts awarded in 1996. These figures indicate continued low support for the SAP/Make-or-Buy policy. The Ministry of Communications awarded 35 percent of R & D contracts in 1996, while the Ministry of Defense awarded 25 percent of the total contracts that same year. Jointly, they awarded a total of 60 percent of all the R & D contracts awarded by the Federal Government of Nigeria in 1996. The numerical profile of the

Ministry of Communication and the Ministry of Defense reveals stronger support for the SAP/Make-or-Buy policy.

The argument or the thought of the bureaucratic-authoritarian regime is that only the military is in a position to save Nigeria. Military juntas are oriented toward patriotic service and think of themselves as able to maintain order and discipline. However, as this analysis shows, the military can often count on the tolerance if not the support of substantial portions of the nation's bureaucracy, elite and the population in general.

Interpretation of the Financial Data

One of the research questions asks what the financial data reveals about the implementation of the policy and whether implementation is related to a perception of conflict or minimal conflict by the different ministries. The data in Tables 11.1 and 11.2 show that the Ministries of Communications and Defense awarded a large number of R & D contracts and a considerable sum of money. In Table 11.2 for example, the R & D contracts that the Ministry of Defense awarded out of its total R & D budget range from 65 percent in 1987 to 100 percent in 1992. It awarded another 71 percent in 1993 and 67 percent in 1994. For the eight years under study, the ministry contracted out an average of 65 percent of its R & D funds to the private sector. The Ministry of Communication also awarded between 37 percent and 99 percent of its R & D budget to the private sector. However, the average R & D fund contracted out during the eight years under study represented 74 percent of its total R & D budget over the period.

In contrast, the Ministries of Agriculture and Energy, Mines and Resources awarded relatively few contracts and monies. The Ministry of Agriculture for example, awarded to the private sector out of its R & D budget between zero percent in 1987 and 20 percent in 1992. The output of crops such as maize and groundnut within the area covered by this project declined by 43.5 percent (Central Bank of Nigeria, 1995). There was however, a sudden increase to 52 percent in 1994. This increase in 1994 was not due to the ministry's support for the SAP/Make-or-Buy policy, but rather a result of diverting 42 percent of the R & D budget to supply fertilizer and agro-chemicals to farmers. The increase in funding did not however, have a positive impact on all the activities of the ministry. The average R & D budget funds contracted out by the Ministry of Agriculture over the eight years period under study, however, was 15 percent. The Ministry of Energy, Mines and Resources contracted out between one percent in 1987 and 22 percent of its R & D budget in 1992. The average funds contracted out in 1993 and 1994 dropped to 10 percent. For the eight years under study, its average R & D budget contracted out to the private sector was only 7 percent. When the results of the interviews are compared with the financial data, a pattern emerges. The Ministries of Communications and Defense perceived minimal conflict between their mandates and the policy and contracted out a substantial number of R & D projects and money. In other words, these particular ministries tended to support the policy verbally, and also contracted out a substantial amount of their R & D work to the private sector.

The Ministries of Agriculture and Energy, Mines and Resources and the Ministry of Communications, perceiving greater conflict between the policy and their mandates, contracted out relatively less R & D. The financial data and the percentage of contracts awarded reveal that the Ministries of Agriculture and Energy, Mines and Resources demonstrated minimal support for the policy both in attitude and deed. By comparing the interview results and financial data, it can be tentatively concluded that the behavior of the Ministry of Agriculture and Energy, Mines and Resources upholds the original prediction about the degree of policy resistance or support. The interview results show that these ministries were less likely to respond positively to the policy, and, although there has been some improvement over time, the relatively small amount of R & D contracted is consistent with the interview results. From the above analysis of the interview results and the financial data, it is reasonable to conclude that federal ministries responded differently to the SAP/Make-or-Buy Policy. Their support, however, depended upon the degree of conflict perceived between their individual mandates and the SAP/Make-or-Buy requirement to contract out.

We are left to explore whether the SAP/Make-or-Buy policy resulted in the development of new technology and whether the economy improved following its enactment. It appears that the policy has not stimulated Nigerian companies to develop technologies that are appropriate for Nigeria.

Technology Development and the Performance of the Economy

Since 1986, when the policy was announced, corporate R & D has increased by only 20 percent, i.e., from 3.3 percent of the corporate budget in 1986 to 3.96 in 1994. The public and private sectors remain dependent upon imported technology. Nevertheless, those firms that have been able to find local substitutes for imported raw materials have performed better under the SAP/Make-or-Buy policy than those still heavily dependent on imports. It also is interesting to note that firms benefiting most from the SAP/Make-or-Buy policy have been small, highly specialized service-oriented, and Nigerian owned. SAP/Make-or-Buy policy has had little impact on the primary target of the policy, that is the major industrial producers.

While some large companies, especially in the manufacturing sector, have taken advantage of the SAP/Make-or-Buy policy, many more have not. SAP/Make-or-Buy therefore cannot be judged a success. The poor performance of SAP/Make-or-Buy policy has been blamed on several factors, among which are inadequate infrastructure (e.g., roads, communications), lack of executive leadership capacity, poor utilization of available manpower, and the absence of a supportive technological base. The creation of contracts and the transfer of substantial amounts of money to the private sector have not produced the desired indigenous technology. Earlier neglect of the private sector, civil war and sustained political instability, as well as the almost total dependence on petroleum exports, are some of the principal elements contributing to the unhealthy state of Nigeria's economy? SAP/Make-or-Buy policy was slated to transcend some of these problems, but it is a minor element in the larger Nigerian picture, and there is little indication of economic improvement in the first ten years of its implementation.

The Central Bank reports a decline in industrial production in the years following the introduction of the SAP/Make-or-Buy policy. The aggregate index of industrial production dropped 22.8 percent in the fourth quarter of 1995 (1985 being 100%). Similarly, declines of 5.0 and 5.1 percent were recorded in 1992 and 1993, respectively. The contraction in industrial production is traced to the manufacturing and mining sub-sectors where output fell by 8.2 and 9.8 percent in 1994 and in the first quarter of 1995. This decline was also observed in the third quarter of 1995 when the index fell by 15.7 percent owing largely to sustained political crisis in Nigeria and the resulting difficulty in accessing foreign exchange for the import of raw materials and machinery spare parts (Central Bank of Nigeria, 1995).

The poor performance of the manufacturing sub-sector was confirmed by a 1996 nation-wide survey conducted by the Central Bank of Nigeria. This survey covered 509 manufacturing establishments in 29 industrial groups, with a response rate of 61.3 percent. The survey showed that the average rate of capacity utilization in the manufacturing industry fell from 37.2 percent in 1993 to 30.4 in 1995. Five manufacturing sub-groups operated above 50 percent capacity utilization, namely, beer (54.3%), wood and cork products (51.1%), soft drinks (50%) and soap and perfumes (50%). Eight others operated above 30 percent. They are: textile (46.6%), cement and cement products (45%), plastic products (42%), drugs and medicine (41%), tires and tubes (32%), vegetable and grain milling (30.5%), fabricated metal products (30%) and bakery products (30%). All the other groups operated at less than 30 percent of their installed capacity. These were structural metal products (24%), paints (23.8%), basic metal products (23%), paper products (23%), printing and publishing (23%) miscellaneous food preparation (26.5%), roofing sheets (21%), radio, television and electrical equipment (18%), sugar and confectionery (17.5%), auto vehicle assembly (15%), and glass products (8%) (Central Bank of Nigeria, 1995).

Expenditure on research and development (R & D) by private sector corporations fell 0.9 percent in 1993 and 26.6 percent in 1994, from 100 percent in 1985. As in previous years, the expenditure on R & D continued to account for a fraction (1.7 %) of total investment expenditure. Performance of R & D enterprises deteriorated further at the end of 1995 reflecting a decline in the levels of output and low overall capacity utilization rates. Interviews conducted in ten companies reveal that the continued devaluation of the Naira caused the cost of imported materials to rise by 229 percent between 1987 and 1995. Similarly, the cost of locally produced raw materials rose by 96 percent in the same time period. In a climate in which borrowing has become exorbitant, many private manufacturers in Nigeria find themselves unable to compete for loans or pay for the foreign exchange needed to bring in foreign products. Moreover, they are unable to reorganize their production techniques, or even cover their basic overhead costs.

The inflation cycle poses still another problem for manufacturers of basic commodities who do not enjoy a large domestic market. Producers who manage to remain in business in spite of the high cost of production, nevertheless, face a situation in which the market for their products diminishes by the day. Consequently, many manufacturers are forced to stockpile their surplus goods in costly warehouses.

Table 11.5 shows the annual capacity utilization of ten Nigerian companies. These companies were expected to be the major source of technology development in Nigeria. However, their capacity utilization records do not indicate any progress in the role they are expected to play in national economic growth.

Table 11.5
Annual Capacity Utilization in Percentages, for Ten Nigerian Companies for 1990, 1993 and 1996

Name of Company	Annual Capacity Utilization (%)				
	1990	1993	% Diff.	1996	% Diff.
Delta Steel Company	8.9	13.2	48.3	18.2	37.9
Ajakuta Steel Company	0	0	0	0	0
Nigerian Refineries	80.2	31.0	-61.3	65.5	111.3
Nigerian Machine Tools Limited	10.0	8.0	-20	10.0	25
Nigerian Paper Mills Limited	11.9	12.8	7.6	3.5	-72.7
Nigerian Newsprint Mfg. Company	12.8	13.3	3.9	3.63	-72.7
Nigerian Sugar Company	71.0	43.3	-39	58.0	33.9
West African Cement Company	68.5	69.8	1.9	64.0	-8.30
Nigerian Cement Company	23.0	19.0	-17.4	12.0	-36.8
Nigerian Marble Mining Company	16.6	16.6	0	7.9	-52.4

Source: Interview conducted in 1995 and 1996. Central Bank of Nigeria, Annual Report, 1995, pp. 81-98.

In 1990 the Delta Steel Company utilization capacity fell from 100 to 8.9 percent. Its capacity increased from 8.9 percent in 1990 to 13.2 percent in 1993. This represents a 48.3 percent increase from 1990. The capacity utilization for the company increased by 37.9 percent in 1996 from 13.2 percent in 1993. The Ajakuta Steel Company, which has been under construction since 1975, is yet to start production. The three Nigerian Refineries produced at a total of 80.2 percent of their capacity in

1990. The level of utilization dropped by 61.3 percent in 1993. However, it increased a little bit from 31 percent in 1993 to 65.5 percent in 1995. This shows a utilization increase of 111.3 percent in 1996. The Nigerian Machine Tools Company manufacturing capacity dropped from 10 percent in 1990 to 8 percent in 1993. It however, increased production by 25 percent in 1996.

Other companies such as the Nigerian Paper Mills limited increased its utilization capacity from 11.9 percent in 1990 to 12.8 percent in 1993. Its production capacity however, decreased by 72.7 percent in 1996 from 12.8 percent in 1993. Similarly, the Nigerian Newsprint Manufacturing Company production capacity dropped from 100 percent installation capacity to 12.8 percent in 1990, increased to 13.3 percent in 1993, and decreased to 3.63 percent in 1996. The Nigerian Sugar Company continued to produce at a fairly higher rate of 71 percent until 1990. Its production capacity however, decreased to 43.3 percent in 1993. In 1996, the company utilization capacity increased by 33.9 percent from its 43.3 percent level in 1993. The West African Poland Cement Company maintained a capacity utilization of 68.5 percent in 1990, 69.8 percent in 1993, and decreased to 64 percent in 1996. The decrease in 1996 represents a negative 8.3 percent of 1993 rate. Nigerian Cement Company capacity utilization dropped from 100 percent in the early 1980s to 23 percent in 1990. The company further decreased its capacity utilization by minus 17.4 percent in 1993. In 1996, its capacity utilization dropped further to 12 percent. The trend of capacity utilization of the Nigerian Marble Mining Company is similar to those of the other companies mentioned above. Its manufacturing installed capacity decreased from 100 percent in 1979 to 16.6 percent in 1990. The company continued to maintain the 16.6 percent utilization capacity till 1993, before a further decrease to 7.9 percent in 1996.

The poor performance of these important companies after nine years of the SAP/Make-or-Buy policy demonstrate that co-ordination and control from the top is difficult to achieve in large and complex organizations. The Nigerian Military Government created a policy but it could not guarantee that implementation would follow a direct path. It even modified the policy in 1987 and again in 1989. Such modifications were in response to obstacles in its implementation phase. Moreover, a procedure for managing unsolicited science and technology proposals from the private sector was developed. In 1989 the policy was expanded again, this time, to cover ongoing R & D and related activities in the natural and social science fields of urban, regional and transportation studies (Central

Bank of Nigeria, 1996).

MOST and MTI continue to play their respective roles in the coordination and administration of the SAP/Make-or-Buy Policy, but their powers remain limited and circumscribed. They can not force the Ministry of Agriculture, or the Ministry of Energy, Mines and Resources to develop specific contracts or allocate funds in ways that they determine to be more effective. The data in fact, reveals considerable dissatisfaction with MOST and MTI, given their attempts at interfering with the work ways of the different ministries. By and large both were judged impediments not facilitator in the work of the ministries. The weakness identified in MOST and MTI, dramatize the weakness in the SAP/Make-or-Buy policy. Moreover, in the context of Nigeria's economic plight, sustained conflict between the military junta and the professional administrators describes a decision-making process that is ill equipped to address national problems.

Implications of the Analysis

This study shows that those who stage coups tend to discount the fact that they have limited experience in politics and limited knowledge of political issues (including issues relating to the economy). They are accustomed to relative simple situations permitting them to issue orders and to expect results accordingly. The bureaucratic-authoritarian regime and their supporter apparently assume that almost any set of able, honest, and devoted person can improve on the government when the military is in control. An authoritarian regime of a military-bureaucratic sort may or may not be associated with a political party. If so, the party is likely to play a restricted role. The regime can be expected, of course, to outlaw political parties and organizations that stand seriously in its way. It is not there to rally mass support or to urge mass participation in political life but rather to get the country through some kind of crisis. It is also likely to want simply to be left alone to do the job. It can be expected to control the media and to repress dissidence in so far as that seems necessary to the preservation of its power.

The implications of this study for the Nigerian government can be summarized as follows: First, governments should not introduce policies which may not be implemented or maintained, no matter how attractive these policies are in principle. Second, policies, which are working, should not be changed without appropriate consultation with those who are involved in its implementation process. Finally, in choosing among policies, priority should be given to those that enhance the stability of the overall policy environment.

In Nigeria, policy touching upon development is made at the level of the Armed Forces Ruling Council. Unfortunately, however, it is not whether good polices are formulated, or even whether the means are provided for the fulfillment of these policies, but whether the policy is implemented, poorly implemented, or not implemented at all. For any policy measure to be successful in Nigeria there is typically one or more government ministries or agencies whose duty it is to formulate in minute detail the modalities required in attaining the goals of the policy. It is essential that those who are to be involved in policy implementation should be included in deliberations before the policy is established. Involvement at the planning stage of a policy generates consensus among those involved in its implementation. It can be argued that without this spirit of participation among implementers, the policy will be judged an imposition, and hence resisted. It was the contention of the bureaucrats in the ministries studied that the absence of discretionary powers was a major reason for the failure of the SAP/Make-or-Buy Policy.

Conclusion

The underlying concern of this paper is whether or not a centralized bureaucratic-authoritarian system can effectively describe the relations between the Nigerian military and the traditional bureaucracy in the process of decision- making and implementation. This chapter found out that a weak bureaucratic-authoritarian relationship in Nigeria resulted in the failure or minimal success of the SAP/Make-or-Buy Policy.

The formulation of SAP/Make-or-Buy policy and the military government's decision to announce it occurred at a time when Nigeria's economy could be regarded as approaching collapse. Economic decline and dislocation can only in part be attributed to ineffective implementation of the SAP/Make-or-Buy policy. What would have been the likely result had the SAP/Make-or-Buy policy been fully implemented as the military expected? Interview findings indicate that few economic benefits would have resulted. Nigeria has experienced frequent breakdowns of equipment and plant closings; the country continues to experience protracted industrial unrest, especially among the oil workers. Nigeria also suffers from low utilization of ready equipment, from foreign exchange constraints, from the high cost of industrial operations, and above all, from political instability. Thus, one can conclude that the ministries were pursuing not only their own interests, but the larger public interests of Nigeria by resisting or opposing an unrealistic policy that had been dictated from above with little or no consultation.

Nigeria in the 1990s remains an underdeveloped, dependent, and technologically backward country (Ake 1985; Nafziager 1997; Aborisade and Mundt 1998). Only when compared with the other nations of sub-Saharan Africa, does Nigeria appear to be developing? Viewed from a global perspective, Nigeria has made little progress in improving its economy. Foreign interests continue their domination in most economic sectors, while Nigerian society struggles to overcome its divisive self-defeating behavior. Coherent political organization, bureaucratic competence and national decision-making are essential requirements of all national development programs but genuine progress is not likely to emerge in Nigeria until the military junta retires to the barracks and new self-governing institutions are elected over a political system anchored in democratic practices.

References

Achike, Okay. (1990). Groundwork of Military Law and Military Rule in Nigeria. Ibadan: University of Ibadan Press.

Adamolekun, L. (1985). Nigeria Public Administration 1960-1980. Ibadan, Nigeria: Heinemann Education Books.

Adamolekun, L. (1986). Politics and Administration in Nigeria. Ibadan, Nigeria: Spectrum Books.

Adamolekun, Ladipo, and Victor Ayeni. (1990). "Nigeria". In Subramanian. Edited by Public Administration in Third World. London: Longman.

Adedeji, Adebayo. (1968). Nigerian Administration and Its Political Setting. London: Hutchinson.

Adedeji, Adebayo. (1981). "Rise and Fall of the Nigerian Civil Service" (Part II & I). West African Magazine (March 30), pp. 687- 692.

Adekson, Bayo. (1978). Towards Explaining Civil Military Instability in Contemporary Sub-Saharan Africa. Ibadan, Nigeria: University of Ibadan Press.

Adeniyi, Emiola. (1989). "Development Planning in Nigeria". Nigerian Trade Journal. (July/September), Vol. 4, 3.

Adu, A.I. (1982). The Civil Service in Commonwealth Africa. London:

George Allen and Unwin Limited.

Adubifa, Akin. (1990). Technology Policy in Nigeria. Ibadan, Nigeria: NISER Press.

Ake, Claude. (1995). "Nigerian Development and the Ogoni Crisis." Policy. Lagos, Nigeria: Daily Times Press.

Ake, Claude. (1995). Political Economy of Nigeria. London: Longman.

Anyanwu, Ahan. (1992). Nigerian Structural Adjustment Program: A Multi-Sectoral Analysis. Enugu, Nigeria: ABIC Books and Equipment Limited.

Apter, D. (1987). Rethinking Development: Modernization Dependency and Postmodern Politics. Newbury Park, Calif: Sage Publications.

Ayida, A. (1987). Reflection on Nigerian Development. Lagos: Heinemann.

Bangura, Yusuf. (1987). "IMF-World Bank Conditionally and Nigeria's Structural Adjustment Program." In The IMF and World Bank in Africa edited by Kjell J. Havenik. Uppsala, Sweden: Scandinavian Institute of African Studies.

Bienen, Henry. (1971). The Military and Modernization. Princeton, New Jersey: Princeton University Press.

Bienen, Henry, and John Waterbury. (1989)."The Political Economy of Privatization in Developing Countries." World Development. Vol.17, 5, pp. 622-632.

Central Bank of Nigeria. (1987-1996). Annual Report. Lagos, Nigeria: Government Press.

Edoho, Felix. (1997). Globalization and the New World Order. Westport, Connecticut: Praeger.

Fadahunsi, Akin, and Igwe B. (1989). Capital Goods and Technological Change and Accumulation in Nigeria Dakar, Senegal: CODESRIA.

Fajana, O. (1987). "Trade and Growth: The Nigerian Experience." World Development. Vol.7, 1, pp.73-78.

Federal Government of Nigeria: Guidelines on Structural Adjustment Program. (1986-1987). Lagos, Nigeria: Government Press.

Friedrich, Carl. (1963). Man and His Government. New York: McGraw-Hill.

Galbraith, John, Kenneth. (1981). The New Industrial State. 2nd Edition. Boston: Houton-Mufflin.

Graf, William. (1988). The Nigerian State, Political Economy, State Class and Political System in Post-Colonial Era. Portsmouth: Heinemann Press.

Ihonvbere, Julius. (1994). Nigeria: The Politics of Adjustment and Democracy. New Brunswick: Transaction Publishers.

Nafziger, Wayne. (1997). The Economics of Developing Countries. Upper Saddle River: Prentice University Press.

Nordlinger, Erik A. (1970). "Soldiers in Mufti: The Impact of Military Rule on Economic and Social Change in Non-Western States." American Political Science Review. Vol. 65. (December) pp. 1131-1148.

Nwosu, Humphrey. (1977). Political Authority and Nigerian Civil Service. Enugu, Nigeria: Fourth Dimension Publishing Company.

Nwosu, Humphrey. (1979). Problems of Nigerian Administration. Enugu, Nigeria: Fourth Dimension Publishing Company.

Obadan, Michael, and Bright Ekerhane. (1988). "The Theoretical Basis of Structural Adjustment Program: An Appraisal. Proceedings of the Nigerian Economic Society 1988 Annual Conference. Ile-Ife: Obafemi Awolowo University Press (May 3-7).

Obasanjo, Olusegun, and Akin Mabogimje. (1991). Elements of Development in Nigeria. Lagos, Nigeria: C & E Publishers.

Odetola, Olatunde. (1982). Military Regimes and Development: A Comparative Analysis of Africa. London: George Allen and Unwin Press.

O'Donnell, Guillermo. (1973). Modernization and Bureaucratic-Authoritarianism: Studies in South American Politics. Berkeley: University of California Press.

O'Donnell, Guillermo. (1976). "Modernization and Military Coup: Theory, Comparisons and Argentine Case." in Lowenthal (ed). Armies and Politics in Latin America. New York: Holme and Meir Press.

Office of the Minister for Science and Technology, New Release. (1990). New Contracting-Out Policy Challenges to Strengthen Nigeria's Industrial Capability. (August 15).

Olukoshi, Adebayo. (1992). The Politics of Structural Adjustment in Nigeria. London: James Carrey Publishers.

Onimode, Bade. (1989). The IMF, the World Bank and the African Debt. (Volume I & II - The Economic Impact). London: Zed Books.

Otobo, E. (1999). "Nigeria." In Public Administration in Africa edited by Oladipo Adamolekun. Boulder, Colorado: Westview Press.

Oyovbaire, S.E. (1980). "Politicization of the Higher Civil Servant in Nigerian Presidential System of Government." Quarterly Journal of Administration (April), pp. 272-280.

Perlmutter, Amos. (1981). Political Roles and Military Rulers. New York: Frank Cass Publishers.

Stepan, Alfred. (1988). Rethinking Military Politics: Brazil and the Southern Cone. Princeton New Jersey: Princeton University Press.

Tarp, Finn. (1993). Stabilization and Structural Adjustment: Macroeconomic Frameworks for Analyzing the Crisis in Sub-Saharan Africa. New York: Routledge.

Treasury Board. (1987). Guidelines for the Implementation of the Make-or-Buy Policy Concerning Research and Development Requirements in the Natural Science. Lagos, Nigeria: Government Press.

Udoekong, Mike. (1990). "Industrialization in Nigeria: An Appraisal." The Nigerian Interpreter, Special Edition (October).

Udogu, Ike. (1995). "The Military Civil Society and the Issues of Democratic Governance: Toward Nigeria's Fourth Republic." Journal of Developing Studies. Vol XI, 2, pp. 162-170.

Ukpabi, S.C. (1972). Military Involvement in Nigerian Politics. Ibadan, Nigeria: Ibadan University Press.

World Bank. (1983-1990). World Development Report. New York: Oxford University Press.

Part IV

How to Achieve Sustainable Development

12 Women, Bureaucracy and Development

Introduction

The history of women in Nigeria's public bureaucracy presents an account of tremendous diversity in the civil service. There can be no mistaking in the widespread and presence of women in the civil service of Nigeria today. Yet female senior public administrators are relatively rare. As the case study in chapters 6 and 8 shows, only two percent of senior public administrators are women in the national, state and local government's civil service in Nigeria (see Tables 12.1 and 12.2). Thus, it appears that women populate the three levels of civil service in Nigeria, but they rarely run them. Equality for women in the civil service is improving, although it is a slow victory, to be sure.

After four decades since Nigeria became an independence nation-state and some experience with quota system, there can be absolutely no doubt about major gain in the opportunity that have become available to women and minority groups in the civil service. However, prejudice continues to exist, as does the glass ceiling that limits women from enjoying truly equal opportunities in the Nigerian public service. Why is this case? Although sufficient time may not have passed to allow more women to work their way into the senior positions of the Nigerian civil service, there appear to be more formidable barriers. Most notably, it is clear that powerful gender role stereotypes persist, narrow-minded beliefs about the kinds of tasks for which women are most appropriately suited. These beliefs originated from religious and in some cases cultural practices.

Women in Nigeria have virtually no formal power in the national and state civil service. Although the national government created Ministry of Women affairs almost a decade ago, there is no doubt that the government shapes and limits women's role in the civil service. Gender is still central to understand the processes through which appointments are made to senior public management positions. Even though the government sometimes promote and patronize women's organizations, Nigerian women are still struggling to find ways to break the glass ceiling imposed on them in the civil service. Well educated women in the civil service in Nigeria continue to face numerous contradictions between what they need to survive and what is possible under current administrative laws, religious, and traditional social structures in the nation.

The few studies that mentioned gender helplessness in African civil service argued that gender does shape the opportunities and constraints women and men face in securing positions in government (Thomas-Sayter and Rocheleau 1995; Adepoju 1994; Kalu 1993). Moreover, as Adepuju pointed out, the systematically inferior position of women inside and outside the civil service and household in Nigeria points to the necessity of treating gender as a force of its own in sustainable development issues in the nation. Although the relative deprivation of women when compared with men varies around Africa, this fact does not diminish the importance of giving women more senior public management positions in Nigeria. If policy is to reach the citizens equitably and the grassroots with effective prescriptions and action for sustainable management of Nigeria's public resources, it will have to address the concerns of women not hired in senior public management positions.

This chapter examines the predicament of prejudice on women in the public service in Nigeria and the struggle to integration women into political leadership and economic development in Nigeria. It argues that the public sector of Nigeria need to introduce diversity management programs as a policy that should be adopted by the national, state and local governments. The chapter also argues that in offering women the opportunity to access economic resources as well as to disentangle their identities from those of their families women will contribute immensely in the sustainable development process in the nation. Further, diversity management programs will provide the space for women in Nigeria to clearly define their role as equal partners in the sustainable development process of the nation. This chapter also presents some theoretical perspectives of the role of women's role in the development process of a nation. Given a labor force and culture with male dominance, is the present use of women in the Nigerian society the best possible one for the country? The concluding section calls for an equal opportunity government policy that will effectively reduce discrimination against women in the civil service and integrate women's interests, social expectations and creation of opportunities for broad economic, social and political participation for all Nigerian women.

Women and Equal Opportunity

The study of feminism and equal opportunity in Nigeria is still in its infancy. Recently, attention to the impact of gender and ethnicity on public institutions has focused largely on perceptions of discrimination, the notion of representative bureaucracy and equal opportunities policies. Most African scholars have argued that the use of the word family is too restrictive and should be replaced with the term intimate. Since current research include studies of couples that cohabitate but are not necessarily married (Abdullah, 1995; Adepoju, 1994; Bank, 1994; Dennis, 1987; Konjo, 1991; Ofei-Aboagye, 1994; Wallace, 1999; Weisner et al. 1997;) the word family might not be appropriate. However, most scholars now accept the idea that a family unit may exist without any form of sanction such as marriage ceremony. In this chapter, the definition of family includes the situation in which individuals are living together regardless of whether they are legally married or not.

There is widespread acceptance of the critical role played by women and public institutions in the development process (see, for example, Turner and Hulme 1997; World Bank 1997). Women act as major actors in the transformation process, whether in terms of their direct involvement in the economy or their more tempered role as catalyst, facilitator and regulator of economic activity. At the same time a growing concern with the representatives of women and the management of diversity within Nigeria's public sector has been a concern. The concern of unequal representation of women in the public sector has affected reform efforts that put stress, human resources management issues such as capacity-building, participatory management styles, constant innovation, entrepreneurial initiative, teamwork, strategic thinking and planning as crucial.

World Bank (1997) report pointed out that when women are not offered equal opportunity in the civil service there is the danger that some skills in a nation will be wasted. The idea that recruitment and promotion are based on merit rather than on some particularistic criteria can contribute significantly to higher levels of morale and performance.

As Esman (1997) has pointed out, ethnic politics largely ignores public administration or socioeconomic development, in much the same way that the literature on economic development overlooks ethnic cleavages. Yet in many societies, particularly in Nigeria ethnicity and gender plays such a fundamental, all-pervasive role in the development process. Gender and ethnic politics is described as "an important dimension in public affairs, pervading the environment in which public administration functions in Nigeria" (Adepoju, 1994).

The report of the civil service reforms of 1988 in Nigeria address the issue of quota system and perceptions of discrimination against women in the public sector. Some African scholars have also strived for what is known as a representative bureaucracy in sub-Saharan African nations (Green 1999; Kalu 1993). The notion of a representative bureaucracy is attributed to Kingsley (1944), with later refinements by Krislov (1974) and Meier (1993), among others. Kingsley's view was that, for an administrative system to respond to changes in the political climate – and there is an assumption that it ought to respond to such changes as a matter of course – it had to represent children, young adults, women and men equally in a society. It should be noted that Kingsley was referring specifically to the homogeneous British society where social classes in the Marxian sense, rather than ethnic groups, were the units of analysis. The notion of a representative bureaucracy in Nigeria means that where the bureaucracy broadly reflects the interests of society, the society should be well represented. In this respect top management should comprise of men, women and young adults in the society. These groups should share a common background and values with the leaders of the governing party in power (Isekhure, 1998). This idea is closely related to the current discourses on public sector reform, that the bureaucracy must be more responsive to the policy direction of the government of the day instead of being purely neutral and impartial.

Lijphart (1977) presents two approaches about the passive and the active. The passive approach presents a more or less sociological/demographic argument. It suggests that the bureaucracy should mirror society as a whole. This approach according to Lijphart is known proportionality, meaning not only that all groups should be represented in decision-making organs, but that they should be represented proportionally. Appointments to the bureaucracy should therefore be allocated among men, women and the other different segments of the population in direct proportion to their numbers. This way, the administrative apparatus of Nigeria will becomes a microcosm of the wider society.

This approach is clearly impractical in Nigeria for three main reasons. In the first place, it fails to recognize that social groups may not be equally predisposed to seeking careers in the public service. To the extent that this is true, the public service of Nigeria will never be fully representative on the basis of proportionality. This had always been the main defense (or rationalization) offered to explain the notable absence of women in senior management positions in the public service. It was argued that they did not apply as they preferred to seek employment in agriculture or commerce (Kalu, 1993). Second, not all groups are qualified to enter based on merit. As Otobo (1999) and Oluwo (1999) pointed out representative bureaucracy in Nigeria depends on an even distribution of formal education. That is, women in the Nigerian society may be underrepresented in the public sector due to historical, religious and cultural patterns of educational development.

The level at which the bureaucracy ought to be representative is a third problem. Modupe Kolawole (1998) argued that socialization experiences among women within the public service tend to diminish the influence of pre-employment experiences, and that upwardly mobile public servants are likely to hold different values and opinions from others with the same social origins. Jerald Greenberg (1999) contend that when one think of a mentor, the image that comes to mind is an older male senior executive helping a younger male junior executive work his way up the public service ladder by introducing him to the "old boy network." By definition, any old boy network is sexist. Indeed, women in Nigeria's public service often seem to have less access to suitable mentor than do men.

Jerald Greenberg (1999) and Modupe Kolawole (1998) presented three reasons why men have more access to mentor than women did. First, there are simply fewer female executives available to serve as mentor for young female employees. Second, women are less willing to enter into mentoring relationships because they anticipate greater risk than men in doing so do. Recent survey in Nigeria found that women expressed more concern than men did about the potential for negative exposure that might come from the increased visibility they assume because of their proteges. This is specifically very important because Nigeria do not have sexual harassment laws. Third, barriers to mentoring exist not only between men and women, but also between members of different religious and ethnic groups. Insofar as mentors and proteges often get together because they have similar backgrounds and share similar attitudes, it is not surprising to find that people from different ethnic and religious groups face difficulties in their mentor – protégé relationships – if they form one at all.

Adamolekun (1999) pointed out the current wave of public sector reform efforts that tacitly approves of an expanded role for technocratic advisors from outside the public sector. The reform policies certainly reduced the role of senior public servants as the sole source of policy advice and almost banishing them to implementation and administration issues. This role also makes it difficult for them to introduce programs that would eliminate discrimination against women. Far from being loyal to their nation, these senior public administrators are more likely to be loyal to their ethnic group and the political hand that feeds them. Thus prejudice against women continues to exist in the civil service of Nigeria, as does the glass ceiling that limits all women from enjoying truly equal opportunities in the nation.

Personnel Management and Women: Discrimination in Practice

The notions of citizenship, politics, and gender relations are revealed in Nigeria through the analysis of how federal, state and local government leaders are open to the equal integration of women in the civil service. An examination of the interaction between male and women in Nigeria suggest that each reinforce each other, but this is not yet shown in the hiring processes of gender.

Table 12.1 and Table 12.2 show profiles of women who are hired at the federal, state and local government levels in Nigeria.

Table 12.1
Profile of Gender in Federal and State Governments in Nigeria

Position Title in Ministry	Gender			Total
	Male	Female	Missing Variable	
Director	3	3	-	6
Asst. Director	9	5	1	15
Manager	24	8	1	33
Asst. Manager	14	5	-	19
Supervisor	44	28	1	73
Professor	5	-	-	5
Others	8	-	-	8
Missing Variable	2	1	3	6
Total	109	50	6	165

Source: Analysis of survey conducted in Nigeria 2000.

Table 12.2
Profile of Gender in Local Government Employees

Position Title	Gender								Total
	M	F	Training Received						
			Ph.D	MA	BA	Dip	NCE	Ex-Army	
LG Chair	150	0	1	3	80	10	6	50	150
Councils	350	15	-	2	160	88	25	90	365
Director of Personnel Mgt.	140	10	-	55	95	-	-	-	150
Treasurers	131	19	-	12	130	8	-	-	150
Engineers	148	2	-	-	145	5	-	-	150
Secretary to LG	149	1	-	2	128	20	-	-	150
Other LG Staff	450	15	-	-	150	300	120	30	600
Total	1518	62	1	74	888	431	151	170	3260

Source: Analysis of survey conducted in Nigeria 2000.

Table 12.1 shows that out of 165 federal and state government employees that responded to the author's survey that was conducted in 2000 only 50 were female. Table 12.2 shows a similar survey conducted at the local government level. The data collected from the 1,580 responses suggest that only 62 females occupied management positions in 150 of the local governments that were randomly selected.

The public personnel management function in Nigeria's public service includes procedures for the establishment of posts, and selection, recruitment and subsequent treatment of persons filling those posts. The latter refers to disciplinary matters, personal/career development, as well as mobility (transfers and promotions). These procedures have four main objectives:

1. To assure that only qualified persons is hired.
2. To assure that public officers are not arbitrarily fired or transferred, and particularly not for reasons of partisan politics.
3. To provide procedures for promotion and/or other mobility, for career development or to accommodate the changing needs of the agency.

4. To provide procedures by which a person's employment can be terminated for unsatisfactory service (Adamolekun 1999).

Although women constitute about 60% of the Nigerian population, there are still a disproportionately low number them in senior leadership positions in all areas. It is therefore clear that women are present in sizable numbers in education, business and industry, and government. The obvious question however is, why aren't there more women in positions of power and leadership? What explanations satisfy the debate about who is qualified to lead in Nigeria?

In Nigeria civil service hiring men into senior management positions can be described as an instrument of controls over female employees. Although this may not be treated by a society as legitimate, the practice still continues. In some ethnic groups where these practices are deemed legitimate their treatment as forms of gender abuse has stirred a huge debate. Often this debate boils down to arguments for cultural relativism versus universal human rights. In most Nigerian families a husband uses this same idea as a reason to physically abuse or discipline his wife. This practice is an acceptable behavior.

As stated above Nigeria has a strong patriarchal structure that maintained the sexual division of labor in the household. This same structure directly restricts women's availability for wage work and indirectly condition the terms of employment for those women who enter the civil service. As the data in chapter six and eight reveals, there is a clear gender differentiation, in terms of occupational status and work condition in Nigeria. Specifically, women in the civil service are characterized by limited and insecure employment opportunities and marked substandard wages, poor work conditions, unstable hours and disadvantageous employment contracts. Women are predominantly employed in low wage jobs or extremely small-scale venture, which shunt them into segregated occupation and repetitious manual production.

Despite the fact that majority of the women who work in the civil service in Nigeria occupy junior positions, there are few women who hold position of power with the civil service. The few women are however, handicapped by the lack of affordable childcare, escalating rate of spousal abandonment, an increasingly high cost of living and gender stereotyping. These conditions deny women in the public service the requisite skills, training, and capital to secure more lucrative and secured employment. Moreover, because Nigerian women tend to be concentrated in transitory, low-paid, and low status jobs that typically replicate their household tasks, proper place as well as of their activities as survival victims.

In the Nigerian public service, the marginalization of women in the nation has two contrasting gender ideologies, which ironically produce the same outcome. The first is related to the aforementioned state- promoted gender identity. The state rhetoric and action imply that women in Nigeria do not need to engage in income-generating activities and that those who do engage in such activities do so for reasons other than economic necessity. The second gender ideology under girding the marginalization of women micro-entrepreneurs is related to gender bias embedded in development practice that perceive women as vulnerable and isolated groups and their activities as a collection of inconsequential endeavors. Gender specific ideologies; such as these, which underpin the marginalization of women within the public sector of Nigeria, are often nuance by cultural, ethnic and religious undertone.

In Nigeria, the rigid and hegemonic nature of prevailing notions of work not only denigrates the work of women but dis-empowers women producers themselves. Interview conducted in Nigeria in summer of 2000 reveals that, although women consider themselves to be producers of goods and providers of services for a large segment of the society, like the society women have a low estimate of the value of their own labor. Hence, it would seem that the particular constructions of gender to which Nigeria working women are subject and which inform their notions of self, not only deny them the value of their daily activities but also undermine the potential of their ministry or public agencies and discourage them from developing enabling notion of self worth.

Finally, the large scale exclusion of women from mainstream senior public management positions and political position at the national, state and local governments despite the fact that they in majority in the nation serves to reinforce this situation.

Policies Towards Equality of Opportunity for Women

While the passive approach emphasizes the sociological or demographic representatives of the Nigerian public service, the active approach places the accent on the cultural, religious and political determination of discrimination against women. From this perspective arise policies such as equal opportunity and other ethnic-conscious instruments designed to benefit the marginalized groups. Equality of opportunity is predicated on the idea of fair competition on the basis of merit, and the role of public policy is to ensure that all qualified individuals (men and women) may enter the competition and be judged according to the same criteria. Thus the state must act to (1) ensure that the competition is equal, and (2) equalize starting points where necessary (Lovenduski 1989: 8).

There has been much debate and political controversy surrounding equal opportunity policies and quota system in Nigeria. At the heart of the debate is the question of whether preferential treatment is justified and, if so, on what grounds. While accepting that there may be reason to challenge the arbitrary criteria on which preferences are to be allocated, there is no alternative but to support Edwards' (1995) position that, in principle at least, they (i.e. preferences to one or other group) are acceptable once they are designed to remove inequality and do not create greater injustices than those they seek to overcome.

Diversity ought to be an end in itself and not a means to achieving some less noble, politically motivated objective. Second, if equal opportunity is intended to serve as compensation for past injustices, then it is flawed as a form of redress since there is seldom anything that links past victims and present beneficiaries. What it does, in effect, is to seriously devalue (or certainly undervalue) the qualifications of those whose forebears stand accused of discriminating against previous generations of the new "in-group." This is surely tantamount to replacing one system of injustice with another.

Government not only must understand the dynamics of family abuse, but also be prepared to offer support and guidance to victims as they move through the difficult period in their life. Repairing the body and spirit is only half the battle; society must be able to make the victims of family abuse completely whole. This has to include financial reimbursement from the offender. The people of Nigeria are beginning to accept the fact that victims of crimes in general and victims of family abuse in particular, have rights and need to be active participants in the criminal justice system. This includes giving their input during sentencing of offenders. The use of victim impact statements is a giant step forward for victims of family violence.

The various policy instruments for ensuring women development are not exclusive to the government's official policies. Legal aid and legal literacy are the most popular components of government's effort to reduce family abuse. To rectify this situation in Nigeria, the Family Law Center is a legal services advisory center offering free legal advice on all family legal problems to low income people. The center's founders were careful not to restrict its services to women because of fears that it would be stigmatized as another "women's liberation project." Such a label might have jeopardized the center's existence for a number of reasons. To be more inclusive the center publishes booklets in four of the main languages in the nation. These publications are free and target school-age children in the hope that they will read it to their mothers while also learning on their own (Akande and Kuye, 1986).

In recent years, some ministries have become increasing proactive in their attempt to eliminate prejudice. Their approach is not just to hire a broader group of people than usual, but to create an atmosphere in which diverse groups can flourish. The ministries above are not merely trying to obey the law or attempting to be socially responsible, but they recognize that diversity is a public issue that needs to be addressed. The Nigerian government should therefore make sure that all its ministries and agencies introduce appropriate diversity management programs. As Otobo (1999) pointed out, the success of the government is determined by its managers ability to naturally tap the full potentials of a diverse workforce that comprise of women, men, young adults and so on.

The introduction of diversity management program in the Nigerian public service would constitute an effort to celebrate diversity by creasing supportive, not just neutral work environments for women and minority ethnic groups in the nation. Governments that adopt the underlying philosophy of diversity management programs is that cracking the glass ceiling requires that women and minorities are not just tolerated but valued in the nation's sustainable development process.

There are some non-official women organizations or associations that are committed to women's development. These non governmental associations include; Association of Working House Wives, Association of Media Women, Army Officers Wives Association, and National Council of Women Society of Nigeria and so on. The interests of these groups are basically confined to the welfare of their members. The activities of the National Council of Women for example, include the operation of child welfare services scheme, and market nurseries to cater for the children of market traders. The council runs adult education programs aimed at increasing political awareness and participation of women in development with particular references to women franchise – the right to vote and be voted for. It also runs a number of hostel accommodations for women in various towns and cities in Nigeria in order to alleviate accommodation problems for women in urban centers.

The formal instrument for women development in the Nigerian administration is the Federal Ministry of Social Development, Youth and Sports. Broad policies and guidelines on women development emanate from this ministry. Prominent among such development programs is the Community Home Economics that include day care center management. This is designed to enlighten women in rural areas on modern methods of home keeping and childcare. Another women development program is the Community Development Training Center. The center undertakes the training of rural women, teachers, and front line women leaders to enable them to motivate the citizens towards undertaking self help projects and to handle the various Day Care Centers (Buchanan, 1993).

The Adult Education program of the Federal Ministry of Education though not an exclusive women policy affair has also presented policy instrument for enhancing women development. Women are largely illiterates in comparison with their male folks and would therefore benefit more from adult education programs of the federal and various state governments. It is pertinent to note that a National Education Agency has been set up by the federal government and, subsequently all the state governments have been directed to set aside five percent of their capital budget on education for the agency (Ibe, 1994).

The Nigerian government has started operating a scholarship scheme for interested female candidates that do exceptionally well in science; technology, mathematics and other sciences related subjects. Two technical colleges have been devoted to the enhancement of women development in the country (Buchanan, 1993). Also indicative of government policy, is the use of mass media to propagate women education. In this vein, both the federal education ministry and state governments seek to encourage parents to send their female children to school. In most Northern states, the official position is to prosecute parents who either withdraw their daughters from school for marriage, encourage their daughters to trade on the streets or farm. The government has also established the Commission for Women's Affairs to enhance the status of women socially and economically. In addition, the government has issued decrees abolishing abuses against women, improving their health status discouraging such practices as early marriage and female circumcision. The President of Nigeria, Olusegun Obasanjo announced the establishment of a new Ministry for Women Affairs in his 2000 budget speech; this is a continuation of General Sani Abacha's legacy of 1995. The rationale for women's ministry is that it will encourage them to enter the labor force and supply a wide range of talents and services demanded by the general public. This in turn will improve productivity and economic growth of the country. In the management of business and industry, however, women are conspicuously absent. It is not the technical, but the sociological aspects of industrial and business management that militates against success for women in the occupation.

Further political pressure on multinational corporations, governments, lenders and international donors by men and women dedicated to sexual equality will be vital to ensure that women's interests are not neglected. These groups range from rural cooperatives to occupational associations, to urban business enterprises, to social welfare, church, and entertainment groups. Although they may not have originated as such, many of these groups have developed an expressly political focus. Through the use of these non-governmental organizations (NGOs), women's protest has assumed widely divergent forms; some organizations are seeking to politicize the private domain in certain contexts. Nonsexist education and training for women and men as well as equal access to jobs, property, and leadership positions must be provided. Nigeria will not achieve its development goals if women's full humanity and citizenship is not acknowledge and vigorously protected.

Even if legal reforms make the economic situation of wives more secured, Nigerian men must be educated on other ways to boost their ego, redirect their anger and curb their chauvinism. Beating ones' wife is surely not an option The media should be used to educate the people of Nigeria, that cultural values that encourage family abuse are no longer valid in the twenty-first century.

Finally, Nigerian women should realize that the degree of success that they will experience in curtailing any opposition from men and in averting gender stereotype in the nation is dependent on their ability to enlist men as allies. The extent to which this would be possible in Nigeria hinges on women's ability to convince men that their new social space and new gender identities are non-threatening, mutually benefiting, and greater than a zero-sum game. In the twenty-first century Nigeria should change the notion of women as specialized homemakers and men as providers. There should be a mutual understanding that both women and men have the obligation to participate in the labor market regardless of gender and domestic responsibilities.

Gender Factor in Development

Women being agents of development is a historical fact and it is a disservice for any country (including Nigeria) to ignore its women population in its development efforts. Therefore, the need for effective participation of women in development should be compelling. Equal opportunities should be provided to them and their male counterparts, both of whom should be seen as partners in progress (Ebosele, 1993; Adepoju, 1994). This partnership role of women in development is slowly being accepted in Nigeria.

In Nigeria feminism obscures the essential struggle and lumps together into interests that might even be practically opposed. The various professional bodies of women and those which are versions of all the political parties in the country today operate to further consolidate a system which opposes the interests of workers and peasants (men and women) alike. They also work principally to advance their own corporate interests and not that of women in general and in abstraction. The "glass ceiling" and the "glass wall" are phrases that were coined to illustrate the obstacles that hinder upward mobility or lateral movement of women in the work place. Many articles offer explanations for the disproportionately low number of women in leadership positions, all of which focus on barriers that keep women from rising in corporations.

It is only when women are freed from the current property relations that they could be regarded as fully liberated. For other injustice which are largely psychological and social, such a humiliation, over-lordship, family abuse, etc., are formed on this basis. The World Bank (1989) summarizes well the economic plight of women: "Modernization has shifted the balance of advantage against women. The legal framework and the modern social sector and producer services developed by the independent African nation (and also most externally sponsored development project) have not serviced women well. Legal systems have discriminated in land titling ... It is often more difficult for women to gain access to information and technology, resources, and credit. Agricultural extension and formal financial institutions are biased towards a male clientele ... There is a wider gender gap in education. As a result, women are less equipped than men to take advantage of the better earning opportunities" (World Bank, 1989: 86-87).

The process of development and urbanization has fortunately liberated a small minority of educated Nigerian women. Many of these professional women play prominent roles in international forums for equal rights, status redress and the emancipation of African women. At the Fourth Regional Conference on Women in Lagos, 1989, Nigeria's formal military leader, General Babangida noted that ... "There are compelling reasons why African women must be integrated in the development process. First is their numerical strength ... They are industrious and enterprising ... They are good managers ... No national development program will be meaningful and thorough if women are not fully involved" (Buchanan, 1993). Nigerian women want to be integrated on an equal footing in the ongoing development process for greater efficiency.

The constraining factors in the advancement of women to the same status as men in Nigeria are daunting in many respects. Therefore in eliciting women participation in development, their inhibiting factors need to be identified and removed in order to equalize access to opportunities.

In the past, women's role in most countries of the world was confined solely to the kitchen and other domestic activities. This view of women's role is still largely held in most African countries, including Nigeria. Women in West Africa are consciously, deliberately and perpetually considered as subordinate to their male counterparts as a matter of tradition and culture that must be unchangeable. In this vein, the relationship between women and their counterpart is that of unequal partners.

This discriminatory practice against women's positive contributions to development has not been obliterated as logically expected from there under development, and unequal access to development opportunities. The importance of this assertion becomes clear when we take a historical excursion into Nigeria's past and even contemporary experiences. For example, Nigeria's political developments in the pre-colonial era cannot be correctly written or understood without the mention of effective leadership of women like Queen Amina of Zaria, who was renowned for her series of conquests and political domination of parts of the old northern states, and Queen Idia of Benin who provided an effective military bastion for her son, Oba Esigie of Benin (Mba, 1982). Apart from these royal names, there are other Nigerian women whose names cannot be divorced from those who have in one way or the other contributed to the socio-economic transformation of the country. In this regard, mention can be made of such indefatigable women political activists as Christy Boyo, Funmilayo Ramsome-Kuti, and Madam Tinubu who flourished in commercial ventures in Lagos, Hajia Gambo Sawaba, Madam Kerry, first woman senator in Nigeria, Franca Afegbua, Second Republic senator, Janet Akinrinade, Ebun Oyagbola, Minister for National

Planning in the Second Republic and female senator in the Fourth Republic, Stella Omu. On purely intellectual plain, women, such as Professor Bolanle Awe, Ebun Clark, Agnes Uduebor, and Grace Alele Williams, first woman President (Vice Chancellor) of a university in Nigeria have made indelible marks in the development of education in the country.

Instances of women's leadership role as shown above are not peculiar to Nigeria. They could be found also in other parts of the world. Women have featured in the monarchical life of Britain and Netherlands of which Queens Elizabeth I and II, and Beatrice of the Netherlands respectively are examples. Contemporarily, the former Prime Minister of Britain (Margaret Thatcher) is a woman. Indira Ghandi was, until her assassination in 1984, the powerful Prime Minister of India, a country of over 800 million people (Mohanty et al, 1991). Golda Meir also ruled Israel. More recently Curazin Aquino and Benazir Bhutto were elected Prime Minister of the Philippines and Pakistan respectively. By her second election to office Benazir Bhutto has become the first female Prime Minister of an Islamic state in the world, a fact that was hither deemed as anathema by Muslim fundamentalist of Zia ul Haq's Pakistan (Egonmwan, 1991). Despite these achievements by women, gender typing of career and leadership in the fields traditionally occupied by males has yet to disappear in Nigeria.

The lack of cooperation between various government services – such as police, courts, social welfare, and health – only exacerbates women's problems. Abused women need many services that cannot be provided by only one agency. The lack of collaboration between agencies results in increased inaccessibility. Although some groups are working to rectify this situation by bringing together non-governmental organizations and governmental departments, government services for abuse women are virtually not enough in Nigeria.

In addition to calls to create special courts and police units to deal with rape, there are also calls for an improvement in the medical treatment offered to survivors in Nigeria. Since this may be the only physician's care they receive, treatment should include more humane aftercare that may be situated in a special examination suite, or some alternative arrangement that affords the victim some basic dignity. The examination and aftercare should comprise of gentle examinations, privacy, medical treatment, showers, emotional support, information about the possible effects of the assault, and referral to the nearest counseling service. As of 1999, there was no specialized rape crisis service or center available in Nigeria. It is interesting that Nigerian activists have solidly embraced extra-legal solutions for dealing with female circumcision, but – at least in terms of the politics of engagement – are so loyal to legal solutions in their efforts against rape and wife beating.

By making FGM and other forms of family abuse an issue in the world press (including Nigerian Press) and among women's groups, there is the tendency that the awareness created would galvanize the stoppage of such practices. This would be a very good example of how human rights issues reach the public, receive international attention, become a topic, and possibly become codified in international law. This has already happened in several Western nations and it is high time Nigerians started respecting their women.

Conclusion

This chapter has sought to examine the issue of managing diversity in the civil service of Nigeria. It argues that the public sector of Nigeria need to introduce diversity management programs as a policy that should be adopted by the national, state and local governments. The chapter also argues that in offering women the opportunity to access economic resources as well as to disentangle their identities from those of their families, diversity management programs will provide the space for women in Nigeria to clearly define their role as equal partners in the sustainable development process of the nation.

The proposed diversity management programs should serve as a key instrument in the recruitment and promotions, and suggests ways in which subjective perceptions of discrimination can be minimized. Transparency is critical. Public disclosure of entrance requirements and examination results, and even of the rationale for confidentiality where this is felt unavoidable, can ensure that injustice and unfairness are met with public censure. The composition of interview panels must be sensitive to issues of ethnicity as well as gender.

Promotions must be subjected to similar pressures. It has been argued that a proper functioning performance appraisal system is indispensable if any element of subjectivity and bias is to be removed from the promotion process. Furthermore, to make a performance appraisal system function effectively, reporting officers should be exposed to training in personnel and diversity management as a matter of course, if only to help develop an appreciation for public personnel management and the importance of performance appraisals within it. It cannot be assumed that those charged with this responsibility are endowed with the knowledge and understanding to treat staff appraisal as a continuous process that begins with the development of a classification system and adequate job descriptions, and is reinforced when public officers agree with their supervisors on specific, measurable, achievable, realistic targets/outputs to be delivered over a given period of time (e.g. quarterly).

Underlying all of this, however, must be the establishment of procedures for conflict resolution at the workplace and a clear-cut and inexpensive grievance procedure that permits public officers who feel they have been discriminated against on ethnic (or any other) grounds to lodge complaints with a competent authority. Subjective perceptions of discrimination are every bit as serious – perhaps even more serious – than discrimination that can be proved to exist on objective criteria. Indeed, the grave danger is in assuming that if allegations of discrimination cannot be substantiated, then it does not exist. As long as it continues to exist in people's minds, the problem will remain a festering sore.

In the twenty-first century, the Nigerian government's civil service needs a new paradigm in the work place that links ability with skill, rather than ability with gender. The precise nature of the jobs assigned to men and women is not important in itself. What is important is that jobs should be given to the people with the right qualifications or skills. Gender typing will not help the country attain its industrialization goals. Given Nigeria's critical economic and political problems, it appears increasingly obvious that suppressing the talents and skills of women in order to protect men's privileges is an enormous waste of human resources that the country can no longer afford. The present situation does not meet the criterion of "the best person for the job." It therefore implies a kind of prodigality that those concerned with public interest can hardly be viewed with equanimity.

Limited gains toward gender equality suggest a reality at odds with seemingly fairer policy formulation. Although some bureaucratic structures are in place to provide for equal wages and equality of opportunity, women's economic position relative to men's have eroded. Enforcement of these myopic policies on gender equality clearly becomes problematic when left to men in top management positions. Culturally and religiously (in case of Muslim) prescribed role for women prevent them from asserting themselves as much as they are capable. It also prevents men from allowing women to function as equal partners. Gender balanced policies and women in senior policy making positions should serve as a model for changing cultural stereotypes. If women's program units are allowed to control significant resources, build useful alliance, and create appropriate incentives, other parts of the public and private sectors would be more likely to respond to policy mandates on gender equality. A look at the past shows clearly that positive strides will not be made without sustained and conscientious efforts by the government.

The various institutions making policies, the new Federal Ministry for Women's affairs and programs should ensure that women are given equal opportunity to contribute in the national development process. With such concrete resolution of the constraints militating against women's participation in development, Nigeria will move faster in its industrialization process.

References

Abdullah, Hussaina. (1995). "Wifeism and Activism: The Nigerian Women's Movement." In the Challenge of Local Feminisms: Women's Movements in Global Perspective edited by Amerita Basu. Boulder, Colorado: Westview.

Adamolekun, Oladipo. (ed.) (1999). Public Administration in Africa. Boulder, Colorado: Westview.

Adeniyi, Tola. (1993). Biography of Chief (Mrs.) H.I.D. Awolowo. Lagos, Nigeria: Daily Times Press.

Adepuju, Aderanti. (1994). "The Demographic Profile: Sustained High Morality and Fertility and Migration for Employment." In Gender, Work and Population in Sub-Saharan Africa, edited by Aderanti Adepoju and Christine Oppong. London: J. Currey.

Akande, Jade O., and Priscilla O. Kuye. (1986). "Nigeria: Family Law Project." In Empowerment and the Law: Strategies of Third World Women, edited by Margaret Schuler, Washington, DC: OEF International, pp. 335-345.

Badejo, D.L. (1985). Women in Nigeria Today. London: England: Zed Books Limited.

Bank, Leslie. (1994). "Angry Men and Working Women: Gender, Violence and Economic Change in Qwaqwq in the 1980s." African Studies, Vol. 53, 1, pp. 89-114.

Buchanan, Enid. (1993). "Women: Struggle for Change." West Africa, (November 1-7), pp. 21-23.

Callaway, Barbara, J. (1987). Muslim Hausa Women in Nigeria: Tradition and Change. New York: Syracuse University Press.

Callaway, Barbara, and Lucy Creevey. (1989). "Women and the State in Islamic West Africa." In Women, the State and Development edited by Sue Ellen M. Charton, Jana Everett, and Kathleen Staudt, pp. 86 –113. Abany: New York: SUNY Press.

Central Bank of Nigeria. (1998). Annual Report and Statement of Accounts. Abuja, Nigeria: Central Bank Publication.

Dennis, Carolyne. (1987). "Women and the State in Nigeria: The case of the Federal Military Government, 1984-1985." In Women, State and Ideology: Studies from Africa and Asia edited by Haleh Afshar, pp. 13-27. Albany, New York: SUNY Press.

Dolphyne, Florence Abena. (1991). The Emancipation of Women: An African Perspective. Accra: Ghana University Press.

Ebosele, Moses. (1993). "Political Emancipation of Women." The Nigerian Observer, Benin City, Nigeria.

Edozien, A. and Adeoye O. (1991). "Privatization in Nigeria." Guardian, May 21, pp. 294-295.

Edwards, J. (1995) When Race Counts The Morality of Racial Preference in Britain and America. London: Routledge.

Egonmwan, Johnson. (1991). Public Policy Analysis: Concepts and Applications. Benin City, Nigeria: Aka and Brothers Press.

Eisenstadt, S.N. (1973). "Modernization: Growth and Diversity." In Tradition, Change and Modernity. New York: John Wiley and Sons.

Esman, Milton. (1997). "Public Administration, Ethnic Conflict, and Economic Development." Public Administration Review, Vol. 57, 6, pp. 527-33.

Green, December. (1999). Gender Violence in Africa. New York: St. Martin's Press.

Greenberg, J. (1999). Managing Organizational Behavior. Upper Saddle River, New Jersey: Prentice Hall.

Ibe, Iro. (1994). "A Look at the Gender Conflict in Africa." Lagos, Nigeria: The Punch Press.

Ifedi, Chuma. (1994). "Women Workers in Multinational Enterprises in Developing Countries." Lagos, Nigeria: Business Concord Press. (June 27), p.7.

Isekhure, N. (1998). 201 Solutions to Vision 2010. Benin City, Nigeria: Oduna Communications.

Kalu, W. J. (1993). "Battered Spouse As a Social Concern in Work with Families in Two Semi-Rural Communities of Nigeria." Journal of Family Violence, Vol. 8, 4, pp. 361-373.

Karanja, Wambuiwa. (1987). "Outside Wives and Inside Wives in Nigeria: A Study of Changing Perceptions in Marriage." In Transformations of African Marriage edited by David Parkin and David Nyamwaya. Manchester, United Kingdom: Manchester University Press.

Kingsley, Donald. (1944). Representative Bureaucracy. Yellow Springs, Ohio: Antioch Press.

Kolawole, Modupe. (ed.) (1998). Gender Perceptions and Development in Africa. Lagos, Nigeria: Arrabon Academic Publisher.

Konjo, Kwame. (1976). "The Dual-Sex Political System in Operation: Igbo Women and Community Politics in Midwestern Nigeria." In Women in Africa edited by Nancy Hafkin and Edna Bay, pp. 45-58. Stanford, California: Stanford University Press.

Konjo, Kwame. (1991). "Nigerian Women's Participation in National Politics: Legitimacy and Stability in an Era of Transition." Michigan State University Working Paper #221. (July).

Krislov, Samuel. (1974). Representative Bureaucracy. Englewood Cliff, New Jersey: Prentice Hall.

Lijphart, Arend. (1977). Democracy in Plural Societies. New Haven: Yale University Press.

Lovenduski, Joni. (1989). "Implementing Equal Opportunities in the 1980s: An Overview." Public Administration, Vol. 67, pp. 7-18.

Mba, Nina, Emma. (1982). Nigerian Woman Mobilized: Women's Political Activity in Southern Nigeria 1900-1965. Berkeley: University of California.

Meier, Kenneth J. (1993). "Representative Bureaucracy: A Theoretical and Empirical Exposition." In James Perry (ed.) Research in Public Administration. Greenwich, Connecticut: JAI Press.

Mohanty, Chandra T., A. Russo and L. Torres. (1991). Third World Women and The Politics of Feminism. Bloomington, Indiana: Indiana University Press.

Nweke, Therese. (1985). "The Role of Women in Nigerian Society: The Media." In Women in Nigeria Today. London: Zed, pp. 201-207.

Obadina, Elizabeth. (1985). "How Relevant Is the Western Women's Liberation Movement for Nigeria?" In Women in Nigeria Today, edited by Elizabeth Obadina. London: Zed, pp. 138-142.

Ofei-Aoagye, Rosemary Ofeibea. (1994). "Altering the Strands of the Fabric: A Preliminary Look at Domestic Violence in Ghana." Signs, Vol. 19, 4, pp. 924-940.

Olowu, D. (1999). "Accountability and Transparency." In Public Administration in Africa edited by Oladipo Adamolekun. Boulder, Colorado: Westview.

Otobo, E. (1999). "Nigeria." In Public Administration in Africa edited by Oladipo Adamolekun. Boulder, Colorado: Westview.

Ramazanoglu, Caroline. (1989). Feminism and the Contradictions of Oppression. London: Routledge.

Robertson, Claire and Iris Berger. (1986). Women and Class in Africa. New York: Africana Publishing Company.

Steinman, Michael. (1991). Women Battering: Policy Responses. Highland Heights, Kentucky: Academy of Criminal Justice.

Thomas-Sayter, B, and Dianne, Rocheleau. (1995). Gender, Environment and Development. Boulder, Colorado: Lynne Rienner Press.

Turner, Mark and David Hulme. (1997). Governance, Administration and Development: Making the State Work. London: Macmillan Press.

Wallace, Harvey. (1999). Family Violence: Legal, Medical, and Social Perspectives. Boston, Massachusetts: Allyn and Bacon.

Weisner, Thomas, Candice Bradley, and Philip Kilbride. (1997). African Families and the Crisis of Social Change. Westport, Connecticut: Bergin and Garvey.

World Bank. (1989). Sub-Sahara Africa: From Crisis to Sustainable Growth: A Long Term Perspective Study. Washington, DC: World Bank.

World Bank. (1997). World Development Report 1997. New York: Oxford University Press (for The World Bank): New York.

World Bank. (1998-1999). World Development Report. New York: Oxford University Press.

13 Managing Ethics and Corruption

Introduction

One of the major problems affecting Nigeria today is corruption. The plague of corruption is so serious that it has affected the development and productivity of both the public and private sectors of the nation. Transparency International recent survey ranked Nigeria as the second most corrupt nation after Russia on earth. Further the Work Bank's Multilateral Investment Guarantee Agency (MIGA) reveals that private savings held by Nigerians outside Africa amounted to US$15 billion (Edoho, 2001). Another interesting aspect of the corruption practice in Nigeria is that all those who are considered millionaires in the nation are former military generals, senior police officers, and former military administrators to states, former state governors, former ministers and state commissioners. It is now a common knowledge that the bulk of Nigeria's hard currencies are lying in private accounts in London, New York, Paris, Zurich, Germany, Geneva and so on. The unaccountable wealth owned by this profile of former senior public administrators reveals that corruption stems from the managerial ineptitude, myopia, and the sheer lack of sustainable directive capacity by the leaders of Nigeria. Agbese (1992) contends that many public administrators see their position as an opportunity or obligation for self and interest group enrichment rather than as a position of public trust.

It has become common tradition in Nigeria for public administrators to behave as though the public service is a "no man business sector." Thus bribery has become a means of concealing ineffectiveness and inefficiency. Police and customs and excise officers are openly seen in public "road blocks" (checking points erected by law enforcement officers in Nigeria) around the nation collecting bribes. When people go to the police station to report a crime, it has become normal practice in some stations for the police to request that the complainants pay bribes. In some cases complainants are asked to provide transportation and paper and writing materials that the police will use to take a statement. If they can not provide what the police demand of them nothing will be done to investigate their case. On the one hand, the police that ought to be the friend of the citizens of the nation are now perceived as enemies of the people, untrustworthy, corrupted and some times act as an accomplice in crime (Isekhure, 1998). On the other hand, from the airports to the sea ports and the other borders of Nigeria Custom officers have created its own modalities for diverting government fund into private pockets. If the borders of Nigeria are well mounted by Custom officers why should there be checking points all over the nation's roads.

If you visit Nigeria, the citizens will tell you that the civil service is the training ground for absolute corruption. If the Nigerian Telecommunications (NITEL) technician does not toss the telephone lines of subscribers just to extort money from citizens, they would probably mess up subscriber's private lines, so that they will be paid again to reconnect such telephone lines. The National Electric Power Authority (NEPA) is not different. It normally would interrupt electricity supply to consumers for several hours each day. Yet at the ending of every month it would send high bills to subscribers to pay. This practice of NEPA has made Nigeria a market for electricity generators. The social predicament of the impact of generating set is that the rich display their wealth as contempt of the poor. The electricity generating sets owned by the rich are constantly working day and night disturbing the peace and quiet of the poor people around. Indeed, several scholars have argued that the cost of importing electricity generating plants into Nigeria since 1970 would have been enough to construct a more viable, effective and workable electricity plant in the nation that would provide light to every home on a regular basis.

There is also the problem of mail pilfering in the Nigeria Post office (NIPOST). To send money or any precious items through the post office is like giving an armed robber your house keys. The corruption problem has also plague the Nigerian National Petroleum Corporation (NNPC), the Ajaokuta Steel Industry, the Aladja Steel Company, Nigerian Ports Authority, the Airport Authority, and the four Refineries in the nation. Isekhure (1998) and Mbaku (1992) contend that Nigeria's public corporations are not only corrupt, but they are down right incompetent. There is a dearth of management skills, absent of commitment, repugnant attitude to work and total absence of accountability. The Nigerian Airways is said to owe several millions of dollars to its creditors. The airline that should have a fleet of jets now has only operational planes. It has now become common practice for the four refineries in the nation to brake down at the same time. Nigeria who is an oil producing nation now imports petroleum more than nations who do not have oil. Thus, the pervasiveness of corruption in Nigeria and how it has affected the sustainable development process could be compared to a cancer that destroys social fabric, kills morale, and dampens constructive innovativeness.

The emergence of the Nigerian military as a governing agent in the post-independence period has further distorted income distribution and promoted corruption as an integral part of the societal norms. According to Isekhure (1998), it was during General Babangida and Abacha that it became obvious that military and political leaders were the pioneers of fraud in Nigeria. These two Nigerian leaders were pioneers in hypocrisy, adepts in corruption, greed in material acquisition, uninformed and absolutely tenacious in holding political power, even when it became obvious that they were no-longer wanted by the citizens of Nigeria. Nigerian news paper reported how one hand, Babangida's administration spent $12 billion that brought more wretchedness, more poverty, more bad government, more dubious business, failed banks, failed public enterprises, failed political parties, failed morality and increasing domestic and foreign debt. In the other hand, how late Abacha's family had handed back to the Nigerian government more than $750 million in state funds illegally amassed by the former leader (Guardian Newspaper, November 11, 1998). African New online November 2nd 1998 also reported how late Abacha left a fortune of between three to six billion dollars of estate. Late Abacha owned about 500 properties including some government buildings that he illegally converted to his own in Nigeria. Abacha's five years in office was marked by kickbacks, bribery, shady dealings and outright theft. Others in Abacha's government were also allegedly siphoned money from the state to amass personal fortunes include former finance minister, Anthony Ani. Former national security adviser Ismail Gwarzo was accused of confiscating about $1.3 billion worth of foreign reserve into his private account (Guardian Newspaper, November 11, 1998).

No doubt, corruption distorts economic incentives, discourages sustainable development, however, the Nigeria's civil servant is not the only ones to blame. Other who seeks favor from the civil servants is also willing to pay bribes in order to obtain unfair advantages or to become rich. As a matter of fact, if those on the supply side are unwilling to pay the bribes, the civil service corruption would be limited to nepotism, illegal levies, and the illegal appropriation of public resources.

According to Mbaku (1992) high inflation and the relatively low salary paid to civil servants in Nigeria has also contributed to the significant increase in corruption. Thus a significant part of the total income for many public administrators are derived from engagement in corrupts outside activities. In addition to low salary and high inflation is the problem of late payment of salary. There were times when the salary of some government employees was not paid for three months. Under such a delicate financial constraints civil servants can not resist bribery. The history of Nigeria shows that regardless of the system of government, military or civilian, government control of the economy will inevitably lead to corruption.

This chapter examines the dynamics of corruption, unethical behavior and mismanagement in the public sector in Nigeria. It argues that state control of the economy and the excessive regulation of the economic activities create the opportunistic behavior that include ethics conflicts due to lack of accountability, inexperience, and ignorance of specific ethical principles by government and business officials in Nigeria. It also argues that any attempt at eradicating corruption in Nigeria must rest on a comprehensive and sustained system of public accountability that takes into account of the interactive nature of the social institutions, political, economic, legal, family, religious, educational and cultural values and norms. The chapter also addresses the question: What can Nigeria do in the twenty-first century to root out corruption, carry out sustainable development and promote entrepreneurship and innovation?

One of my objectives in this chapter is to sketch a framework for thinking about the ethical responsibilities of professional managers in Nigeria in the twenty-first century. My focus here is on professional ethics rather than the comparative merits of substantial policies. To do so, I consider the nature of the relationship between government officials in federal and some state governments, their clients in the private sector and the environment they evolve, and the dilemmas they sometimes raise for professionals. Further, we provide some suggestions on how to manage ethics in both the public and private sectors in the twenty-first century.

Why we Need Ethics and Morality

Much of the growing literature in the area of ethics, morality, and public policy concerns the values that should be considered in attempting to select better policies (Schelling 1981; Amy 1984; Shaw 1991; Weimer and Vining 1992; Donaldson and Werhane 1996; Boatright 1997). This literature draws from the work of Jeremy Bentham (1748 - 1832), Immanuel Kant (1724 - 1804), John Stuart Mill (1806 - 1873), Lawrence Kohlberg (1927 - 1987), and Ross (1930). They present ethics as a set of rules that define right and wrong conduct. These ethical rules state when behavior is approved and when it is considered unacceptable and wrong. In a broader sense, ethics also includes the processes of (1) making distinctions between questions of fact and belief, (2) deciding what moral principles apply to a situation, and (3) deciding how issues are defined. It reminds government officials in Nigeria that no single value, such as economic efficiency, can provide an adequate basis for all decision making; rather, moral principles and the values they represent are fundamental to ethics.

According to Edwin Coulter (1996), ethics is a form of morality that is different in degree. Morality is society's definition of right and wrong, and it generally prevails throughout society. Ethics, on the other hand, is an individual code of right and wrong that is relevant to who a person is and where he or she is. It is a code of right and wrong for one person that may be quite different from a code of right and wrong for another person. Thus, any manager with an ounce of imagination would realize that the ethics of his or her profession concerns the concept of justice. When a manager does anything that undermines the possibility of a better relationship between the people he or she is dealing with and the society as a whole, this bureaucrat is behaving unethically. If a senior government official charges fees for a free government service or takes kickbacks or diverts public funds to his or her personal use, this individual is being not only unjust, but unethical.

To understand better the issue of ethics and morality we propose the addition of two concepts: equity and justice. These four terms are closely related but not identical; all are directly pertinent to the behavior of public officials.

Ethics

Ethics often refers to the choice between what is good or bad or right or wrong. In ethical theory, good is first defined; then the right action is considered to be a way of achieving that good. Ethics is concerned with moral duty and obligation. A synonym for ethics is morality. As Aristotle stated, ethics deals with the conduct of human action. In public management, ethics focuses on how the public administrator should question and reflect "in order to be able to act" responsibly. Ethics requires inquiry and contemplation into the truth that is, seeking "the right answers to one's question" (Kaplan and Ross 1968).

Morality

Morality refers to good character and right actions that build and support character. Synonyms for "moral" include ethical, righteous, noble, and virtuous, which in turn suggest that morality imply equitable conduct, fairness, moral eminence, and freedom from the taint of questionability.

Equity

Equity implies conformity to acceptable standards of natural rights, law, and justice. Equitable behavior is devoid of prejudice, favoritism, or fraud. It also implies the qualities of justness, fairness, and impartiality.

Justice

Justice implies qualities of justness, fairness, impartiality, integrity, and honesty. Aristotle used justice to mean practicing virtue toward others and conforming to truth, fact, and reason. He thought that achievement of justice in a society contributed to the development of friendship between people and an atmosphere in which ethical behavior could take place (Kaplan and Ross 1968). Justice can be defined as that type of human behavior that disavows undue interference in the lives or affairs of others and, whenever possible, prohibits other people from committing such transgressions. Under this concept, people are respected for their own basic worth and regarded as coequals. The just person is one who consciously governs his or her actions so as not to disturb the proper concerns of others. If it can be fairly stated that injustice, the opposite of justice, leads to conflict and insecurity in a society, then it can be inferred that justice can help a society achieve harmony and stability.

Ethical ideas do influence our attitudes, but very little. Socrates believed that knowledge is virtue, and Plato put up arguments to prove that our knowledge of moral ideas and values can make us good (Donaldson and Werhane 1996). This view, as we observe in some African nations, is mistaken. There are criminals among intellectuals, the military and political leaders in African societies and public institutions. Many of them should be sent to jail, but their knowledge and social position enables them to act against morality and the law, and to escape punishment. The most ethically deprived sectors of Nigerian societies are not the illiterates, the mass of workers and farmers, or even the innocent youth who are reacting to the example of the larger society. The most immoral or unethical people in Nigeria are the elites, be they business-people, presidents, ministers, military or police officers, civil servants or professionals.

The consequentialist theory of ethical reasoning, also referred to as the teleological theory, concentrates on the consequences of human action, and evaluates all actions, in terms of the extent to which they achieve desirable results. Another consequentialist notion also holds that a right action must maximize overall good; that is, it must maximize good or bad from the standpoint of the entire human community (Donaldson and Werhane 1996). The best acceptable label for this type of consequentialism is utilitarianism. The eighteenth century philosopher Jeremy Bentham coined this term, although its best-known proponent was John Stuart Mill in the nineteenth century. As formulated by Benham, the principle of utility states that an action is right if it produces the greatest balance of pleasure or happiness and unhappiness in light of alternative actions. Mill supported a similar principle, using what he called "the proof of the principle of utility" namely; the recognition that the only proof of something being desirable is that someone actually desires it (Hellriegel and Slocum 1994).

John Boatright (1997) identified two groups of ethical concepts, usually teleological and deontological theories. The deontology theory comes from Immanuel Kant. He believed that ethical reasoning should concern activities that are rationally motivated and should utilize precepts that apply universally to all human actions. Kant argued that the proper focus for ethical judgments should not be consequences but moral precepts, the rules, norms, and principles that guide human action. Kant stresses that the only thing that can be of good or worthwhile without any provisos or stipulations is an action of the will freely motivated for the right reasons. Other goods such as wealth, beauty, and intelligence are certainly valuable but are not good without qualification because they have the potential to create both good and bad effects. Deontologists typically hold that certain actions are right not because of some benefits to an individual or group but because of the nature of these actions or the rules from which they follow (Ross 1930; Phillips 1984; Carson 1985; Danley 1983). Thus, "do unto others as you would like them to do unto you," and bribery is wrong because of its very nature, regardless of the consequences.

John Locke (1632 - 1704) and Rawls also present moral rights or ethical arguments that complement the work of Immanuel Kant. Locke claims that every person is born with, and possesses, certain basic rights that he referred to as “natural rights.” These rights are inherent in a person's nature; they are possessed by everyone equally, and cannot be taken away. On the other hand, Rawls asks an interesting question: Which principle of justice would a rational person formulate if he were behind a “veil of ignorance”? That is, if one does not know whether he is young or old, male or female, rich or poor, highly motivated or an introvert, or anything about his status in society. Unable to predict which principles, if picked, will favor him or her personally, Rawls argues, such a person will be forced to choose principles that are fair to all (Rawls 1994)? This approach to ethics, therefore, holds that management decisions should be consistent with fundamental rights and privileges such as those of life, freedom, health, privacy, and property. Employees, customers, and the general public should also have the right not to be intentionally deceived on matters about which they should be informed. These principles could in turn be the values of a just society. In a just society, the concepts of fairness, equity, and impartiality are supported by three implementing principles. First, the distributive justice principle requires managers not to treat individuals differently on the basis of arbitrarily defined characteristics. Second, the fairness principles, requires employees to support the rules of the organization when the following conditions are met, the organization is just or fair, and the employees have voluntarily accepted benefits provided by the organization or have taken advantage of opportunities offered in order to further their own interests. Employees are then expected to follow the organization’s rules, even though the rules might restrict their individual choices. Third, the natural duty principle requires that managers base decisions on a variety of universal obligations. These obligations are the duty to help others who are in need or in jeopardy, provided that the help can be given without excessive personal risk or loss; the duty not to harm or injure another; the duty not to cause unnecessary suffering; and the duty to support and comply with just institutions.

The teleological theory postulates that the rightness of action is determined solely by the amount of good consequences it produces. Actions are justified by virtue of the ends they achieve, rather than some feature of the actions themselves. Thus, the concept of goodness is fundamental in teleological theory, and the concepts of rightness and obligation, or duty, are defined in terms of goodness.

According to utilitarianism, one's obligation, or duty, in any situation is to perform the action that will result in the greater possible balance of good over evil. A great deal depends on what is regarded as good and what is regarded as evil. Pleasure is taken to be ultimately the only good, and evil is the opposite of pleasure, or pain. But utilitarianism can be understood more broadly, so that goodness is human well being (Donaldson and Werhane 1996). Whatever makes human beings generally better off or provides some benefits is good, and whatever makes them worse off or harms is bad. Generally utilitarianism does not attempt to resolve these differences but accepts each person's own conception of what being better off means for him or her. The fact that an action would provide some benefit or inflict some harm is generally a morally relevant reason for or against performing it. So utilitarianism is able to explain why actions such as lying, breaking a promise, stealing, and assault are wrong and their opposites, such as truth telling, promise keeping, and respect for property, are right. Lying, for example, creates false beliefs that often lead people to make disadvantageous choices, and if lying was to become common, trust would be eroded, with a resulting decline in welfare for everyone.

Jeremy Bentham and John Stuart Mill perceived utilitarianism as a revolutionary theory, both because it accurately reflected human motivation and because it had clear application to the political and social problems of their days. If one could measure the benefit or harm of any action, rule, or law, they believe, one could sort out good and bad social and political legislation as well as good and individual actions. To several utilitarians, some pleasures are quantitatively better than others are. Intellectual pleasures, for example, are said to be higher than physical pleasures. According to Mill, "it is better to be Socrates unsatisfied than to be a pig satisfied." By this, Mill believed that the optimal situation was one of "greatest happiness for the greatest number."

Utilitarian is divided into two groups: act utilitarian and rule utilitarian. Act utilitarian emphasizes the consequences of providing the greatest good for the greatest number. Rule utilitarian, on the other hand, relies primarily on following predefined rules or standards in order to obtain the greatest good for the greatest number. In sum, utilitarian reasoning obligates us only to include the interests of everyone in our calculation, not to act in a way that advances individual interests. Thus, an action is right if and only if it produces the greatest balance of pleasure over pain for everyone, and an action is right if and only if it conforms to a set of rules, the general acceptance of which would produce the greatest balance of pleasure over pain for everyone.

Many of the conflicts between managers and consumer groups, employee groups, and government agencies may be a result of the tendency of managers to use act or rule utilitarianism as their ethical guide. In contrast, nonmanagement groups may tend to rely more on the justice and moral rights approaches to justify their actions. Public and private managers in Nigeria often have difficulty anticipating the consequences of their decisions and behavior, as required under act utilitarianism. However, a manager can usually tell whether he or she is following a rule or code of professional ethics, as stipulated under utilitarianism. For example, under act utilitarianism a manager might agree to pay a bribe because it is necessary in order to get a job done that benefits the whole organization? Under utilitarianism, any idea of bribery would be rejected because it is against the rules of the organization. An ethical problem may arise, however, whenever one responds to the demands of a law, governmental policy, or even an ethical principle that simultaneously jeopardizes the welfare of people with whom one works. This thorny ethical dilemma typically causes considerable distress because a manager must choose between legitimate loyalties.

Managing Corruption in Practice

There are several factors that relate to the decline in public confidence in the Nigerian federal and state governments. One is that unethical government contributed to a climate where rhetoric flourished that is flamboyantly antigovernment, anti-public sector, and especially anti-management.

Roger and Njoku (2001) contend that the Nigerian government must start by developing a public administration that is responsive to the needs of the people. The implication is that the nation's civil service must be competent and possess a significant level of professionalism. Hiring decisions should be based on merit and superior qualification. Senior positions should be awarded to individuals who posses the ability and expertise to efficiently perform assigned duties. Public administration position should not be used as rewards for political support or swapped for bribes, or used to meet obligation to one's ethnic groups. Incompetent, unqualified, and unprofessional civil servants contribute significantly to failures in development, force the nation to remain essentially underdeveloped and contribute to corruption (Mbaku, 1992).

Senior bureaucrats, military juntas, and managers in both the public and private sectors can do many things to help improve organizational productivity. They could develop new approaches to old problems, recommit to quality, demonstrates a concern for process and method, improve use of time to reduce the cost of what is done, and contribute to the pleasantness of the environment. Public productivity improvement requires an infusion of professionalism in public management. The public interest is intimately related to administrative decisions, giving them direction and meaning in all they do. As this relationship involves moral duty and obligation on the part of the public administrator, it involves ethics. Ethics, then, becomes crucial to the entire range of activities with which the public administrator is involved. Professionalism means a commitment to an ethic or a need to do better from top to bottom. Managing means is more than living well it is more than presiding, and it is more than keeping everyone happy. It is a passion and an obsession.

The problem of accountability is apparent in every sphere of life in Nigeria because of the sentiment of the nation's society. Nigerians can generally be considered as a "generous but selfish" group of people. Sometimes government officials and managers in the private sector willfully and maliciously engage in acts they know to be in violation of the ethical standards of their profession. This perception of a nation's people is not fair, but most top management, be it military junta, director in the ministry, or private sector, have turned the notion of civic virtue around to mean the accommodation of self-interest, – the pursuit of private advancement with little or no concern for public interest. The majority of the public servants who are corrupt wake up every morning and go to work with the "me" mentality. A weakened sense of civic virtue, failure to feel accountable to the public, and placing personal priority and gain over those of the public all contribute to the presence of corruption in public policymaking and implementation, thus creating many problems for sustainable development in the nation.

Avarice, expediency, and other self-serving motives that blur judgments and boundaries are common among those guilty of ethical violations. Nevertheless, well-meaning political leaders, military juntas, police officers, and senior management personnel are also vulnerable to the ethical dilemmas in the nation. A variety of factors complicate ethical judgment in many sub-Saharan nations. These factors include personal trust, public and private sector managers' reputation, and the status of current and future employment, continued access to public policymakers, and inadequate/unclear guidelines and laws. Many of these factors involve implications that go well beyond ethical issues (for example, ethnic and religious values) in Nigeria. The range of unethical behavior in the nation may also be associated with the legacy of colonial regimes, inexperience, ignorance of specific ethical principles, and lack of accountability by public managers.

The development of professional ethics and a code of conduct, either collectively or individually, may be viewed as an attempt to correct some of the unforeseen ethical dilemmas; however, ambiguities concerning the consequences of available alternatives and poor enforcement of punishment have made public officials undermine the need to stay above these ethics. Corruption directly and indirectly affects the implementation of public and private programs. The deployment of huge sums of money by public managers in Nigeria into private use results in the abandonment of development projects or their unsatisfactory completion. Given the spiraling rate of inflation in the nation, the time spent by government officials negotiating "kickbacks" increases the costs of projects. Corruption also lowers the morale of subordinate officers who work under corrupt superiors.

Corruption in government institutions frequently leads to organizational goal displacement. Most multimillionaires in Nigeria today are either presidents or heads of state, former presidents, military generals, senior police officers, ministers, or senior bureaucrats. In pursuit of private goals, several officials in public institutions may form cliques and informal groups to maximize their benefits. These actions are all come at the expense of the attainment of institutional development goals. In effect, public and private institutions that are corrupt and that steadily suffer goal displacement can hardly be expected to be efficient or practice management ethics.

The nation has systematically moved from a communal world into a modern society that had its beginning in the colonial period of the nineteenth century. Before the nineteenth century the basic social, organizational, political, and moral character of Nigerian communal society was grounded in the peasant communal system. While morality has its basis in economic and social organization it also has historical character. With the introduction of European colonial regimes, capitalism, and management ethics, a new value system began to emerge in the nation.

The capitalist mode of production does not emphasize communal enterprise; rather, it emphasizes individual enterprise and acquisition. Individualism and the notion of survival of the fittest galvanize competition not among groups but among individuals. Individual conscience becomes the source of moral judgment. What is good or right is no longer what the community approves but what the individual feels and decides for him. What we need to understand is the basis of this change, and how it will affect public management in the twenty-first century.

In developed societies such as the United States and Japan, there has been great success in social and economic development through cooperation between public and private enterprises. Nations such as Canada, France, England, and Germany have also accomplished their social objectives through public management and administration of social resources. Although Nigeria's public organizations exist along-side private enterprises, their rate of success has been very discouraging when compared with European and North American nations.

Why are the differences in public management success and ethics so great? Several scholars have argued that inadequate executive capacity, technology, internal conflicts and corruption combine in various ways to impair the efficiency of both public and private administrators in Nigeria. I will add lack of management ethics and accountability to the list. Even when Nigerian citizens are trained in Europe and North America, they return home to the nation only to undermine the management ethics they were taught.

While ethics – oriented reforms have been gaining widespread acceptance since the 1970s, it is only recently, in the face of indebtedness and growing economic crises, which such reforms have caught on in several African nations. By the 1990s, several African countries had instituted far-reaching economic reforms – trade liberalization, deregulation, and the divestiture of state-owned companies. These economic reforms represent fundamental departures from earlier practices. The unsuccessful implementation of the neo-liberal policy agenda that constitutes structural adjustment has been the central concern of a growing body of literature that often focuses on the issues of regime type and democratic transition. However, none of the literature has focused on the dilemma of management ethics in Nigeria and how it could be resolved for a better practice in the twenty-first century. One question we like to raise is whether the military and bureaucracy in Nigeria are participants in national underdevelopment rather than development.

Although there is some degree of corruption in every government, the background to bad management ethics in Nigeria, as compared to other Third World nations lies in its political economic history. First, there is the factor of unequal distribution of income, which can be traced to the colonialization process. However, the political independence that Nigeria attained in 1960 in the control of their economy and society did not address this inequality of income (Olaniyan 1996). The lack of challenge to this unequal distribution of resources led to a polarization of society, with small but very powerful groups (sometimes-ethnic groups) dominating the economy and the political system. In pursuit of private goals, several officials in public institutions form cliques and informal groups in order to maximize their benefits, all at the expense of the attainment of institutional goals. The national and state governments of Nigeria also have great trouble in securing tax income; this in turn complicates the maintenance of fiscal balance and the provision of public services equally to the citizens. The exclusion of lower level civil servants, lower-level professionals and intellectuals, ordinary wage earners, and junior political activists in the distribution of material rewards in the nation reinforced the general problems of accountability and, lack of justice and motivation activities to increase creativity by subordinates in the management of government services. Patronage appointments are often given to people who lack competence. Second, the polarization of Nigeria also opened the way for populist leaders who built their popularity on their charisma and on their ability to form coalitions between different groups in the country. Once in power, these Nigerian leaders practice unethical management of the nation's resources, by bestowing favors on their supporters with little concern for macroeconomic stability, justice, and equity. For example, Joseph Mobutu, former president of Zaire, increased real wages for his special guard and left the other military personnel as well as civil servants in his nation unpaid for several months. There are many public officers like Joseph Mobutu of Zaire in Nigeria. While the salary of teachers and many civil servants were not paid for several months between 1993 and 1994, soldiers from the rank of captain and major were given car allowances. The ordinary rar k soldiers were also bestowed proportional allowances as well. Third, Nigerian import substitution policies were still in place when the debt crisis broke out. This meant that import dependence was high and export capacities were weak. External adjustments, necessary in order to cope with the balance-of-payments problems and the debt crisis, were thus more costly.

The nature of politics since the 1960s in several African nations (including Nigeria) has been such that the premium of political power is so exceedingly high that political contestants regard victory in election as a matter of life and death and are determined to capture or retain power by all means. Therefore, elections are not free and fair. The evidence of rigging and fighting in Nigeria conclusively proves that the party in control of government has not built confidence among the citizens in the way it has managed the nation's affairs, despite the huge material resources that have been invested.

In the Nigerian context, for instance, imputes ethnic hostility to intense competition for leadership, not just power but perceived control over resource allocation. Duddley (1973:75) postulates that "politics in Nigeria . . . is not about alternative policies, but about the control over men and resources." According to Diamond (1988), the state is the primary locus of wealth, providing access to resources and offering opportunities for class formation. Thus, "those who aspire to the positions in the dominant class must aspire to political power and the basis of class formation results in an extraordinary premium on political power. Since the state is a major avenue for public wealth, Edoho (1997) argued, that the instrumentalities of state are frequently used to grant favors, thereby rendering politics a zero sum game. In light of this scenario, the ethics of business penetrated politics, the ethics of politics penetrated business; the ethics of gangster penetrated both."

The inability of the leaders of Nigeria to cultivate financial discipline and stringent management of the economy led to the twin problems of a national budget deficit and a weak balance of payments so that there is little prospect for economic development. Corrupt, inept, and insensitive leadership for the past three decades has led to the ultimate collapse of legitimacy and has led to immorality and impropriety. Thus, the nonspecifically of ethics codes and other regulations has caused confusion as to what is moral or unethical for Nigerian public managers.

Many disputes arise over the question of the significance of the end results of several policies proposed for the management and development of Nigeria. The government's involvement in the relocation of sites of city capitals and the creation of new states and local governments at the time of debt crisis shows lack of pragmatic management skills. Involved is a relative waste of national resources, as in that several government officials have misappropriated funds in connection with the construction of roads and other government projects.

Corruption, strikes, decline in agriculture revenue, heightened world economic recession, and the failure of Nigerian leaders to make the most of their mandate have led to the underdeveloped nature of the nation's economy. Because the government is the major source of wealth and politics, it has been relatively easy for those in military authoritarian regimes to amass personal wealth. Ordinary people now regard the Nigerian police as extortionists and uniformed bandits. Custom departments and their check-points have also become hotbeds of corruption, over-staffing, bribery, and extortion. Peter Koehn (1990) asserts that the salaries and fringe benefits of public servants pale in significance the more indirect opportunities for individual enrichment that government service provides, and he claims that most public managers have principally devoted their ample social prestige and political power to reaping personal or corporate group benefits.

These maladaptive patterns in Nigeria mean that the very infrastructure created to carry out good management is, in fact, one of the main obstacles to its achievement. Thus, unethical politicians, military generals, senior management personnel, and professionals have grossly misdirected much of the wealth of the nation, thereby causing many ambitious development projects to suffer. The prime emphasis for Nigerian leaders in high-level political and military circles seems to be personal achievement rather than national development, and their rhetoric on nationalism often conceals the backwash effect of their abuse of public trust. When these abuses, excessive greed, and lack of genuine patriotism are disclosed, as they were under General Gowon, Babangida and Sani Abacha of Nigeria and in comparison with former president Mobutu Sese Seko of Zaire and Houphouet- Boigny of Cote d' Ivoire, people become alarmed and call for action to address the contradiction. In the 1970s, Idi Amin of Uganda used government as an instrument of ethnic warfare and was, in addition, ruthless in eliminating persons and groups who seemed to threaten his corrupt rule. Through roughly the same years, Equatorial Guinea was ruled by a despot so brutal that, according to estimates by Amnesty International, nearly half the population of the country fled. Olukoshi Adebayo et al. (1994) assert how the formal president Seyni Kountche of Niger helped to liquidate the Development Bank of the Republic of Niger by owing 468.5 million CFA francs. How could a nation's president who sought to adjust the structure of the economy, on the one hand, decide, on the other hand, to incapacitate it financially? Deliberate borrowing of money from national banks by some Nigerian leaders, senior military and police officers, and political elites without seeking to repay their debt is not only unethical; it is also counter productive and unjust and does nothing to enhance equity in a nation. One of the main jobs of the police, as in all societies, is to enforce the laws of a country; they often work with the courts and civil administrators. In Nigeria, however, when the courts, military juntas, police officers mediate coercive violence and their close relatives/associates have the option of not obeying the court's decision. This type of unethical behavior has often raises questions such as, what constitutes justice and morality. Are some persons above the laws of a nation?

In sum, corruption directly or indirectly affects the implementation of management principles and sustainable development in Nigeria. Deployment of huge sums of money into private use results in the abandonment of projects or their unsatisfactory completion. Given the spiraling rate of inflation in Nigeria, the time spent by government officials in negotiating kickbacks increases the costs of projects. The enduring social effects of structural adjustment policies that contribute to a high unemployment rate and lower education and health standards raise considerable doubt about the future of management in the states of Nigeria. The problems are part of the issues that structural adjustment programs were supposed to redress. In effect, public institutions that are corrupt and that steadily suffer goal displacement can hardly be expected to be efficient.

Towards Professional and Ethical Public Service

The complexity of the causes of unethical management and the persistence of a weak professional code of conduct in Nigeria makes the selection of a pragmatic method of management very necessary for the twenty-first century.

Exit, Voice, and Disloyalty

Albert Hirschman (1970) asserts the notion of "Exit, Voice, and Loyalty" in his book. He explores how people can react when they are dissatisfied with the organizations in which they participate. According to Hirschman, they may exercise voice by working to change the organization from within, or they may simply exit the organization for another. In Hirschman's framework, loyalty helps determine how much voice is exercised before exit is chosen. We find it useful to use Hirschman's concepts of voice and exit, then to add disloyalty. Note that we shall abandon the concept of loyalty because our goal here is how to provide solutions to unethical practices.

Management personnel in Nigeria could exercise various combinations of voice, exit, and disloyalty when they confront value or ethical conflicts. If managers notice unethical acts or policies in their organizations, they might try to change them through protest or objections within their agencies. If supervisors lack either the inclination or the authority to reverse these policies, then they might next make their objections formally through memoranda to supervisors and to successive superiors until they reach the highest-ranking official with authority to change the policy. Table 13.1 shows how the exit, voice and loyalty can be applicable in Nigeria.

Table 13.1
Indicators of Accountability and Transparency in Nigeria

Type of Mechanism	General Perception of Effectiveness
Exit	
Internal market	Low
External market	Low
Contracts	
Voice	
Elections	Low
Referenda	Nil
Grievance ventilation	Low
Participation/decentralization	Low
Interest Groups	Low
Information freedom	Nil
Media and public opinion	Low
Loyalty	
Codes of conduct/regulation	Low
Merit system	Nil
Discipline	Low
Inspectorates	Low
Performance-based compensation	Nil
Hierarchy	Low

Source: Adopted from Olowu, Dele. 1999. "Transparency and Accountability." In Oladipo Adamolekun edited Public Administration in Africa. Boulder, Colorado: Westview Press.

At the same time, they might speak out against the policy at staff meetings whenever they have the opportunity. At some point, however, they will have exhausted all the avenues of protest within the agency that are legitimate. If they are successful in reversing the policy or unethical behavior, then they can take comfort in having disposed of their ethical problem. If they are, however, unsuccessful, they might want to try another approach. An ethically justifiable option at this time will be to resign from the organization.

Dele Olowu (1999) pointed out that exit opportunities are utilized in cases where goods and services can be produced by a variety of service providers. A variant of the exit option is the use of internal markets for service bids that are not appropriate for provision by the private sector. He further contend that voice mechanism in Africa provide opportunities for citizens to voice their concerns about maltreatment or misuse of position or public resources by officials.

Combining voice with the threat of exit by issuing an ultimatum is likely to be ethically superior to simply resigning. Why does some one find a particular policy or behavior so objectionable, while others approve of it? Perhaps the answer is that some individuals have a better-developed ethical sense or are more principled. On the other hand, the reason for disagreement may be that both the employees and their superiors hold morally justifiable values that happen to conflict. Although there may be some concern about maintaining diversity within African public agencies, the danger of selective attrition seems less serious when it results from legitimate differences of opinion rather than from a clash between expediency, such as basic principles. Another action to consider is disloyalty to the agency. Individuals might share or leak confidential information of their agency's plan to journalists, interest groups leaders, or other persons who can interfere with them. Even if you are not a pure Kantian, anytime they do not act openly and honestly, they should closely scrutinize the morality of their actions. Further, an important moral tenet is that one takes responsibility for one's action. One also forfeits the opportunity to continue your protest within the agency.

Whistle-Blowing

Another possibility is that individuals speak out until silenced. This approach is often referred to as whistle blowing. Individuals might also be justified acting covertly if they were convinced that they could prevent serious harm that might occur in the future by remaining in the public organization. The management strategy here is that the government official's obligation to honesty in the twenty-first century arises from a public trust as well as private virtue so that public dishonesty, unjustified by other overriding values, lessens the forces of confidentiality. Rather than waiting for a code of ethics for Nigeria, perhaps managers should work toward an ethos for the new professionals of the twenty-first century. Managers of both public and private sectors in the nation should explicitly recognize their obligations to protect the basic rights of others, to support the democratic processes as expressed in their respective constitutions, and to promote personal integrity. These values should generally dominate their responsibility to clients in their ethical evaluation.

Discrimination against one person or ethnic group is preferential treatment for another, so one is as much a part of the nation's unethical practice as the other. But whereas preferential treatment once occurred mainly for the benefit of some ethic groups (for example, Hausa-Fulani people), now it occurs more for the benefit of other groups (Yoruba or Igbo people). Arguments concerning preferential treatment and unethical management practices may be either backward or forward-looking. So far as the backward-looking argument is concerned, the main issue arises when remedial measures appear to benefit the undeserving at the expense of the innocent. The question then arises whether the issue should be considered purely in terms of individuals or whether whole ethnic groups or communities are involved. With respect to the forward-looking argument, the obvious question concerns the kind of society desired for the twenty-first century and the kinds of methods that are acceptable in promoting its achievement. Preferential treatment, and more especially ratio hiring and promotion in management, may be justifiable simply as the most effective attack on their previous unethical discrimination system in Nigeria.

The social precondition of trust is also essential to solving the problems of unethical behavior in Nigeria. Social arrangements in the twenty-first century should encourage trust formation by restructuring incentives. Trust should involve the belief that the trusted person or institution has sufficient insight to treat another person's cause as if it were his own. If individuals are to trust their institutions in this fashion, then some mediation is necessary to integrate the individual and the institution into common standpoint. This mediation would require the state to enter into the subjective consciousness of the people and at the same time encourage the people to begin to participate in the state. This action would ensure that individuals understand the state's role in furthering their rational interests and that the state should remain sensitive to the appropriately formulated needs of its citizens. Under these circumstances, an ethical society is likely to protect rights, hinder unjustified coercion, and foster the ability to pursue ends. In order to ground a viable form of ethical life, an ethical tradition must contain certain specified kinds of durable norms. Thus, an ethical tradition for the twenty-first should be grounded in durable and universally applicable management norms or principles that should be at least potentially consistent with the realization of a substantial ethical life in Nigeria.

Social Responsibility

The concept of social responsibility is the next approach to solving the problems of ethical conflict in Nigeria in the twenty-first century. Social responsibility can be divided into three strategies: affirmative, stakeholder, and traditional. The traditional strategy holds that management in Nigeria should serve the interests of shareholders. This means that the overriding managerial obligations of managers in Nigeria in the twenty-first century are to maximize shareholders' profits and their long-term interest. This approach will encourage both public and private managers to be socially responsible and use their resources to engage in activities designed to increase profits so long as they stay within the rules of the game, by engaging in open and free competition without deception or fraud. The stakeholder strategy suggests that managers in Nigeria should have obligation to identifiable groups that are affected by, or can affect achievement of, an organization's objectives. These stakeholders should commonly include important customers, competitors, government agencies, unions, employees, debt holders, trade associations, important suppliers, shareholders, and consumer groups. The majority of managers who accept the stakeholder's strategy for the twenty-first century would probably endorse John Boatright's (1997) interpretation of a firm's obligation – that the first social responsibility of business is to make enough profit to the cover costs of the future. If this social responsibility is not met, no other social concerns can be met. The rationale for Nigerian leaders should include the general idea that a better society creates a good environment for business.

Duties and responsibilities concerning lawmaking, law observance, and law enforcement are very critical. Mechanisms such as control through general criminal and civil laws, federal laws and regulations, control exerted by peers, specific legal controls from state licensing boards, and civil litigation of malpractice complaints would protect the public from unlawful, incompetent, and unethical actions perpetrated by managers and public leaders. Members of the executive, legislative, and judicial branches of government, from local councils to national government, should be among those who need to think of the probable consequences of action and inaction, seeking relevant knowledge and adjusting their behavior accordingly to improve ethical and moral standards in Nigeria. Through a committee system or otherwise, legislators or members of public assemblies should have an obligation to see to it that desirable legislation are considered and that unethical values are avoided.

Law observance should be a duty for everyone. To ignore this duty, violating laws either systematically or capriciously is to act unethically. The greater the proportion of people who are irresponsible about law observance, the greater the danger to the social order and management ethics, and the more government will be undermined. Law enforcement needs to occur responsibly in Nigeria in the twenty-first century. This means that enforcement of law must be carried out as consistently as possible, and with regard for the rights and interests of all those affected.

Since liberal democracy depends on morality that is not produced or sustained spontaneously, law must be allowed to play a critical role in the nation. Law would serve as the authoritative voice of the political community, establish punishments for certain kinds of behavior, and educate the people. When law is used to enforce certain ethical standards, it should be viewed as the norm of the society. According to Rousseau, the power of law should be limited to the preservation of morality, not the creation of a new morality. Prudence would dictate, therefore, that some morally undesirable actions are too much a part of the nation to be eradicated, but law can still be a powerful teaching tool. It could be used to create ethical and virtuous institutions, as well as help limit the growth of vices that threaten the liberal society.

The affirmative strategy for management in Nigeria in the twenty-first century should hold that managers be obligated (1) to avoid problems by anticipating changes in their environment, rather than simply reacting to them, (2) to blend the organization's objectives seamlessly with those of stakeholders and the general public, and (3) to take concrete, proactive steps to promote the mutual interests of the organization, its various stakeholders, and the general public. This strategy draws heavily from the justice and moral rights ethical approaches. This strategy requires five categories of obligations and managerial behavior from Nigerian managers in the twenty-first century.

1. The search for legitimacy. Managers must consider and accept broader criteria for measuring the organization's performance and social roles than those required by law and the marketplace.
2. Operating strategy. Managers would be obliged to maintain or improve the current standards of the physical and social environment. They must be willing to compensate victims of pollution and other organization-related hazards, even in the absence of clearly established legal grounds.
3. Response to social pressures. Managers must accept responsibility for solving current problems in Nigeria. They must be willing to discuss activities with outside groups and make information freely available to them and be receptive to formal and informal input from outside groups in decision making.
4. Ethical norms. Managers of Nigeria must take defined position on issues of public concern in the twenty-first century. They must advocate ethical norms for all in the organization, the industry, and business in general.
5. Political and legislative activities. Nigerian managers in the twenty-first century must show willingness to work with outside groups for enactment of public policies, for example, environmental protection laws, and equitable distribution of development projects around their respective nations. They must promote honesty and openness in government and in their own organization's lobbying activities.

Social Audit

One important dimension to a successful implementation of ethical reform in Nigeria should be the need to conduct social audit periodically. Social audit will entail an attempt to identify measure, evaluate report on, and monitor the effects of the organizations on their stakeholders and society as a whole. Social audit, in contrast to a financial audit, focuses on social action rather than on fiscal accountability. A social audit is an important measurement of achievement under the affirmative social responsibility strategy. Conducting such an audit is typically viewed as an optional activity under the stakeholder strategy. A government ethics program needs to be audited periodically to see if all its elements are fully in place and working well. The audit should include a survey of members' opinions and perceptions of the program and the agency's ethical climate.

Besides being diagnostically useful, a survey is another way to communicate the importance of ethics. Thus, the affirmative social responsibility strategy draws on the moral rights and justice approaches. It obligates Nigeria's respective organizations to focus on social responsibility by utilizing national resources to help meet society's needs.

A new public management approach emerged in the late 1990s in the United States that will be useful to Nigeria in the twenty-first century. The new managerial strategy borrows heavily from the public choice approach, and it seeks a customer-driven method to public policy. Public choice posits the individual as a consumer of government services and theorizes that both consumer choice and administrative efficiency will be enhanced if governments can be made to compete for individuals, and purchases of goods and services in a market. To achieve results, public managers in Nigeria must make better use of market like completion in the provision of goods and services. This may be accomplished by (1) privatization (contracting out services to the private sector) (2) reorganizing government agencies in such a way that they might be able to compete with one another, and (3) making public administration more customers driven. The new public management favors an organizational structure that is decentralized and business-like in order to promote responsiveness.

In order to achieve favorable ethical standards for the twenty-first century, Nigeria must encourage creativity. To be creative in management a nation must invest six resources just as it would on individuals. The six resources are knowledge, intellectual abilities, thinking styles, motivation, personality, and environment. It takes approximately ten years for a person to acquire expertise in a management field; therefore, Nigeria must adopt a long-term perspective and give employees that time to develop before they are assigned critical tasks. Ethics training must be included in employee career development processes. Employees should be frequently reminded that ethical behavior is expected to be their work habit. In the twenty-first century, synthetic ability is the most important. Therefore, the Nigerian government would do well to include in the management team some people with high synthetic ability and encourage all team members to use that particular ability. The membership of the management team should be limited to only those who have the high practical ability that is required in the twenty-first century. Managing performance is the only sure way to get desired results consistently. Factoring ethics into the process of managing performance is the best way to ensure that work objectives are achieved in an ethical manner and that other on-the-job behaviors are ethical. Managers and subordinates should be sensitized to the fact that ethical behaviors are valued and expected and that there will be accountability for unethical behavior.

Thinking-style preference should focus on selecting for promotion only those who have the style that the government or institution has encouraged. In entry-level jobs and lower levels of management, following guidelines may be adequate, but at higher levels, a manager needs to be capable of creating those policies or guidelines. Nigerian public managers should prefer the styles that get rewarded. Seeing a colleague gets rewarded for using an inventing style encourages a person to try it himself. The best thing a manager can do to encourage an inventing style is to serve as a role model and use that style himself.

A personality profile is essential in the twenty-first century in Nigeria. People who have their own way of thinking and doing things often appear strange to people who are more conventional. Therefore, organizations in Nigeria should be concerned with keeping sufficient diversity inside the organization to sense accurately the variety outside it because an individual has only limited experiences from which to make the connections that may suggest an innovation. Motivation is probably the single most important thing managers in Nigeria can do to encourage creativity on a project. The motto for the twenty-first century should be, "Have fun, put love where you work, and go in the opposite direction to achieve an edge over your competitors." All work and no play kill the potential of discovery, mastery, and openness to change and flexibility and hinder innovation and invention. Because the future cannot be predicted with much accuracy, both Nigerian governments and the creative management teams need to manage the risk involved in playing with creative ideas in their respective environments.

A point implicit in the above should be made explicit: The comparisons that are made in judging questions of ethics and equal treatment are made within the national framework. Ideally, the framework should no doubt be universal in Nigeria. Persons living in Abuja, Akure, Benin City, Ibadan, Lagos, Enugu, Owerri, Jos, Bauchi, Kaduna, Port Harcourt, Asaba, Sokoto, Kano, Ilorin, Minna, and Yola should have equal treatment and equality of opportunity and national reward when compared with each other. But it would be utopian to make comparisons on this basis. When we talk about ethics in management and equality of opportunity, we are talking about what happens within the boundaries of a nation-state or jurisdiction. Nevertheless, Nigerian leaders of the twenty-first century should realize that good management is as important to the public interest as is charismatic leadership.

If the critical consciousness of public managers was raised and they became more aware of the moral issues of equity and justice, they would be in a better position to solve the main ethical problems they face. Our experience, involving many on-the-job public officials and the principles of justice, enables us to set workable guidelines for the behavior of public managers in the twenty-first century. An extensive ethical dialogue along these lines would produce most of the following principles for official behavior in Nigeria:

1. Administrative action will not abridge any person's right to basic liberties so long as these are compatible with a system of liberty for all.
2. Offices and positions will be open to all under conditions of fairness and equality.
3. Official decisions and actions in program execution will benefit the less advantaged members of the public served at least as much as the more advantaged members.
4. Administrative processes will be open to public review; information will be freely shared.
5. Public administrators will openly participate in policy discussions, and supply relevant information to interested parties but accept decisions forthcoming from the policy process as guides for their own behavior.
6. Parties at interest to administrative decisions and actions will be consulted and involved in agency decisions pertinent to their interests.
7. Principles of basic human rights, as spelled out in the Nigerian Constitution, will guide administrative behavior.
8. Administrative behavior must be such as to stand the test of public review for fairness, honesty, and impartiality.
9. Administrative action will be as concerned with the growth and development of affected persons as with program efficiency.
10. Administrators will neither seek nor accept favors or advantages resulting from their positions.
11. Administrators will be responsible for their agencies or ministry's achieving its defined goals, but they will search for and make public unintended consequences of their programs.
12. Public managers will monitor their programs and fellow employees for honest and ethical behavior, bringing notice where violations occur.

The author is aware that these guidelines for ethical dialogue would represent, in practice, something of a bombshell in Nigeria. However, the 12 items would add up to a heavy charge on public officials in the nation, with the intention that their effect would be to render their behavior more ethical, and moral, equitable, and just. Jerald Greenberg (1999) contends that codes of ethics are especially effective when they are used in conjunction with training programs that reinforce a government organization's values. In the absence of such training, too many codes come across as "window dressing" and are ignored, if they are even read at all. The author believe that despite the somewhat different emphasis on many of these principles, they would prove more valuable as guides to ethical dialogue in problem solving situations than most "code of ethics" now in use. They would offer ways to control corruption and abuses of office but go on to include human development and democratic procedures as matters relevant to ethical, moral, and just behavior in the twenty-first century.

Conclusion

This chapter has argued that public positions should not be used as rewards for political support or swapped for bribe. It argues that the weak or diffuse sense of national interest created by numerous and regular changes in government invalidate the notion of democracy. Nigeria must develop a public administration that is responsive to the needs of the people. National, state and local of governments must establish merit system for employment and promotion, as well as implement strict and code of conduct. The new ethics would replace the code of conduct that has been the functioning model for decades. Government efforts toward improving the ethical responsibility of public employees tend to focus on legalistic and organizational strategies. Organizational strategies designed by the bureaucracy, as practiced today; do not provide a satisfactory solution. One thing that is clear from the analysis of this chapter is that Nigeria will not become a sustainable developed nation if an effective rule of law is not put in place.

Public servants salary should be increased according inflation rate. They also should be paid regularly. There should be programs set up to educate civil servant that their position should not be seen as an obligation for self and group interest. National interest should be the number priority of all the public servants. Ethical programs should be introduced to change the societal norms. This can only be achieved through instilling values different from those that are currently acceptable. The family, church, mosque, and schools have an important role to play in changing the values and current social norms of the nation. Greater senses of national identity need to be introduced in all aspects of life. This will help provide accountability and transparency. Citizens need to accept that self-interest need not take second place to rights, justice, and fairness in public dealings.

Although each public servant must be personally responsible for his or her own behavior on the job, given the fragility of the human conscience, government must also be responsible for a work-place that is conducive to ethical behavior. Constitutional rule and disciplinary actions backed by an efficient and effective enforcement system that ensures cooperation and compliance, is the most effective means of addressing corruption. Thus, the quality of ethical choice in social processes largely depends on the participants' willingness to go beyond personal biases to consider their responsibility to the general public.

Utilitarianism maintains that morally right action is the one that provides the greatest happiness for the greatest number of people. Not only does it enable us to justify many of the obligations of individuals and organizations – such as refrain from bribery in the case of Nigerian public and private managers – but the principle of utility also provides a strong view about justice.

References

Adamolekun, Oladipo. (1999). Edited Public Administration in Africa. Boulder, Colorado: Westview Press.

Adler, J. (1987). "Moral Development and the Personal Point of View." In Ethics in Business, edited by J. Kittay and S. Meyers, New Haven, Connecticut: Yale University Press.

Agbese, P. (1992). "With Fingers on the Trigger: Military as Custodian of Democracy in Nigeria." Journal of Third World Studies. Vol. 9, 2, pp. 220-53.

Akinterinwa, B. (1994). "The Experience of Niger: Adjusting What Structure?" In Structural Adjustment in West Africa, edited by Adebayo Olukoshi. Lagos, Nigeria: Pumark.

Amy, D. (1984). "Why Policy Analysis and Ethics Are Incompatible." Journal of Policy Analysis and Management. Vol. 3, 4 (Summer), pp. 573-591.

Boatright, J. (1997). Ethics and the Conduct of Business. Upper Saddle River, New Jersey: Prentice-Hall.

Brumback, G. (1991). "Institutionalizing Ethics in Government." Public Personnel Management. Vol. 20, 3, pp. 353-364.

Carson, T. (1985). "Bribery Extortion, and the Foreign Corruption Practices Act." Philosophy and Public Affairs. Vol. 14, 2, pp. 66-90.

Clor, H. (1996). Public Morality and Liberal Society. Notre Dame, Indiana: University of Notre Dame Press.

Coulter, E. (1996). Principles of Politics and Government. (Sixth Edition), Madison: Brown and Benchmark.

Danley, J. (1983). "Towards a Theory of Bribery." Business and Professional Ethics Journal. Vol. 2, pp. 19-39.

Diamond, L. (1988). Class, Ethnicity and Democracy in Nigeria. Syracuse, New York: Syracuse University Press.

Donaldson, T. and P. Werhane. (1996). Ethical Issues in Business. Upper Saddle River, New Jersey: Prentice-Hall.

Duddley, B. (1973). Instability and Political Order: Politics and Nigeria in Crisis. Ibadan, Nigeria: Ibadan University Press.

Dworkin, R. (1978). "Liberalism." In Public and Private Morality, edited by S. Hampshire. Cambridge, Massachusetts: Cambridge University Press.

Edoho, F. (1997). Globalization and the New World Order. Westport, Connecticut: Praeger.

Edoho, F. (2001). Management Challenges for Africa in the Twenty-first Century. Westport, Connecticut: Praeger.

Eells, R. (1977). Bribery and Extortion in World Business: A Study of Corporate Political Payment Abroad. New York: Macmillan.

Fleishman, J. and B. Payne. (1980). Ethical Dilemmas of the Education of Policymakers. New York: Hastings Center.

Greenberg, Jerald. (1999). Managing Behavor in Organizations. Upper Saddle River, New Jersey: Prentice Hall.

Guardian Newspaper, November 11 (1998). Lagos, Nigeria.

Harsch, E. (1993). "Accumulator and Democrats: Challenging State Corruption in Africa." Journal of Modern African Studies. Vol. 31, 1, pp. 31-48.

Heady, F. (1991). Public Administration: A Comparative Perspective. New York: Marcel Dekker.

Hellriegel, D. and J. Slocum. (1994). Management. New York: Addison-Wesley.

Hirschman, A. (1970). Exit, Voice, and Loyalty. Cambridge, Massachusetts: Harvard University Press.

Isekhure, Nosakhare. (1998). 201 Solutions to Vision 2010. Benin City, Nigeria: Oduna Communications Press.

Kaplan J. and Ross, W. (1968). The Pocket Aristotle. New York: Washington Square Press, pp. 246-250.

Keith-Spiegel, P. and G. Koocher. (1995). Ethics in Psychology. Hillsdale, New Jersey: Lawrence Erilbaum.

Koehn, P. (1990). Public Policy and Administration in Africa: Lessons from Nigeria. Boulder, Colorado: Westview.

Mbaku. J. M. (1994). "Bureaucratic Corruption and Public Policy Reform in Africa." Journal of Social Political and Economic Studies. Vol. 19, 2, pp. 149-75.

Olaniyan, O. (1996). Foreign Aid, Self-Reliance, and Economic Development in West Africa. Westport: Praeger.

Olowu, Dele. (1999). "Transparency and Accountability." In Public Administration in Africa edited by Oladipo Adamolekun. Boulder, Colorado:Westview Press.

Phillips, M. (1984). "Bribery." Ethics Journal. Vol. 94, 3, pp. 621-626.

Rawls, J. (1994). The Theory of Justice. London: Oxford University Press

Rogers, H. and Bernard Njoku. (2001). "Corruption and the Nation-State: Improving the Ethical Climate in Nigeria." Conference Proceedings of International Academy of African Business and Development. Washington DC. (April), pp. 147-152.

Ross, W. (1930). The Right and the Good. Oxford: Oxford University Press.

Schelling, T. (1981). "Economic Reasoning and the Ethics of Policy". Public Interest. Vol. 63 (Spring), pp. 37-61.

Shaw, W. (1991). Business Ethics. Belmont, California: Wadsworth.

Tong, R. (1986). Ethics in Public Policy Analysis. Englewood Cliffs: Prentice-Hall.

Weimer, D. and A. Vining. (1992). Policy Analysis: Concepts and Practice. Englewood Cliffs, New Jersey: Prentice-Hall.

14 Broad-Based Sustainable Development

Introduction

This text is about the relationship between the army junta and federal bureaucracy in Nigeria. The overall process is illustrated by several case studies. Nigeria's Structural Adjustment policy, and the difficulties encountered when the federal ministries responded differently, often adversely, to its implementation is also used to reveal the relationship between the military and public administrators in the nation. As background, the study has traced Nigeria's problems with political development, and especially the roles played by the nation's military rulers and higher bureaucrats since the country gained its freedom from British colonialism.

If the future could be predicted, policymakers and public managers could rationally work toward accomplishing known results. Unfortunately, the future is contingent upon many complex social, political, economic, and technological factors. Even if we were able to quantify these factors today, there is no guarantee that they would remain constant in the future. This suggests that predicting the twenty-first century of public management is an impossible task. However, forecasting the twenty-first century is a risky business at best, but trend analysis and speculation about future possibilities may help us understand what events are likely to be continued and how we may avoid certain undesirable consequences if particular scenarios are implemented.

The predicament encountered with centralized economic decision-making and the pervasive nature of policies pursued in Nigeria has provided a painful but critically important lesson. Military intervention and the patrimonialization of the nation's apparatus are fundamentally in conflict with the process of economic development. Economic progress blossoms best when economic freedom, expressed through the market place, is promoted and enhanced. The precipitating cause of the elusiveness of development in Nigeria is the manifest irrelevance of centralized economic decision-making. Government intervention in economic affairs is now equated with economic retardation and has, consequently, become a discredited policy framework. The significant truth is that bad government is the biggest single reason for poverty in Nigeria, and less government is the most effective single remedy. Further, the rule of law suffered during the military regimes in Nigeria. In order for Nigeria to develop in the twenty-first century, the rule of law has to be revived to the fullest capacity.

Nigerian leaders must eschew government ownership and intervention in favor of market-oriented policies in the twenty-first century. Government intervention in economic affairs has not and cannot result in a dependable relationship between economic development and economic management. Consequently, government intervention, as a policy option, must be terminated except in those few special circumstances that pertain to the national good. Just as political expediency in the past four decades reinforced the somewhat intellectually feasible preference for some form of centralized government socioeconomic decision-making as the basis for nation-building and as the means toward modernization, it is now necessary to disengage from such a policy framework and implement liberalized economic policies. After almost half a century of independence and the right to develop and implement policy indigenously, the majority of the social infrastructures are worse than what they used to be.

The experimentation associated with post-independence socioeconomic policy in Nigeria has brought disastrous results – so disastrous, as a matter of fact, that it seems incredible that the model that was once viewed as attractive and worthy of imitation by so many nations is now a dilemma. However, like so many of sub-Saharan nations themselves, those policies are now considered bankrupt, and it is time to attempt to eradicate the whirlpool of despair that the military and its exclusive policymakers have created.

Policy reform, then, is a matter of urgency in order to move toward achieving the rising levels of growth necessary to sustain an improved standard of living and create an atmosphere that is not antidemocratic, antisocial, anti-progressive, or anti-entrepreneurial – reform that would create opportunities for people to make their own choices. Allowing people to make choices would enable a nation's economy to respond more quickly to the ever-changing world economy and even to take advantage of the opportunities that such change may offer. Policy reform in the twenty-first century may be difficult, but it is absolutely essential in to produce the growth that Nigeria requires meeting the needs of its citizens. Reform represents the initial steps in the long journey back toward sustainable economic progress. Policy reform here is used to refer to those policies that effectively promote development through market-oriented principles and reduced government intervention.

Implementing policy requires that the leaders of Nigeria assume a stance of good leadership. Good leadership can assure good government that, in turn, can assure stability and continuity, without which investment and production will continue to falter. Good government or governance can provide the environment to facilitate economic progress. Good governance is taken to mean the exercise of legitimate power and authority in the management of national affairs. Its dimensions are political, tactical, and institutional. It is good government and also implies political accountability, bureaucratic transparency, information and expression, and capacity-building capability. In addition, it requires a professionally competent and honest civil service and sound fiscal management.

The reform policies the Nigerian government pursues in the twenty-first century would also determine the pace of sustainable development. The behavior of government plays an important a role in stimulating – or impeding, for that matter – economic progress as does, for example, the behavior of entrepreneurs. Thus, the creativity and skill of the leadership of Nigeria, and their advisers, play a key role in the process of sustainable development.

Military and Bureaucracy

Nigeria's military juntas have had as their central purpose the restoration of public order, and the promotion of economic development. Far from being a cohesive, united, corrective force, however, the Nigeria military reflected all the ethnic and social tensions that have plagued the country since independence. Nevertheless, the most intense disorder and the higher incidence of unrest came when the country was led by civilian regimes. The military's justification for the exercise of political power was its declared capacity to eliminate corruption and preserve law and order. But under military rule, although relative stability was improved, the Gowon,

Babangida and Abacha regimes allowed corruption to increase and it was more widespread and more flagrant than during the brief periods of civilian government. Thus, the declared corrective intentions of the military regimes in the first period (1966-79), as well as the more recent military governments under Buhari, Babangida and Abacha are little more than empty phrasings.

The problems of corruption, the ever increasing incidence of robbery and brigandage, the frequent industrial strikes, the miserable performance of the economy, the high inflation, the uneven development of the country, the low modernization, and sustained inter-ethnic rivalry have led to the paralysis of the military government. This confirms Henry Bienen's (1970) observation that the military lacks the wisdom, skills, training and mind-set for social and economic development. The military rules in an arbitrary manner, perhaps even more so than during the British colonial administration.

Interviews conducted in 1997 and 2000 among key military officers, federal public servants, and development program coordinators, show a most inequitable distribution of resources and opportunities, but sustained dependence on the higher public bureaucracy. It is the latter's advice and counsel that is needed in the making of public policy. Here again, the colonial legacy is most pronounced. But in spite of the bureaucracy's continuing importance, it suffers from poor education, a lack of ethical training, and a high degree of formalism and impersonality. Moreover, the bureaucracy is a culturally oriented institution that is burdened by the pressures of ethnicity, insistent on the maintenance of quotas, and too easily given to personal expression, to self-pleading and opportunistic bargaining. President Obasanjo has taken a positive step by signing a contract with the United State military to train the Nigerian army on how to conform to democratic role. It is the hope of the author that such training will yield the required results in the future.

The civil service reform of 1988 introduced more professionalism and accountability, but corruption has persisted. Moreover, the creation of still more states caused a rapid growth in the administrative services, and recruitment into the public bureaucracy has followed the principle of federal supremacy. A substantial effort was made to enlist personnel with an understanding of development administration. But the junta did not follow through in implementing these reforms. Given its tendency to reduce the role of the bureaucrats, the army junta failed to understand how administrators assist the government in identifying and carrying out appropriate development policies, how they can be used to stimulate economic growth, promote social equity, strengthen public sector management, and generally improve international operations. Moreover, the military administration, under the influence of the IMF and World Bank, bypassed development administration and promoted the work of the private sector. Thus neither professionalism nor development administration has received the necessary support from the central authorities. The undermining of the civil service tradition was another cost of the AFRC's general structural adjustment policies and the SAP/Make-or-Buy Policy.

The fact that successive military juntas have continued to divide and subdivide the country into more and more administrative states/zones may give them more opportunity to thwart secessionist movements, but the process also multiplies over and again the number of untrained, inexperienced and easily corrupted bureaucrats at the lower level. It is difficult to see political development in such circumstances. The more centralizing military elites also appear to have created a situation where the decentralized, less professional bureaucrats in the different states enjoy significant advantages over the administrators who man the federal ministries. Does this help to explain the frequent coups, and counter coups, the changes at the top of the ruling juntas and the clash of interests between the junta and higher bureaucracy in the federal ministries? In other words, Nigeria's tribal/ethnic problems are not resolved by dividing the country into 36 states. To the contrary, we see a confused army high command, as well as a higher federal bureaucracy that is increasingly more insecure, in fact so insecure that it is given to considerable inter as well as intra-organizational conflict. Effective decision-making is only possible in conditions that promote cooperation between the military and higher bureaucracy in Nigeria, but such cooperation has diminished markedly. The Nigerian situation indicates a break down in civil-military decision-making, and hence repeated failures in achieving stated national goals.

The welfare of public servants in Nigeria needs to be addressed. Public administrators are underpaid, lacking in motivation, a sense of purpose and direction. The only sense of direction that they have is how they could use their position to enrich themselves. The national interests have become secondary to personal interest. Some national, state, and local employees are often paid their salary late or not at all for several months. This delay in payment has galvanized corruption among civil servants. To make matters worse state and local government have neither published or audited their accounts in the past 25 years. That is one of the reasons why vast amounts of money seep into pockets of corrupt senior public administrators. Thus the civil service situation in Nigeria can is describe as deplorable, ineffective, wasteful, and sloppy and operate a spoil system in its recruitment and promotion programs. The author believes that the Nigerian government has outgrown and outlived its policies, structure and rules for carrying out government business and for managing its citizens and the economy. For change to take place in the government several norms have to be changed. The government of President Obasanjo must start addressing the problems of the public service by developing a professional public administration that is competent and based on a merit system.

The environment within which Nigeria public administrators and military work shapes their attitudes and the environment are made of system and structure. The systems however, reinforce the mentality that change is not necessary. Therefore, the Nigerian leader job is to encourage its people, public administrators, and military to question and challenge those systems that prevents great performance. Many organizational systems in Nigeria require a total overhaul. These institutions include the governing systems, administrative systems, organizational behavior and processes. The government need to introduce an inter relationship management program that will enable both public administrators and all public institutions to understand that every change process must begin with a picture of the destination shared by everyone. Citizens, Public administrators and the military must be re-trained to accept that self-interest need not take second place to rights, justice, and fairness.

Dependence on External Technology and Raw Materials

Nigerian private sector firms did not generate the anticipated new technologies promised by the SAP/Make-or-Buy Policy. Nigeria continues its dependence on external technology and raw materials. Structural adjustment was supposed to reduce Nigeria's external debt and redress its payment imbalance. But the drain on its external foreign exchange reserves continues, and its foreign debt grows with the steady importation of foreign-made equipment and spare parts, as well as raw materials.

Therefore, the country's economic problems remain and conditions can only worsen. Nigeria will still be in search of a technology that utilizes locally available resources, and produces products that satisfy domestic need well into the twenty-first century.

It is noteworthy that the structural adjustment program over-turned almost two decades of indegenization and self-reliance programs in other areas of the Nigerian economy. SAP/Make-or-Buy is still a comparatively new policy but its adequacy, is open to question, especially with regard to the negligible impact it has had on the country's private sector firms. Presumably, the private sector firms, which through their manufacturers association constituted one of the forces behind the detailed strategy for the resolution of Nigeria's technological problems, have already received a significant portion of the estimated $250 million of R & D contracted out by government ministries and agencies. This research reveals that the four ministries studied awarded R & D contracts amounting to $163.67 million to private firms. These firms had convinced government of their ability both to create employment and to put Nigeria in the forefront of new technology. Presumably also, the military policy-makers believed these objectives were attainable. But the realization that these firms are not delivering either jobs or new technologies leads one to question how well the SAP/Make-or-Buy policy is being implemented or whether there is too much "slippage" between the intent of the policy and its actual output.

Related to the matter of "slippage" between policy intent and policy output are the reasons underlying two important modifications to the SAP/Make-or-Buy Policy in 1987 and 1989? The first of these modifications was tied to ministerial budgets that had already been set. Therefore, the need existed to provide interim financing while the ministries and agencies geared their budgets to accommodate the contracting out requirements of the policy. Similarly, in 1989 the policy was expanded to cover ongoing R & D and related studies in the natural sciences, as well as an urban, regional and transportation topics. This later modification to the policy was supposed to encourage an expansion of funding for contracting out purposes.

Implications

The implications of this study for the Nigerian government can be summarized as follows: First, governments should not introduce policies which may not be implemented or maintained, no matter how attractive these policies are in principle. Second, policies, which are working, should not be changed no matter how costly they may seem in terms of resource mis-allocation. Finally, in choosing among policies, priority should be given to those that enhance the stability of the overall policy environment. Although the SAP/Make-or-Buy policy recognizes three of the four elements in any public policy (i.e., goals, means and constraints), the true picture cannot emerge if the fourth element is not analyzed. This fourth element pertains to the roles and power of the policy implementers or bureaucrats. In Nigeria, policy touching upon the development of technology is made at the level of the Armed Forces Ruling Council. Unfortunately, however, it is not whether good policies are formulated, or even whether the means are provided for the fulfillment of these policies, but whether the policy is implemented, poorly implemented, or not implemented at all.

The core element of the SAP/Make-or-Buy Policy therefore lies in its implementation. For any policy measure to be successful in Nigeria there is typically one or more government ministries or agencies whose duty it is to formulate in minute detail the modalities required in attaining the goals of the policy. Such a ministry or agency must necessarily be staffed by experienced bureaucrats. It is also essential that those who are to be involved in policy implementation should be included in deliberations before the policy is established. Involvement at the planning stage of a policy generates consensus among those involved in its implementation. It can be argued that without this spirit of participation among implementers, the policy will be judged an imposition, and hence resisted.

In order to avoid the possible problems that are most likely to arise during implementation, there is often the need to give the bureaucrats a role in modifying aspects of the policy. Such powers should be exercised discretely, but in such a way that displays confidence in bureaucratic decision-making. It was the contention of the bureaucrats in the ministries studied that the absence of discretionary powers was a major reason for the failure of the SAP/Make-or-Buy Policy.

It is clear, the objectives of the SAP/Make-or-Buy Policy have not been achieved. Moreover, certain policy measures that were introduced such as the policy guidelines, were not developed with the ministerial consultation they required. Nevertheless the policy did heighten awareness of the need for new indigenous technology, even if it is still awaited. Coherent political organization, bureaucratic competence and national decision-making are essential requirements of all national development programs but genuine progress is not likely to emerge in Nigeria until the military junta retires to the barracks and new self-governing institutions are erected over a political system anchored in democratic practices.

The analysis in the text reveals that an increase in a series of factors such as human and physical capital accumulation or a decrease in the growth of labor force can obtain an increase in GDP per capita in Nigeria. On the other hand, considering an international area, controlling the behavior of real equilibrium exchange can contribute more in sustainable growth of GDP.

Fostering Decentralization and Citizens Empowerment

Present problems and future challenges can become avenues for innovative projects as public managers begin to take morally responsible and proactive actions toward promoting the public interest. However, to be responsive to new ideas and possibilities, public managers must take critical action to create organizational changes. For problems to be solved and for the quality of work life to be improved, structures and processes of public ministries and agencies must be rendered more adaptive, collaborative, and innovative. This requires the development of a decentralized and humanized workplace.

Policymakers and higher-echelon public managers will also have to design new forms of organizations that will give more power in decision making to lower-level managers and employees, facilitate diversity of ideas and interests, and allow opportunities for learning and self-improvement. Potentials for individual growth and learning are denied under a system of a rigid bureaucratic-authoritarian regime that stresses conformity and loyalty of its members. Centralized management, such as prevails during a military regime, in which the head of state controls the national government, and at the same time appoints military administrators at the state level, only promotes a hierarchical consciousness in which employees must assume loyalty, conformity, commitment, and dedication to the head of state in order to be assigned tasks and responsibilities. There has been no meaningful dialogue between superiors and subordinates, central bureaucrats and local government officials, and between military juntas and civil servants in Nigeria. The channel of communication that has been in place is very dictatorial or authoritarian in nature. This type of communication process is essentially vertical and involves little mutual learning or understanding and needs to be reformed if the nation wants to achieve broad-based sustainable development in the twenty-first century.

Decentralization is a sometimes-confusing term. As Devas (1997) points out, decentralization, as most often used, means some form of transference of power from the national to state and local governments, thereby strengthening local autonomy. But it can also mean decentralization of management whereby lower levels of governance are given discretionary authority to manage programs and are held accountable to a higher-level authority for meeting performance standards. Several pressures have emerged in nations around the world to advance decentralization. A popular, widely held notion is that decentralization fosters democracy (Slater 1997). Citizens are believed to have a more effective voice at the grass-roots level. Decentralization structures help reduce the level of political volatility by offering citizens on the periphery channels the opportunity for political participation by presenting, the opportunities to express demands, and by reducing the distance to points of political access.

Following decades of centralization planning in Nigeria, there is a growing perception that federal bureaucracies have become so bloated and distanced as to produce great inefficiencies and to render them increasingly ineffective. Decentralization would move policy input and decision making out from the federal government to where varieties of needs can be accommodated and varying state and local governments accounted for. For example, reform-minded bureaucrats in France and Italy promoted decentralization to regions so as to gain bureaucratic efficiency and to relieve the national government of "bureaucratic overload" (Rousseau and Zariski 1987, 270).

A decentralized public management system must be sustained through sharing of management's power with lower-level employees in Nigeria. Executive power in the twenty-first century should be defined as the moral and honorable exercise of authority within a set of ground rules to which the national and state bureaucrats, senior directors, military juntas, lower-level managers, and employees as a whole have agreed. Through the process of empowerment, employees will have the opportunity to develop their abilities to solve problems and to improve themselves. Empowering people through decentralization does not imply abandonment of organizational authority. It simply opens up humanistic possibilities for improving organizational effectiveness by establishing collaborative relationships between ministries and their civil servants. Amitai Etzioni (1984) describes the development of mutuality as one dimension for renewing management. He stated that "mutuality is not an altruistic affair. There is an expected reciprocity of affection and respect. Individuals are so composed that they need to receive affection and respect regularly, just as batteries need recharging" (31).

In comparison, Japanese management is paternalistic; there is a great deal of mutual respect and affection between military juntas, senior bureaucrats, and lower-level employees; and management's efforts to promote the welfare of civil servants are based on both organizational interests and human concerns. Nigerian management's relationship to lower-level employees, on the other hand, is basically authoritarian. This needs to change in the twenty-first century. The successful experiences of self-management and industrial democracy in Scandinavian nations are based on the common beliefs among government executives, politicians, clergymen, unions, managers, and workers about the values of enhancing democracy in the workplace. Lastly, decentralization is not only advanced as a curative to federal bureaucratic inefficiencies and a way to promote diversity rather than standardization, but also as a means to partially relieve federal government fiscal woes. Restructuring will enable the federal government to push financial burdens downward.

Education for Raising Consciousness

The education of Nigerian public managers and citizens to understand democratic values and processes is imperative because democratic administration needs the participation of competent public employees as well as input from active citizens. Education can take various forms, ranging from the traditional pedagogical methods of learning in class to long-distance learning that sometimes characterizes adult education.

There has been a lot of enthusiastic interest in constitutional engineering, political parties, politicians, elections, and election monitoring in Nigeria for transition into a democratic government in the near future. But the role of workers has particularly been ignored even when the new and traditional political parties and human rights and prodemocracy movements have had to rely on this particular constituency in their contestation for power. Yet Nigeria cannot afford to ignore the popular institutions and constituencies that determine the dynamics of politics and shape the overall character of the transition from military regime to a multiparty system (Ihonvbere 1994; Soyinka 1996; Lemarchand 1993).

Why are efficiency-enhancing changes sometimes combined with inefficient elements? Why do nations adopt particular reforms at particular times? Why, at other times, do they delay adopting reforms that would clearly increase aggregate welfare? Scholars have suggested a number of answers to these questions, both in general and in the context of particular cases. These mostly focus on three sets of factors, the interests of actors, the nature of political institutions, and the policy choice of individual reformers.

Institutions

By institution I mean the rules of the game in a society or, more formally, the humanly devised constraints that shape human interaction. For a given distribution of interests and power among social actors, various scholars have argued that different political institutions can induce different policy outcomes.

What type of institutions is most conducive to enacting and implementing economic reform policy in Nigeria in the twenty-first century? One common view is that institutions that insulate economic decision-makers from interest group pressures improve the chances of efficiency-enhancing reform. At its most extreme, the argument has been made that military political institutions permitted Nigeria to ignore populist pressures, demobilize social organization, and implement economic reform (O'Donnell 1973; Ihonvbere 1994). Democratic institutions, some argue, preclude such insulation. More limited claims have been made about particular institutional structures within democracies. Stephen Haggard and Robert Kauman (1995) contended that constitutions that strengthen executive and insulate economic ministries are seen as promoting reform. Independent Central Banks tend to be more financially conservative than those more dependent on government or parliament politicians, who are more likely to yield to populist temptations.

Empirical studies have found no clear relationship between democracy or military regimes and reform, and the evidence on executive strength or insulation and reform varies depending on the geographical scope of the study (Haggard and Kaufman 1995; Hellman 1996). What is important for every government is the concern of strengthening the institutions of the state to make them more effective in advancing the welfare of its citizens and in managing society in line with the nation's mandated authority.

As institutions or organizations (military and bureaucratic) get older and tend to become less innovative and slower in solving problems, training programs should be planned with assistance from outside change agents, and organizational members may be given the opportunity to pursue educational programs to satisfy their personal need for learning. Adult education institutions should be developed to address these needs in the twenty-first century.

Education for critical consciousness should also be emphasized at schools of public policy and administration in Nigerian universities. When students complete their college education, they would have learned various analytical skills, and scientific, political, humanistic, ethical, and moral responsibilities toward the public. The administrators of the twenty-first century should become reflexive individuals who can recognize that their technical expertise is embedded in a context of meanings. They must understand what their actions to others (clients and other employees) – and what the other's actions – mean to them. Reflexive administrators, if they are also proactive individuals, will have the ability to learn about both themselves and their relationships to the social world of Nigeria. Their perception of the social world will become clearer as they carry on meaningful dialogues with employees, clients, and the public.

Through training, military juntas and administrators can learn the meaning of participation and the use of shared power. They can become aware of the significance of democratic values and processes and develop a sense of responsibility for representing, in the day-to-day execution of administrative tasks, the interests of the general public.

Civil Society and Interests

Various terms have been used to describe the organizations that make up the social network that constitutes civil society. The most common term used today is non-governmental organization. Charities, youth groups, service clubs, church groups, trade unions, hobby groups, advocacy groups, community organizations, grassroots community groups, community improvement and betterment groups, self-help groups, and all other kindred organizations are of civil society. The socio-cultural function of civil society groups is to promote social cohesion; combat isolation, alienation, and anomie; train future leaders; develop organizational skills; and raise the self-confidence and self-esteem of members. What this diverse group of NGOs has in common is that each sets its members to work to produce a good or service that adds value to the lives of either the member themselves or their communities. The political functions of civil society groups are to increase participation in political processes, provide voice and political empowerment to members, and force governments to be open and more responsive.

Most simply, interest-based arguments contend that particular policies survive only if they serve the material interests of the most powerful coalition of actors. As we alluded to in Chapters 3 and 11, the structural adjustment policy reforms were delayed or never introduced during General Buhari's regime because the most powerful coalition had reason to oppose them. Therefore, in the twenty-first century, Nigeria should encourage the development of democratic institutions "manufacture consent" and cooping societal groups through participatory mechanisms. The kind of balance of power between citizens and government that such institutions would create may make bargains between them more credible. Even if democratic deliberation complicates the enactment of radical economic development in Nigeria, it is likely to make their implementation more effective.

What policies are necessary to promote the development of social capital in civil society in Nigeria in the twenty-first century? Most important is protection for the human rights of free speech, association, and assembly. These rights protect the people who advocate starting civil society organizations, organize people to come together and form the group (association) and hold meetings and group activities (assembly). For civil society to develop in Nigeria effectively, two levels of protection of these human rights are necessary:

1. The various governments of Nigeria must not prohibit or repress these activities. The government may do this out of a belief in these human rights or because it lacks the will or ability to actively mobilize itself to

carry out such repression. It is the latter condition that often allows civil society to get off to a flying start toward democratization in the waning days of dictatorship, when the government takes no positive steps to encourage such organizations yet lacks the will or resources to effectively repress them.

2. The federal government of Nigeria must protect civil society activity from repression by their nongovernmental enemies; repression of unions by employers; repression of poor people's organizations by local elites; and repression of radical or innovative political and cultural groups by defenders of traditions and orthodoxy.

Generally, security of the human right to organize is the single most important step in encouraging the expansion and normalization of existing informal or even underground social network (Diamond 1992; Weaver, Rock, and Kusterer 1997). People who belong to a multiplicity of organizations, each with a different overlapping membership, have pluralist connections to their society and pluralist interests to defend. Secular civil society thus lessens the risk of religious strife and civil conflict.

Individuals

The success or failure of economic reform efforts in the twenty-first century will depend in part upon the particular policies chosen by the individual reformer. In the twenty-first century, interest-based or institution-based approaches often view the outcomes of politics as straightforwardly deducible from the interests of powerful social groups or the institutional constraints within which they pursue them. The characteristics of the individuals involved in the formulation of the structural adjustment policy may explain why the policy failed.

What we can learn from the structural adjustment policy is that interest and institutions provided the constraints that explain why some economic development programs were completely infusible in Nigeria in the 1980s and 1990s and why others were possible. But I argue that the factors that best explain the timing of individual reform successes and failures relate to changes in the particular policies adopted by the central policymakers. Successful economic development requires both the opportunities provided by interests and institutions and the ability of a policy entrepreneur to identify these opportunities and to exploit them to the full through appropriately designed policies. As the military and public administrators begin to show their new attitudes toward citizens, citizens in turn are likely to raise their consciousness and become more active and cooperative clients.

The comparative perspective in Nigerian public administration must be renewed, but with different assumptions. Comparative administration in Nigeria during the 1960s and up to the 1980s was basically the testing of British and American theories by comparing different administrative systems through deductive inquiry, that is, application of predetermined categories of concepts to explain differences and similarities. Although a deductive approach is necessary for the development of common theoretical knowledge, an inductive process of understanding the unique characteristics of different situations may also offer new knowledge that may be valuable in new contexts. A practical suggestion is for students and practitioners of Nigerian public management to consider ways of improving their condition through a phenomenological or inductive understanding of policy and administration in other nations. As an example, study of participate management, health care policy, crime prevention, education policy, technology policy or environmental policy, as practiced in Japan and certain European nations could be very suggestive; so might be the comparative study of long-term and short-term planning, budgeting processes, public involvement in decision-making, and matters of this nature. A synthesis of comparative studies presents opportunity for public learning in an era of information and technology.

Accountability, Transparency and Effective Governance

By now it should be apparent to the readers of this book that Nigeria's potential for development in the twenty-first century will be shaped by a number of factors. Some ingredients of effective governance are systemic to the whole government and the way it relates to people and organizations in the nation. Reforms in these areas could improve governance in all ministries and agencies. The payoff from these systemic reforms is potentially greater than improving the skills of one manager at a time or improving the manageability of one agency at a time.

Accountability in this text means holding people responsible for their performance and holding public and private sector managers responsible for the results of their decisions. Accountability can range from the narrow, technical concept of financial accountability, which holds people responsible for correct handling of the money they control, to the broad concept of political accountability, which holds officials responsible for living up to the expectations they created while campaigning for election. In analyzing accountability in Nigeria in the twenty-first century, it is necessary to consider (1) who is being held responsible; (2) to whom they are being held responsible; and (3) how they are being held responsible.

Democracy and political participation will increase in Nigeria in the twenty-first century when accountability is supplemented by additional lines of responsibility to create a built-in system of checks and balances. This happens when government officials are responsible not only to their bureaucratic superiors on the organizational chart but also to a political party or constituency organization that they must keep satisfied and to a professional association that insists on its own standards for their performance. Thus, a lawyer working in an environmental protection agency may have to account for his or her actions, not only to a direct superior but also to environmental monitoring groups and to the standards of professional competence and ethics of the bar association. To measure accountability or performance in a government agency, it will be ideal to compare the annual performances of particular agencies in terms of cost-effectiveness and efficiency. In essence, this requires keeping track of the agency's output and comparing the ratio of those outputs to the expenses involved. One increasingly common approach to measuring and monitoring governmental effectiveness is through public opinion polls. The poll is not a precise measure of actual governmental performance, but it has several advantages. It can help Nigeria to measure legitimacy very effectively, and it would increase democratic accountability if the opinion polling is performed regularly and independently and if the results are announced publicly.

Both accountability and an effective rule of law require open and public procedures, in other words, transparency. They would also require that information about the economy and society be regularly and objectively collected and widely published. Without information about policy and program results, policy and program accountability are almost meaningless. Transparency and good information systems should be two characteristics of a system of effective governance in the twenty-first century in Nigeria. Dele Olowu (1999) contend that reforms aimed at enhancing the accountability and transparency of Nigeria's public administrators would therefore need to empower the people through a variety of institutions that can provide leverage for the public to demand and assert accountable performance. He further stated that such institutions would include vibrant medium and small-scale private sector organizations, effective local governments that are accountable to the people rather than to the central government. These institutions should also be able to enforce the rule of law whenever their policies were deliberately violated.

Economic Stabilization and Sustainable Development

Proponents of neoclassical economic theory, led by the World Bank and the International Monetary Fund, argue that the solution to this problem requires rolling back the role of the federal government to get it to do only those things that governments have to do and can do well (Fisher 1998; Weaver, Rock, and Kusterer 1997; World Bank 1997; Nafziger 1997). This limits the role of government to providing those public goods that the private sector can not provide, including national defense, protection of persons and property, and enforcement of contracts. It also includes maintaining a sound system of money and credit, undertaking some public works and agricultural research, and financing public health and public education. The neo-classical economic model also requires removing price control, reducing regulatory rigidity, eliminating legal monopolies, and improving the functioning of governments so that private enterprise can flourish.

Other factors that Nigeria should consider in the twenty-first century include the following: First, the potential for development will depend on the amount of natural resources and human capital that Nigeria continues to produce. A nation such as Nigeria with very rich soil, low population density, a high educational level, and a lot of petroleum for export and domestic use has obvious advantages over an impoverished, overpopulated nation such as Rwanda or one lacking a lot of natural resources such as Niger, Benin, or Chad. Second, the international political and economic order will create constraints and opportunities for Nigeria. If the nation as well as other developing nations is to make economic progress, the industrial countries will have to keep their doors open to

Nigeria's and other sub-Saharan nation exports. Further, industrialized nations are unlikely to commit large sums to foreign aid in the twenty-first century, nor is it clear how productive such aid has been in the past. Nigeria will still require technical advice in agriculture, population control, environmental preservation, and fiscal management.

Nigerian leaders should realize that they couldn't make history alone. In the future they will be constrained by the political and socioeconomic structures of the nation and of the international community. The student protest that brought President Suharto's 32 years regime to an end in 1998 could happen or spill-over to Nigeria if good leadership is not demonstrated by the leaders of Nigeria. Thus, both economic and political progress will ultimately depend on the quality of government leadership. Political skills, democracy, decency, honesty, and courage will make the difference between success and failure of leaders in the twenty-first century in the nation.

Economic transformation in the twenty-first century will involve a change in the rules of the game. It would entail expansion of the economic space in which producers can compete – and hence dismantling of state participation, intervention, and discrimination. The economic reforms of the twenty-first century should expand the scope of competition, primarily within domestic industry and to a higher extent between domestic and foreign producers. These reforms should also expose public enterprises to competition. Intensified competition does not necessarily lead to a change in the rules of the game. In the Nigerian system where the new politicians have no visible means of subsistence, intensified political competition could as well enhance the use of the state for plunder. Future plunder would require retention of means of control over industry and trade. There is optimism in the wind that the political rules of the game will change for good in the twenty-first century. It is in these portents that Nigeria must look for a potential change in economic rules for industrial development, as it was intended under the structural adjustment policy.

Fiscal policy in the future must be reformed to reduce the fiscal deficit and economic inefficiencies in public expenditures and to redress the imbalances in public expenditures and taxation. The first would help reduce inflationary pressures in the economy as part of macroeconomic stabilization, and the second would improve economic efficiency. For example, subsidies on transportation, fuel, and fertilizer encourage firms to consume more of these. Value-added taxes (VATs) are recommended because they can raise a lot of revenue and are fairly easy to administer.

Fiscal reform for the twenty-first century should also promote decentralization of government, allowing local governments to raise revenue and spend it for local infrastructure and services. Decentralization as an important part of fiscal reform has been discussed in detail earlier in this final chapter.

An important part of reducing the fiscal deficit is the closing, privatization, or reform of state-owned enterprises (World Bank 1995). Privatization is meant to reduce economic inefficiency and income inequality. This has turned out to be an extremely difficult thing to do in Nigeria (especially), and the international financial institutions (IFIs) have lost their early single-minded enthusiasm for privatization. Instead of trying to privatize, the IFIs have recommended that developing nations (including Nigeria) remove the monopoly status of state-owned enterprises and allow private firms to compete with them.

The economic policy reform espoused by the World Bank and the International Monetary Fund has not gone unchallenged. Critics take exception to almost every aspect of the World Bank's structural adjustment model. They have demonstrated that except for Hong Kong none of the highly successful exporters in East Asia have liberalized their trade policies along neo-liberial lines (Fisher 1998; Nafziger 1997; Weaver, Rock and Kusterer 1997; Gillis et al. 1992). While borrowing money from the World Bank, the Chinese have assiduously avoided taking its advice. Korea is also widely known for the highly interventionist role its government played in its development. It must give us pause that most of the really successful have economies followed policies quite contradictory to those being pushed by advocates of neo-liberal, laissez-faire structural adjustment.

Why has government intervention in markets in East Asia not resulted in economic inefficiency and slow growth? The simple answer to the question is that the incentives provided by interventionist governments in East Asia rewarded results. Exporters were rewarded for export success; farmers were rewarded for growing food. In fact, the governments in Korea and Taiwan established elaborate mechanisms for tracking a firm's performance over time and rewarding it for success or punishing it (for example, through tax audits) for poor performance. This was possible because the governments saw export success and meeting food needs as critical to national survival, had enough freedom from interest groups to design strategies that rewarded success, and were characterized by relatively honest and competent bureaucracies. This example demonstrates that when this combination exists, the alternative can work. Thus, in the twenty-first century Nigeria's policymakers can learn something from the East Asian alternative approach to neo-liberial macroeconomic policies. The example from Asia demonstrates that non-Western nations need not model themselves on Western countries to attain development. Japan, for example, successfully modernized in its own way. Nonetheless, "culturally appropriate" development remains the most romantic yet difficult to achieve of the models available. On the basis of cross national analysis and research on the problems facing Nigeria, there has been an emerging consensus that the nation's policy and reform agenda needs to focus on the following in order for it to attain sustainable development in the twenty-first century. Nigeria's instruments of reform must focus on:

1. Accelerating trade liberalization to enhance the competitiveness of domestic producers and speed up Nigeria's integration into global economy.
2. Fostering private sector development as the principal engine of growth – but focus on the primary sector and the use of local raw materials.
3. Promote all aspect of ethical, fairness, justice and good governance.
4. Foster human resources and social development.
5. Build administrative and managerial capacity as an essential step in carrying out the needed reforms effectively.
6. Opening the banking sector to healthy, competition and international best practices in bank management, particularly through privatization; and strengthen the legal framework for banking activities (Cleeve 2001).

Democratic Programs and Nation Building

The shortest and surest path to democracy in Nigeria is to foster the growth of its prerequisite institutions. In a new democratic system, democratization efforts must take the form of capacity building, or institutional development work, in these key areas: law enforcement, education, the media, and organized civil society. In the absence of this prior institutional development, more direct democratizing reforms of the system of government are unlikely to succeed in the first place or to sustain themselves even if they are initially successful. Given the anti-nation ideology of the new global order, the ethnic and religious tensions that are rampant in Nigeria and the built-in economy of affection, nepotism, and corruption that characterize the nation, state building becomes a difficult process. Historically, state building preceded democratization and was generally accomplished by coercive means through conquests or in the process of resisting conquests. Unlike in the twentieth century, nation building has now become fused with democratization.

This fusion has serious implications to the manner in which the process of nation building can take place as well as to the nature of democracy. In regard to nation building, it implies that integrating the disparate groups and determining the relations between them and the nation can only be accomplished through collective decisions of all the parties involved and on the basis of carefully negotiated terms that are acceptable to all of them. Such negotiated terms also imply that if such agreements are not reached, the option of secession is available to ethnic groups. For this reason, democratization of the terms of nation building may involve the risk of accelerating nation disintegration (Mayer, Burnett, and Ogden 1996). However, few ethno-national movements in Nigeria have demanded to form their own states.

Ethno-nationalists in Nigeria will clearly face serious dilemma in future. On the one hand, they will find integration with the state under existing terms and conditions of unevenness unacceptable. On the other hand, they will realize the risks nation disintegration and fragmentation entail.

The aim of future politicians in Nigeria should be to occupy and retain territories, be its vote's representative, and be accountable for its money or power. They should be naturally inclined to use baits and sticks in doing so; favors, subsidies, and discrimination should be their basic instruments, and they have no reason to favor fair, transparent, non-discretionary, or non-distorting policies in general. But they should pursue such policies if they provide political advantage or prevent political loss. Reforms should always follow crises because crises hold the possibility of political loss. Therefore, reform in public policy should be undertaken as a stop-loss strategy. But that also means that quick-fix public policies that resolve internal or external crises are more likely to be adopted than fundamental, lasting structural reforms; and such reforms should be stopped once the crises are overcome.

Future reforms do not have to be born out of a crisis – like was the case of the structural adjustment policy. They should be formed as part of political strategy in non-critical times if politicians can see a way of making political capital out of them. Nigerian economists in the twenty-first century need to develop pathology of unreformed public policies as a tool for use in political battles.

There are many good reasons why such pathology does not emerge in Nigeria. In many nations, an independent economic profession does not exist. The government as a priesthood to do propaganda for it recruits the economists that are available. Funds, official secondments, and other awards go to the priests. The government does not publish objective, usable information. Clearly, policy reformers survive better in large, open, diversified societies in which the government is the sole source of patronage and information. But where there is political competition, there will be a scope for the use of economic ideas and viewpoints as political weapons. Generating them is not a popular occupation among economists and public policy analysts; it is plodding empirical work, and where the government is powerful, propagating heterodox ideas may carry few rewards and serious punishments. But the fact cannot be ignored that economic ideas have a force of their own, that they are potential political weapons. Generally speaking, politicians to build up loyal constituencies should use subsidies, concessions, and other economic favors. By the same token, they must harm opposing politicians who constitute a potential market for reformist ideas in the twenty-first century, in Nigeria.

There is another reason why this sort of post-reform economic research is important. Most reforms raise detailed empirical questions and present complicated choices. The more these have been anticipated and studied, the more likely it is that the reforms will be of a high quality. The questions will often be legal; reforms do very often require a change in law. Hence, understanding of law among economists and public policy analysts, and vice versa, is essential for sound reforms. Policy changes usually have a budgetary dimension; and resistance to them will generally depend on their financial effects on constituents. Therefore, knowledge of the technicalities of public finance and accounting also contributes to good reform. The military, bureaucrats, and politicians in Nigeria cannot afford to assume that lawyers and accountants will provide the relevant inputs, for specialist human resources of all sorts are scarce in unreformed governments due to brain drain.

The term *brain drain* is used here to mean the emigration or "overflow " of high-level persons or professionals who would otherwise be under-utilized and discontented in their home country. Studies sponsored by the World Bank lend further support to the idea that human resource development has an important bearing on economic growth (Human Development Index 1997; World Bank Report 1996). There is reason to believe that the relationship is two-way and mutually supporting. On the one hand, growing economies can and do devote increasing resources to improvement of educational, health, and nutritional standards. But it is also apparent that investment in human resources helps to accelerate economic growth. It does this by increasing labor productivity, encouraging greater physical investment, and reducing the dependency burden of the population. These contributions to growth are especially evident in the case of education. A major weakness of the manpower planning approach in Nigeria is that people with more education are increasingly doing jobs that previously were done by less-educated persons, and this has resulted in brain drain or emigration of professional workers from the nation.

There are many policies that Nigeria will have to consider in the twenty-first century to stop the problem of brain drain. One approach would be to establish political stability and appropriate public institutions. The national and state governments in Nigeria could reduce the overflow of highly technical, professional, and managerial skills by encouraging students and trainees to take programs relevant to the nation's interests. They should also provide good pay and benefit systems that are comparable to what professionals may earn if they emigrate. Further, Nigeria should provide the necessary technical tools, laboratories, and professional environments that would attract and challenge well trained personnel to remain in the nation. Developed nations could be invited to periodically provide refresher conferences, seminars, workshops, and training to Nigerian professionals and highly skilled personnel to reduce their emigration abroad.

The industrial revolution needed as part of a broader strategy for sustainable development in Nigeria will involve structural change on a number of levels: geographical, sectional, managerial, technological and societal. This has led most observers to emphasize the complexities and difficulties of making the necessary changes; industry in particular has stressed the need for a very gradual shift. However, because of the continuing lack of appreciation in environmental policy circles of the dynamic nature of industrial development, these difficulties have been overstated. Industrial development is a process of constant restructuring, as seen in the far-ranging changes in industry composition and location since the 1970s and in the rapid diffusion of personal computers during the 1980s. The issue is now how to harness this dynamic potential for sustainable development.

Innovations of the need for time sit uneasily with industry's manifest ability to adapt to new circumstances and the pressing urgency of the human and environmental situation. Policymakers, industrialists and environmentalists have largely failed either to explore or act upon the multiple benefits that could flow from the pursuit of a vigorous ecoindustrial policy. The continuing resistance to such a fast tract to sustainable industrial development in Nigeria is thus evidence not only of lack of imagination and courage, but also a clear statement that most military, political and business leaders still do not take the sustainability imperative seriously.

It is essential to focus on the grass root or rural community level when making sustainable development operational. Processes that meet basic needs while protecting the environment and empowering the poor, thus internalizing the necessary trade-off, have been labeled 'primary environmental care' similar in many respects to primary health care. Primary environmental care is as little able to solve all environmental and poverty problems in a country or region as primary health care can solve all health-related problems. But there is ample experience that sustainable development will not be possible in the absence of the involvement and empowerment of the intended beneficiaries of the development process.

Policies Toward the Private Sector

The private sector in Nigeria is composed of mostly agriculture, and it is larger than the government or public sector. In the past the military and bureaucrats set targets for production, employment, investment, exports, and imports for the private sector but usually have no binding policies to affect the target. This was one of the problems the structural adjustment/make-or-buy policy had in the nation. Beyond forecasting, the usefulness of target figures for the private sector depends on the reliability of data, the persuasiveness of the policymaking process, and policy implementation or control over the private sector.

Implementing public policy in the private sector means

government trying to get people to do what they would otherwise not do, invest more in equipment or improve their job skills, change jobs, switch from one crop to another, adopt new technologies, and so on. Some policies for the private sector in the twenty-first century in Nigeria may include the following:

1. Reducing monopolies and oligopolies. Good governance is vital not just to ensure the rule of law and protect against international organized crime but also to maintain and expand social and economic infrastructure.
2. Investigating development potential through scientific and market research and natural resources surveys.
3. Promoting private and public saving.
4. Providing adequate infrastructure (water, power, transportation, and communication) for public and private agencies.
5. Promoting better resource utilization through inducements and controls.
6. Providing the necessary skills through general education and specialized training.
7. Seeking out and assisting entrepreneurs. Small enterprises that can export should be supported in making this leap. Otherwise, production will continue to be dominated by larger and less labor, intensive firms. Small enterprises vulnerable to imports may merit temporary protection.
8. Improving the legal framework related to land tenure, corporation, commercial transactions, and other economic activities.
9. Managing new technology. Labor-saving technologies that are developed elsewhere and require advanced skills may be inappropriate in Nigeria. Though vital, technological change will always be a double-edged sword, and its relationship with poverty reduction is complicated and poorly understood. The benefits of investment in technology can be maximized if it is accompanied by strong policies to create human capital and foster small enterprises.
10. Creating markets, including commodity markets, security exchanges, banks, credit facilities and insurance companies (Nafziger, 1997).

Political economy and development theories of sequencing of reforms have a general utility but are not usually relevant to particular situations: The window of opportunity for public policy is usually narrow in Nigeria; however, the military, bureaucrats, and politicians should do what they think is advantageous or easy, irrespective of what economists or policy analysts tell them. Democratic principles and other empirical rules should guide whatever they do in the twenty-first century.

First, politicians tend to think that removal of concession merits compensation. This generally does not make economic sense, especially in the case of urban concessions over rural areas. But it is good political sense if it buys peace or prevents secession of a valuable constituent. Policy-makers in the twenty-first century should ensure that the compensation does not become worse than the concession it replaces. Generally, one short, lump-sum compensation is better than an income stream. But the two are equivalent only where there is a functioning financial market in which one can be reliably converted into the other.

Second, one is on safer grounds in deregulating real controls than monetary or financial controls. Investment takes time, so market structures generally change slowly; even a hurried, one-shot deregulation is likely to hurt some one soon. Developments in finance, trade, and construction, on the other hand, can be extremely rapid; reforms in these areas call for more forethought, negotiations, bargaining, conflict and compromise, or consensus building.

Third, it often helps to divide the constituencies and tackle them one by one. For instance, if a subsidy scheme involves both subsidy to consumers and one from low-cost to high-cost consumers, it is sometimes strategically advantageous to turn it into a fixed-rate subsidy, thereby eliminating the cross-subsidy between producers. Similarly, if privatization involves closure and sale of assets, it is politically advisable first to pay off workers and thereby reduce the number of interested parties. Current military and bureaucrats as well as the new politicians of the 1990s are fond of saying that the best is the enemy of the good. This is not a very wise saying, but dividing up the best into elements and sequencing them often make it more practicable.

The fourth empirical rule for Nigeria in the twenty-first century is that booms are a good time to remove constraints on competition, and slumps are a good time to remove consumer subsidies and concessions. In general, the money value of concessions and distortions varies considerably over time, and study of their variation can help in timing their removal with the least disruption.

Political and economic development in the twenty-first century in Nigeria requires openness, nondiscrimination, transparency, negotiation, and consensus building. This factors are not only required by the military, the bureaucrats, the politicians and the policymakers; they should also be required by other interest groups, ethnic or tribal groups, political parties, and so on. To present these as the absolute good for the future will convince no one, but these factors will help in building a viable political stability, which will then spill over to economic development. Nigeria can no longer afford to formulate and implement policies that would fail like the structural adjustment/make-or-buy policy. The "vision 2010" economic development program being proposed is a good policy path. However, the Nigerian military should be more committed to establishing viable political stability and institutions before embarking on such a "vision." Under the current political turmoil the nation is too dark for its citizens to have the appropriate "bright vision."

Conclusion

In this last chapter, I examined the predicaments facing Nigeria and how they have become more manifest in each attempt to attain democratic rule and economic reform. This approach provides an opportunity to observe how respect for human rights, democratization, and broad-based sustainable development efforts have interacted with market-oriented economic policies in the past three decades in Nigeria. Without these contextual factors, economic reform would have not occurred either quickly or as they did. While economic crisis and debt clearly played a greater role in Nigeria's structural adjustment program, it is clear that the military and bureaucracy did not foresee the deep restructuring that eventually occurred.

In the 1990s, there has been a clear rethinking of interest in participatory approaches to development. Beneficiaries' participation in designing and implementing projects, the empowerment of women and other disadvantaged groups, grassroots involvement in decision making and planning, and participatory rural appraisal are the rage (Weaver, Rock and Kusterer 1997; Fisher 1998). Much of the neoclassical or neo-liberial economics, macro-policy, relative prices, and structural adjustment approach are decidedly pass in the late 1900s, and Nigeria needs to learn from this transition.

Interestingly, in the 1980s, macro-policy, getting prices right, stabilization, and structural adjustment reigned supreme. In the 1970s, participation and empowerment of the poor, particularly in rural areas or integrated rural development, were popular, and macro-policy and relative prices were forgotten. Those of us who can remember that far back have asked, be we doomed to repeat history? Unless macro policymakers and grassroots activists develop more mutual respect and engage in dialogue with each other in Nigeria, the twenty-first century will be grim indeed.

The cycle of military regimes, decline in citizen participation, and faulty macroeconomic policy needs to be broken in Nigeria. It is important to foster dialogue between the major two disparate communities of grassroots activists and macro policymakers and advisers, though this will not be easy. Policymakers, particularly economists, and grassroots activists have vastly different beliefs about the influence of incentives, such as higher prices, on individual (for example, small farmer) behavior. Grassroots activists are more likely to emphasize the effect of structures and institutions on group behavior and outcomes.

This difference in perspective leads to radically different policy prescriptions. Whereas economists working for the military recommend restructuring incentives, activists emphasize the need for collective action. To the activist, the economists' incentives are part of the military structure of domination that perpetuates poverty. To the military, the grassroots activists' call for participation is doomed to failure.

Both groups are right and wrong. There is ample evidence that prices and incentives both matter. With the military government's proactive confiscators tax policies toward small farmers – either through overvalued exchange rates or by paying farmers a small percentage of the world price for their products – farmers do not produce for the market, and rural poverty results. But it is equally clear that unless those same small farmers find ways to solve collective problems, such as maintaining irrigation canals and ditches or farm-to-market roads, they will be unable to take advantage of market opportunities.

Both markets and organization matter in the twenty-first century. Macro-policies have a better chance of success if micro-practices reinforce them. Similarly, collective action has a better chance of success if macro-policies are supportive. This insight into the linkages between macro policies and micro- collective action provides the basis for building a shared vision of development between Nigerian communities, one in which growth is equitable, poverty is reduced, and there is more, rather than less, participation.

Finally, although we see the need for adjustment, we remain agnostic concerning the impact of the World Bank, the IMF, and other donor-financed neo-liberal or laissez-faire structural adjustment on sustainable development. However, a hopeful view of public policy, cautioned by appropriate realities and a willingness to meet challenges and opportunities, is fully warranted in the twenty-first century.

References

Brautigam, D. (1997). "Substituting for the State: Institutions and Industrial Development in Eastern Nigeria." World Development. Vol. 25, pp. 1063-1080.

Carroll, T. (1992). Intermediary NGOs: The Supporting Link in Grassroots Development. West Hartford, Connecticut: Kumarian Press.

Cleeve, E. (2001). "Globalization and Development in Sub-Saharan Africa." Corruption and the Nation-State: Improving the Ethical Climate in Conference Proceedings of International Academy of African Business and Development. Washington DC. (April), pp. 268-273.

Devas, N. (1997). "Indonesia: What do we Mean by Decentralization?" Public Administration and Development. Vol. 17, pp. 351-367.

Diamond, L. (1992). The Democratic Revolution: Struggles for Freedom and Democracy in Developing World. New York: Freedom House Press.

Etzioni, A. (1984). An Immodest Agenda: Rebuilding America Before the 21st Century. New York: McGraw-Hill.

Fisher, J. (1998). Nongovernments: NGOs and the Political Development of the Third World. West Hartford, Connecticut: Kumarian Press.

Gillis, M., D. Perkins, M. Roemer, and D. Snodgrass. (1992). Economics of Development 3rd ed. New York: W. Norton.

Guy, G. (1983). Development by People: Citizen Construction of Just World. New York: Praeger.

Haggard, S. and R. Kaufman. (1995). The Political Economy of Democratic Transitions. Princeton, New Jersey: Princeton University Press.

Hellman, J. (1996). A Competitive Advantage: Political Competition and Economic Reform in Post Communist Transition. Cambridge: Harvard University Press.

Holmberg, J. (1992). Making Development Sustainable: Redefining Institutions, Policy, and Economics. Washington DC: Island Press.

Ihonvebere, J. (1994). Nigeria: The Politics of Adjustment and Democracy. New Brunswick, Connecticut: Transaction.

Lemarchand, R. (1993). African Troubled Transitions. Journal of Democracy. Vol. 3, 4 (October), pp. 98-110.

Mayer, L., J. Burnett and S. Ogden. (1996). Comparative Politics: Nations and Theories in a Changing World. Upper Saddle River, New Jersey: Prentice-Hall.

Nafziger, W. (1997). Economics for Developing Countries. Upper Saddle, New Jersey: Prentice-Hall.

O'Donnell, G. (1973). Modernization and Bureaucratic-Authoritaritarian Studies in South American Politics. Berkeley: University of California Press.

Olowu, Dele. (1999). "Accountability and Transparency." In Public Administration in Nigeria edited by Oladipo Adamolekun. Boulder, Colorado: Westview Press.

Putnam, R. (1993). Making Democracy Work. Princeton New Jersey: Princeton University Press.

Rouseau, M. and R. Zariski. (1987). Regionalism and Regional Devolution in Comparative Perspective. New York: Praeger.

Slater, R. (1997). "Approaches to Strenthening Local Government: Lessons from Sri Lanka." Public Administration and Development. Vol. 17, pp. 251-265.

Snavely, K. and R. Beck. (1994). "Defining the Role of Non-Prorit Corporation in Community Economic Development." Journal of the Community Development Society, Vol. 24, pp. 213-228.

Syinka, W. (1996). The Open Sore of A Continent: A Personnal Narrative of the Nigerian Crisis. New York: Oxford University Press.

Tarrow, S. (1994). Power in Movement: Social Movements, Collective Action and Politics. New York: Cambridge University Press.

Weaver, J., M. Rock, and K. Kusterer. (1997). Achieving Broad-Based Sustainable Development. West Harford, Connecticut: Kumarian Press.

World Bank. (1995). World Bank Annual Report. New York: Oxford University Press.

World Bank. (1997). World Bank Annual Report. New York: Oxford

University Press.
World Bank. (2000). World Bank Annual Report. New York: Oxford University Press.
World Bank. (2000). Human Development Index. New York: Oxford University Press.

Selected Bibliography

Abosrisade, O. and R. Mundt. (1998). Politics in Nigeria. New York: Longman.

Aboyade, O. (1980). "Nigerian Public Enterprises as an Organizational Dilemma." In Administration for Development in Nigeria edited by P. Collins, Lagos, Nigeria: African Education, pp. 83 - 98.

Achike, O. (1978). History of the West African Frontier Force. London: Longman.

Achike, O. (1990). Groundwork of Military Law and Military Rule in Nigeria. Ibadan, Nigeria: University of Ibadan Press.

Adamolekun, L. (1983). Public Administration: A Nigerian and Comparative Perspective. London: Longman.

Adamolekun, L. (1985). Nigeria Public Administration, 1960-1980. Ibadan, Nigeria: Heinemann Educational Books.

Adamolekun, L. (1986). Politics and Administration in Nigeria. Ibadan, Nigeria: Spectrum Press.

Adamolekun, L. and V. Ayeni. (1990). "Nigeria". in Public Administration in Third World Nations, edited by V. Subramanian. London: Longman. 120 - 145.

Adamolekun, L. edited (1999). Public Administration in Africa. Boulder, Colorado: Westview Press.

Adams, P. (1995). "Democracy Delayed in Nigeria". Christian Science Monitor Vol. 3, 2 (October), pp. 5 - 11.

Adedeji, A. (1968). Nigerian Administration and Its Political Setting. London: Hutchinson.

Adedeji, A. (1981). "Rise and Fall of the Nigerian Civil Service. Part I and II." West African Magazine. (March 30), pp. 670 - 687.

Adekson, B. (1978) Towards Explaining Civil Military Instability in Contemporary Sub-Sahara Africa. Ibadan, Nigeria: University of Ibadan Press.

Adeniyi, E. O. (1989). "Development Planning in Nigeria". Nigerian Trade Journal Vol. 4, 3 (July - September), pp. 11 - 25.

Adeola, F. (1996). "Environmental Contamination, Public Hygiene, and Human Health Concerns in the Third World: The Case of Nigerian Environmentalism." Environment and Behavior. Vol. 28, 5, pp. 614 - 646.

Adler, J. (1987). "Moral Development and the Personal Point of View." In Ethics in Business, edited by J. Kittay and S. Meyers. New Haven, Connecticut: Yale University Press.

Adu, A. (1982). The Civil Service in Commonwealth Africa. London: George Allen and Unwin.

Adubifa, A. (1990). Technology Policy in Nigeria. Ibadan, Nigeria: NISER Press.

Ahmad, S. (1994). Nigeria: The Political Economy of Oil. Oxford: Oxford University Press.

Ahmadu, B. (1962). My Life. London: Cambridge University Press.

Aihe, D. (1985). Selected Essays on Nigerian Constitutional Law. Benin City, Nigeria: Idodo Umeh Publishers Limited.

Aina E. and N. Adedipe. (1991). The Making of the Nigerian Environment Policy. Ibadan, Nigeria: Ibadan University Press.

Ajayi, S. (1988). "Issues of Over-evaluation and Exchange Rate Adjustment in Nigeria." Washington, DC: Prepared for Economic Development Institute of the World Bank.

Ajayi, T. (1962). Milestone in Nigerian History. Ibadan, Nigeria: Oxford University Press.

Ajayi, T. (1965). Christian Mission in Nigeria, 1841-1891. London: Longman.

Ake, C. (1985). "Indigenization: Problems of Transformation in Neo-Colonial Economy." in The Political Economy of Nigeria, edited by C. Ake. New York: Longman.

Ake, C. (1985). The Political Economy of Nigeria. London: Longman.

Ake, C. (1995). "Nigerian Development and the Ogoni Crisis." Nigerian Policy Magazine. Lagos, Nigeria: Daily Times Press (July): Vol. 5, pp. 13 - 15.

Akin-Aina, W. (1994). "Logic in the Illogical." Newswatch News Magazine, Lagos, Nigeria. July 25, p. 9.

Akinterinwa, B. (1994). "The Experience of Niger: Adjusting What Structure"? in Structural Adjustment in West Africa, edited by A. Olukoshi. Lagos, Nigeria: Pumark.

Albrow, M. (1970). Bureaucracy. London: Pall Mall Press.

Aldrich, H. and C. Zimmer. (1986). "Entrepreneurship through Social Networks." In the Art and Science of Entrepreneurship, edited by D. Sexon, and R. Smilor. Cambridge, Massachusetts: Ballinger.

Allison, G. (1971). Essence of Decision-Making: The Cuban Missile Crisis. Boston: Little Brown.

Almond, G. and G. Powell, (1966). Comparative Politics: A Development Approach Boston: Little Brown.

Almond, G. and J. Coleman. eds. (1960). The Politics of Developing Areas. Princeton,

Aluko, A. (1995). "New Developments in the Admiralty Jurisdiction of the Federal High Court in Nigeria." Journal of African Law. Vol. 39, 1, pp. 20 - 45.

Amanor, K. (1994). The New Frontier: Farmer's Response to Land Degradation: A West African Study. UNRISD, New Jersey: Zed Books.

Amy, D. (1984). "Why Policy Analysis and Ethics Are Incompatible." Journal of Policy Analysis and Management, Vol. 3, 4 (Summer), pp. 573 - 591.

Anderson, B. (1991). Imagined Communities: Reflections on the Origin and Spread of Nationalism. New York: Verso.

Anderson, J. (1984). Public Policy-Making. New York: Holt, Rinehart and Winston.

Anderson, K. (1991). "Radical Criminology and the Overcoming of Suffering." In Criminology as Peacemaking, edited by. H. Pepinsky and E. Quinney Bloomington: Indiana University Press.

Andrain, C. (1988). Political Change in the Third World. Boston: Unwin Hyman Press.

Anyanwu, A. (1992). Nigerian Structural Adjustment Program: A Multi-Sectoral Analysis. Enugu, Nigeria: ABIC Books.

Appiah-Opoku, S. (1994). "Theoretical Orientation of Environmental Assessment in Canada: Application to the Third World." Environments Vol. 22, 3, pp. 103 - 110.

Appiah-Opoku, S. (1997). "Indigenous Institutions and Environmental Assessment: The Case of Ghana." Environment Management Vol. 121, 2, pp. 159 - 171.

Apter, D. (1965). The Politics of Modernization: Protest and Change. Englewood Cliffs, New Jersey: Prentice-Hall.

Apter, D. (1987). Rethinking Development: Modernization Dependency and Postmodern Politics. Newbury Park, California: Sage.

Aristotle. (1958). Politics. Translated and edited by E. Barker. London: Oxford University Press.

Art, R. (1983). "Bureaucratic Politics and American Foreign Policy: A Critique." Policy Science. Vol. 4, 4 (December), pp. 120 - 145.

Ascher, K. (1992). The Politics of Privatization: Contracting Out in the NHS and Local Authorities. London: Macmillan.

Ascher, W. and R. Healy. (1990). Natural Resource Policy Making: A Framework for Developing Countries. Washington, DC: Durham.

Ashorth, W. (1983). Contracts and Finance. London: H.M. Stationery Office.

Atanda, A. (1966). The Missionary Impact on Modern Nigeria. London: Longman.

Aughey, A. (1983). "Mrs Thatcher Philosophy." Parliamentry Affairs. Vol. 36, 3, 389 - 398.

Aweto, D. (1990). "Plantation Forestry and Forest Conservation in Nigeria." The Environment. Vol. 10, pp. 127 - 137.

Awolowo, O. (1947). Path to Nigerian Freedom. Ibadan, Nigeria: University of Ibadan Press.

Awolowo, O. (1981). Awo on the Nigerian War. Ibadan, Nigeria: Tribune Press.

Ayida, A. (1987). Reflection on Nigerian Development. Lagos, Nigeria: Heinemann.

Ayida, A. and H. Onitiri. eds. (1971). Reconstruction and Development in Nigeria. Ibadan, Nigeria: Oxford University Press.

Babbie, E. (1992). The Practice of Social Research. 6th edition. Los Angeles: Wadsworth Publishers.

Bangura, Y. (1987). "IMF-World Bank Conditionality and Nigeria's Structural Adjustment Program." In The IMF and the World Bank in Africa edited by Kjell J. Havenik. Uppsala, Sweden: Scandinavian Institute of African Studies, 95 - 116.

Banton, M. (1983). Racial and Ethnic Competition. Cambridge: Cambridge University Press.

Baranshamaje, E. (1995). The African Virtual University (AVU): Concept Paper. Netscape Navigator. 1 - 27.

Barbier, E. (1989). "The Economic Value of Ecosystems." In Tropical Wetlands. Gatekeeper Series, no 89 - 102. London: Environmental Economics Center. 1 - 12.

Bates, A. (1971). Markets and States in Tropical Africa. Berkeley: University of California Press.

Baucus, D. and S. Humans. (1994). "Second-Career Entrepreneurs: A Multiple Case Study of Entrepreneurial Process and Antecedent Variables." Entrepreneurship Theory and Practice. (Winter).

Beinaart, W. (1994). Twentieth - Century South Africa. New York: Oxford University Press.

Bendix, R. (1945). "Bureaucracy and the Problem of Power." Public Administration Review. Vol. 5, pp. 194 - 209.

Bendor, J. and H. Thomas. (1992). "Rethinking Allison's Models." American Political Science Review. Vol. 86, pp. 2 - 8.

Benien H. and V Diejomaoh. (1981). The Political Economy of Income Distribution in Nigeria. New York: Holmes and Meier.

Benn, S. (1967b) "Rights." In The Encyclopedia of Philosophy edited by P. Edwards. New York: Oxford University Press. Vol. 7, 8, p. 195.

Benn, S.I. (1967) "Equality, Moral and Social." In The Encyclopedia of Philosophy edited by P. Edwards. New York: Oxford University Press. Vol. 3, 4, p. 38.

Bennet, L. (1995). International Organization: Principles and Issues, 2nd ed. Englewood Cliffs, New Jersey: Prentice-Hall.

Bennett, R. (1993). Police at Work. Beverly Hills, California: Sage.

Bennis, W. (1986). Changing Organizations. New York: McGraw-Hill.

Bhagwati, J. (1978). Anatomy and Consequences of Exchange Control Regimes Cambridge, Massachusetts: Ballinger National Bureau of Economic Research (NBER).

Bienen, H. (1983). The Political Economy of Income Distribution in Nigeria. New York: Holmes and Meier.

Bienen, H. (1971). The Military and Modernization. Princeton, New Jersey: Princeton University Press.

Bienen, H. (1971). The Military and Modernization. Princeton, New Jersey: Princeton University Press.

Bienen, H. (1976). "Transition from Military Rule: The Case of Western State of Nigeria." In Political Participation Under Military Regime. edited by H. Bienen and D. Morell. Beverly Hills, California: Sage. 64 - 70.

Bienen, H. (1978). Armies and Parties in Africa. New York: Africana Publishing Company.

Bienen, H. and V. Diejomaoh. (1981). The Political Economy of Income Distribution in Nigeria. New York: Holmes and Meier.

Bienen, H., and J. Herbst. (1996). "The Relationship between Political and Economic Reform in Africa." Comparative Politics. Vol. 29 (October), pp. 23 - 42.

Bienen, H., and J. Waterbury. (1989). "The Political Economy of Privatization in Developing Countries." World Development. Vol. 17, 5, pp. 622 - 650.

Biesteker, T. (1987). Multinationals, the State, and Control of the Nigerian Economy. Princeton, New Jersey: Princeton University Press.

Binder, L. (1986). "The Natural History of Development Theory." Comparative Studies in Society and History. Vol. 28, 1, pp. 3 - 33.

Biobaku O. (1965). "Colonialism in Nigeria." in Christian Mission in Nigeria. edited by J. Ajayi. London: Longman.

Biobaku, S. (1980). "Educational Evolution in Nigeria: Growth Without Development," A Paper presented at the Institute of African Studies Seminar Series, University of Ibadan.

Blassa, B. (1981). The Newly Industrializing Countries in the World Economy. New York: Pergamon Press.

Blau, P. (1956). Bureaucracy in Modern Society. New York: Random House.

Blau, P. (1989). The Dynamics of Bureaucracy. Revised edition. Chicago: The University of Chicago Press.

Blau, P. and W. Richard (1982). Formal Organizations. San Francisco: Chandler Publishers.

Boatright, J. (1997). Ethics and the Conduct of Business. Upper Saddle River, New Jersey: Prentice-Hall.

Bollen, K. (1979). "Political Democracy and the Timing of Development." American Sociological Review. Vol. 44, 5, pp. 572 - 587.

Bonoma, T. (1985). "Case Research in Marketing: Opportunities, Problems, and Process." Journal of Marketing Research. Vol. 12 (May), pp. 199 - 208.

Botkin, J. and J. Mathews. (1992). Winning Combinations. New York: John Wiley.

Boulding, E. and R. Kahn. ed. (1984). Power and Conflict in Organizations. New York: Basic Books.

Brams, S. (1975). Games Theory and Politics. New York: Free Press.

Brautigam, D. (1997). "Substituting for the State: Institutions and Industrial Development in Eastern Nigeria." World Development. Vol. 25, pp. 1063 - 1080.

Braybrooke, D. and C. Lindblom. (1963). A Strategy of Decision. New York: The Free Press.

Breemer, V., C. Drijver. and L. Venema. (1995). Local Resource Management in Africa. New York: Wiley and Sons Publishers.

Brownsberger, W. (1983). "Development and Government Corruption-Materialism and Political Fragmentation in Nigeria." Journal of Modern African Studies. Vol. 21, 2, pp. 225 - 245.

Brumback, G. (1991). "Institutionalizing Ethics in Government." Public Personnel Management. Vol. 20, 3, pp. 353 - 364.

Cairncoss, S. (1981). "Government and Implementation." New Scientist and Science Journal. Vol. 7 (September), pp. 135 - 150.

Callaghy, T. (1993). "Political Passion and Economic Interests: Economic Reform and Political Structure in America" in Responses to Africa's Economic Decline, edited by Hemmed J. New York: Columbia University Press.

Cammack P., D. Pool, and W. Tordoff. (1993). Third World Politics: A Comparative Introduction. Baltimore: Johns Hopkins University Press.

Carrol, J. and Johnson, E. (1990). Decision Research: A Field Guide. Thousand Oaks CA: Sage.

Carroll, T. (1992). Intermediary NGOs: The Supporting Link in Grassroots Development. West Hartford, CT: Kumarian Press.

Carson, T. (1985). "Bribery Extortion, and the Foreign Corruption Practices Act." Philosophy and Public Affairs, Vol. 14, 2, pp. 66 - 90.

Carver, R. (1989). "Examining the Premises of Contracting Out." Public Productivity and Management Review. Vol. 13 (Fall), pp. 13 - 26.

Cawthra, G. (1994). Policing South Africa. London: Zed Books Limited.

Central Bank of Nigeria (1990). Annual Report and Statement of Accounts. Lagos, Nigeria: CBN Press.

Central Bank of Nigeria. (1986). Annual Report and Statement of Accounts. Lagos, Nigeria: CBN Press.

Central Bank of Nigeria. (1987). Annual Report and Statement of Accounts. Lagos, Nigeria: CBN Press.

Central Bank of Nigeria. (1988). Annual Report and Statement of Accounts. Lagos, Nigeria: CBN Press.

Central Bank of Nigeria. (1993). Annual Report and Statement of Accounts. Lagos, Nigeria: CBN Press.

Central Bank of Nigeria. (1994 - 1995). Annual Report and Statement of Accounts. Lagos, Nigeria: CBN Press.

Central Bank of Nigeria. (1996 - 1998). Annual Report and Statement of Accounts. Lagos, Nigeria: CBN Press.

Chang, S. and Jones, R. (1992). "Approaches to Privatization: Established Models and a US Innovation." Government Finance Review. Vol. 8, pp. 17 - 21.

Chhibber, A. and J. Wilton. (1986). "Macroeconomics Policies and Agricultural Performance in Developing Countries." Finance and Development. Vol. 23, 3, pp. 6 - 9.

Chokor, B. (1993). "Government Policy and Environmental Protection in the Developing World: The Example of Nigeria." Environmental Management, Vol. 17, 1, pp. 15 - 30.

Chokor, B. and A. Odemerho (1991). "Land Degradation Assessment by Small-Scale Traditional Farmers in Nsit Community of Nigeria." Department of Geography and Regional Planning: University of Benin, Nigeria. Mimeograph.

Choksi, A. (1979). "State Intervention in the Industrialization of Developing Countries: Selected Issues." World Bank Staff Working Paper no. 341. World Bank: Washington, DC.

Chowdhury, K. (1996). "Literacy and Primary Education." Working Papers. Human Capital Development and Operations Policy, 1 - 19.

Church, T. (1982). "The Old and the New Conventional Wisdom of Court Delay." Justice System Journal. Vol. 7, pp. 395 - 412.

Cleeve, E. (2001). "Globalization and Development in Sub-Saharan Africa." Conference Proceedings of IAABD, International Conference, Washington DC (April 4-7), 268 - 274.

Clor, H. (1996). Public Morality and Liberal Society. Notre Dame, Indiana: University of Notre Dame Press.

Cohen, M., March, J. and Olsen, J. (1972). "A Garbage Can Model of Organizational Choice." Administrative Science Quarterly, Vol. 17, 2, pp. 1 - 25.

Coleman, J. (1958). Nigeria: The Background to Nationalism. Berkeley: University of California Press.

Collier, D. (1979). The New Authoritarianism in Latin America. Princeton, New Jersey: Princeton University Press.

Collins, Paul. (1980). Administration for Development in Nigeria. Lagos, Nigeria: African Education Press.

Consedine, J. (1995). Restorative Justice: Healing the Effects of Crime. Lyttleton, New Zealand: Ploughshares Publication.

Coser, L. (1966). The Functions of Social Conflict. Glencoe, Illinois: The Free Press.

Cosgel, M. (1996). Metaphor, Stories and the Entrepreneur in Economics. History of Political Economy. Durham, North Carolina: Duke University Press.

Cosgel, S. and R. Jones (1992). Metaphor, Stories and the Entrepreneur in Economics: History of Political Economy. Durhman, North Carolina: Duke University Press.

Coulter, E. (1996). Principles of Politics and Government. (Sixth Edition), Madison: Brown and Benchmark.

Cox, F. L. Erlich, and J. Tropman. (eds.) (1990). Strategies of Community Organization: Macro Practice. Ithaca, New York: Peacock.

Cribb, R. and B. Colin. (1995). Modern Indonesia: A History Since 1995, New York: Longman.

Crick, B. (1962). In Defense of Politics. London: Weidenfeld and Nicolson.

Criminal Procedure Act of Nigeria. (1963). Lagos, Nigeria: Federal Government Printing Press.

Crouch, H. (1986). "Patrimonialism and Military Rule in Indonesia." In The State and Development in the Third World. edited by A. Kohli. Princeton, New Jersey: Princeton University Press.

Crozier, M. (1984). The Bureaucratic Phenomenon. Chicago: The University of Chicago Press.

Currie, E. (1986). Confronting Crime: An American Challenge. New York: Pantheon.

Cyert, R. and J. March. (1989). A Behavioral Theory of the Firm. Englewood, New Jersey: Prentice-Hall.

Dahrendorf, R. (1968). Essay in the Theory of Society. Standford, California: Standford University Press.

Daily Times, Lagos, Nigeria. October 27 (1960). 2 - 3.

Danley, J. (1983). "Towards a Theory of Bribery." Business and Professional Ethics Journal. Vol. 2, pp. 19 - 39.

David-West, T. (1994). "Nigerian Federalism and The Virus of Disunity." The Guardian Press. (January 2), pp. 5 - 6.

Davies, C. (1984). "Environmental Institutions and the Reagan Administration". In Environmental Policy in the 1980s, edited by Vig and Kraft Washington, DC: CQ Press.

Davies, J. (1962). "Towards a Theory of Revolution." American Sociological Review. Vol. 3, pp. 5 - 19.

Dawa, M. (1991). "Deforestation: A Traditional Approach to the Problem and Remedies." Paper presented at the Annual Conference of the Environment and Behavior Association of Nigeria, Kaduna.

De Waal, A. (1997). Famine Crimes: Politics and the Disaster Relief Industry in Africa. Bloomington, IN: Indiana University Press.

Decalo, S. (1986). Coups and Military Rule in Africa: Studies in Military Style. New Haven: Yale University Press.

Dent, M. (1975). "The Third Military Coup in Nigeria." World Today 5 (September): 23 - 31.

Dent, M. (1978). "Corrective Government: Military Rules in Perspective," in Soldiers and Oil: The Political Transformation of Nigeria, edited by K. Panter-Brick. London: Frank Cass, 101 - 137.

Desai, A. (1997). The Economics of Transition to An Open Market Economy. Paris: OECD Development Center.

Deutsch, K. (1953). Nationalism and Social Communication: An Inquiry into the Foundation of Nationality: Cambridge, Massachusetts: MIT Press.

Deutsch, K. (1957). Political Community and the North Atlantic Area. Princeton, New Jersey: Princeton University Press.

Devas, N. (1997). "Indonesia: What do we Mean by Decentralization?" Public Administration and Development. Vol. 17, pp. 351 - 367.

Dexter, A. (1970). Elite and Specialized Interviewing. Evanston, Illinois: Northwestern University Press.

Diamond, L. (1987). "Ethnicity and Ethnic Conflict." The Journal of Modern African Studies. Vol. 25, 1, pp. 117 - 128.

Diamond, L. (1988). Class, Ethnicity and Democracy in Nigeria. Syracuse, New York: Syracuse University Press.

Diamond, L. (1992). The Democratic Revolution: Struggles for Freedom and Democracy in Developing World. New York: Freedom House Press.

Dibie, R. (1994). "ECOWAS: Is Functionalism the Answer to Regional Economic Integration in West Africa." Journal of Ethno-Development. Vol. 3, 3, 54 - 63.

Dibie, R. (2000). "Making the Economic Community of West African States (ECOWAS) Sustainable in the Twenty-first Century: Any Lesson From the European Union?" Journal of Comparative Education and International Relations in Africa. Vol. 3, 1-2, pp. 63 - 85.

Dibie, R. (2001) ed. Politics and Policies in Sub-Saharan Africa. New York: American University Press.

Dibie, R. and F. Edoho. (2001). "Business-Government Partnership in Nigeria: A Framework for National Development." Journal of African Business, Vol. 2, 2, pp. 95 - 115.

Dike, E. (1994). Economic Transformation in Nigeria. Zaria, Nigeria: Ahmadu Bello University Press.

Doern, G. (1970). "The Political Realities of Science Policy-Making in the Federal Government." Science Forum. Vol. 15, 2 (June), pp. 20 - 31.

Doern, G.B. (1972). Science and Politics in Canada. Montreal: McGill-Queen's University Press.

Donaldson, T. and P. Werhane. (1996). Ethical Issues in Business. Upper Saddle River, New Jersey: Prentice-Hall.

Dos Santos, T. (1970). "The Structure of Dependence." American Economic Review. Vol. 9 (May), pp. 5 - 15.

Downs, A. (1967). Inside Bureaucracy. Boston, Massachusetts: Little Brown.

Downs, A. (1972). "Up and Down with Ecology-The Issue Attention Cycle." Public Interest. (Summer): 38 - 50.

Drucker, P. (1979). The Age of Discontinuity. New York: Harper & Row.

Duddley, B. (1973). Instability and Political Order: Politics and Nigeria in Crisis. Ibadan, Nigeria: Ibadan University Press.

Duddley, B. (1982). An Introduction to Nigerian Government and Politics. Bloomington, Indiana: Indiana University Press.

Duncan, A. (1992). Structural Adjustment and African Farmer. London: Heinemann.

Dunn, W. (1977). Public Policy Analysis. Englewood Cliffs. New Jersey: Prentice-Hall.

Dworkin, R. (1978). "Liberalism." In Public and Private Morality, edited by S. Hampshire, Cambridge, Massachusetts: Cambridge University Press.

Dye, T. (1976). Policy Analysis: What Governments Do, Why They Do It and What Difference It Makes. Birmingham, Alabama: University of Alabama Press.

Dye, T. (1997). Understanding Public Policy. 5th edition. Englewood Cliffs, New Jersey: Prentice-Hall.

Dye, T. and H. Zeigler. (1981). The Irony of Democracy. 5th edition, Monterey, California: Brooks Cole.

Dyer, G. (1992). The Entrepreneurial Experience. San Francisco, California: Jossey-Bass.

Easton, D. (1965). A Framework for Political System Analysis. Chicago: University of Chicago Press.

Easton, D. (1971). The Political System: An Inquiry into the State of Political Science. 2nd edition, New York: Knof.

Eckaus, R. (1977). Appropriate Technology for Developing Countries. Washington, DC: National Academy of Science.

Economist Intelligence Unit (1994 - 1995). Business International, Country Profile: Nigeria. New York: Annual Survey of Political and Economic Background.

Edoho, F. (1997). Globalization and the New World Order: Promises, Problems and Prospects for Africa in the 21st Century. Westport, Connecticut: Praeger.

Edoho, F. (2001). Management Challenges for Africa in the Twenty-first Century. Westport, Connecticut: Greenwood.

Edoho. F. (2001). "Information Technology Transfer: A Human Resource Dimension." Conference Proceedings of IAABD, International Conference, Washington DC (April 4-7): pp. 268 - 274.

Edwards, G. and I. Sharkansky. (1978). The Policy Predicament. San Francisco, California: Freeman.

Eells, R. (1977). Bribery and Extortion in World Business: A Study of Corporate Political Payment Abroad. New York: Macmillan.

Egborge. A. (1991). "Industrialization and Heavy Metal Pollution in Warri River." 32nd Inaugural Lecture, University of Benin, Benin City, Nigeria, 1 - 32.

Egonmwan, J. (1991). Public Policy Analysis: Concept and Application. Benin City, Nigeria: Aka and Brothers Press.

Egunjobi, L. (1993). "Issues in Environmental Management for Sustainable Development in Nigeria." The Environmentalist. Vol. 13, 1, pp. 33 - 40.

Ehiametalor, E. (1991). "The Impact of 6+3+3+4 System of Education on National Development," A Paper presented to the Committee of Heads of Federal Government Establishments in Bendel State, Nigeria. August, 30.

Ehiametalor, E. and Oduaran, A. (eds.) (1991). Fundamentals of Adult Education, Benin City, Nigeria: Nigerian Educational Research Association, 88 - 100.

Ehindero, S. (1988). Police and The Law of Nigeria. Lagos, Nigeria: Daily Times Press.

Eisenstadt, S. (1966). Modernization: Protest and Change. Englewood Cliffs, New Jersey: Prentice-Hall.

Ekeh, P. (1975). "Colonialism and the Two Publics in Africa: A Theoretical Statement." Comparative Studies Society and History. Vol. 17, 1, pp. 21 - 40.

Ekuehare, B. (1983). "The Foreign Exchange Effects of the Development of the Nigerian Textile Industry." The Nigerian Journal of Economic and Social Studies. Vol. 25, pp. 37 - 56.

Epelle, S. (1960). The Promise of Nigeria. London: Pan Books.

Erocal, D. (1991). Environmental Management in Developing Countries. Development Center of the Organization for Economic Cooperation and Development (OECD).

Esman, M. (1994). Ethnic Politics. Ithaca, New York: Cornell University Press.

Esman, M. (1974). "Administrative Doctrine and Developmental Needs." In The Administration of Change in Africa: Essays in the Theory and Practice of Development Administration in Africa edited by E. Morgan. New York: Cornell University Press.

Essien, E. (1990). Nigeria Under Structural Adjustment. Ibadan, Nigeria: Foundation Publishers.

Estes, R. (1995). "Social Development Trends in Africa 1970 - 1994: The Need for a New Paradign." Social Development Issues. Vol. 17, 1, pp. 18 - 100.

Etzioni, A. (1968). The Active Society: A Theory of Societal and Political Processes. London: Collier-Macmillan.

Etzioni, A. (1981). A Complex and Comparative Organizations; An Analysis of Power Involvement and Their Correlates. New York: Free Press of Glencoe.

Etzioni, A. (1984). An Immodest Agenda: Rebuilding America Before the 21st Century. New York: McGraw-Hill.

Etzioni, A. (1989a). Modern Organizations. Englewood Cliffs, New Jersey: Prentice-Hall.

Etzioni, A. (1989b). Readings on Modern Organizations. 2nd edition New York: Holt, Rinehart and Winston.

Evans, D. (1984). Appropriate Technology and Its Role in Development. In Appropriate Technology in Third World Development, edited by P Kosh. Westport, Connecticut: Greenwood Press.

Fadahunsi, A. and B. Igwe. (1989). Capital Goods and Technological Change and Accumulation in Nigeria. Ibadan, Nigeria: Ibadan University Press.

Fafunwa, A. (1974). History of Education and Nigeria, London: George Allan and Unwin.

Fafuwa, A. (1992). "Each-One-Teach-One: The Nigeria Strategy." The Spider, Vol. 6, 2.

Fajana, O. (1987). "Trade and Growth: The Nigerian Experience." World Development. Vol. 7, 1, pp. 73 - 78.

Falola, T. (1996). Development Planning and Decolonization in Nigeria. Miami, Florida: Florida University Press.

Federal Environmental Protection Agency (1989). Our National Environmental Goals. Lagos, Nigeria: FEPA.

Federal Environmental Protection Agency Report (1991). The Nigerian Environment 3: 1 - 12.

Federal Environmental Protection Agency Report (1997). Lagos, Nigeria: Federal Ministry of Information and Culture Press.

Federal Government Guidelines on Structural Adjustment Program (1986 - 1987) Lagos, Nigeria: Government Press.

Federal Government of Nigeria (1987). Federal Ministry of Trade and Industry Annual Report . Lagos, Nigeria: Government Press.

Federal Government of Nigeria (1988). Federal Environmental Protection Agency Degree. Federal Ministry of Information and Culture, Lagos, Nigeria.

Federal Government of Nigeria (1996). Federal Office of Statistics Annual Abstract. Lagos, Nigeria: Government Press.

Federal Ministry of Agriculture (1997). Annual Report. Abuja, Nigeria: Government Press.

Federal Ministry of Industries (1988). Industrial Policy of Nigeria Policies, Incentives Guidelines and Institutional Framework. Lagos, Nigeria: Government Press.

Federal Ministry of Information (1986). A New Horizon. Lagos, Nigeria: Federal Ministry and Culture.

Federal Office of Statistics Annual Report and Data (1989 - 1997). Lagos, Nigeria: Government Press.

Federal Republic of Nigeria (1988). Official Gazette: Privatization and Commercialization Decree. Lagos, Nigeria: Government Press.

Federal Republic of Nigeria (1990 - 1992). Guidelines for the National Rolling Plan, Lagos, Nigeria: Government Press.

Federal Republic of Nigeria (1991). Approved Budget of the Federal Republic of Nigeria, Lagos, Nigeria: Government Press.

Federal Republic of Nigeria (1992) Views and Comments of the Federal Government on the Report of the Commission on the Review of Higher Education in Nigeria, Lagos, Nigeria: Federal Director of Printing.

Feit, E. (1968). "Military Coups and Political Development: Some Lessons from Ghana and Nigeria." World Politics. Vol. 20, 2 (January), pp. 179 - 193.

Finer, S. (1969). The Man on Horse Back: The Role of the Military in Politics. London: Pall Mall Press.

Fisher, J. (1998). Non-governments, NGOs and the Political Development of the Third World. West Harford, Connecticut: Kumarian Press.

Fleishman, J. and Payne, B. (1980). Ethical Dilemmas of the Education of Policymakers. New York: Hastings Center.

Frainso, M. (1963). "The Structure of Development Administration." In Development Administration, Concepts and Problems, edited by J. Swerdlow. Syracuse, New York: Cornell University Press.

Frank, A. G. (1969). Latin America: Underdevelopment or Revolution? New York: Monthly Review Press.

Fransman, M. (1985). "Conceptualizing Technical Change in Third World in 1980s: An Interpretive Survey." The Journal of Development Studies. Vol. 21, 4 (July): 572 - 652.

Fransman, M. (1986). Economic Development. Boulder, Colorado: Westview Press.

Freire, P. (1970). Pedagogy of the Oppressed. New York: Seabury.

Freire, P. (1973). Education for Critical Consciousness. New York: Seabury.

Freire, P. and Macedo, D. (1987). Literacy: Reading the World and the World. South Hadley, Massachusetts: Bergin & Garvey.

Frieden, J. (1991). Debt, Development, and Democracy. Princeton, New Jersey: Princeton University Press.

Frieden, J. and Rogowski, R. (1996). "The Impact of the International Economy on National Policies: An Analytical Overview." In Internationalization and Domestic Politics, edited by R. Keohane and H. Milner. Cambridge: Cambridge University Press.

Friedrich, C. (1963). Man and His Government. New York: McGraw-Hill.

Friedrich, C. (1968). Constitutional Government and Democracy. Boston, Massachusetts: Blaisdell.

Friedrich, C. (1968). Trends of Federalism in Theory and Practice. New York: Praeger.

Frohock, F. M. (1979). Public Policy: Scope and Logic. Englewood Cliffs, New Jersey: Prentice-Hall.

Funga, F. (1991). "Pouvoir, ethnies et regions." Dialogue Vol. 149 (Nov.- Dec.): 5 - 16.

Furtado, C. (1973). "The Concept of External Dependence in the Study of Inter-development." in The Political Economy of Development and Underdevelopment edited by C. Wilber, New York: Random House, 18 - 123.

Gabriel, A. and Powell, M. (1966). Comparative Politics: A Development Approach. Boston, Massachusetts: Little Brown.

Galbraith, J. (1981). The New Industrial State. 2nd revised edition Boston, Massachusetts: Houghton-Mifflin.

Gann, L, and Duignan, P. (1981). Colonialism in Africa, 1870-1960. New York: Cambridge: University Press

Gartner, C. (1993). "From Unemployment to Entrepreneur: A Model of Factors that influence the Choice of Self-Employment Among Outpaced Middle and Upper-Level Managers." Academy of Management. 2 (August): 23 - 35.

Geertz, C. (1994). "Primordial and Civic Ties" in, Nationalism, edited by Hutchinson and Anthony D. Smith Oxford: Oxford University Press.

Gersick, C. (1991). "Revolutionary Change Theories: A Multilevel Exploration of the Punctuated Equilibrium Paradigm." Academy of Management Review. Vol. 16, 10 - 36.

Gillis, M., Perkins, D., Roemer, M. and Snodgrass, D. (1992). Economics of Development. 3rd edition New York: W. Norton.

Glickman, H. ed. (1995). Ethnic Conflict and Democratization in Africa. Atlanta, Georgia: African Studies Association.

Goodsell, C. (1985). The Case for Bureaucracy. 2nd edition Chatham, New Jersey: Chatham House.

Gordon, M. (1964). Assimilation in American Life: The Role of Race, Religion, and National Origins. New York: Oxford University Press.

Government of the Federal Republic of Nigeria. (1986). National Education Policy. Lagos, Nigeria: Government Printing Press

Graf, W. 1988. The Nigerian State, Political Economy, State Class and Political System in Post-Colonial Era. Portsmouth, New Hampshire: Heinemann Press.

Grainger, I. P. (1987). The Literacy Campaign Zimbabwe. Journal of Social Development in Africa, 2, no. 2: 49 - 58.

Greenberg, J. (1999). Managing Behavior in Organizations. 2nd edition. Upper Saddle River, New Jersey: Prentice-Hall.

Greene, Jack. (1993). Managing Police Work. Beverly Hills, California: Sage.

Grindle, H. (1986). "Civil-Military Relations and Budgetary Politics in Latin America." Armed Forces and Society. 13, no. 2: 255 - 275.

Grindle, M. and Thomas, J. (1991). Public Choice and Policy Change: The Political Economy of Reform in Developing Countries. Baltimore: The Johns Hopkins University Press.

Grosse, S. (1994). "The Roots of Conflict and State Failure in Rwanda. The Political Exacerbation of Social Cleavages in a Context of Growing Resources Scarcity." Department of Population Planning and International Health, School of Public Health, Ann Arbor.

Gruber, W. and D. Marquis. eds. (1969). Factors in the Transfer of Technology. Cambridge: MIT. Press.

Guest, R. (1982). Organizational Change: The Effect of Successful Leadership Homewood, Illinois: Richard D. Irwin.

Gunilla, A, and. B. Beckman. (1987). Industry Goes Farming: The Nigerian Raw Material Crisis and the Case of Textiles and Cotton. Research Report No. 80. Uppsala, Sweden: Scandinavian Institute of Africa Studies.

Gurr, R. (1970). Why Men Rebel. Princeton, New Jersey: Princeton University Press.

Gurr, R. (1993). Minorities at Risk: A Global View of Ethno-Political Conflict. United States Institute of Peace Press, Washington, DC.

Gurr, R. (1989). "Drowning in a Crime Wave." The New York Times (April 13).

Gutteridge, W. (1964). Military Institutions and Power in the New States. London: Methuen.

Gutteridge, W. (1975). Military Regimes in Africa. London: Methuen.

Guy, G. (1983). Development by People: Citizen Construction of Just World. New York: Praeger.

Haberler, G. (1958). International Trade and Economic Development. in. Economics of Trade and Development edited by Thebberge D. New York: John Wiley and Son.

Hagen, E. (1962). On the Theory of Social Change: How Economic Growth Begins. Homewood: Dorsey Press.

Haggard, S. and Kaufman, R. (1989). "Economic Adjustment in New Democracies." In Fragile Coalitions: The Politics of Economic Adjustment, edited by J. Nelson. New Brunswick: Transaction.

Haggard, S. and R. Kaufman. (1995). The Political Economy of Democratic Transitions. Princeton New Jersey: Princeton University Press.

Hague, D. and R. Smith, B. ed. (1981). The Dilemma of Accountability in Modern Government: Independence Versus Control. London: Macmillan.

Halisi, C. (1997). "From Liberation to Citizenship: Identity and Citizenship in Black South Africa Political Thought." Comparative Studies in Society and History Vol. 39, (January): 66 - 85.

Hall, R. (1982). Organizations Structure and Process. Englewood Cliffs, New Jersey: Prentice-Hall.

Halperin, M. (1974). Bureaucratic Politics and Foreign Policy. Washington, DC: Brookings Institute.

Handelman, H. (1996). The Challenge of Third World Development. Upper Saddle River New Jersey: Prentice-Hall.

Hanke, S. (1987). "Prospects for Privatization." New York: The Academy of Political Science, 24 - 60.

Harowitz, D. (1985). Ethnic Groups in Conflict. Los Angeles, California: University of California Press.

Harowitz, D. (1990). "Making Moderation Pay: The Comparative Politics of Ethnic Conflict Management." In Conflict and Peacemaking in Multiethnic Societies edited by Joseph Montvile, Lexington, Massachusetts: Lexington Books.

Harris J. (1971). "Nigerian Entrepreneurship in Industry," in Entrepreneurship and Economic Development, edited by P. Kilby, New York: Free Press.

Haruna, P. (2001). "Reflective Public Administration Reform: Building Relationship, Bridging the Gap in Ghana." African Studies Review Vol. 44, 1, pp. 37 - 57.

Heady, F. (1991). Public Administration: A Comparative Perspective. New York: Marcel Dekker.

Heilroner, R. (1970). Between Capitalism and Socialism: Essays in Political Economics. New York: Random House.

Heinz, A., H. Jacob, and R. Lineberry. (1983). Crime in City Politics. New York: Longman.

Hellman, J. (1996). A Competitive Advantage: Political Competition and Economic Reform in Post Communist Transition, Cambridge: Harvard University Press.

Henig, R. (1985). Public Policy and Federalism: Issues in States and Local Politics. New York: St. Martin's Press.

Henry, N. (1999). Public Administration and Public Affairs. Upper Saddle River, New Jersey: Prentice-Hall.

Herman, C., C. Kegley, and J. Resenau. (1987). New Direction in the Study of Foreign Policy. Boston: Allen and Unwin.

Hirschman, A. (1958). The Strategy of Economic Development. New Haven, Connecticut: Yale University Press.

Hirschman, A. (1970). Exit, Voice, and Loyalty. Cambridge, Massachusetts.: Harvard University Press.

Hollomon, J. and A. Harger. (1998). America's Technological Dilemma. Technology Review. Vol. 11, 2 (July). 34 - 50.

Holmberg, J. (1992). Making Development Sustainable: Redefining Institutions, Policy, and Economics. Washington DC: Island Press.

Horton, J. (1966). "Order and Conflict Theories of Social Problems." American Journal of Sociology. Vol. 21 (May/June): 23 - 35.

Huntington, S. (1964). The Soldier and the State. Cambridge, Massachusetts: Harvard University Press.

Huntington, S. (1968). Political Development and Political Decay. World Politics. Vol. 7, 3, pp. 386 - 430.

Huntington, S. (1969). Political Order in Changing Societies. Cambridge, University Press.

Huntington, S. (1987). Understanding Political Development. Boston, MA: Little Brown.

Hutchful, E. (1985). "Oil Companies and Environmental Pollution in Nigeria." In The Political Economy of Nigeria, edited by Ake. London: Longman.

Hyden, G., and I. M. Bratton. (eds.) (1992). Governance and Politics in Africa. Boulder, Colorado: Lynne Reinner.

Ignatief, M. (1993). Blood and Belonging: Journeys into the New Nationalism. Toronto: Penguin.

Igwe, B. and J. Ndekwu. (1985). Technological Choice Decision-Making Ibadan, Nigeria: NISER Press.

Ihonvbere, J. (1991). "Economic Crisis, in Sub-Saharan Africa: Debt, Dimensions, and Prospects for Recovery." Journal of International Studies Vol. 27 (July): 23 - 39.

Ihonvbere, J. (1995). "The State and Environmental Degradation in Nigeria: A Study of the 1988 Toxic Waste Dump in Koko." Journal of Environmental Systems, Vol. 23, 3, pp. 207 - 227

Ihonvbere, J. (1997). "Organized Labor and the Struggle For Democracy in Nigeria." African Studies Review. Vol. 40, 3 (December): pp. 77 - 110.

Ihonvebere, J. (1994). Nigeria: The Politics of Adjustment and Democracy. New Brunswick, Connecticut: Transaction.

IIchman, W. (1969). "Productivity, Administrative Reform and Anti-Politics." In Political and Administrative Development, edited by R. Braidanti. Durham, North Carolina: Duke University Press, 472 - 526.

Ikein, A. (1990). The Impact of Oil on a Developing Country: The Case of Nigeria. New York: Praeger.

Ikime, O. (1969). Niger Delta Rivalry and the European Presence 1884 - 1936. London: Longman.

Imoko, D. (1990). "The Development of Nigerian Manufacturing Sector." The Nigerian Interpreter. Vol. 10, 3 (October): 10 - 21.

Industrial Policies of Member Countries. (1981). Paris: Organization of Economic Cooporation and Development.

Interview with General Ibrahim Babangida. (1998). New York Times. New York: New York Times.

Isekhure, N. (1998). 201 Soulutions to Vision 2010. Benin City, Nigeria: Oduna Communications Press.

Jackman, R. (1978). "Politicians in Uniform: Military Governments and Social Change in Third World." American Political Science Review. Vol. 70, 3 (December): 125 - 40.

Jagun, D. (1993). "Nigeria: The Basis of Union." Lagos, Nigeria: The Nigerian Guardian. (April 8): 3 - 7.

James, V. (1993). African Ecology: Sustaining the Biological and Environmental Diversity of a Continent. Jefferson, North Carolina: McFarland.

Janowitz, M. (1964). The Military in the Political Development of New Nations. University of Chicago Press.

Janowitz, M. (1977). Military Institutions and Coercion in Developing Nations. Chicago: University of Chicago Press.

Jemibewon, D. (1978). A Combatant in Government. Ibadan, Nigeria: Heineman.

Jenkins, I. (1980). The Social Order and The Limits of Law. Princeton, New Jersey: Princeton University Press.

Jennings, E. (1990). "Public Choice and the Privatization of Government: Implications for Public Administration." In Public Management, edited by C. Hyde and J. Shafritz, Chicago: Nelson-Hall.

Jequier, N. (1976). Appropriate Technology Problems and Promises. Paris: Organization for Economic Cooperation and Development Publications.

Jones, C. (1984). An Introduction in the Study of Public Policy. Monterey, California: Brooks/Cole.

Jones, L. (1991). Performance for Public Enterprises. Washington, DC: World Bank.

Jubril, A. (1986). "Education and Public Policy in Nigeria." In Towards Education in Nigeria for the 21st Century, edited by S. Oriafo and U. Gbenedio. Benin City, Nigeria: Institute of Education, University of Benin.

Kaplan J. and Ross, W. (1968). The Pocket Aristotle. New York: Washington Square Press, 246 - 250.

Kaplinsky, R. (1990). The Economies of Small Appropriate Technology in a Changing World. Washington, DC: Appropriate Technology International.

Karagodin N and Rkov N. (1987). "The New Stage of Scientific and Technological Revolution." Social Science Vol. 18, 2, 120 - 142.

Katz, D. and R. Kahn (1986). The Social Psychology of Organizations. New York: Wiley.

Katz, J. (1992). Modeling Entrepeneurial Career Progressions: Concepts and Considerations. St. Louis, Missouri: Center for Entrepreneurial Studies.

Kawewe, S. (1998). "The Inability of the United Nations to Reform Practices that Endanger Third World Children. New Global Development." Journal of International and Comparative Social Welfare. Vol. 5, 21, 15 - 26.

Kawewe, S. and R. Dibie. (1999) "United Nations and the Problem of Women and Children Abuse in Third Nations." Social Justice Journal. Vol. 26, 1 (Spring), pp. 78 - 98.

Kaynes, J. (1936). The General Theory of Employment, Interest and Money. New York: Harcourt Brace.

Kegley, C., and E. Wittkopf. (1987). American Foreign Policy: Patterns and Process. New York: St. Martin's Press.

Kegley, C., and E. Wittkopf. (1995). World Politics: Trend Transformation. New York: St. Martin Press.

Keih, G. and P. Agbese. (1996). "The Military and the Crisis of Underdevelopment." Third World in Perspective Journal. Vol. 1, 3, 35 - 50.

Keith-Spiegel, P. and G. Koocher. (1995). Ethics in Psychology. Hillsdale, New Jersey: Lawrence Erilbaum.

Kellas, J. (1991). The Politics of Nationalism and Ethnicity. London: Macmillan Education.

Keohane, R. and H. Milner (1996). Internationalization and Domestic Politics. Cambridge: Cambridge University Press.

Keohane, R. and J. Nye. (1977). Power and Interdependent World Politics in Transition. Boston: Little Brown.

Kettl, D. (1993). Sharing Power: Public Governance and Private Markets. Washington, DC: Brookings Institute.

Kilby, P. (1969). Industrialization in an Open Economy: Nigeria 1945 - 1966. Cambridge, New York: Cambridge University Press.

Kilby, P. (1983). "An Entrepreneurial Problem." American Economic Review, Vol. 73, 2, 107 - 111.

Kinder, D. and A. Weiss (1978). "In Lieu of Rationality: Pyschological Perspective on Foreign Policy Decision-making". Journal of Conflict Resolution. Vol. 22, 4, 707 - 735.

Kingdom, J. (1984). Agendas, Alternatives and Public Policies. Boston, Massachusetts: Little Brown.

Kirk-Green, A. (1964). Crisis and Conflict in Nigeria: A Documentary Source Book 1966 - 1970. London: Oxford University Press.

Knight, F. (1921). Risk, Uncertainty and Profit. Chicago: University of Chicago Press.

Koehn, P. (1983). "The Role of Public Administrators in Public Policy Making Practice and Prospect in Nigeria." Public Administration and Development, Vol. 3, 4, 256 - 268.

Koehn, P. (1984). "The Evolution of Public Bureaucracy in Nigeria." In. Administrative Systems Abroad, edited by J. Tummala . Boulder, Colorado: Westview, 188 - 228.

Koehn, P. (1990). Public Policy and Administration in Africa: Lessons from Nigeria. Boulder, Colorado: Westview.

Kolawole, M. (1998). Gender Perceptions and Development in Africa. Lagos, Nigeria: Arrabon Academic Press.

Kopp, R. and M. Hazilla. (1990). "Social Cost of Environmental Quality Regulations A General Equilibrium Analysis," Journal of Political Economy, Vol. 98, 853 -73.

Kraft, M. and Axelrod, R. (1984). "Political Constraints on Development of Alternative Energy Sources. Lessons from the Reagan Administration." Policy Studies Journal (December): 319 - 330.

Kraft, M. and V. Norman. (1990). "Environmental Policy from the Seventies to the Nineties Continuity and Change." in Environmental Policy in the 1990s, edited by V. Norman Vig and Michael E. Kraft. Washington, DC: CQ Press.

Krueger, A. (1993). "Virtuous and Vicious Circles in Economic Development." American Economic Review. Vol. 3, 5 (May), 21 - 34.

Krueger, N. (1993). "Growing Up Entrepreneurial: Developmental Consequences of Exposure to Entrepreneurship." Academy of Management. Vol. 2, 6, 30 - 42.

Krupp, S. (1981). Pattern in Organization Analysis. New York: Holt, Rinehart, and Winston.

Lairson, T, and D. Skidmore. (1993). International Political Economy: The Struggle for Power and Wealth. New York: Harcourt Brace Jovanovich College Publishers.

Lal, D. (1986). "The Political Economy of Economic Liberalization." World Bank Economic Review. Vol. 1, 2, 273 - 299.

Lall, S. (1982). Developing Countries as Exporters of Technology: A First Look at the Indian Experience. London: Macmillan.

Lasch, C. (1979). The Culture of Narcissism. New York: Warner Books.

Laski, H. (1975). The State in Theory and Practice. London: George Allen and Unwin.

Lasswell, H. (1950). Politics: Who Gets What, When, How. New York: P. Smith Press.

Lawson, C.O. (1974). The Role of the Civil Servants in Military Regime. Quarterly Journal of Administration. Vol. 3, 4 (January): 127 - 131.

Lelyveld, J. (1985). Move Your Shadow: South Africa, Black and White. New York: Penguin.

Lemarchand, R. (1993). "African Troubled Transitions." Journal of Democracy. Vol. 3, 4 (October): 98 - 110.

Lemarchand, R. (1994). Burundi: Ethnocide as Discourse and Practice. New York: Cambridge University Press.

Lemarchand, R. (1995). "Four Models for Resolving Ethnic Conflict." African Voices. Vol. 4, (Summer), 1 - 37.

Leo-Paul, D. (1996). Entrepreneurship in a Remote Sub-Arctic Community. Entrepreneurship Theory and Practice. Waco, Texas: Baylor University.

Lester, J. (1990). "A New Federalism? Environmental Policy in the States." In Environmental Policy in the 1990s: Toward A New Agenda, edited by Vig and Kraft Washington DC: Congressional Quarterly Press.

LeVine, R. (1966). Dreams and Deeds. Chicago: University of Chicago Press.

Lewis, D. (1982). Louder Voices: The Corporate Welfare Bums. Toronto: James Lewis and Samuel Publishers.

Lewis, M. (1992). "The Political Economy of Public Enterprise in Nigeria." Ph.D. Dissertation, University of Michigan.

Lewis, W. (1969). Some Aspects of Economic Development, Benin City, Nigeria: Ethiope Publishing Corporation.

Lijphart, A. (1980). "Federal, Confederal, and Consociational Options for the South African Plural Society." In Conflict and Compromise in South Africa edited by R. Rotberg and J Barrat. Lexington, Massachusetts: Heath.

Lijphart, Arend. (1977). Democracy in Plural Societies: A Comparative Exploration. New Haven, Connecticut: Yale University Press.

Lindblom, C. (1965). The Policy Making Process. Englewood Cliffs. New Jersey: Prentice-Hall.

Lindblom, C. (1993). "The Science of Muddling Through." In Classical Readings in American Politics. edited by P. Nivola. and D. Rosenbloom. New York: St. Martin's Press.

Lipset, S. M. (1959). "Some Social Requisites of Democracy: Economic Development and Political Legitimacy." American Political Science Review. Vol. 53, 5, 69 - 105.

Longregan, J. and K. Poole. (1990). "Poverty, the Coup Trap, and Seizure of Executive Power." World Politics, Vol. 42, 2, 151 - 83.

Luckham, R. (1971). The Nigerian Military: A Sociological Study of Authority and Revolt. London: Longman.

Luckhman, R. (1974). "The Nigerian Military: Disintegration or Integration?" In Military Regimes. edited. by P. Bricks. London: Longman.

Lynch, T. (1996). Public Budgeting in America. 4th edition Englewood Cliffs, New Jersey: Prentice-Hall.

Macneil, I. (1988). Contracts, Instruments for Social Cooperation, East Africa: Text, Cases, Materials. South Hackensack, New Jersey: F. Rothman.

Malloy J. (1992). "Contemporary Authoritarian Regimes." In Encyclopedia of Government and Politics. edited. by M. Hawkesworth and M. Kogan. New York: Routledge.

Malloy, J. (1977). "Authoritarianism and Corporatism in Latin America." In Encyclopedia of Government and Politics edited by M. Hawsworth and M. Kogan, New York: Routledge.

Malthus, T. (1951). Principles of Political Economy. New York: Augustus Kelly.

Mamdani, M. (1996). Citizen and Subject. Contemporary Africa and the Legacy of Late Colonialism. Princeton, New Jersey: Princeton University Press.

Maniruzzaman, T. (1987). Military Withdrawal from Politics: A Comparative Study. Cambridge, Massachusetts: Ballinger.

Manor, J, ed. (1991). Rethinking Third World Politics. New York: Longman.

Maravcsik, M. (1983). "The Role of Science in Technology Transfer." Research Policy. Vol. 12, 5 (October): 287 - 96.

March, J, ed. (1985). Handbook of Organizations. Chicago: Rand McNally.

March, J. (1978). "Bounded Rationality, Ambiguity and the Engineering of Choice." Bell Journal of Economics. Vol. 9, 3, 587 - 608.

March, J. and Z. Shapira. (1982). "Behavioral Decision Theory and Organizational Decision Theory." In Decision Making: An Interdisciplinary Inquiry, edited by G. Ungson and D. Braunstein. Belmont, California: Wadsworth.

March, J., and H. Simon. (1958). Organizations. New York: John Wiley.

Marger, M. (1997). Race and Ethnic Relations. New York: Wadsworth.
Marx, K. (1967). Das Capital: A Critique of Political Economy. New York: International Publishers.
Mathews, J. (1991). Preserving the Global Environment. New York: Norton and Company.
Mauer, M. (1996). "The Drug War's Unequal Justice." The Drug Policy Letter. Vol. 28 (Winter), 10 - 13.
Mayer, L., J. Burnett, and S. Ogden. (1996). Comparative Politics: Nations and Theories in a Changing World. Upper Saddle River, New Jersey: Prentice-Hall.
Mazrui, A. (1986). The Africans: A Triple Heritage. Boston, Massachusetts: Little Brown.
McCall, G. and J. Simmon, eds. (1969). Issues in Participant Observation: A Text and Reader. Boulder, Colorado: Addison-Wesley.
McClelland, D. (1961). The Achieving Society. Princeton, New Jersey: Princeton University Press.
McCormick, J. (1995). Comparative Politics in Transition. New York: Wadsworth.
Meehan, E. (1985). The Theory and Method of Political Analysis. Homewood, Illinois: Dorsey.
Melson R. and H. Wolpe. (1970). "Modernization and the Politics of Communalism: A Theoretical Perspective. "American Political Science Review. Vol. 54 (December): 3 - 17.
Michaell, C. (1984). "Public Opinion and Environmental Politics in the 1970s and 1980s." in Environmental Policy in the 1980s, edited by N. Vig and M. Kraft Washington, DC: CQ Press.
Michele, R. (1968). Political Parties: A Sociological Study of the Oligarchical Tendencies of Modern Democracy. Glencoe, Illinois: The Free Press.
Miles, W. (1994). Hausaland Divided: Colonialism and Independence in Nigeria and Niger. Ithaca, New York: Cornell University Press.
Miliband, R. (1983). The State in Capitalist Society. London: Quarter Books.
Millar, M. (1995). The Third World in Global Environmental Politics. Boulder: Lynne Rienner Publishers.
Milovanovic, D. (1997). Chaos, Criminology, and Social Justice. Westport, Connecticut: Praeger.
Miners, N. (1971). The Nigerian Army, 1956 - 1966. London: Methuen.
Ministry of Science and Technology (1994). Federal Science Programs, 1989 - 1994 Lagos, Nigeria: Government Press.
Ministry of Science and Technology (1995). Technology Policy 1986 - 1994. Lagos, Nigeria: Government Press.
Mises, L. (1980). "La accion humana. Tratado de economia." (Editorial): Madrid Times.
Mitchell, W. (1958). "The Polity and Society: A Structural Functional Analysis Mid-West." Journal of Political Science. Vol. 2, 1, pp. 403 - 440.
Mitrany, D. (1966). A Working Peace System. Chicago, Illinois: Quadrangle Press.
Moe, T. (1984). "The New Economics of Organization." American Journal of Political Science. Vol. 28, 4 (November): 739 - 777.
Moe, T. (1990). Political Institutions: The Neglected Side of the Story: Journal of Law, Economics and Organization. Vol. 6, 2, 213 - 253.
Mohan, B. (1997). Toward New Global Development. International Social Work. Vol. 4, 4, pp. 433 - 450.
Morley, J. (1996). "White Grams Burden." The Drug Policy Letter. Vol. 28 (Winter), 17 - 19.

Morrison, D. and H. Stevenson. (1972). "Cultural Pluralism, Modernization and Conflict: An Empirical Analysis of Sources of Political Instability in African Nations." Canadian Journal of Political Science. Vol. 5, 1, March, 90.

Mueller, D. (1979). Public Choice. Cambridge, New York: Cambridge University Press.

Myint, H. (1971). Economic Theory and Underdeveloped Countries. London: Oxford University Press.

Nafziger, W. (1969). "The Effect of the Nigerian Extended Family on Entrepreneurial Activity." Economic Development and Cultural Change. Vol. 18 (October): 25 - 33.

Nafziger, W. (1993). The Debt Crisis in Africa. Baltimore: Johns Hopkins University Press.

Nafziger, W. (1997). The Economics of Developing Countries. Upper Saddle River New Jersey: Prentice-Hall.

Nankani, H. (1990). "Lessons of Privatization in Developing Countries." Finance and Development. Vol. 27, 43 - 35.

National Institute of Justice. (1997). Assessing Criminal Justice Needs. Washington, D.C: NIJ. August.

Naude, W. (1996). "Financial Liberalization and Interest Rare Risk Management in Sub-Saharan Africa." Center for the Study of African Economics, Working Paper Series.

Ndegwa, P. (1985). Africa's Development Crisis and Related International Issues. London: James Currey.

Ndegwa, S. (1997). "Citizenship and Ethnicity: An Examination of Two Transition Moments in Kenyan Politics." American Political Science Review. Vol. 91, 3, (September): 25 - 41.

NERC (1977). National Policy on Education, Lagos, Nigeria: Federal Ministry of Information.

Neubauer, D. (1992). American's Courts and the Criminal Justice System. Monterey, California: Brooks/Cole.
New Jersey: Princeton University Press.

Newsum H. and O. Abegunrin. (1987). United States Foreign Policy Towards Southern Africa: Andrew Young and Beyond. New York: St. Martin's Press.

Nieburrg, H. (1986). In the Name of Science. Chicago: Quadrangle Books.

Nigeria Interpreter (Special Edition) (1990). Lagos, Nigeria: Federal Ministry of Information.

Nigeria Technical Committee on Privatization and Commercialization (1989). Second Progress Report. Lagos, Nigeria: Government Press.

Nigeria: A Complete Fact-finder (1995). Ibadan, Nigeria: Tee-Rex Limited.

Nigerian Constitution of (1979). Lagos, Nigeria: Federal Government Printing Press.

Nigerian Constitution of (1989). Lagos, Nigeria: Federal Government Printing Press.

Nigerian Year Book (1993). Lagos, Nigeria: Daily Times Press.

Nincic, M. (1988). United States Foreign Policy: Choices and Tradeoffs. Washington, DC: Congressional Quarterly.

Nnoli, O. (1980). Ethnic Politics in Nigeria, Enugu, Nigeria: Fourth Dimension Publishers.

Nordlinger, E. (1977). "Soldiers in Mufti: The Impact of Military Rule Upon Economic and Social Change in Non-Western States." American Political Science Review. 65 (December). 1131 - 1148.

Norman, O. (1996). Economic Development and Environmental Policy. New York: Kegan Paul International.

Nussbaum, B. (1993). "Corporate Refugees: After the Pain, Some Find Smooth Sailing." Business Week, April 12, 58 - 65.

Nwagwu, N. (1992). "Financing Education in Nigeria: Issues and Innovations" in Towards Education in Nigeria for the 21st Century, edited by Oriafo, S. and U. Gbenedio, Benin City, Nigeria: Institute of Education, University of Benin.

Nwankwo, N. (1988). "Case Studies on the Environmental Impact of Oil production and Marketing in Nigeria." in Environmental Issues and Management in Nigerian Development, edited by P. Sada and Odemerho. Ibadan, Nigeria: Evans Brothers.

Nwosu, H. (1977). Political Authority and Nigerian Civil Service. Enugu, Nigeria: Fourth Dimension.

Nwosu, H. (1979). Problems of Nigerian Administration. Enugu, Nigeria: Fourth Dimension.

O'Donnell, G. (1973). Modernization and Bureaucratic-Authoritarianism Studies in South American Politics. Berkeley: University of California Press.

O'Donnell, G. (1976). "Modernization and Military Coup: Theory, Comparisons and the Argentine Case." In. Armies and Politics in Latin America, edited by J. Lowenthal. New York: Holme and Meir Press.

Obadan, M. and B. Ekuerhane. (1988). "The Theoretical Basis of Structural Adjustment Program: An Appraisal." Proceedings of the Nigerian Economic Society 1988 Annual Conference May 3 - 7, 1988. Ile-Ife, Nigeria: Obafemi Awolowo University Press.

Obadan. M. and B. Chokor. (1991). "Environment and Economics in Nigeria. Report of the Nigerian Environmental Study/Action Team. Ibadan, Nigeria: 1 - 63.

Obasanjo, O. (1993). "Hidden Agenda." West Africa. Lagos, Nigeria: Daily Times Press. (January 25 - 31): 97.

Obasanjo, O. and A. Mabogimje. (1991). Elements of Development in Nigeria. Lagos, Nigeria: C and A Press.

Obiozor, G. (1985). Nigerian Participation in United Nations. Enugu, Nigeria: Fourth Dimension.

Odetola, O. (1982). Military Regimes and Development: A Comparative Analysis of Africa. London: George Allen and Unwin.

Oduaran, A (1995). "Mass Literacy Education Policy and Delivery in Nigeria." Commissioned Paper by the Delta State Agency for Adult and Non-Formal Education. Asaba, Nigeria, June 19, 1 - 5.

Oduaran, A. (1986). "The Right to Learn, Community Development and the Sufferance of Vanishing Generals." In The Right to Learn: Role of Non-Formal Education in Nigeria, edited by M. Omolewa. Ibadan, Nigeria: Nigerian National Council for Adult Education (NNCAE).

Oduaran, A. (1987). "The Trouble with Self-Reliance in Nigeria: How Community Education can Help." in Issues in Nigerian Adult and Community Development Education edited by A. Oduaran. Benin City: Nigerian National Council for Adult Education (NNCAE).

Oduaran, A. (1989). "Learning and Earning in Africa: Orientation, Problems and Prospects." In Adult Education: Theory and Practice, edited by J. Osuala and J. Mereni. Benin City, Nigeria: University of Benin Press.

Oduaran, A. (1993). "Education, Employment and Rural Development in Nigeria', in: Towards Education in Nigeria for the 21st Century, edited by S. Oriafo and U. Gbenedio Benin City: Institute of Education, University of Benin.

Office of the Minister for Science and Technology (1990). New Contracting-Out Policy Challenges Industry to Strengthen Nigerian. News Release. Lagos, Nigeria: Government Press. Vol. 7, 4 (August 15).

Ogowewo, T. (1995). "The Problem with Standing to Sue in Nigeria." Journal of African Law. Vol. 39, 1, 1 - 15.

Ogowewo, T. (1996). "The Role of Target Management in a Tender Offer: The Position in Nigerian Law." Journal of African Law. Vol. 40, 1, 21 - 36.

Ogun, O. (1990). "The Monetary Effect of an Export Boom: 1950 – 1985." Ph.D. dissertation, University of Ibadan, Nigeria.

Ohonbamu, O. (1970). The Psychology of the Nigerian Revolution. New York: International Publications.

Ojigbo, O. 1980. Nigeria Returns To Civilian Rule. Lagos, Nigeria: Tokion.

Ojo, A. (1997). "Nigeria Today." In Nigerian Information Network. Boston: MIT Press, pp. 22 - 40.

Okafor, F. (1988). "Rural Development and the Environment: Degradation Versus Protection." In Environmental Issues in Nigerian Development, edited by P. Sada and D. Odemerho. Ibadan, Nigeria: Evans Brothers.

Oke, B. (1990). "Structural Adjustment and the Role of the Central Bank of Nigeria: The Nigerian Experience and Future Direction." Central Bank of Nigeria Economic and Financial Review. Vol. 28, 1, 36 - 38.

Okonkwo, C. (1986). The Police and the Public in Nigeria. London: Sweet and Maxwell.

Ola, C. 1984. Town and Country Planning and Environmental Laws in Nigeria. Ibadan, Nigeria: Ibadan University Press.

Ola, R. and S. Hume. (1994). Government and Local Development in Western, Benin City, Nigeria: Ambik Press.

Olagunju, T., A. Jinadu, and S. Oyovbaire. (1993). Transition to Democracy in Nigeria (1985 - 1993). Ibadan, Nigeria: Spectrum.

Olaniyan, O. (1996). Foreign Aid, Self-Reliance, and Economic Development in West Africa. Westport, Connecticut: Praeger.

Olashore, O. (1991). The Challenges of Nigeria's Economic Reform. Ibadan, Nigeria: Fountain.

Olayiwola, A. (1996). "Political Communication in Nigeria." In Political Communication in Action. edited by D. Patetz. Cresskill, New Jersey: Hampton.

Olorunsola, V. (1972). The Politics of Cultural Sub-Nationalism in Africa. Garden City, New York: Anchor Books.

Olowu, D. (1999). "Accountability and Transparency." In Public Administration in Africa, edited by L. Adamolekun. Boulder, Colorado: Westview Press.

Olowu, D., S. Bamidele and J. Erero. (1991). Nigerian Public Administration: Past, Present and Future. Ibadan, Nigeria: Shaneson Limited.

Olson, M. (1982). The Rise and Decline of Nations. New Haven, Connecticut: Yale University Press.

Olukoshi, A. (1992). The Politics of Structural Adjustment in Nigeria. London: James Carrey.

Olukoshi, A., O. Olaniran and F. Aribisala. (1994). Structural Adjustment in West Africa. Lagos, Nigeria: Pumark.

Omojokun, S. (1979). "History of the Nigerian Army Since 1960." Paper presented at the Nigerian Army Day Celebration. Lagos, Nigeria: July 6, 1979.

Omolewa, M. (1983). "On the definition and Scope of Mass Education in Nigeria, 1946 - 1960." Education and Development, Vol. 3, 2 (July): 216.

Omolewa, M. (1983). Adult Literacy Census in Nigeria, Ibadan, Nigeria: Afrografika Publication.

Omolewa, M. (1993). "The Plausibility of Education for All by the year 2000 AD." in Towards Education in Nigeria for the 21st Century, edited by Oriafo S. and U. Gbenedio. Benin City, Nigeria: Institute of Education, University of Benin.

Omuta, G. (1985). "The Petroleum Factor in Environmental Decay in Isoko Local Government Area, Bendel State, Nigeria." Geo-Journal. Vol. 11, pp 173 - 181.

Onimode, B. (1989). Alternative Development Strategies for Africa. London: Institute for African Alternatives.

Onimode, B. (1989). The IMF, the World Bank and the African Debt. Vols. 1 and 2, The Economic Impact. London: Zed Books.

Onitiri, H. (1961). "Nigerian International Economic Relations. A Survey." Nigerian Journal of Economics and Social Studies. Vol. 3, (November): 13 - 38.

Onwukwe, D. (1994). "Why Police Can't Combat Crime Wave." Nigerian Daily Champion, July 30, 5 - 6.

Orlans, H. (1983). Contraction for Knowledge. San Francisco, California: Tassey-Bass.

Osagie, E. and Oyelabi, J. (1974). "Net Foreign Exchange Cost of Manufacturing Industries in Nigeria." Economic Bulletin of Ghana. Vol. 4, 36 - 43.

Oshiekwere, P. (1994). "Democracy and Integrity." Lagos, Nigeria: The Nigerian Guardian, Lagos, June 9, 5 - 7.

Ostheimer, J. (1973). Nigerian Politics. New York: Harper and Row.

Ostrom, E., Schroeder, L. and W. Sussan. (1993). Institutional Incentives and Sustainable Development. Boulder CO: Westview.

Ostrum, V. and Ostrum, E. (1971). "Public Choice: A Different Approach to the Study of Public Administration," Public Administration Review, Vol. 13, 274 - 286.

Otobo, E. (1999). "Nigeria." In Public Administration in Africa, edited by L. Adamolekun. Boulder, Colorado: Westview Press.

Oyediran, O. (1978). Survey of Nigerian Affairs. Ibadan, Nigeria: Oxford University Press.

Oyediran, O. (1979). Nigerian Government and Politics Under Military Rule, 1966 - 1979. New York: St. Martin's Press.

Oyediran, O. and Adigyn Agbaje. (1999). Nigeria: Politics of Transition and Governance 1986 - 1996. Dakar, Senegal: CODESRIA.

Oyejide, A. (1998). "Trade Policy and Regional Integration in Development Context: Emerging Patterns, Issues and Lessons for SUB-Saharan Africa." Journal of African Economics. Vol. 7, 1, 108 - 145.

Oyejide, T. (1986). "The Effects of Trade and Exchange Rate Policies on Agriculture in Nigeria." Ibadan, Nigeria: IFPRI Research Paper, No. 55. October.

Oyovbaire, S. (1980). "Politization of the Higer Civil Servant in Nigerian Presidential System of Government." Quarterly Journal of Administration. Vol. 3, 2 (April): 2 - 16.

Oyovbaire, S. (1984). Structural Change and Political Process in Nigeria. African Affairs. Vol. 4, 1 (January): 20 - 31.

Pack, H. (1994). "Productivity or Politics: The Determinant of Indonisian Tariff Structure." Journal of Development Economics. Vol. 44, 2, 441 - 451.

Packer, H. (1968). The Limits of the Criminal Sanction. Palo Alto: Stanford University Press, 155 - 157.

Pattnayak, S. (1996). "Modernization, Dependency and the State in Asia, Africa and Latin America." International Journal of Comparative Sociology. Vol. 37, 274 - 286.

Pearce, D., Markanda, A. and B. Barbier. (1990). Sustainable Development: Economics and Environment in the Third World. London: Earthscan Publication.

Pepinsky, H. (1995). "Peacemaking Pimer." Peace and Conflict Studies. Vol. 2, 2, 32 - 53.

Pepinsky, H., and E. Quinney. (1991). The Geometry of Violence and Democracy. Bloomington: Indiana University Press.

Perkins, C., Stephen J. and Beck A. (1995). "Jails and Inmates, 1993 - 94." Bureau of Justice Statistics Bulletin. NCJ-151651, September.

Perlmutter, A. (1981a). Political Roles and Military Rulers. London: Frank Cass.

Perlmutter, A. (1981b). "The Comparative Analysis of Military Regimes: Formations, Aspirations and Achievements." World Politics. Vol. 33, 1, 96 - 120.

Perrow, C. (1980). Organizational Analysis: A Sociological View. Belmont, California: Brooks and Cole.

Perrow, C. (1981). "The Analysis of Goals in Complex Organizations." American Sociological Review, Vol. 26, 8, (December): 20 - 41.

Perrow, C. (1982). Complex Organization: A Critical Essay. Glenview, Illinois: Scott, Foreman.

Peters, J. (1995). The Nigerian Military and the State. London: Tauris I. B.

Petulla, J. (1987). Environmental Protection in the United States: Industry, Agencies and Environmentalists, San Francisco, California: San Francisco Study Center.

Phillips, A. (1990). The 1988 Nigerian Civil Service Reforms and Their Post-1992 Prospects. Ibadan, Nigeria: NISER Publication.

Phillips, A. and O. Ajakaiye. (1993). Nigerian Economy and Society: Economic Policy and Development. Ibadan, Nigeria: NISER.

Phillips, A. and E. Ndekwu. (1992). Structural Adjustment Programs in a Developing Economy: The Case of Nigeria. Ibadan, Nigeria: NISER.

Phillips, C. (1964). The Development of Nigerian Foreign Policy. Evasnston: Northwestern University Press.

Phillips, M. (1984). "Bribery." Ethics Journal. Vol. 94, 3, 621 - 626.

Picard, L. (1994). Policy Reform for Sustainable Development in Africa: The Institute Imperative. Boulder Rienner.

Polanyi, M. (1989). "The Republic of Science: Its Political and Economic Theory." Minerva. Vol. 1, 4, 44 - 55.

Portney, P. (1990). Public Policies for Environment Protection, Washington, DC: Resources for the Future.

Presthus. R. (1962). V. Weberian. "Welfare Bureaucracy in Traditional Society." Administrative Science Quarterly. Vol. 4, 3 (May): 15 - 24.

Public Service Review Commission Report (1987). Lagos, Nigeria: Federal Ministry of Information.

Putnam, R. (1993). Making Democracy Work. Princeton New Jersey: Princeton University Press.

Rains, G. (1995). "Another Look at East Asian Miracle." World Bank Economic Review. (September): 509 - 534.

Randall, V. and R. Theobald. (1985). Political Change Underdevelopment. London: Macmillan.

Rawls, J. (1994). The Theory of Justice. Oxford University Press, London.

Redcliff, M. and D. Goodman, eds. (1991). Environment and Development in Latin America: The Politics of Sustainability. Manchester, England: Manchester University Press.

Rhaods, S. (1993). Modern Economic Analysis. Upper Saddle River, New Jersey: Prentice-Hall.

Riggs, F. (1964). Administration in Developing Countries. Boston, Massachusetts: Houghton Mifflin.

Ripley, R. (1985). Policy Analysis in Political Science. Chicago: Nelson Hall.

Rogowski, R. (1989). Commerce and Coalition: How Trade Affects Domestic Political Alignments. Princeton, New Jersey: Princeton University Press.

Rondinelli, D. (1993). Development Project as Policy Experiments: An Approach to Development Administration. New York: Routledge.

Rosenberg, M. (1988). The Logic of Survey Analysis. New York: Basic Books.

Rosenbloom, D. (1998). Understanding Public Management, Public Policy and Law. Upper Saddle River, New Jersey: Prentice-Hall.

Ross, W. (1930). The Right and the Good. Oxford: Oxford University Press.

Rostow, W. (1978). The World Economy: History and Prospect. Austin: University of Texas Press.

Rouseau, M. and R. Zariski. (1987). Regionalism and Regional Devolution in Comparative Perspective. New York: Praeger.

Rupert, J. (1998). "Military Talking with Opposition to Find Safe Way to Leave Power." Washington DC: Washington Post Foreign Service, June 23.

Rushefsky, M. (1990). Public Policy in the United States: Towards the Twenty-First Century. Pacific Grove, California: Brooks/Cole.

Saasa, O. (1985). Public Policy Making in Developing Countries: The Utility of Contemporary Decision Making Models. Public Administration and Development. Vol. 4 (June), 309 - 21.

Sahn, D. (1994). Adjusting to Policy Failure in Africa Economies. Ithaca, New York: Cornell University Press.

Sandbrook, R. (1993). The Politics of African's Recovery. New York: Cambridge University Press.

Sandbrook, R. (1990). "Taming the African Leviathan." World Policy Journal (Fall): 673 - 701.

Sapolsky, H. (1982). Polaris System Development: Bureaucratic and Programmatic Success in Government. Cambridge, Massachusetts: Harvard University Press.

Savas, E. (1987). Privatization: The Key to Better Government. Chatham, New Jersey: Chatham House.

Schaar, J. (1981). "Community or Contract: William Faulkner and the Dual Legacy." In The Problem of Authority, edited by J. Diggins and M. Kann. Philadelphia: Temple University Press.

Schaffer, B. (1969). "The Deadlocks in Development Administration." In Politics and Change in Developing Countries: Studies in Theory and Practice of Development, edited by Schaffer, B. Cambridge University Press.

Schelling, T. (1981). "Economic Reasoning and the Ethics of Policy". Public Interest. Vol. 63 (Spring), 37 - 61.

Schultz, T. (1975). "The Value of the Ability to Deal with Disequilibria." Journal of Economic Literature. Vol. 13, 51 - 67.

Schumpeter, J. (1942). The Theory of Economic Development. Cambridge, Massachusetts: Harvard University Press.

Schumpeter, J. (1954). History of Economic Analysis. New York: Oxford University Press.

Schwab, R. (1988). "Environmental Federalism," Resources, 92, Washington DC: Resources for the Future.

Schwarz, W. (1968). Nigeria. London: Pall Mall.

Schwelb, E. (1968). "Human Rights." In International Encyclopedia of the Social Sciences edited by D. Gills. Vol. 6, New York: Crowell Collier and Macmillan.

Selznic, P. (1986). TVA and the Grass Roots: A Study in the Sociology of Formal Organization. New York: Harper and Row.

Shapiro, M. (1990). "Toxic Substances Policy", in Public Policies for Environmental Protection, edited by Portney, P. Washington, DC: Resources for the Future, 195 - 242.

Shaw, W. (1991). Business Ethics. Belmont, California: Wadsworth.

Sheffey, A. (1978). Conservation Commission in Massachusetts. Washington, DC: Robert G. Healy, Land Use and the States (Washington DC).

Shleifer, A., and Treisman, D. (1997). The Economics and Politics of Transition to an Open Market Economy. Paris: Organization for Economic Cooperation Development Center.

Simmel, G. (1988). "Conflict and, Transition." in The Web of Group-Affiliations, edited by K. Woff and Bendix R. Glencoe, Illinois: Free Press.

Simon, H. (1958). Administrative Behavior. 2nd ed. New York: Macmillan.

Simon, H. (1980). Public Administration. 1st edition New York: Knof.

Sinaceur, M. (1977). "What is Interdisciplinary?" International Social Science Journal , Vol. 26, 4, (June): 20 - 45.

Skidmore, J. and J. Laison. (1993). International Political Economy in Developing Nations. New York: St. Martin's Press.

Skocpol, T. (1985). "Bringing the State Back." In Strategies of Analysis in Current Research. edited by J. Evans. Cambridge University Press.

Slater, R. (1997). "Approaches to Strengthening Local Government: Lessons from Sri Lanka." Public Administration and Development Vol. 17, 251 - 265.

Snavely, K. and R. Beck. (1994). "Defining the Role of Non-Profit Corporation in Community Economic Development." Journal of the Community Development Society, Vol. 24, 213 - 228.

So, A. (1990). Social Change and Development: Modernization, Dependency, and World System Theories. Newbury Park California: Sage.

Soyinka, W. (1972). The Man Died. New York: Harper.

Soyinka, W. (1996). The Open Sore of A Continent: A Personnal Narrative of the Nigeria Crisis. New York: Oxford University Press.

Stack, J. (1992). The Great Game of Business. New York: Currency Books.

Staley, E. and R. Morse. (1965). Modern Small Industries for Developing Countries. New York: McGraw-Hill.

Stepan, A. (1988). Rethinking Military Politics: Brazil and the Southern Cone. Princeton: Princeton University Press.

Stepan, A. (1986). "The New Professionalism of International Warfare and Military Role Expansion." In Armies and Politics in Latin America. edited by J. Lowenthal. New York: Holmes and Meir.

Stevenson, H. and J. Gumpert. (1985). "The Heart of Entrepreneurship." Harvard Business Review. Vol. 63, 2, 85 - 94.

Stevenson, H. and J. Jarillo-Mossi. (1990). A paradigm of Entrepreneurrship: Entrepreneurial Management. Strategic Management. Vol. 11, 17 - 27.

Stewart, F. and Ranis, G. (1990). Macro-Policies for Appropriate Technology: A Synthesis of Findings, in Appropriate Technology for Development, edited by F. Stewart. New York: St. Martin's Press.

Stolper, W. (1976). "Problem of Development Planning," In Leading Issues in Economic Development. edited by Gerald Meier New York: Oxford University Press.

Subramanian, V. (1990). Public Administration in Third World. London: Longman.

Suleiman, E. and J. Waterbury. (1990). The Political Economy of Public Sector Reform and Privatization. Boulder: Westview.

Summers, L. and Thomas. V. (1993). "Recent Lessons of Development." The World Bank Research Observer. Vol. 3 (July): 235 - 249.

Tamuno, T. (1972). The Evaluation of the Nigerian State. London: Longman.

Tarp, F. (1993). Stabilization and Structural Adjustment: Macroeconomic Frameworks for Analyzing the Crisis in Sub-Saharan Africa. New York: Routledge.

Tarrow, S. (1994). Power in Movement: Social Movements, Collective Action and Politics. New York: Cambridge University Press.

Technical Committee on Privatization and Commercialization (TCPC) (1990) Fourth Progress Report. Lagos, Nigeria: Government Press.

Technical Committee on Privatization and Commercialization (TCPC). (1991). Fifth Progress Report. Lagos, Nigeria: Government Press.

The Europa World Year Book (1997). Vol. 1. London: Europa Publications Limited.

Theen, R. and F. Wilson. (1996). Comparative Politics. Upper Saddle River, New Jersey: Prentice-Hall.

Theobald, R. (1990). Corruption, Development and Underdevelopment. Durham, North Carolina: Duke University Press.

Thomas-Slayter, B. and D. Rocheleau. (1995). Gender, Environment and Development in Kenya. Boulder, Colorado: Lynne Rienner.

Thompson, J. (1967). Organizations in Action; Social Science Bases of Administrative Theory. New York: McGraw Hill.

Thompson, V. (1964). "Objectives for Development Administration." Administrative Science Quarterly. Vol. 9, 4, 91 - 98.

Thompson, V. (1971). Modern Organization. New York: Alfred A. Knof.

Timmons, J. (1990). New Venture Creation: Entrepreneurship in the 1990s. 3rd edition. Boston Massachusetts: Irwin.

Tong, R. (1986). Ethics in Public Policy Analysis. Englewood Cliffs: Prentice-Hall.

Transition Program in Trouble in Nigeria (1998). Washington Post. May 3rd - 4th.

Treasury Board (1987). Guidelines for the Implementation of the Make-or-Buy Policy Concerning Research and Development Requirements in the Natural Sciences. Lagos, Nigeria: Government Press.

Turner, M. and D. Hulme. (1997). Governance, Administration and Development. West Hartford, Connecticut: Kumarian Press.

Uchendu. O. (1993). "Interest Rate Policy, Savings and Investment in Nigeria," Central Bank of Nigeria Economics and Financial Review. Vol. 3, 34 - 52.

Udoekong, M. (1990). "Industrialization in Nigeria: An Appraisal." Nigerian Interpreter, (Special Edition). Vol. 2, 1 (October): 5 - 33.

Udogu, I. (1995). "The Military, Civil Society and the Issues of Democratic Governance: Toward Nigeria's Fourth Republic." Journal of Development Studies. Vol. 11, 3, 2 - 25.

Udogu, I. (1997). Nigeria and the Politics of Survival as a Nation-State. Westport, Connecticut: Greenwood Publishers.

Ugorji. E. (1995). Privatization/Commercialization of State-Owned Enterprises in Nigeria. Comparative Political Studies. Vol. 27, 4 (January): 537 - 560.

Ukpabi, S. (1972). Military Involvement in Nigerian Politics. Ibadan, Nigeria: University of Ibadan Press.

Umar, D. (1998). Interview with Colonel Abubakar Dangiwa Umar. Lagos, Nigeria: Tell Magazine. Vol. 10 (August): 3 - 10.

United Nations (1948). Universal Declaration of Human Rights. New York: Author.

United Nations (1982). Scientific and Cultural Organization. Review of Education in Africa: Statistical Review. Document of the MINEDAF-V, Conference of Ministers of Education and Those Responsible for Economic Planning in African Member States, Harare, Zimbabwe.

United Nations (1997). Human Development Index and Report. New York: Oxford University Press.

Urevbu, A. (1994). "Impact of Science and Technology on Everyday Life: An African Perspective." Impact of Science and Technology. Benin City, Nigeria: University of Benin Press.

Van de Ven, A. (1992). "Suggestions for Studying Strategic Processes." Strategic Management Journal. Vol. 20, 169 - 188.

Vesper, K. (1990). New Ventures Strategies. Englewood Cliffs, New Jersey: Prentice-Hall.

Vig, N. (1990). "Presidential Leadership: From the Reagan to the Bush Administration." in Environmental Policy in the 1990s, edited by N. Vig and M. Kraft, Washington, DC: CQ Press.

Wade, R. (1990). Governing the Market: Economic Theory and the Role of Government in East Asian Industrialization. Princeton, New Jersey: Princeton University Press.

Walden Annual Report on Nigeria (1995). Los Angeles, California: Walden.

Walton, J. and D. Seddon, D. (1994). Free Markets and Food Riots: The Politics of Global Adjustment. Oxford: Blackwell.

Weaver, J. and K. O'Keefe. (1991). The Evolution of Development Economics. Washington, DC: American University Press.

Weaver, J., Rock, M. and K. Kusterer. (1997). Achieving Broad-Based Sustainable Development. West Harford, Connecticut: Kumarian Press.

Weber, M. (1922). The Theory of Social and Economic Organization. Translated by Handerson, A.and P. Talcott. Fair Lawn, New Jersey: Oxford University Press.

Weber, M. (1946). "Bureaucracy." in From Max Weber: Essays in Sociology. Translated and edited by H. Gerth, and C. Mills. New York: Oxford University Press.

Weimer, D. and A. Vining. (1992). Policy Analysis: Concept and Practice. Englewood Cliffs, New Jersey: Prentice-Hall.

Weiner, M. and Huntington, S. (ed.) (1987). Understanding Political Development. Boston: Little Brown.

Welch, C. (1970). Soldier and State in Africa. Evanston, Illinois: Northwestern University Press.

Wheatley, M. (1993). Leadership and the New Science. San Francisco, California: Barett Kohler.

White, J. (1981). Public Administration in Nigeria 1914 - 1948. London: Longman.

Wiarda, H. (1996). American Foreign Policy: Actors and Processes. New York: Harper Collin College.

Widner, J. (1994). Economic Change and Political Liberalization in Sub-Saharan Africa. Baltimore: Johns Hopkins University Press.

Wildavsky, A. (1992). The New Politics of the Budgetary Process. New York: Harper Collins.

Wilensky, H. (1987). Organizational Intelligence: Knowledge and Policy in Government and Industry. New York: Basic Books.

Wilfred, D. (1985). The IMF Policy Paradigm: The Macroeconomics of Stabilization, Structural Adjustment, and Economic Development. New York: Praeger.

Willoughby, K. (1990). Technology Choice: A Critique of the Appropriate Technology Movement. San Francisco, California: Westview.

Wilson, J. (1968). Varieties of Police Behavior. Cambridge, Massachusetts: Harvard University Press.
World Bank (1994). Adjustment in Africa: Reform, Results, and the Road Ahead. New York: Oxford University Press.
World Bank (1983). World Development Report. New York: Oxford University Press.
World Bank (1985). World Development Report. New York: Oxford University Press.
World Bank (1986 - 1989). World Development Report. New York: Oxford University Press.
World Bank (1990 - 1993). World Development Report. New York: Oxford University Press.
World Bank (1990). Towards the Development of an Environmental Action Plan for Nigeria. World Bank, Washington, DC.
World Bank (1992). Development and the Environment. New York: Oxford University Press.
World Bank (1994 - 1995). World Development Report. Infrastructure for Development. International Bank for Reconstruction and Development. New York: Oxford University Press.
World Bank (1997). Human Development Index. New York: Oxford University Press.
World Bank (1997). World Development Report. New York: Oxford University Press.
World Bank (1998). World Development Report. New York: Oxford University Press.
World Bank (2000). Human Development Index. New York: Oxford University Press.
World Bank (2000). World Development Report. New York: Oxford University Press.
Yalokwu, P. (1992). "Education Funding for Quality Education in Nigeria." In Towards Education in Nigeria for the 21st Century, edited by S. Oriafo and U. Gbenedio Benin City: Institute of Education, University of Benin.
Young, F. (1984). The Contracting Out of Work: Canada and United States of America. Industrial Relations Experience. Kingston, Ontario: Industrial Relations Center, Queen's University Press.
Zartman, W. ed. (1983). The Political Economy of Nigeria. London: Longman.
Zehr, H. (1990). Changing Lenses: A New Focus for Crime and Justice. Socttdale, Pennsylvania: Herald Press.
Zolberg, A. (1968). "Military Intervention in the New States of Africa." In The Military Intervenes: Case Studies in Political Development, edited by H. Bienen. New York: Russel Sage, 25 - 46.

Index